FOURTH EDITION

Perspectives on Social Change

Robert H. Lauer
U.S. International University

Allyn and Bacon
Boston London Toronto Sydney Tokyo Singapore

To Jeanette, Jon, Julie, and Jeff
and to a future illuminated by hope

Series Editor: Karen Hanson
Series Editorial Assistant: Laurie Frankenthaler
Production Administrator: Annette Joseph
Production Coordinator: Susan Freese
Editorial-Production Service: Kailyard Associates
Cover Administrator: Linda K. Dickinson
Manufacturing Buyer: Megan Cochran

A Division of Simon & Schuster, Inc.
160 Gould Street
Needham Heights, Massachusetts 02194

Library of Congress Cataloging-in-Publication Data

Lauer, Robert H.
Perspectives on social change / Robert H. Lauer. — 4th ed.
p. cm.
Includes index.
ISBN 0-205-12575-1
1. Social conflict. 2. Social change. I. Title.
HM101.L368 1990 — 90-37560
303.4—dc20 — CIP

Printed in the United States of America
10 9 8 7 6 5 4 3 2 1 95 94 93 92 91 90

Contents

Preface

One of James Fenimore Cooper's fictional characters said the entire country was in "a constant state of mutation." Few would argue that the situation has altered—if anything, the rate of change is accelerating. Moreover, the changes that continually confront us are defined variously as baffling, outrageous, appropriate, acceptable, inevitable, and so forth. Probably, one could even find all such adjectives applied to the same change, such as the changing situation of racial minorities. The point is that social change elicits some kind of response, for change is both inescapable and consequential in our lives. Some observers would even argue that change is the most crucial factor in our well-being (or lack of well-being). The study and understanding of change, therefore, are linked to the quality of human life.

This book is addressed to all those who are concerned about change. It is not an exhaustive study of all aspects of change, but it indicates the most important issues and problems. Some topics in this book are of great importance but have been neglected in other texts: the role of youth in change, the relationship of violence to change, and strategies for effecting change. Other topics have been treated more or less adequately by others but must be understood by any serious student of change: theories, mechanisms, and patterns of change in the world today.

I hope the reader of this book will gain a broad understanding of the basic concerns in the area of social change. I hope the reader will be both stimulated and prepared to explore the various facets of change in greater depth, for the opportunities for creative and significant work are many.

This book will be most valuable if the reader understands its plan of organization. The divisions are, of course, arbitrary; one could use any of a number of different schemes. Basically, the book is divided into sections designed to answer some important questions:

- What is change, and what kinds of assumptions underlie discussions of change? (Part One—Introduction)
- How might we explain change? (Part Two—Theoretical Perspectives on Change)
- What is the driving force of change? (Part Three—Mechanisms of Change)
- What is one of the most important forms or patterns of change today? (Part Four—Patterns of Contemporary Change)
- And what are the important considerations in effecting and guiding change? (Part Five—Applied Sociology: How to Bring about Change)

This largely follows the pattern of the first three editions. However, the fifth part has been changed and expanded to two chapters to reflect the current interest in applied sociology. It shows how sociology can be a practical discipline, using materials not only to understand change but to actually bring it about. In addition to the revisions in Part Five, I have deleted some material that seemed no longer pertinent or useful, and I have updated all chapters.

The reader will soon discover that some materials could have been placed in more than one section. Ogburn and Veblen could have been discussed as theorists rather than as representatives of the notion that technology is a crucial mechanism of change. Two considerations guided the choice of location: first, I wanted to cover, at least briefly, all the most important thinkers; and second, I wanted to deal with mechanisms, patterns, and strategies apart from their inclusion in specific theories. The second point should both clarify theories and aid further theoretical development.

But mechanisms, patterns, and strategies are always an implicit or explicit part of theories, and most students of social change employ implicit or explicit theoretical perspectives in their analyses. Consequently, it was necessary to make some arbitrary decisions. My arbitrariness thus confessed, I trust it will not distract the reader from seriously digging into the subject of change.

Acknowledgments

Many minds other than the author's are involved in writing a book. I would like to acknowledge my indebtedness to four teachers who have been particularly influential in my own intellectual development: Paul Campisi, Gunter Remmling, Wolf Heydebrand, and Robert Boguslaw. I am also grateful to those who used the earlier editions and made suggestions for improvement. Special thanks to Hosein Azadi, University of Nebraska–Lincoln, who reviewed this work in its early stages.

Finally, in the course of the writing of this book, many people were important to me in terms of their support and encouragement. I am grateful for a family that has been rich in those qualities. They have been an enclave of love in a violent world.

PART ONE

Introduction

Sociology emerged out of the turbulence of the nineteenth century as a science of social order and social change. Auguste Comte, who has been called "the sire of sociology," fathered a discipline that would illuminate not only the bases of a viable structure of society but also the course of human development. But the children drifted away from the father's vision; the greater portion of twentieth-century energies were expended on what C. Wright Mills called *grand theory* and *abstracted empiricism.* As a result, sociology was in the embarrassing position of confronting a rapidly changing world with a paucity of tools of understanding. There are indications that the second half of the century is different—works on social change have begun to proliferate.

There are, however, certain impediments that must be cleared away in order for fruitful work to be carried on in the area of social change. One impediment is definitional. Social change has often been discussed without being defined—it has been used by researchers to refer to everything from attitude change to the historical evolution of societies. We will begin, therefore, by defining and illustrating what is meant by *social change.* The other impediments to be discussed are what I have called the *myths* of change; they are assumptions that impede our understanding, and the first chapter seeks to dispel them.

CHAPTER ONE

Social Change: Meaning and Myths

The world may yet, as T. S. Eliot suggested, end with a whimper rather than a bang. In the meantime, it plunges breathlessly into a hazy future, convulsed by conflict, writhing in the agony of injustice, and searching with a kind of urgent desperation for a meaningful human existence. Such a world demands an understanding of social change. The perspectives of past thinkers are helpful and are a necessary foundation both for understanding the present and for constructing new perspectives for the future. But some past writings tend to suffer from confusion about the meaning of change and, in addition, have been rooted in assumptions that we can now see to be false. Theories of change have been built upon myths about change. These myths hinder our understanding and impede the construction of new perspectives. To understand social change, therefore, we must begin by defining the concept and by shedding the mythical from our thought.

The Meaning of Change

Much of the literature on change proceeds without ever clearly defining what is meant by the concept. Social change is treated as though its meaning were intuitively evident. But neither is its meaning intuitively evident nor do all scholars mean the same thing by it. In fact, some talk about change in terms that others would say do not reflect change at all. For example, survey research in Detroit has shown that from 1956 to 1971, the percentage of men who agree that there are some kinds of jobs that women should not hold declined from 65 to 48 percent.[1] In other words, by 1971, fewer Detroit men held a negative attitude toward women working in all kinds of jobs. Is that change? Some would say yes, while some feminists might argue that nothing really changed because the male attitudes were not reflected in substantial female gains in the job market.

• Change Is Pervasive

What, then, do we mean by *social change?* Most definitions speak of change in very broad terms. Wilbert Moore, for example, has defined *change* as the "significant alteration of social structures," meaning by *social structures* the "patterns of social action and interaction."[2] Moore included in his definition various expressions of structures: norms, values, and cultural phenomena. Obviously, such a definition is broad. Other definitions are similarly broad; thus, *social change* has been defined as "variations or modifications in any aspect of social process, pattern, or form," and as "any modification in established patterns of interhuman relationships and standards of conduct."[3]

Such definitions are not without merit, for they suggest that social change is a complex phenomenon that is pervasive at various levels of social life. If the definitions cover virtually the whole of social life, it is because the whole of social life is continually changing. What differs is the rate of change. Attitudes about a particular phenomenon (such as male attitudes about women working) may change more or less quickly than the pertinent social institution (the percentage of women in various sectors of the economy). But the discrepancy at any point in time reflects differing rates, not change versus nonchange.

In other words, the position taken in this book is that change is normal and continual (see discussion later in this chapter of the myth of deviance). The important questions to ask relate to the direction and rate of change at various levels of social life. Some disputes about change occur because people forget about the various levels and the differing rates. For some, there is no change, or at least no significant change, unless the institution itself has changed. For others, even changes in attitudes reflect significant alterations in social life.

In this book, social change will be viewed as an inclusive concept that refers to alterations in social phenomena at various levels of human life from the individual to the global. The various levels, some representative areas of analysis within each level, and some representative units of analysis are given in Table 1-1. Change may be studied at one or more levels, using various units of analysis. Obviously, attitude change in this scheme is as legitimate and important as institutional change. The important point to keep in mind, however, is that changes that are significant at one level are not necessarily significant

Table 1-1 • Levels of Analysis in Social Change

Level of Analysis	*Some Representative Areas of Study*	*Some Representative Units of Study*
Global	International organization; international inequality	Gross National Product; trade data; political alliances
Civilization	Life cycle of civilizations or other patterns of change (e.g., evolutionary or dialectical)	Artistic, scientific, and other innovations; social institutions
Culture	Material culture; nonmaterial culture	Technology; ideology; values
Society	Stratification system; structure; demography crime	Income, power, and prestige; roles; migration rates; murder rates
Community	Stratification system; structure; demography; crime	Income, power, and prestige; roles; population growth; murder rates
Institutions	Economy; polity; religion; marriage and family; education	Family income; voting patterns; church attendance; divorce rates; proportion of people with college education
Organizations	Structure; interaction patterns; authority structure; productivity	Roles; friendship cliques; administration/production ratio; output per worker
Interaction	Types of interaction; communication	Amount of conflict, competition, or neighboring; identity of frequent and infrequent participants in interaction
Individual	Attitudes	Beliefs about various matters; aspirations

at other levels. Attitude change may or may not lead to, or reflect, changes in interpersonal relationships, organizations, or institutions.[4] Or there may be a time lag involved, with changes at one level occurring more slowly than changes at another. In any case, it is my position that alterations at any level of social life may be properly regarded as social change. Our research should therefore focus on the directions and rates of change at the various levels and on the relationships between changes at differing levels. As the latter suggests, distinguishing between levels does not mean that changes at a particular level are independent of changes at other levels. My point is, rather, that we must recognize the level at which we are working and refrain from drawing unwarranted conclusions about other levels.

The importance of keeping levels in mind is illustrated by a study of rural communities in Bolivia conducted by McEwen and his associates.[5] The research sought to identify the kinds of changes that occurred in rural areas after the 1952 revolution. Although many revolutions involve little more than a "changing of the palace guard," the Bolivians experienced radical change after 1952 in the form of a breaking up of the feudalistic hacienda system, new labor and social welfare legislation, and a nationalization of much of the mining industry. To what extent did such societal and institutional changes affect communities? The researchers investigated six rural communities, two of which were agricultural villages and four of which were market towns. They found that profound changes had occurred generally in rural Bolivia, but that the impact varied from community to community. The changes that occurred included the following:

> *a decline of the hacendado class following the weakening of their economic base; the disappearance or slackening of lines of control over hacienda peons; the organization of peasant unions as corporate interest associations having a variety of legal and political as well as economic and social responsibilities; the extension of a national political role for the peasants . . . ; and the strengthening of old as well as the creation of new economic opportunities, especially for ex-hacienda peons—all of which effects have undermined the traditional social stratification.*[6]

All of these changes, of course, were congruent with the aims of the revolutionary movement. Nevertheless, individual communities in Bolivia were affected differently, and some were virtually untouched by the revolution. For example, in the small market town of Villa Abecia, the researchers found that economic power was in the hands of a few *patrons* (landlords), who controlled land, water, and labor—a situation that was little different from that of prerevolutionary days. In part, the *patrons* were able to retain their power because most of them joined the revolutionary party and because they secured control over the local Agrarian Reform Court. Consequently, while some villages were considerably changed, others were like Villa Abecia, where the *campesinos* (rural dwellers, peasants) comprise the majority but "conform to the classic, prerevolutionary pattern, that of the deferential, illiterate peon, resigned for generations to an impoverished and precarious existence, living in crude huts in the vineyards and fields, dressed in homespun and working long hours."[7] The societal and institutional changes that occurred in Bolivia were not reflected in every community. Societal and institutional change does not mean that similar changes will occur in the community, just as attitudinal change does not mean that there has been a similar change in a social institution. Social change is normal and continual, but in various directions, at various rates, and at multiple levels of social life. To understand change, we must be clear about our level or levels of analysis.

• Change Is Patterned

Change is patterned as well as pervasive. Indeed, if there were no pattern, we could develop no theories of change. Some patterns require a detailed verbal description, such as the pattern of modernization that we will discuss in Part IV. Some patterns can be summarized fairly well in the form of a graph, such as the pattern of diffusion and adoption of innovations discussed in Chapter 7. Moore has identified ten geometric patterns that can be found in various theories, including rising straight lines (ongoing progress theories), rising cyclical curves (progress with fluctuations), and level cyclical or sinusoidal curves (fluctuations with neither progress nor regress over long spans of time).[8] The point is that change is not a purely capricious or nebulous process. There is a form or a pattern to change that allows us to understand, describe, and analyze it.

We can illustrate the patterned nature of change by a few examples from the United States. Our concern here is not to get a comprehensive picture of changing American society, but only to get a little better sense of how change is a patterned process by looking at some American examples.

In general, as many observers have pointed out, American society over the past two centuries has become larger, more diverse, urbanized, more scientifically and technologically oriented, and industrialized, and has exhibited change in all social institutions (government, education, the economy, religion, and the family). Some of the changes have been in the form of a fairly continual upward trend. For example, America has become increasingly urbanized throughout its history. As Figure 1-1 shows, the proportion of Americans living in urban areas has increased fairly steadily. Officially, we became an urban nation in

1920, when the census returns first showed a majority of the population living in urban areas. By 1980, 73.7 percent of the population was classified as urban. The proportion of Americans who were urban dwellers doubled in the first three-quarters of the twentieth century.

Various other kinds of change have also followed the pattern of a generally upward trend. Population growth has been continual throughout our history, fueled by immigration, a declining death rate, and a birth rate higher than the death rate. These three components of population change illustrate other patterns of change (see Figure 1-2). The birth and death rates have followed a long-term downward trend,

Figure 1-1 • Proportion of American Population Living in Urban Areas (in percent)

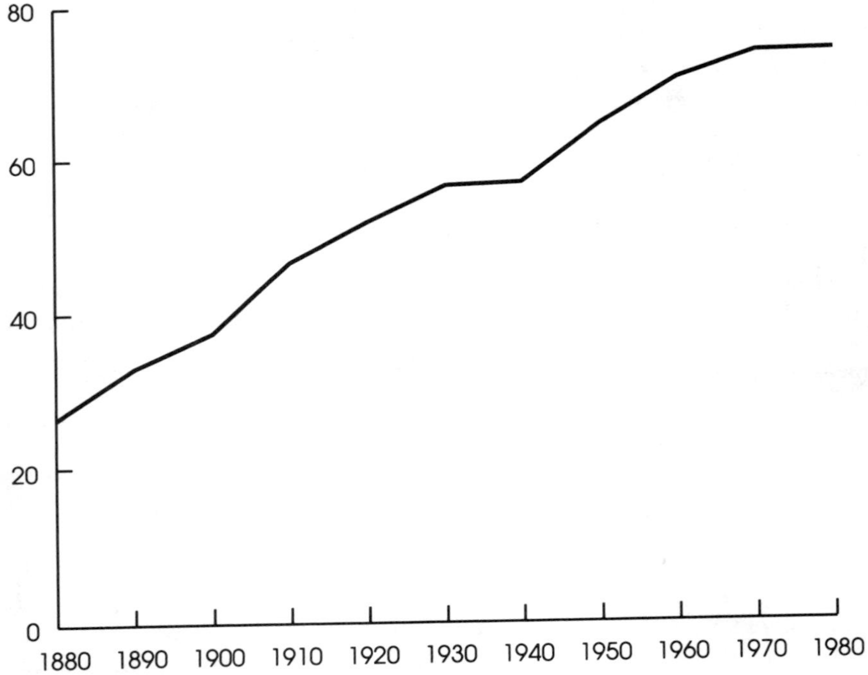

Source: Plotted from data in *Social Indicators, 1976* (Washington, D.C.: U.S. Government Printing Office, 1977); *Historical Statistics of the United States* (Washington, D.C.: U.S. Government Printing Office, 1975); and *Statistical Abstract of the United States* (Washington, D.C.: U.S. Government Printing Office, 1989).

with fluctuations and some short-term reversals of the trend. The reversal in the birth rate trend during the 1940s and early 1950s resulted in the well-known "baby boom" in America. The immigration rate has fluctuated much more than either the birth or death rate throughout most of American history. Until the 1930s, when the pattern became a slight upward trend with small fluctuations, immigration followed a cyclic pattern.

A variety of changes have been cyclical.[9] Business cycles are perhaps one of the more well-known cyclical phenomena. There are also cycles in organizational behavior and social behavior. For instance, the government tends to oscillate between liberalism and con-

Figure 1-2 • Components of Population Change in America: 1860-1986 (per 1,000 population)

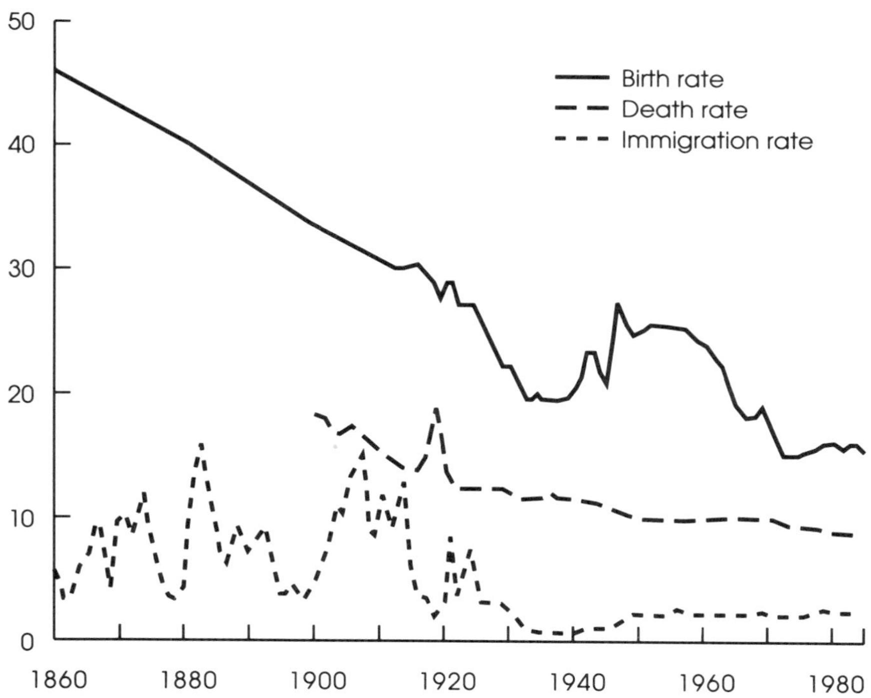

Source: Historical Statistics of the United States (Washington, D.C.: U.S. Government Printing Office, 1975), and various editions of *Statistical Abstract of the United States* (Washington, D.C.: U.S. Government Printing Office).

servatism. Fads and fashions appear and disappear. Marriage rates, divorce rates, and murder rates, among others, all tend to fluctuate over time. In some cases, there is a long-term upward or downward trend along with the fluctuations, but the cycles are clearly seen.

There are a variety of other kinds of patterns. Some things change in curvilinear fashion, increasing and then leveling off and sometimes decreasing. For example, the proportion of Americans who are members of a religious body increased throughout most of our history, reached a peak in the 1960s, then began to decline (see Figure 1-3). For other things, the long-term trend may be upward or downward, but the trend is not so much continual as it is cyclical or spasmodic. Often, a particu-

Figure 1-3 • Proportion of American Population Who Are Members of a Religious Body: 1890-1985 (in percent)

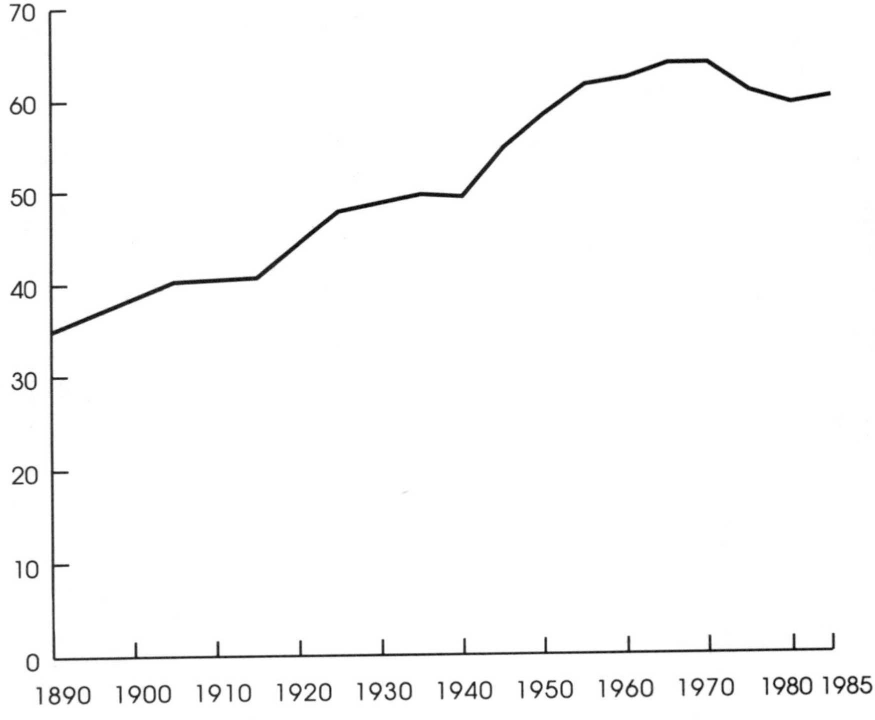

Source: Derived from data in various editions of *Statistical Abstracts of the United States* (Washington, D.C.: U.S. Government Printing Office).

lar trend will have a number of sharp deviations from the general pattern, deviations that reflect particular circumstances or events. For example, divorce rates show a long-term upward trend along with cyclic variations. In addition, there have been some periods of dramatic change. At the time of the 1890 census, less than one-half of 1 percent of females 14 years and older were reported as divorced. For the 1970 census, the number had risen to 3.86 percent. But the pattern was not one of continual increase. The rate rose gradually through the 1920s, declined until 1935, then began to rise again. The rate rose sharply from 1940 to 1946, declined again to 1958, rose gradually until 1967, then began another sharp increase into the late 1970s. In the 1980s, the rates once again began a slight decline (see Figure 1-4).

In sum, there are patterns to social change. There are many different patterns, some of which can be shown graphically as we have done above. Of course, the full meaning of such changes requires a verbal as well as a graphical description. That is, patterns of change have meanings that need to be interpreted. For example, Norval Glenn has looked at trends in the United States from the 1950s to the 1980s.[10] Among other things, he noted that there has been a weakening of allegiance to political parties (increasing numbers of people define themselves as independents); a decline in the number of people who agree with many traditional Christian beliefs (such as accepting the Bible literally); increasing approval for nontraditional, nonfamily roles for women; and increasing approval of premarital sexual relations. Glenn notes that all of these trends offer support for the idea of some social critics that modern individualism is increasing. That is, since the 1950s, Americans have tended more and more to withdraw their allegiance from groups and institutions and the values fostered by them and focus instead on themselves and their own needs and desires. Thus, Glenn took a number of long-term, upward and downward trends and gave additional meaning to them by showing how they can reflect a larger master trend of growing individualism.

In addition to their value in enabling us to understand change, patterns of change have implications for the quality of human life, and any particular pattern may have manifold consequences. For example, we mentioned the "baby boom" that lasted into the 1950s, as shown in Figure 1-2. The result of this birth rate pattern was a great expansion of the school-age population and a corresponding increase in the numbers of facilities and of teachers. The subsequent downturn in the trend, on the other hand, resulted in a diminishing school-age population in the 1970s and 1980s and led to considerable financial and personnel troubles in educational circles. In addition to education, birth rates have an impact on various other aspects of social life, such as the economy,

Figure 1-4 • U.S. Divorce Rates: 1925-1985 (per 1,000 population)

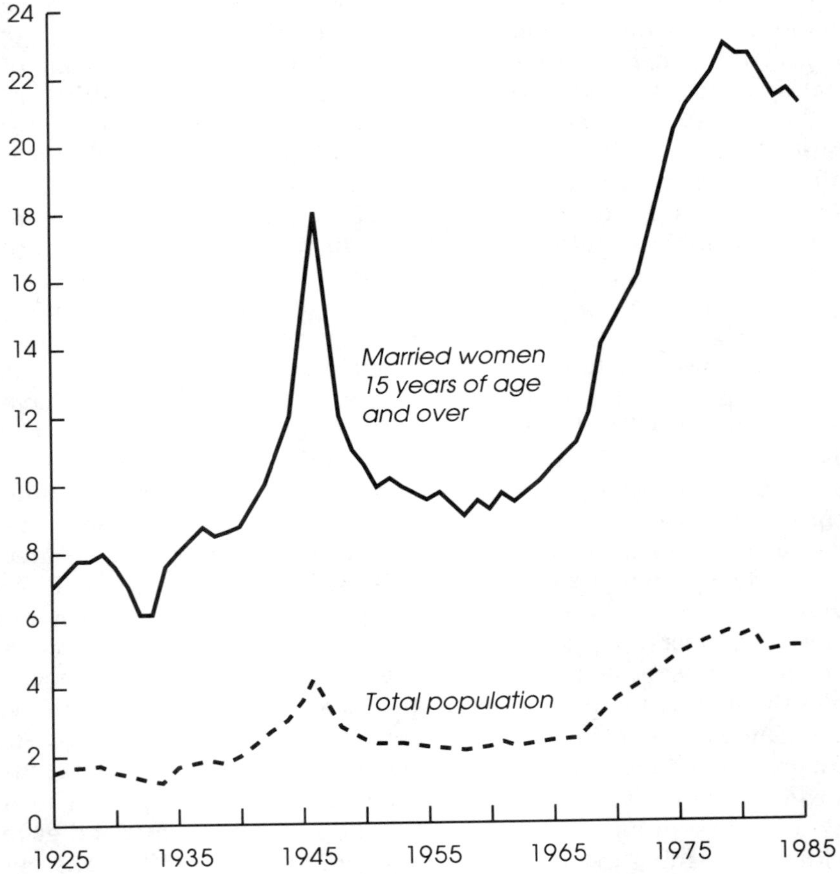

Source: National Center for Health Statistics, "Advance Report of Final Divorce Statistics, 1984," *Monthly Vital Statistics Report* 35 (Hyattsville, Md.: Public Health Service, 1986), p. 2.

people's health, crime rates, government programs, and the environment.

As we shall see in subsequent chapters, the theorists of change underscore the importance of patterns. They all posit particular patterns to social change. They do not necessarily agree on what is the basic pattern, but they all insist that social change is not a capricious process.

The Myths of Change

• The Myth of Deviance

A considerable amount of sociological thinking has conceived of change as in some sense a violation of the normal.[11] That is, the normal state of affairs in society is persistence; institutions or values or cultural patterns are thought to be stable over time. This reflects a conservative strain that has pervaded sociology throughout its history. While Comte, for example, acknowledged the role of human action in social progress, he reduced that role to one of implementing intellectual reform. Utopia, which for Comte was a scientific society, would come when people began to think scientifically. The role of the sociologist was to induce scientific thinking.

A variety of theoretical perspectives have appeared in sociology since Comte, but in recent decades the dominant note has been structural-functionalism, which gives primary attention and support to social orders characterized by stability and integration. This focus on stability (and the consequent neglect of change) assumes that static analyses can be made without coming to terms with change, and that an understanding of social change demands a prior and thorough understanding of social statics.[12] Sociologists working within this perspective, then, have been far more concerned with structures than with processes, and even when they have dealt with processes, they have dealt with them within structurally limited bounds. Persistence and regularities have been viewed as the normal state of affairs; change has been viewed as a kind of social deviance.

A thorough understanding of structures does not guarantee an understanding of change. This should be clear from the manner in which change has been kept at the periphery of sociological interest during the decades of structural-functionalist dominance. There has been a continuous refinement of structural analysis, rather than a transition to studies of change.

In more recent work, some structural-functionalists are attempting to make use of the perspective by correcting past deficiencies with regard to change (see the discussion in Chapter 4).

It is more realistic and fruitful, then, to see change as inherent "in the very nature of things,"[13] including the very nature of social life. Whether we are talking about the physical world, the history of the human race, or the human intellect, we find that "nothing remains what, where and as it was, but everything moves, changes, comes into being and passes out of existence."[14] Reality is not static. As the ancient Greek philosopher Heraclitus correctly observed, all being is "in flux, is constantly changing, constantly coming into being and passing away."[15]

The ubiquity of change may be easily accepted for transitional societies in the contemporary world. It has, for example, been asserted that change is ubiquitous in modernizing societies, in the United States, and in any society that strives to fulfill human needs.[16] But I am arguing for the ubiquity of change in all societies, including ancient and primitive ones. With respect to ancient society, we may take China as an example. The Hegelian idea of a China bound by a stagnant social structure is no longer tenable. It has become increasingly clear that China's history was "full of upheavals, abrupt transitions, and gradual changes."[17] In the so-called Axial Period, for example, China was in considerable flux, along with the other major societies of the time. From 900 to 200 B.C., the structure of both Chinese society and Chinese thought was undergoing continual change.[18] The centuries following that period present a marked contrast with the rapidly changing society of the Axial Period but do *not* present a society staying virtually unchanged over a long span of time. For example, a study of the region of Hangchow in the thirteenth century concludes that the "impression of order and prosperity given by the South China of the thirteenth century is illusory. Behind it lie the continuous and tragic impoverishment of the State, destitution and disaffection in the countryside, and the struggle of factions within the ruling class."[19] Among the changes occurring in Hangchow from the beginning of the twelfth to the end of the thirteenth century were rapid population growth; the emergence of a class of merchants between the small elites and the masses of the people; commercial expansion, and the concomitant increased wealth of the merchants; and a deterioration of the elites, as evidenced by increased corruption and factional conflict. Such changes spanned two centuries; thus, what was unusual about China was not the lack of change but the unusually slow rate of change. The same argument may also be advanced with respect to primitive societies.[20]

Change, in other words, is normal. Whether we are dealing with the individual[21] or social level, change is of the essence. Humans must either grow or decay: "The pure conservative is fighting against the essence of the universe."[22] Early evolutionary theory in sociology had many flaws, but one of its central tenets was valid—the ubiquity and normality of change. The problem of social change, therefore, becomes one of the *rate* of change rather than of its presence or absence. What demand investigation are such questions as why certain societies and certain times exhibit unusually rapid or unusually slow rates of change; what factors affect rates and how; and whether there is an optimal rate of change for human well-being.

• *The Myth of Trauma*

The notion that change is abnormal is often associated with a second idea—change is traumatic. Change has been called an "ordeal," a "crisis," and a "foreign and unwanted agent."[23] Indeed, it is not difficult to gather evidence that seems to support the myth of trauma.

There is, for example, some evidence that mental illness is related to social change. Not every kind of change is associated with mental illness, however. Rather, certain changes in conjunction with various other social and psychological factors seem to increase mental stress. For example, rates of hospitalization increase for people who migrate from one place to another and for those who are in a state of cultural transition; but lower rates of admission to mental hospitals occur during the changes from war to peace and peace to war.[24] Social change per se, then, does not lead to mental stress or emotional illness.

The traumatic nature of change may also be supported by the large number of social and psychological impediments to change that have been identified.[25] These impediments could be seen as defense mechanisms against the trauma of change. Indeed, there are manifold ways in which people resist change; any change agent faces an incredible array of problems when seeking to lead people in new directions. In some cases, the value system itself seems to possess built-in resistance to any change. The values may, for example, minimize the importance of material aspirations, or disparage the cultural ways of others, or demand interpersonal and intergroup relationships that are incongruent with a modernized society.

Certain attitudes also impede change. Economic development will lag unless people acquire attitudes of cooperation, the desire for advancement, respect for manual work, and so forth.[26] Even change that promises to fulfill such basic needs as medical care may be resisted because, for example, of traditional attitudes about the propriety of a woman being examined by a male doctor.

Other factors that inhibit change are rigid stratification systems, a high degree of social inequality, community fragmentation, vested interests, and even cultural motor patterns. An example of the latter is provided by the reputedly low efficiency of certain Indian factory workers.[27] The Indian workers who service machines have been far less efficient at the job than their European counterparts. However, the machines require the worker to stand or sit on a high stool. Although the Indians are able to work efficiently for hours while squatting, they tire quickly when forced to stand or sit. The failure of the Indian workers to adapt to the machines is rooted in a cultural motor pattern rather than in some psychic trauma inherent in change.

Finally, there are social-psychological factors that inhibit change. The government, for example, is generally conceded to be crucial to much change in the contemporary world. The success or failure of the developing nations of the world is crucially linked with actions of the central governments; no nation in the contemporary world is modernizing on the basis of the activities of individual entrepreneurs alone. The peasants' perception of the government, however, often involves considerable suspicion and distrust. Thus, a Nigerian effort to introduce new fertilizer to the peasants failed, in spite of the fact that the innovation would have greatly increased productivity. The peasants rejected the fertilizer because of past negative experiences with officials, distrust of the British government, and a lack of understanding of both the use and the usefulness of the new fertilizer.[28]

All of the above could be interpreted as social and psychological protective mechanisms that have evolved out of the need to cope with the trauma of change. The argument could be clinched by citing the numberless concrete instances of resistance to change, including resistance to railroads, the automobile, the typewriter, alternating current, tractors, umbrellas, street lighting, and even potatoes.[29]

In Chapter 13, we will look in more detail at the bases upon which change is resisted. Suffice it to say that, while there are many reasons people resist change, none is related to any trauma intrinsic to change. Nevertheless, the assumption of trauma has often been made, and that assumption is a negative value judgment about change that is likely to lead to the assertion of persistence and stability as the natural and desired state of affairs for humans. The fallacy of this myth, however, is clearly seen in the obverse side of the question—the changes that are welcomed, initiated, or both, by people themselves. If people clearly resist change at times, they just as clearly value it at other times. For example, it has often been assumed that one of the critical problems of industrializing a traditional society is securing commitment of an industrial labor force. People have been known to be frustratingly sporadic in coming to work in the factories. Nevertheless, commitment to industrial work is not always a problem. For example, a study of the labor force in Pune, India, found the workers to be thoroughly committed to working in the factories; most remained in their jobs for years, with only some of the more educated workers leaving the factories to seek other kinds of employment.[30] Industrialization is neither inevitably resisted nor inherently inconsistent with a traditional culture. It is only when we assume that a factory in Asia or Africa or Latin America must operate exactly like its American counterpart that we will encounter serious problems of resistance.

Peasant societies do not cling tenaciously to the existing order; the peasant wars of the twentieth century bear ample witness to the peasants' desire for change. One reason peasants value change is that the peasant community is not often the stable and harmonious society that is depicted in the concept of *Gemeinschaft*, or "folk society." On the contrary, many peasants find life a "continual anguish" and eagerly seek change.[31] Lerner pointed out that in all the Middle Eastern countries he studied, the rural villagers admitted to their unhappiness, while modernizing individuals reported much less unhappiness. Traditional society is receding in the Middle East "because relatively few Middle Easterners still want to live by its rules."[32]

Social change, then, is not inevitably resisted. At times it may be, but at other times people may deliberately initiate change. The effort may have sufficient intensity to effect radical change within a single generation.[33] At this point, a qualification needs to be introduced. For while change per se cannot be viewed as traumatic, the rate of change seems to be related to experienced stress. Rapid change may generate considerable stress. Hezel reported that rapid change experienced by the people on the island of Truk in Micronesia contributed to that society developing the highest rate of suicide in the Pacific.[34] Toffler coined the phrase "future shock" to describe the psychic disruption that results from experiencing too much change in too short a time.[35] One study of health records of military personnel concluded that "a cluster-year of life-changes was seen to occur immediately prior to an illness or to a clustering of illnesses.[36] When the rate of life-changes (including such changes as death of a spouse, divorce, marital problems, a new line of work, a child getting married, personal successes, and new religious patterns) was high, with many changes occurring in a short period of time, physical or mental illness tended to follow the changes. The greater the total score of "life-change units" (the various changes were weighted, with death of spouse being the most heavily weighted and minor infraction of civilian law the least weighted), the greater the probability of a major health change.

It should be noted that the changes dealt with in the above study were of kinds that would be perceived both as desirable and as undesirable. Some of the changes, such as personal successes, would be highly valued; some, such as death of a loved one, would be highly undesirable. It was not merely the kind of change that the authors found to be related to stress, but the rate of change.

These findings have been challenged, however. In a test of the "future shock" thesis, I found a direct relationship between anxiety level and perceived rate of change among a group of subjects.[37] The greater the perceived rate of societal change, the higher the anxiety level. This relationship was moderated when the changes were defined as desirable. Independent research by Vinokur and Selzer came to a similar conclusion.[38] They found that accumulated life-changes were directly related to self-reported tension and distress, but the relationship did not hold true for desirable changes.

Thus, the perceived desirability or undesirability of change is the crucial factor in whether or not the change generates psychic distress. A high rate of change, then, appears to generate more stress than a low rate. At this point, however, we do not know why some people seem to suffer as a result of high rates while others do not. A high rate of change is not always associated with trauma, at least not with severe trauma. In a comparison of two communities in the American West, one rapidly changing and one stable, researchers found that people in the changing community perceived no more stress in their lives and reported no more symptoms of stress (such as sleep problems, nervousness, anxiety, and depression) than did those in the stable community.[39] The only difference was that those in the changing community felt less integrated into the town than did those in the stable community. The researchers did not measure perceptions of the people, but it is possible that those in the changing community defined the changes as largely desirable. (It was called a "boom" town, one in which the economy was growing rapidly.) At any rate, it seems that the most stress occurs when people perceive the changes to be both rapid and undesirable.

Although the evidence is sparse and more difficult to obtain, a relatively low rate of change may also generate stress. The relationship, in other words, may be curvilinear—both too high and too low rates of change generate stress. This implies an optimal rate of change for human well-being. Such an optimal rate in the organizational context has been suggested by Starbuck, who pointed out that members of organizations will be unhappy in both "an overly stable environment" and "an overly variable one."[40] Seidenberg has written about the "trauma of eventlessness," a situation in which the absence of sufficient stimuli can have traumatic consequences. "A lack of external events and appropriate internal responses can constitute a trauma no less than the 'dramatic' assaults against the ego. More than that, the anticipation of more and more eventlessness similarly constitute a danger of severe proportions to one's well-being."[41] As an example, he relates the case of a woman who suffered a breakdown when she became aware that without some kind of change her future would be nothing more than a duplication of a past "characterized by submission to authority, absence of choice, and a general exclusion and isolation from the significant stimuli of life."[42] If rapid change is a source of stress, so may be change that is too slow.

• The Myth of Unidirectionality and Utopia Apprehended

Some of the first sociologists set forth theories of social evolution that posited a uniform end, and, in some cases, a uniform path to that end, for all societies. Comte, for example, described social evolution in terms of an ineluctable sequence that was leading to a predestined end. Some contemporary thinkers have continued to propagate this notion, while others have admitted to diverse pathways—though still to a predestined end. In any case, the end is the same—a modern, industrial society that has an obviously Western appearance.

This myth of unidirectionality—the idea that all societies are ultimately heading toward one particular end—is sometimes called *the theory of convergence* and sometimes *the contradiction between tradition and modernity.* It is basically a form of technological determinism, although the extent of that determinism varies among theorists. That is, no one argues that each industrial society will be a carbon copy of every other industrial society, but industrialization is often seen as a powerful process that effects a considerable amount of standardization. Consequently, the uniformities of industrial society are perceived to be of far greater significance than any diversity.

Thus, it has been maintained that certain societal patterns (patterns that are similar to those of the West) are inevitable for any society that accepts Western technology.[43] Probably the most noted exponents of this position are Clark Kerr and his associates, who set forth the idea of the "logic" of industrialism.[44] This logic does not demand a singular path, but it does insist upon a singular end, namely, *pluralistic industrialism.* The pluralistic industrial society is one in which there is a system of checks and balances in the midst of an incessantly changing technology. Conflict between diverse interest groups is regulated by a "web of rules" constructed by the state, by managers, and by various associations. The state is very powerful, with considerable economic responsibility. The productive enterprise itself is dominant and possesses "substantial authority" in order to maximize efficiency.

Kerr and his associates argue that a number of factors lead toward uniformity in the pluralistic industrial society. These include the passage of time—the further the society moves away from the traditional base, the more potent the logic of industrialism becomes; technology; the push of progress; the imperatives of education and equality; the omnipresent state; the dominance of the productive enterprise; and the compulsion of comparisons (people in various societies will strive for progress and participation in society upon the basis of their knowledge of the achievements of competing societies).

The idea that all societies are ultimately becoming similar easily turns into the myth of utopia apprehended, which is the argument or assumption that a modern, industrial society represents the ultimate in human achievement. The solution for world problems, then, lies in helping the developing nations to modernize (where *modernize* is equivalent to *Westernize*) as quickly and painlessly as possible. The sooner they become like the West, it is believed, the sooner the human race will enjoy peace and fulfillment. Utopia has already been apprehended cognitively; it only becomes a matter of time and will until it is apprehended in reality throughout the world. The inherent flaws in modern society are thereby ignored; the modern social structure is held to require only refinement, not radical change.[45]

Undoubtedly, there is some truth in the myth of unidirectionality. The dominance of the state for contemporary industrial growth seems to be an imperative for the developing nations. But this is not equivalent to saying that all industrial and industrializing societies are becoming alike with respect to the role of the state. Furthermore, the myths of unidirectionality and utopia apprehended seem to be contradicted by a substantial amount of evidence. The assumption that industrialization demands particular social forms may be shown to be false in some very basic respects. In the first place, the supposed antithesis between tradition and modernity is false. In his study of Cantel, Guatemala, Nash found that a considerable amount of traditional life can continue and even flourish at a higher level in the process of industrialization.[46] An accommodation was worked out between a textile mill and the community such that the factory proceeded with its business of production and the community continued with its institutions.

Factory work schedules in Cantel were accommodated to traditional holidays and to the traditional obligations of the people in the civic area. The traditional requirements of male participation in civic affairs sometimes demanded a man's full time for anywhere from a period of weeks to as much as two years. Nevertheless, the men who worked in the factory were allowed to devote the required time to civic duties without penalty. Further, factory work did not affect the world view of the Cantelenses; factory and nonfactory workers were found to hold similar beliefs. The traditional modes of thinking were not transferred to the factory, but neither was the rationality implicit in the factory transferred to everyday experience.

The persistence of tradition is particularly evident in the Orient. Scholars generally agree that Japan has modernized while maintaining and utilizing premodern, traditional institutions.[47] Japanese society has not moved along the path from tradition to modernity; rather, Japan is a nation that employs both tradition and the modern and holds them together in a viable contradiction that has resulted in rapid development. A 1966 study of nearly one thousand Japanese students found that although Japanese political behavior is outwardly similar to that of Westerners, that behavior has not been truly westernized; traditional Japanese values still persist.[48]

Vogel's study (in the late 1950s) of the role of kinship structure in urbanization and modernization provides a good example of the way in which Japanese tradition has facilitated change.[49] Urbanization in Japan has proceeded in a much more orderly fashion than it did in Europe and the United States and has been controlled somewhat by kinship organization. Typically, one son would remain in the rural area and inherit the family property, while others would migrate to the city and seek work there. The rural family was responsible for attempting to place the migrating sons in jobs by making contacts in the city. Both employer and employee depended upon such personal connections. Once settled in the city, the migrant was no longer bound by the traditional family customs and was free to adopt urban customs. In other words, the son who remained behind accepted the responsibility for caring for the parents and the family customs, leaving the migrants—once they found work—free to pursue their own lives and careers. In addition, the migrants were motivated to develop the necessary skills to remain in a good economic position, for once in the city, the migrant was no longer considered a member of the rural kinship group and was not expected to return home. Since a crucial need of an industrializing society is skilled labor, the kinship system facilitated the former by motivating migrants to become the latter.

The Japanese pattern is more or less characteristic of the nations of East Asia in general, for those nations have not adopted the Western way in its entirety, but rather have exercised great selectivity. Some aspects of Western society have been accepted, but others have been ignored or rejected outright. Those elements that were borrowed did not have the same effects as they had in the West. A modernized East Asia, therefore, will probably reflect the West neither in its overt cultural patterns nor "in its more fundamental ideals and values."[50]

There is, then, no inherent conflict between tradition and modernity such that the more modern a nation becomes, the more it must necessarily shed its tradition. Traditionalism, the commitment to the past and its ways, can severely hamper change. However, tradition itself, as Japan has clearly shown, can be a vehicle for change rather than a barrier. Even traditional ideas that seem, on the surface, to resolutely resist change may actually serve to facilitate it—at least certain kinds of change. An instance of this is the Indian concept of *dharma,* which involves the individual's duty to fulfill his or her own part of a network of mutual obligations and privileges. On the surface, it would seem that adhering to *dharma* would negate any kind of change, since those obligations and privileges emerge from the past. Nevertheless, in addition to maintaining the social order, the concept admits to flexibility, to modification of duty as the social milieu changes. "The accommodative characteristics of the *dharma* concept has [sic] allowed for change without overthrow of basic principles."[51] Thus, transformation is compatible with the concept, and much of the change in India during and since the days of Ghandi may be seen as a working out (rather than a rejection) of *dharma.*

Industrialization does not demand the obliteration of tradition nor does it impose a particular social structure upon a people. The logic of industrialism is said to require the priority of the economic. Nevertheless, the relation between the economy and polity in the United States and the Soviet Union, two highly industrialized nations, is obviously not the same. All efforts at industrialization in Communist China have been marked by the absolute priority of the political.

A similar argument with respect to the family has been set forth by Goode, who finds a considerable variety of family forms congenial with industrialization; there is no necessary destruction of traditional family patterns.[52] In an Arab village studied by Tannous, there was an initial conflict between the silk factory, with its typical emphasis on individual profit, and the traditional Lebanese kinship group, which had been the basis of community organization. The problem was resolved not by the disintegration of kinship obligations, but by a new form of factory enterprise. Each factory was the work of an enterprising individual who was supported by the compound family unit. The factories were always referred to in terms that indicated kinship group ownership, and the traditional kinship obligations were transferred to the factory situation.[53]

In general, then, it is not possible to justify the idea of a singular end for modernizing societies nor is it possible to justify the idea of a singular path to that end. The study of two Indonesian towns that were in the pretakeoff period of economic development concluded that the path toward economic takeoff may involve considerable diversity in terms of cultural patterns and social structures. One town was characterized by a highly individualistic, modernized Moslem, economically motivated setting; the other was group-centered, orthodox Hindu, and politically motivated.[54]

Another example is the Arab city of Tripoli, which was changing in the 1960s from an agrarian-commercial to a light industrial economic base. Some of the aspects of the Western industrial nations emerged in Tripoli—trends toward universal education, professionalism, modernized travel and communication, and expanded governmental programs, for example. These trends became an addition to, rather than a displacement of, the agrarian-commercial patterns. And "when we consider certain values, sentiments, and qualities of interpersonal relationships, we shall find cultural patterns which differ considerably from comparable ones which have been associated with the Western industrial city."[55]

Finally, it has been shown that some of the factors we often associate with modernization on the basis of Western experience may show a negative correlation with sustained growth in the developing nations. At certain levels of development, such factors as degree of literacy, growth of the mass media, formal education, and urbanization may correlate negatively with sustained growth.[56] The reason for this becomes clear if we consider education. When many of the developing nations first gained their independence, they faced a serious shortage of educated personnel to assume positions of responsibility in the polity and economy. The economy, however, may not expand rapidly enough to absorb an educated elite, particularly if the emphasis has been on universal education. Furthermore, the cost of maintaining a massive public education system may seriously impair the accumulation of capital necessary for economic development. At the same time, education is associated with power and with the material advantages of the West, so that there is a general demand for universal education. The net result may be that the government finds itself in a situation in which it is politically necessary, but economically unfeasible, to maintain large-scale education.

If, then, the idea of unidirectionality is a myth, the question arises as to whether anything can be said about the process of modernization apart from specific situations.A more realistic view than the unidirectional one is suggested by Black, who foresees a possible "universalization of functions, but not of institutions."[57] Modernization confronts a society with certain basic problems; but the answers that are given to those problems may vary considerably. A variety of institutional forms may prove to be adequate.

There are a number of reasons why there will be diverse societal answers to the problem of modernization. One is that the developing nations of the world have seen both the desirable and the objectionable in industrialized societies. The ideologies of the leaders of the developing nations always, therefore, have a nationalistic hue that rejects both the Soviet and the American patterns as appropriate *in toto* for their own societies.[58]

Second, although I have used the terms *modernization* and *industrialization* interchangeably, modernization may proceed apart from industrialization. That is, industrialization may be viewed as an essentially economic pattern of development, while modernization refers to the social and political changes that are often, though not necessarily, associated with industrialization. In the West, industrialization and commercialization were bound up with the process of modernization; but some non-Western development has involved commercialization and bureaucracy without industrialization."[59]

A third reason developing nations will pursue their own unique courses is that neither modern nor traditional societies are homogeneous entities. Just as modern, industrial societies exhibit differing systems, so do the traditional societies reveal considerable variations.[60] The developing nations are starting from diverse bases and aiming at diverse ends. The myths of unidirectionality and utopia apprehended are just that—myths. Our future is not converging toward some social system that is essentially an extrapolation of the contemporary West. Whatever logic there is in industrialism, it does not foreordain the shape of the future.

• *The Myth of Semantic Illusion*

As pointed out above, it has sometimes been assumed that static analyses can be made without coming to terms with change, and that an understanding of social change demands a prior and thorough understanding of social statics. This error may be compounded by assuming that every static analysis has implications for change, so that ultimately the difference between theories of change and theories of statics is merely a semantic illusion. This position has been argued forcefully by Kim Rodner.[61]

Rodner maintains that change theories are not distinguishable from nonchange theories by the variable of time. Rather, what are called *social change theories* are characterized by one or both of two properties that are not related to time: (1) the precision in stating the temporal connective and (2) the degree of compoundedness of the theory. As an example of the precision in stating the temporal connective, he refers to the theory of Davies regarding the cause of revolution. That theory can be expressed in terms of increasing temporal precision, from the folk law that thwarted hopes sometimes produce social uprisings to the more temporally precise law that some exact temporal quantity of an extended increase in expectations and the satisfaction of those expectations, followed by an unexpected reversal of short duration, may cause revolution. What the sociologist means by *laws of change,* according to Rodner, is the greater temporal precision in the second as opposed to the first formulation.

As to the degree of compoundedness, Rodner is referring to the difference between a single law and a series of laws that can be linked together into an explanatory chain. The latter, with its greater complexity, would have more obvious temporal implications.

Thus, the myth of semantic illusion concludes that all theories have implications for both change and statics, for all are saying essentially the same thing. The only difference is in the degree of precision with which the theory is formulated. This conclusion is false. All theories may indeed imply certain dynamics; all may imply movement of some kind; all certainly recognize that social life is not an inert entity. But all theories do not imply change—except, perhaps, in the negative sense that change is some kind of deviance or in the functionalist sense that change is merely an elaboration of a particular system. In addition, some theories regard change as natural, while others view it as that which occurs through some kind of coercion.

Whether change or persistence is seen as the basic reality is important. The difference between nonchange and change theories is more than semantic illusion; it is a difference in fundamental attitude toward change and the legitimacy of change. The theorist who works in the context of a nonchange theory provides—willingly or not—an ideological basis for the status quo. The people who operate on the assumption of the normality of persistence rather than of change will tend to inhibit—willingly or not—change in their society.

This latter point is illustrated by the exceedingly slow rate of change in China for hundreds of years prior to the twentieth century. The Chinese viewed persistence as the basic reality. They valued order, which was derived from the Mandate of Heaven, given to the Emperor that he might "organize a moral system and establish the moral order."[62] Change in this context was severely limited in scope. Certain recurrent processes were legitimate and even inevitable. The Chinese both perceived and expected the tempo of change to be slow. As Hsueh Fu-ch'eng, writing in 1879, put it: "According to the way of heaven, there is a small change once every several hundred years, and a great change once every several thousand years."[63] The difference between the Chinese view of reality and that of those people who held that reality is continual change was not one of mere illusion. The

Chinese expectation of a slow rate of change was matched by the reality of Chinese society.

Conclusion

Once we have clarified what we mean by *change* and cleared away the myths about change, we are in a position to begin the task of understanding change. Some of the theories to be discussed in the following chapters will make the assumptions that we have called *myths*. This does not mean, however, that nothing can be gained from a study of these theories. Many insights will come through the examination of past perspectives. The point is, however, that new perspectives on change must be constructed, and these new perspectives will be most fruitful if they assume that change is normal; that change carries with it no intrinsic trauma; that diverse patterns of change and a range of future alternatives are open to any society; and that whether one assumes change or persistence as the basic reality has important practical as well as theoretical consequences.

Endnotes

1. Otis Dudley Duncan, Howard Schuman, and Beverly Duncan, *Social Change in a Metropolitan Community* (New York: Russell Sage Foundation, 1973), p. 24.
2. Wilbert E. Moore, *Order and Change: Essays in Comparative Sociology* (New York: Wiley, 1967), p. 3.
3. In, respectively, Henry Pratt Fairchild, ed., *Dictionary of Sociology* (Ames, Iowa: Littlefield, Adams & Co., 1955), p. 277; and George A. Lundberg, Clarence C. Schrag, Otto N. Larsen, and William R. Catton, Jr., *Sociology*, 4th ed. (New York: Harper & Row, 1963), p. 583.
4. Attitude research has been the subject of considerable controversy and has yielded ambiguous results. See Robert H. Lauer, "The Problems and Values of Attitude Research," *The Sociological Quarterly* 12 (1971): 247-52. An excellent, concise discussion of the perplexing relationship between attitudes and behavior may be found in Irwin Deutscher, *Why Do They Say One Thing, Do Another?* (Morristown, N.J.: General Learning Press, 1973).
5. Willliam J. McEwen, *Changing Rural Society: A Study of Communities in Bolivia* (New York: Oxford University Press, 1975).
6. Ibid., p. 12.
7. Ibid., p. 61.
8. Wilbert E. Moore, *Social Change* (Englewood Cliffs, N.J.: Prentice-Hall, 1963), pp. 34-39.

9. Leon Martel, *Mastering Change* (New York: New American Library, 1986), Chapter 4.

10. Norval D. Glenn, "Social Trends in the United States: Evidence from Sample Surveys," *Public Opinion Quarterly* 51 (1987): S109-26.

11. See, for example, Talcott Parsons, Robert F. Bales, and Edward A. Shils, *Working Papers in the Theory of Action* (Glencoe, Ill.: Free Press, 1953), pp. 102-3; Talcott Parsons, "Some Considerations on the Theory of Social Change," *Rural Sociology* 26 (1961): 219-39; Richard T. LaPierre, *Social Change* (New York: McGraw-Hill, 1965), pp. 38-39; and Robert A. Nisbet, *Social Change and History* (New York: Oxford University Press, 1969), p. 270.

12. See Talcott Parsons, *The Social System* (Glencoe, Ill.: Free Press, 1951), pp. 483-86; and Wilbert E. Moore, "A Reconsideration of Theories of Social Change," *American Sociological Review* 25 (1960): 817.

13. Alfred North Whitehead, *Science and the Modern World* (New York: Macmillan, 1925), p. 179.

14. Frederick Engels, *Anti-Duhring*, trans. Emile Burns (New York: International Publishers, 1939), p. 26.

15. Ibid., p. 27.

16. By, respectively, C. E. Black, *The Dynamics of Modernization* (New York: Harper & Row, 1966), p. 47; Daniel Bell, *The End of Ideology* (New York: Free Press, 1960), pp. 35-36; and Amitai Etzioni, *The Active Society* (New York: Free Press, 1968).

17. Etienne Balazs, *Chinese Civilizations and Bureaucracy*, trans, H. M. Wright, ed. Arthur F. Wright (New Haven: Yale University Press, 1964), p. 15.

18. Don Martindale, *Social Life and Cultural Change* (Princeton: Van Nostrand, 1962), pp. 93-161.

19. Jacques Gernet, *Daily Life in China on the Eve of the Mongol Invasion, 1250-1276*, trans. H. M. Wright (Stanford: Stanford University Press, 1962), pp. 16-17.

20. See, for example, R. M. MacIver and Charles H. Page, *Society: An Introductory Analysis* (New York: Rinehart and Co., 1937),p. 512; and Raymond Firth, *Elements of Social Organization* (London: Watts & Co., 1951), pp. 80-121.

21. The Swiss psychiatrist Paul Tournier, in his *The Meaning of Persons*, trans. Edwin Hudson (New York: Harper & Row, 1957), p. 100, says: 'The perfectly stable being is nothing but an automaton, without life—a thing."

22. Alfred North Whitehead, *Adventures of Ideas* (New York: Mentor Books, 1933), p. 273.

23. By, respectively, Eric Hoffer, *The Ordeal of Change* (New York: Harper & Row, 1952); Robert A. Nisbet, *Social Change and History*, p. 282; and Richard T. LaPierre, *Social Change*, p. 39.

24. H. B. M. Murphy, "Social Change and Mental Health," *Milbank Memorial Fund Quarterly* 39 (1961): 385-445.

25. For a brief account of some of these factors, see Philip Hauser, "Cultural and Personal Obstacles to Economic Development in the Less Developed Areas," *Human Organization* 18 (1959): 78-84. A more extensive treatment is provided by George Foster, *Traditional Cultures: And the Impact of Technological Change* (New York: Harper & Row, 1962), pp. 64-142.

26. Gunnar Myrdal, *Asian Drama*, vol. 3 (New York: Pantheon, 1968), p. 1873.

27. Bert F. Hoselitz, "Tradition and Economic Growth," in *Tradition, Values, and Socio-Economic Development*, ed. Ralph Braibanti and Joseph Spengler (Durham: Duke University Press, 1961) p. 89.

28. Ronald Cohen, "The Success That Failed: An Experiment in Culture Change in Africa," *Anthropologica* 3 (1961): 21-36.

29. See Bernard Barber, *Science and the Social Order* (Glencoe, Ill.: Free Press, 1952), p. 213; and W. I. Thomas, *Primitive Behavior: An Introduction to the Social Sciences* (New York: McGraw-Hill, 1937), pp. 726-27.

30. The original study was Richard T. Lambert, *Workers, Factories, and Social Change in India* (Princeton: Princeton University Press, 1963). A follow-up study attempted to discern reasons for moving among those workers who did leave the factory. Only education was moderately related to departure. See Richard T. Lambert, Ralph B. Ginsberg, and Sarah J. Moore, *The Transformation of an Indian Labor Market: The Case of Pune* (Philadelphia: John Benjamins, 1986).

31. Joseph Lopreato, *Peasants No More* (San Francisco: Chandler, 1967), p. 65.

32. Daniel Lerner, *The Passing of Traditional Society* (Glencoe, Ill.: Free Press, 1958), pp. 398-99. The portrait of peasant life as generally unsatisfactory (by our standards, and sometimes by theirs as well) is found rather consistently in the literature. A good summary of the main features of that portrait is found in Everett M. Rogers and Rabel J. Burdge, *Social Change in Rural Societies*, 2nd ed. (New York: Appleton-Century-Crofts, 1972), pp. 418-28.

33. Anthony Wallace, "Revitalization Movements," *American Anthropologist* 58 (1956): 264-81.

34. Francis X. Hezel, "Truk Suicide Epidemic and Social Change," *Human Organization* 46 (1987): 283-91.

35. Alvin Toffler, *Future Shock* (New York: Random House, 1970).

36. Richard H. Rahe, Joseph D. McKean, Jr., and Ranson J. Arthur, "A Longitudinal Study of Life-Change and Illness Patterns," *Journal of Psychosomatic Research* 10 (1967): 366.

37. Robert H. Lauer, "Rate of Change and Stress: A Test of the 'Future Shock' Thesis," *Social Forces* 52 (1974): 510-16.

38. Amiram Vinokur and Melvin L. Selzer, "Desirable Versus Undesirable Life Events: Their Relationship to Stress and Mental Distress," *Journal of Personality and Social Psychology* 32 (1975): 329-37.

39. Richard S. Krannich and Thomas Greider, "Personal Well-Being in Rapid Growth and Stable Communities: Multiple Indicators and Contrasting Results," *Rural Sociology* 49 (1984): 541-52.

40. William H. Starbuck, "Organizational Growth and Development," in *Handbook of Organizations*, ed. James G. March (Chicago: Rand-McNally, 1965), p. 472.

41. Robert Seidenberg, "The Trauma of Eventlessness," *The Psychoanalytic Review* 59 (1972): 102.

42. Ibid., p. 103.

43. George A. Theodorson, "Acceptance of Industrialization and Its Attendant Consequences for the Social Patterns of Non-Western Societies," *American Sociological Review* 18 (1953): 477-84.

44. Clark Kerr, John T. Dunlop, Frederick H. Harbison, and Charles A. Myers, *Industrialism and Industrial Man* (Cambridge: Harvard University Press, 1960), pp. 282-288.

45. For a critique of the theory of modernization along these lines, see Michael Walzer, "The Only Revolution: Notes on the Theory of Modernization," *Dissent* 11 (1964): 432-40. For examples of the explicit argument or implicit assumption that a modern, industrial society is utopia apprehended, see Ernest Gellner, *Thought and Change* (Chicago: University of Chicago Press, 1964), pp. 69ff; C. E. Black, *The Dynamics of Modernization* (New York: Harper & Row, 1966), pp. 129ff; Francis R. Allen, *Socio-Cultural Dynamics* (New York: Macmillan, 1971), pp. 340ff; and Brigitte Berger, *Societies in Change* (New York: Basic Books, 1971), pp. 13-14, 174.

46. Manning Nash, *Machine Age Maya* (Chicago: University of Chicago Press, 1967).

47. A brief summary, some references, and divergent viewpoints regarding the Japanese experience are provided in a number of articles in the *Journal of Social Issues* 24 (1968): 1-158.

48. F. Kenneth Berrier, "Japanese Values and the Democratic Process," *Journal of Social Psychology* 68 (1966): 129-38.

49. Ezra F. Vogel, "Kinship Structure, Migration to the City, and Modernization," in *Aspects of Social Change in Modern Japan*, ed. R. P. Dore (Princeton: Princeton University Press, 1967), pp. 91-111.

50. John K. Fairbank, Edwin O. Reischauer, and Albert M. Craig, *East Asian: The Modern Transformation* (Boston: Houghton Mifflin, 1965), p. 9.

51. Joan Bondurant, "Traditional Polity and the Dynamics of Change in India," *Human Organization* 22 (1963): 10.

52. William J. Goode, "Industrialization and Family Change," in *Industrialization and Society*, ed. Bert F. Hoselitz and Wilbert E. Moore (Paris: UNESCO-Mouton, 1963), pp. 239-55.

53. Afif I. Tannous, "Social Change in an Arab Village," *American Sociological Review* (1941): 651-62.

54. Clifford Geertz, *Peddlers and Princes* (Chicago: University of Chicago Press, 1963).

55. John Gulick, "Old Values and New Institutions in an Lebanese Arab City," *Human Organization* 24 (1965): 51.

56. S. N. Eisenstadt, ed., *Readings in Social Evolution and Development* (Oxford: Pergamon Press, 1970), p. 23.

57. Black, *The Dynamics of Modernization*, p. 49.

58. Paul E. Sigmund, ed., *The Ideologies of the Developing Nations* (New York: Praeger, 1967).

59. David E. Apter, *The Politics of Modernization* (Chicago: University of Chicago Press, 1965), pp. 43-44.

60. Donald N. Levine, "The Flexibility of Traditional Culture," *The Journal of Social Issues* 24 ((1968): 129-42.

61. Kim Rodner, "Logical Foundations of Social Change Theory," *Sociology and Social Research* 51 (1967): 287-301.

62. Hajime Nakamura, *Ways of Thinking of Eastern Peoples,* ed. Philip P. Wiener (Honolulu: East-West Center Press, 1964), p. 271.

63. Quoted in Ssu-yu Teng and John K. Fairbank, *China's Response to the West* (New York: Atheneum, 1967), p. 142. For a more extended discussion of these points, see Robert H. Lauer, "Temporality and Social Change: The Case of 19th Century China and Japan," *The Sociological Quarterly* 14 (1973): 451-64.

PART TWO

Theoretical Perspectives on Change

"When I even hear the word *theory*," an intelligent student said to me, "I go into a panic." A considerable number of students have expressed similar concerns about dealing with theory. Theories need not unsettle us. In fact, we use theories all the time. In simplest terms, a theory is an explanation. We act on the basis of theories about individuals, society, and the world in which we live, i.e., ideas that explain what individuals, society, and the world are all about. Some theories explain problems in society on the basis of the evil nature of humans; individuals who relate to other individuals with mistrust may be acting on the basis of such a theory.

In a more formal sense, a theory is a set of logically related propositions that explain some phenomenon. This may be easily illustrated by Durkheim's famous effort to explain suicide.[1] Durkheim argued that one type of suicide, which he called *egoistic*, varies inversely with social integration. Specifically, the suicide rate will be less (1) among families in which there are children (domestic integration increases with children in the home), (2) during times of national crisis (an external threat increases political integration), and (3) among Catholics as opposed to Protestants (Catholics form a more integrated religious group than the highly individualistic Protestants).

Durkheim's theory of egoistic suicide can be summed up in one sentence: the suicide rate of any group varies inversely with the degree of social integration of that group. However, we have said that a theory is a *set* of propositions, and there is such a set of propositions implied in what Durkheim has said. Merton has spelled these out with respect to religious groups:

1. Social cohesion provides psychic support to group members subjected to acute stresses and anxieties.
2. Suicide rates are a function of unrelieved anxieties and stresses to which persons are subjected.
3. Catholics have greater social cohesion than Protestants.
4. Therefore, lower suicide rates should be anticipated among Catholics than among Protestants.[2]

Durkheim's theory, in sum, is an effort to explain the phenomenon of suicide. Likewise, all the theories we shall examine in this part are attempts to explain social change. What causes change? What is the pattern of change? What is it that changes? Why does change occur in the particular direction we observe rather than in some other, just as reasonable, alternative way? These are the kinds of questions the various theories attempt to answer. The kinds of answers provided by the theories allow us to categorize them. Thus, some theories are based on sociohistorical processes (chapters 2 and 3); some emphasize analytical rather than empirical materials (Chapter 4); and some stress the importance of social-psychological factors in change (Chapter 5).

Endnotes

1. Emile Durkheim, *Suicide*, trans. John A. Spaulding and George Simpson, ed. George Simpson (New York: Free Press, 1951).
2. Robert K. Merton, *Social Theory and Social Structure* (Glencoe, Ill.: Free Press, 1957), p. 97.

CHAPTER TWO

Sociohistorical Theories: Cyclic

Where is the human race heading? Are we plunging recklessly toward the annihilation of civilization, or groping our way with agonizing slowness toward utopia? The question as framed sounds reasonable to modern, Western ears, but to many people throughout history it would provide an inadequate number of alternatives. A more common way of explaining the direction of change has been to conceive of it as cyclic. The Greeks, Romans, and Chinese, among others, thought of human life as enmeshed in vast historical cycles rather than in a particular linear direction.

In the Chinese view, for example, the universe was thought to be in continual flux, but that flux followed a "fixed and therefore predictable pattern consisting either of eternal oscillation between two poles or of cyclical movement within a closed circuit; in either case the change involved is relative rather than absolute, since all movement serves in the end only to bring the process back to its starting point."[1] Because of this cyclic pattern, Chinese historians gave world history neither a beginning nor an end. Time was a series of cycles based on planetary motions, and could therefore be thought of as "extending indefinitely into the past and future for as long as the planets themselves exist."[2]

The difference between this view and that of the modern West was expressed clearly by the scholar Yen Fu, who pointed out that while the Chinese neglected the present because of their love of antiquity, Westerners were struggling in the present in order to overcome the past and transcend it. The Chinese, he observed, believed that a "period of order and a period of disorder, a period of prosperity and a period of decline" was the normal course of human history. By contrast, Westerners believed that "daily progress should be endless."[3]

In contrast with the dominant Western view, then, some theorists have tried to explain the course of history by viewing it in terms of an ongoing series of cycles. That there are cyclic variations in social life is indisputable, of course. Some of these are familiar to us—such as business cycles—but there are a large number of intriguing cycles at every level of human life. For example, at the individual level there are numerous cyclic variations in physiological functions—diurnal variations in temperature and blood pressure, among others. At various other levels, we find a great number of cyclic phenomena, including cyclic patterns of wars, creativity, crime, marriage and birth rates, religious and scientific activity, and labor problems. The theories to be examined in this chapter, however, argue for cycles at the level of civilizations or societies. We shall examine three such theories; in detail they differ considerably, but each in some fashion stresses a cyclic pattern. Each also thereby asserts that what may appear as an upward or downward linear direction of change is actually only the phase of a cycle; ultimately, the direction will reverse itself.

Nomadic versus Sedentary: Ibn Khaldun

At a time when most people thought of history in terms of Providence, a remarkably perceptive Arab scholar endeavored to identify causal factors in the historical process.[4] Ibn Khaldun (1332-1406) was born in Tunis, and was a descendant of an aristocratic family that included many prominent political figures and scholars. Khaldun himself spent the greater part of his life in political service, where he was able to observe political turmoil in northwest Africa; for by the fourteenth century, the expanding civilization of Islam had begun to decline. Khaldun was struck by the disintegration of the Islamic world, and he determined to explain it.

For four years, Khaldun retired from political life in order to write his "universal history." To start with, he felt that existing approaches to the writing of history were totally inadequate. For Khaldun perceived that the mere chronicling of events was at best a beginning task of the historian; what was needed was an explanation, an identification of the pattern of changes. This explanation, or pattern, is contained in *The Muqaddimah,* the introduction to his history. It is this work, rather than the history itself (which he entitled *Book of Lessons and Archive of Early and Subsequent History, Dealing with the Political Events concerning the Arabs, Non-Arabs, and Berbers, and the Supreme Rulers Who Were Contemporary with Them*), for which he can justly be called one of the world's great thinkers.

The *Muqaddimah* explores the manifold factors involved in social change. Khaldun examines the influence of the physical environment on people, the forms of primitive and advanced social organization, intergroup relationships, the nature of leadership, urban life, and various cultural phenomena (arts, crafts, sciences, and so forth). In other words, he not only made a bold new advance in trying to ascertain causal factors in change; he also recognized that those factors would be numerous and diverse.

As a result, Khaldun may be regarded as a pioneer of sociological thought, identifying and utilizing six "basic principles on which sociology must rest."[5] These principles are as follows:

1. Social phenomena follow lawful patterns. These patterns are not as rigid as those operative in the physical world, but they exhibit sufficient regularity to be recognized and described. This, of course, represents a radical departure from the notion that social life follows the immutable will of Providence or the unpredictable caprices of fate.
2. The laws are operative at the societal level. While the individual, therefore, is not a mere pawn of vast historical forces, neither is he able to escape the limitations imposed upon his behavior by societal laws. Contrary to the American expectation that if all is not well with the social order a change of president may resolve our problems, Khaldun asserted that reformers in corrupt states would be neutralized by overwhelming social forces.
3. The laws of the social process must be discovered through gathering much data and observing relationships among the variables. Both written records of the past and present observation can provide the data. This emphasis on the empirical grounding of social knowledge represents another departure, in this case a departure from the more common rational and mystical perspectives of the fourteenth century.
4. Similar social laws are operative in societies that are structurally similar. Societies may be separate both in time and in space, yet be characterized by similar laws because of similar social structures.
5. Societies are characterized by change. The rate of change may vary considerably. Khaldun thought that in some past eras, not many significant changes had occurred for long spans of time. But in his own time, it seemed as though "the entire creation had changed and the whole world been altered, as if it were a new and repeated creation, a world brought into existence anew."[6]
6. The laws that apply to the change are sociological, not biological or physical, in nature. Khaldun considers the impact of the physical environment on human behavior, noting such things as the effects of

heat on the inhabitants of tropical zones and the effects of air and food. He argues that great civilizations can only arise in the temperate zones, that hot air creates mirth, that heavy, starchy foods make people dull of mind. But these are not crucial factors in understanding history. The thrust of history must be understood in terms of social phenomena such as solidarity, leadership, occupation, and wealth. Social change must be seen in terms of social variables that alone can account for the change.

Furthermore, Khaldun builds his theory of change on the premise that humans are social creatures. "Human social organization is something necessary."[7] This was expressed in the philosophical saying that man is by nature political. That means simply that humans must have "the social organization for which the philosophers use the technical term *town*."[8] This social nature derives from the fact that each person must rely on others to help in the activities necessary for existence—cooking, planting, making utensils and tools. No one is self-sufficient. Human needs can be fulfilled only through the cooperative efforts of many.

At the same time, Khaldun believed in humans' innate aggressiveness. Like Hobbes, therefore, he argued that people required strong authority in order to restrain aggression. A sovereign is required who will have absolute authority over his or her subjects, and prevent them from attacking one another. This "royal authority is a natural quality of man which is absolutely necessary to mankind."[9] A human being is a creature who was made to be ruled by a sovereign.

The importance of these assumptions regarding the social nature and innate aggressiveness of humankind will become clear as we turn to Khaldun's theory of change. That theory involves two contrasting forms of social organization—the nomadic (Bedouins) and the sedentary. The theory is an attempt to explain the Bedouin success in overthrowing a number of North African civilizations.

Both Bedouins and sedentary people are "natural groups," i.e., groups that result from differing ways of making a living. The Bedouins live a Spartan existence; their life is difficult and simple. They subsist in the desert and make their living through the raising of camels. This distinguishes them from most Berbers and non-Bedouins, who cultivate grain and engage in agriculture, and from a number of other groups who make their living from such animals as sheep and cattle. The Bedouins are unable to secure any but the bare necessities of existence. Their way of life generates in them great courage and a high degree of self-determination. There is also intense solidarity among the Bedouins; indeed, the rigors of existing in the desert demand the cooperative efforts that arise from group solidarity. The net result of all this is that the Bedouins are "the most savage human beings that exist."[10]

Solidarity is a crucial aspect of Bedouin life and a key concept with Khaldun. Those people who possess it are likely to conquer those who lack it; given equal numbers, the antagonist united by a sense of "group feeling" is always stronger than and superior to the opponent that is composed of differing groups. But why do some groups possess solidarity and others lack it? Khaldun identifies a number of sources of Bedouin solidarity, including the exigencies of desert life mentioned above, kinship bonds, and religion.

Kinship ties are important in creating solidarity in that people possess a natural urge to protect their blood relatives from attack or injustice. Religion is important in that it restrains the savage Bedouin nature; religious zeal neutralizes the competitiveness and envy which group members might otherwise feel toward one another and provides shared goals and a common perspective.

In sum, as a religious, kinship-oriented group living under severely demanding environmental conditions, the Bedouins emerge in Khaldun's writing (and, no doubt, did emerge in reality) as a horde of Genghis Khans-ruthless, tough, and both willing and able to overwhelm every opponent.

In spite of this portrait of human ferocity, Khaldun does not mean to disparage the Bedouins. Quite the contrary, in fact, for the Bedouin way of life existed before the sedentary, and the latter represents a process of degeneration in almost every respect except material goods. "Sedentary people" are those who live in cities and countries and make their living either by the crafts or by commerce. A sedentary person presents a contrast to the nomad.

Sedentary people are primarily interested in pleasures of various kinds. They crave luxury and success, and eagerly immerse themselves in every kind of worldly indulgence. They become more and more removed from the goodness that was to be found among the Bedouins; the souls of sedantary peoples are "coloured with all kinds of blameworthy and evil qualities."[11] This life of indulgence makes them lazy; their life of ease erodes the Bedouin qualities of courage and strength. Energy, fortitude, and vigor are swallowed up in the cesspool of riotous, self-indulgent living.

The qualities that made for survival and triumph melt away from sedentary people. Group solidarity and religion weaken and finally crumple before the onslaught of unrestrained indulgence in pleasure. People who once might have joined together in zestful cooperation become alienated and worse: they are "devoted to lying, gambling, cheating, fraud, theft, perjury, and usury."[12] Like an Arab Savonarola, Khaldun lays bare the utter corruption of sedentary life.

Yet the picture is not totally bleak. For Khaldun does acknowledge that the crafts and sciences are brought to perfection only in a large sedentary civilization. The cultural development of the human race cannot occur when the individual struggles at the subsistence level. Some measure of luxury and surplus are necessary for science and the crafts to develop beyond very simple levels.

Sedentary life, then, is secular, individualistic, and relatively affluent. This is the obverse of the nomadic life in virtually every characteristic. Morally, spiritually, physically, and culturally, sedentary and nomadic people live in two different worlds.

We have, then, been presented with two contrasting forms of social organization, and their resulting personality types. In the description itself, we have already seen hints of Khaldun's theory of change; that theory is based on conflict, the clash between nomadic and sedentary people. The desert nomads covet the luxuries of the city; "urbanization is found to be the goal to which the Bedouin aspires."[13] The nomads, therefore, continually attack and conquer cities and towns; the sedentary inhabitants of the urban areas are no match for the fierce Bedouins. As a result of the conquest of the urban areas, a state or empire is formed. But once the conquerors settle in the cities, they fall prey to the degeneration of the sedentary peoples they conquered. It is only a matter of time before a new horde of nomads sweeps over the empire. Thus, there is a cycle of change, with empires being established, decaying into a state of vice and impotence, and falling before the power of a new generation of desert nomads. The state is established and overthrown by conflict. History is an ongoing cycle of growth and decay, of conquest and collapse.

Khaldun describes the natural history of the empire that is established (and that will sooner or later fall) in terms of three generations and five stages.[14] An empire, like an individual, has a "natural life span," which is generally no more than three generations or about 120 years. The first generation includes those who swept over the land to conquest; once settled in the cities, they retain the strength and solidarity of their desert existence. The effects of sedentary living begin to appear, however, in the second generation. Luxury and royal authority replace rigorous living and solidarity. There is the remembrance of the qualities of the past, and some hope of recapturing them. But by the third generation, the very qualities of desert life have been forgotten. By this point, sedentary living has taken its toll; the empire has become "senile and is worn out," and the fourth generation faces destruction.

Khaldun describes this same process in terms of five stages. In the first, the nomads have succeeded in overthrowing all opposition and establishing a new empire. In the second, consolidation takes place as the new ruler secures control over the domain. The third stage is one of "leisure and tranquility"; the quest for more and more experiences of luxury has begun, and there is an expansion of the culture (such as development of governmental functions, erection of buildings and monuments). Peace continues in the fourth stage, which, however, is marked by preservation of what has been obtained in the past rather than by any new expansion of culture. Traditionalism characterizes the fourth stage. Finally, the fifth stage is one of degeneration. The ruler wastes money on luxury on himself, and his "inner circle." He is surrounded with those who are incapable of carrying on the affairs of state. The ruler alienates the people and loses the support of many of the soldiers. The empire has been seized by a social sickness that is relentless and chronic; there is no cure for its illness—it can only await its destruction.

As this summary of Khaldun's thought shows, this great Arab thinker set forth numerous insights about social change that demand that he be ranked among the most perceptive of social theorists. He recognized the complexity of social life and tried to account for the multitude of factors that would bear upon the question of change. Environmental, social, and social-psychological factors are all considered. In the general context of a conflict theory of change, Khaldun looked at the importance of the physical environment, the social structure, the role of leadership and personality, and the crucial importance of group cohesiveness. He perceived the importance of occupation (ways of making a living) in understanding personality types. He examined the roles of religion and leadership in effecting change. We have not discussed the latter in detail, but Khaldun gives considerable attention to it. He points out, for example, that what matters to the subjects is not the ruler's appearance or intellect but the kind of relationships he establishes with his subjects. The ruler who relates to his people in a despotic manner is engaging in an act of self-destruction; the ruler must be concerned for the needs of the subjects and must seek to gain their love. In fact, it is the ruler's failure in benevolence and obsession with luxury and self-indulgence that pave the way for the degeneration and fall of the sedentary civilization.

In sum, writing at a time and place where explanations were likely to be clothed in fatalistic terms, Ibn Khaldun set forth an incisive theory of change. Among the important insights of his work are the following:

1. The historical method offers the best approach to understanding social change.
2. The factors involved in change are many and diverse; no single factor (such as personality or technology) can adequately account for change.
3. Differing forms of social organization create differing personality types.
4. Conflict is the basic mechanism of change.
5. A variety of social-psychological factors—leadership, personality, group cohesiveness—help us to understand both the antecedents and the outcome of intergroup conflict.
6. Change tends to be pervasive, occurring in all the social institutions; religion, the family, the government, and the economy are all involved in the process.

Challenge and Response: Arnold Toynbee

Like Khaldun, whom he called an "Arabic genius," Arnold Toynbee (1889-1975) sees a process of birth, growth, stagnation, and disintegration in social life.[15] Toynbee takes as the unit of his study societies or civilizations rather than nations or periods of time. The study of any particular nation is unintelligible as a "thing-in-itself"; it must be seen as part of a larger process. We cannot, for example, understand England by merely studying the history of that nation itself; rather, we must see England in terms of its place in Western Christendom. The focus of study, therefore, is not England or the United States or any other particular nation, but the civilizations of which any nation is but a part.

There are, according to Toynbee, twenty-one such civilizations (e.g., the Egyptian, the Indic, the Sumerian, the Babylonian, the Western). Six civilizations arose spontaneously from primitive societies: the Egyptian, the Sumerian, the Chinese, the Mayan, the Minoan, and the Indic. Each of these arose independently of the others, and they appeared in widely separated areas. All the other civilizations derive from these original six. In addition, there have been three abortive (Far Western Christian, Far Eastern Christian, Scandinavian) and five arrested (Polynesian, Eskimo, Nomadic, Ottoman, Spartan) civilizations.

What caused a civilization to arise out of a primitive society? The latter is oriented toward the past, and remains static; societies in the process of civilization, by contrast, are in "dynamic motion along a course of change and growth."[16] Toynbee first examines racial and environmental explanations and rejects them. There is no superior race, and there are no environments that could create civilizations themselves because of their facilitating characteristics. Rather, civilizations arise out of responses to challenges: the causal mechanism is not an entity but a relation, and that relation may be one of human-nature or human-human. For example, the Egyptian civilization arose as the result of an adequate response to the challenge of the swamps and jungles of the Nile Valley, while other civilizations emerged from the challenge of intergroup conflict.

The point is that it is not easy conditions that cause civilizations to arise, but rather adverse conditions. A civilization emerges on the throes of struggle; it comes into being only by surmounting barriers, not by traveling an open, smooth road. A number of different kinds of challenges may comprise the adversity necessary for the rise of a civilization. Toynbee talks about five different stimuli: hard countries, new ground, blows, pressures, and penalizations.[17] *Hard country* refers to a difficult physical environment, such as that provided by the "watery chaos of the lower valley of the Yellow River."[18] *New ground* refers to land that has not been settled and tilled. *Blows* include sudden military defeats, while *pressures* indicate a situation of continuing external threat. Finally, *penalizations* refer to those classes and races who have historically been subjected to various forms of oppression, discrimination, and exploitation.

Obviously, when we have a challenge, we do not always have the kind of response that generates a civilization. The challenge may be so severe that no adequate response can be made. There is, therefore, not a direct relation between challenge and response, but a linear one. That is, a broad range of degrees of difficulty can evoke an adequate response; but at the extremes—challenges that are overly weak and overly severe—adequate response is not possible. If the challenge is too severe, a civilization may abort or become arrested,in its development; in such cases, the challenge has sufficient force to prevent normal development, though it is not so severe as to cause defeat.

The first criterion, then, of whether or not an adequate response will be made is the severity of the challenge. The second criterion of adequate response is the presence of an elite in charge of the response. The growth of the civilization hinges on the behavior of a creative minority. "All acts of social creation are the work either of individual creators or, at most, of creative minorities."[19] But the bulk of humankind tends to remain mired in past ways. The task of the minority, therefore, is not simply to create new social forms and processes, but to "contrive some means of carrying this sluggish rear-guard along with them in their eager advance."[20] Led by the elite, the civilization grows through a series of successful responses to continuing challenges.

What is the meaning of the growth of a civilization? Toynbee calls it a process of "etherialization," a shift of emphasis from some lower sphere of being or of action to a higher."[21] This means the conquest of initial obstacles so that energy is released for responding to challenges which are now internal rather than external and spiritual rather than material in nature. Such growth means increasing self-determination, and it involves continual differentiation among the parts of the society. This differentiation occurs because some parts will respond successfully, while others will succeed through imitating those that make adequate response; and still others will fail to be either creative or imitative and so will succumb. The net result is the development of a unique style in each civilization. The Hellenic civilization, for example, had a "predominantly aesthetic outlook on life as a whole," while the Indic and Hindu civilizations tended "towards an outlook that is predominantly religious."[22]

No civilization continues to grow indefinitely. Commonly, there is a breakdown, which occurs when the creative elite no longer functions adequately, the majority no longer gives its allegiance to and imitates the elite, and social unity disintegrates. The breakdown and disintegration are common but not inevitable. There may also be a petrifaction, as illustrated by the history of Egyptiac Society and the Far East. In the state of petrifaction, the society continues on after it should have completed its life-course (as measured by Toynbee's theory and his analysis of other societies). For example, Egyptiac Society survived for nearly two thousand years after it had apparently become moribund, continuing in a state of "life-in-death." In other words, during the second half of its existence (roughly the sixteenth century B.C. to the fifth century A.D.) Egyptiac Society continued as an identifiable civilization, but it was stagnant as far as cultural production was concerned. Like an individual who has lost virtually everything but the capacity to breathe and eat and cling to life, Egyptiac Society lingered on but contributed nothing of value.

Most civilizations do not petrify; they break down. And when that breakdown occurs, it follows a characteristic pattern: there is a societal fission, with the civilization rupturing into the three opposing groupings of dominant minority, internal proletariat, and external proletariat. Each of the three groupings, in turn, creates a "characteristic institution: universal state, universal church and barbarian warbands."[23] The creation of a universal state means that the elite now imposes itself on the masses by force; it has transformed itself into a ruling class. This is not done deliberately to exploit the masses, but as a desperate effort to hold together the crumbling civilization. The internal proletariat, made up of those who are "in" but not "of" the society, turns against the elite and forms a universal church. The external proletariat, those who were culturally influenced by the growing civilization but who are no longer charmed once the breakdown has occurred, then ceases to imitate and becomes hostile toward the civilization. The boundary between the civilization and the external proletariat becomes a military frontier; "this temporary and precarious balance of forces inevitably tilts, with the passage of time, in favour of the barbarians."[24]

Like Khaldun, Toynbee concerned himself with social-psychological aspects of change. Having portrayed the "schism in the body social," therefore, he proceeds to discuss the "schism in the soul." Societal fission is mirrored in the individual psyche; during the time of disintegration, the varied ways of behaving, feeling, and living that characterized the growing civilization are replaced by "alternative substitutes." For example, rather than being sustained by the sense of exhilaration and vigor that pervaded the growing society, the people struggle with a sense of drift (beyond human control) and a sense of sin.

The stage of disintegration, like the stage of growth, has its creative individuals who fashion a response to the challenges. In the growing stage, they led the masses in making successful responses to the varied challenges. In the disintegration stage, they come as saviors of, or deliverers from, the society. Specifically, there are four types of saviors who appear. The "saviour with the sword" is the founder and upholder of the universal state. The "saviour with the time machine" is the "archaist" or the "futurist." The former is one who saves by restoring a golden era of the past; the latter is one who saves by leaping into the unknown of the future (by revolution that severs the society from the past). The "philosopher masked by a King" represents a solution that employs neither the sword nor the time machine, a solution first proposed by Plato. It demands a union of philosophy and political power; either philosophers must become kings, or kings must become philosophers. This solution will fail, argues Toynbee, because of the essential contradiction between the detachment of the philosopher and the coercive intervention of the king. Finally, there is the "God incarnate in a man." It is only those saviors who have presented themselves as gods who offer hope, or, more accurately, it is only Jesus Christ who can deliver us from death. It is for this kind of argument that Toynbee has been accused of burying history in an Anglican churchyard.

The disintegration of a civilization does not proceed at a uniform pace, nor does it equally affect all parts of the civilization. There is a rhythm: "In military language the rhythm may be expressed as rout-rally-rout-rally-rout."[25] For example, the universal state represents a rally after the rout of a time of distress. Finally, whereas the growing civilization is marked by increasing differentiation, the disintegrating civilization is marked by increasing standardization. Dominant minorities "uniformly" create philosophies and universal states; internal proletariats "uniformly" find a higher religion which is expressed through a universal church; and external proletariats "uniformly" gather in warbands to launch their assault upon the civilization.

Toynbee was concerned about the prospects of Western civilization as well as the fate of past civilizations. He suggested a number of basic problems that would have to be confronted and somehow resolved, problems that are as pressing today (if not more so) as they were over thirty years ago when Toynbee wrote about them. One is the problem of war, which was a primary cause of the breakdown and disintegration of civilizations of the past. With the development of the atom bomb, the control of war has become an imperative.

A second basic problem is that of class conflict. Industrialization means that the bulk of material goods need no longer be monopolized by a privileged few. People will no longer be content unless they are free from want. There is a question of whether we are willing to pay the price, since the production of sufficient goods to satisfy the masses of people requires a number of "turns of the screw" in regimenting workers, who must submit to the bondage of mechanized work. In their efforts to resist this regimentation, the workers joined together in trade unions, which only increased their regimentation. Furthermore, the middle class found itself mired in regimentation in the form of bureaucracy:

> *It looked as if the regimentation imposed by industrial technology might be taking the life out of the pre-industrial spirit of private enterprise; and this prospect opened up a further question. Would the technical system of mechanized industry be able to survive the social system of private enterprise? And, if not, would the Western civilization itself be able to survive the death of a mechanized industry, to which it had given hostages by allowing its population to increase in the Machine Age far beyond the numbers that any non-industrial economy could support?*[26]

As the quote suggests, a third basic problem identified by Toynbee is population growth. If that can be solved, he said, we will need to address the problem of leisure. All of these problems remain crucial to human well-being. Perhaps the one that Americans recognize least is that of social class, the inequalities that exist in a nation that boasts of equality of opportunities. Are the inequities between people in different social classes so serious and so grievous that they will lead to a decline and fall of Western civilization? Even if the problem of class is somehow resolved, will our civilization be able to cope with the threat of war or the problems raised by overpopulation? Toynbee not only identified some of the basic problems; he also reminded us by his survey of history that no civilization is immune to decline.

In sum, the picture that Toynbee draws for us of the history of humankind is one of continuing cycles of birth, growth, breakdown, and disintegration of civilizations. Toynbee sees this whole process as being intimately tied up with the functioning of elites and their relationships with the masses, both the internal and external proletariats. Further, as he grapples with the complexity of societal change, Toynbee tries to avoid the extremes of determinism and historicism. It is questionable whether he is able to do this. For example, we may ask whether a challenge is of the proper severity to elicit a civilization-building response. There is no way to answer the question except by ex post facto analysis; if a civilization develops, the challenge was of sufficient but not too much severity, while an aborted or arrested civilization points to an overly severe challenge. As Toynbee himself observed, there are no predetermined outcomes to challenges, which are "therefore intrinsically unpredictable."[27]

Nevertheless, there is value in striving, as Toynbee did, to identify critical factors involved in social change without making those factors either deterministic or capricious. In addition, Toynbee stresses for us again the centrality of conflict in change, the important role of elites and the elite-masses relationship, and the significance of social-psychological factors in understanding change.

Oscillating Sociocultural Modes: Pitirim Sorokin

Pitirim A. Sorokin (1889-1968), our final example of a thinker who sees cyclic variations in the historical process, was born in Russia, sentenced to death by the Communists in 1918, and exiled in 1922. He spent the remainder of his life in the United States, where he wrote several important works about social mobility, sociological theory, and sociocultural change.[28] A brilliant and prolific scholar, Sorokin covered virtually the whole of Western history in his effort to determine historical patterns of change. In his *Social and Cultural Dynamics*, he analyzed change from 600 B.C. to around A.D. 1935, focusing on Western civilization (including the Graeco-Roman), but bringing in some materials from Chinese, Hindu, and Arabian cultures.

Like Toynbee's, Sorokin's writing covers an immense and impressive span of time and humanity. However, Sorokin criticized Toynbee's methodology. Toynbee's "civilizations," argued Sorokin, are arbitrarily defined and of little scientific use; basically, this is because Toynbee fails to distinguish between systems and congeries. The civilizations identified by Toynbee are in reality a "conglomeration of many systems and congeries."[29] As such, they are not the integrated wholes envisioned by Toynbee, and they cannot be treated as units of analysis.

Sorokin himself employed the "logico-meaningful" method; this method involves the discovery of some central principle around which a system is organized and which gives meaning to each of the elements of the system, thereby integrating them into the whole. In such a system, there will be a "logical compatibility and specific dependence or interdependence of each meaning-element upon other meanings-elements," and the same relationship will hold true between the meanings-elements and the overall system.[30]

This method yields, according to Sorokin, three sociocultural systems, or supersystems," which will be described below. Sorokin endeavored to show how all the elements of one of the supersystems tend to be characterized by the one pervasive principle of that particular supersystem. To do this, he had to examine such aspects of culture as art, systems of truth, religion, ethics, law, philosophy, and the family. These varied aspects of culture were subjected to both qualitative and quantitative analysis. Qualitatively, the various aspects of culture had to be defined in accord with whether they exhibited the principle of one or the other of the three supersystems. Quantitatively, the rate of occurrence of each of the three principles in each facet of culture had to be estimated for each period of time throughout the centuries covered in the study. For example, the percentage of thinkers who held to an ethics of happiness versus the percentage who advocated an "absolute" ethics (such as the moral commands of a religion) was computed for each century, and was found to vary from certain periods in which all thinkers held to an absolute ethics to periods in which the distribution was nearly even.

Sorokin, then, finds that sociocultural history is a cyclic variation between three supersystems which represent fairly homogeneous cultures. A great culture is not a "mere dumping place of a multitude of diverse cultural phenomena," but a "unity or individuality whose parts are permeated by the same fundamental principle and articulate the same basic value."[31] The three systems are the ideational, which is pervaded by the principle of God as true reality and value; the sensate, which is pervaded by the principle that the sensory world is the true reality and value; and the idealistic, which is a combination of the other two—that is, reality and value are partially sensory and partially suprasensory.[32] Thus, ideational culture is spiritual and nonmaterial in its emphasis; sensate culture is material and hedonistic in its emphasis; and idealistic culture manages a balance between the ideational and the sensate, usually with the former somewhat dominant over the latter. Christian medieval Europe exemplifies the ideational culture; the time around the birth of Christ and the present are sensate cultures; idealistic systems (such as Europe in the thirteenth and fourteenth centuries) tend to emerge during the transition from the ideational to the sensate.

The distinction between the various systems may be clearer if we contrast some features of an ideational and a sensate culture. In the ideational culture, individuals perceive their basic needs as spiritual; in the sensate, people focus on their physical needs and attempt to gratify the senses. In an ideational culture, truth is revealed by God through various individuals, and is apprehended by mystic experiences, intuition, or direct revelation. In the sensate culture, truth is gained through the senses, and if a statement is not verifiable by the senses it cannot be said to be true. Ideational liberty is an inner freedom, "rooted in the restraint and control of our desires, wishes, and lusts."[33] Sensate liberty is the individual's ability to do whatever he or she wants; it is freedom from external constraints. Ideational art focuses on the "supersensory kingdom of God"; it is symbolic and religiously oriented. Sensate art focuses on the empirical world, and seeks to provide people with sensual gratification. We could carry on the contrast through the whole of culture, for every aspect of culture may be characterized as ideational, idealistic, or sensate. It should be noted, however, that Sorokin does not claim total homogeneity for any empirical culture; none of the supersystems is actually found "monopolistically without the coexistence, as a minor or equal stream, of the other systems."[34] With only a few exceptions, the art, philosophy, religion, and science of any period will have some segments that differ from the dominant principle of the time. If the great bulk of the fine arts in the tenth to eleventh centuries A.D. was ideational, we must not lose sight of the fact that a small number of works were idealistic and a few were sensate. Even when, for example, most paintings and sculpture were religious in nature, at least a few were secular.

We also must not conclude from Sorokin's scheme that a particular supersystem is merely a recapitulation of a former supersystem, so that the cycles of change mean that, for example, our sensate culture is a return to the type of culture that existed at the time of Christ. Here we can use the distinction between form and content. In simple terms, a box is always a box, in the sense that its shape remains constant. Yet a box filled with explosives is different from that same box filled with food. The form is the same, but the content can vary significantly. Likewise, our present sensate age is similar to the sensate age at the time of Christ in terms of the emphasis on the material aspects of life, but obviously there are significant differences in the content of the two material or sensate cultural systems.

There is, then, no linear pattern in history. Cycles of cultural patterns characterize the social process—history is an oscillation between opposing cultural forms such as materialism-idealism, ethics of absolute principles-ethics of happiness, determinism-indeterminism, and visual (sensate)-formal, symbolic (ideational) emphasis in the fine arts. How and why does a culture change from one mode to another? Sorokin noted that there are both quantitative and qualitative aspects to the growth and decline of a sociocultural system. In order to understand those aspects, we must first note the three components of an empirical sociocultural system, namely, the system of meanings, the vehicles, and the human agents. Every empirical system has a system of meanings (based on the dominant sociocultural principle): the Constitution and laws of the United States are an example of a system of meanings at the core of the American system. Second, there is a system of empirical vehicles that "objectify" the meanings. The vehicles that objectify the U.S. Constitution and laws include speech, written documents and literature, ceremonies, and buildings such as courts. Finally, there are the human agents who "bear the system of meanings, who actualize it and realize it through the media of the vehicles."[35]

Returning to the question of the growth and decline of sociocultural systems, Sorokin maintained that quantitative growth referred primarily to a quantitative increase in either the vehicles or the human agents or both. For example, the legal system may be expanded to include an increased number of courts, lawyers, and lawsuits along with an increase in the number of laws. Qualitative growth, on the other hand, involves some kind of improvement of the system of meanings, its vehicles, its human agents, or all three components. Qualitative growth is "movement toward the optimum integration of the system."[36] Qualitative growth, for Sorokin, seems to imply at the societal level what has been called *self-realization* or *self-actualization* at the individual level. Thus, qualitative growth would mean that the legal system would more and more approximate perfect equity among the members of the society and that lawyers would more and more conform to the highest ethical and professional standards.

Is there any relationship between quantitative and qualitative growth? At some points—at earlier stages of development—the two kinds of growth may proceed simultaneously. At later stages, the relationship between the two may be one of independence or even inverse. Thus, "a fairly uniform symptom of disintegration in any great supersystem of culture is the substitution of quantitative colossalism for a sublime quality."[37] For example, in its most creative period (sixth to fourth centuries, B.C.) Greece produced temples (including the Parthenon), statues, and drawings of relatively modest size, music of relative simplicity, and literature that was moderate in terms of number, size, and production. "Nothing was measured by the number of copies sold or by the size of valuable objects."[38] In the Hellenic and later Roman periods, however, quality deteriorated, and greater and greater quantity, in terms of both size and number, became the basis of aesthetic judgment (Sorokin's own judgment, of course, identifies this as deterioration). Whether the art, temples, literature, and other facets of culture of the later period were indeed generally inferior because of the value on "colossalism" may be disputed, but Sorokin saw in the differences clear evidence of a culture declining qualitatively along with an increasing stress on quantity.

Like cultural growth, cultural decline is both quantitative and qualitative. Quantitative decline involves decreasing vehicles or human agents or both. The legal system may decline through a diminishing number of law schools and lawyers, obsolescence, and failure to replace laws and legal literature. Qualitative decline involves some kind of deterioration of the system of meanings or in the interdependence among the system of meanings, vehicles, and human agents. Contradictions may develop between the ideals and actual behavior of lawyers, to continue our example. Ambiguities and contradictions may increase in the statutes. The purpose of the law may be distorted by the behavior of judges.

Finally, a system dies when its system of meanings deteriorates to the point where it is no longer recognizable or when the vehicles, human agents, or both are all lost. The actual "life span" of any system varies enormously—but most are finite. Some small systems—fashions and fads—have rather short life spans. Religious systems may continue for thousands of years. An individual system of religion, like individual systems of philosophy, law, or art, or like political regimes, tends to come into being, to be articulated by its vehicles and human agents over some period of time, and then to pass "into the realm of pure meanings."[39]

Thus, both systems and supersystems pass through the phases of growth and decline. But how does this change occur with respect to the relation between the whole and its parts? Sorokin summed up the answer in a series of propositions. First, in a closely integrated system, the change will occur as a whole; all parts will change together. Second, if the system is not closely integrated, change may occur in some subsystems without occurring in others; only significant change in the more important parts of the system will effect change throughout so that the entire culture will experience change. Third, if a culture is merely a grouping of congeries, any part may change without affecting any other part. Fourth, if the culture is composed of the "coexistence" of a number of systems and of congeries, the culture will change differently in its varied parts; namely, all the important parts will change together, while the congeries will change independently of one another. All of this simply says that various elements will change either concomitantly or independently of one another, depending on the extent to which they are integrated. Even when various elements are changing in the same direction, there may be some leading or lagging; music may change in a particular direction before painting and sculpture at one time and may lag behind at another time. Indeed, regardless of the degree of integration, there has probably never been a culture where all the elements changed together simultaneously.[40]

While our discussion has only touched on the basics of Sorokin's thought, it does show that his thought is truly cyclic: history is the oscillation from one to another of the three sociocultural supersystems. An important question arises as to the mechanism of change—what causes the shift from one mode to another? Sorokin suggested three possible explanations of sociocultural change. First, change may be the result of factors external to the sociocultural system. If, for example, we look for explanations of change in the family, we seek factors in the economy (industrialization), or demographic changes, or perhaps even biological factors as causal mechanisms. This assumes that the family is a more or less passive grouping, which will remain as it is unless it is disturbed by outside forces.

A second explanation that has been offered is the theory of immanence. In this theory, change occurs because of internal factors in the system. In other words, it is of the nature of the system to change: "It cannot help changing, even if all its external conditions are constant."[41] And the third explanation seeks both internal and external causes of change. Sorokin opted for the "principle of immanent change . . . supported by the externalistic principle, within certain conditions and limits."[42] If that sentence sounds like an evasive answer, Sorokin's writing basically supports the principle of immanence. He stressed the fact that any actual sociocultural system must necessarily change by virtue of its activity: any system that exists and that is active in some sense is thereby changing. External factors do have some influence, but internal factors provide the main impetus for change, and any particular change may be initiated via the meanings-components, the vehicles, or the human agents.

Sorokin's insistence on internal factors as mechanisms of change places him with all those process and dialectical thinkers who have argued that change is normal and continual. This, as noted before, is also the position taken in this book. The important question is not why something changes, but why it changes in the direction it does and what factors impel it in that direction. Sorokin offered broad directions in his three sociocultural systems, and said that any of the three components of a system could serve as a mechanism of change.

In spite of his assertion that change can be initiated in human agents, however, Sorokin's system of thought implies that human beings are more the helpless tools of vast, impersonal forces than manipulators of their own destinies. At times, this view of humankind becomes explicit. The "crisis" of mankind, he wrote in 1941, was not created by Hitler, Stalin, or Mussolini; rather, "the already existing crisis made them what they are—its instrumentalities and puppets."[43] Even if we won the war, he predicted, the crisis would remain unchanged. For the basic crisis was not the actions of certain men or nations, but the overly developed sensate culture of the West.

And this leads to one final point of Sorokin's. Like Spengler, Sorokin saw the West as being in stage of decline (though he did not foresee the same future as Spengler did). Our sensate culture, he argued, is "overripe." The future holds only disintegration of that culture, including the degeneration of values, the proliferation of force and fraud, the loss of freedom, the growth of tyranny, the deterioration of the family, and the loss of creativity.[44] This is not to underrate the achievements of sensate culture, for it "wrote truly the most magnificent page in the whole history of mankind and culture."[45] Its mission is now completed; the day of its death has already passed, and it lingers on to torment us. It is "tired and exhausted. It deserves a rest. It should hand on the torch of creativeness to other forms of culture."[46] Of course, the other form of culture that will succeed our sensate culture must be either an ideational or an idealistic culture.

In sum, Sorokin offers us an imaginative and impressive theory of cyclic change that is supported by an immense amount of data. Any work of this scale is subject to many criticisms and will make numbers of assertions which are debatable. Nevertheless, Sorokin, like our two other cyclic theorists, shows us the utility of a historical approach to the study of change. Like the others, he treats change as normal rather than as a kind of aberration. In one way he is less pessimistic than Khaldun or Toynbee, for to him the disintegration of a sociocultural system does not mean a return to some level of barbarism and a consequent fresh start. The death of our sensate culture, for example, means that we shall journey toward "the magnificent peaks of the new Ideational or Idealistic culture" and that thereby "the creative mission of Western culture and society will be continued."[47]

One of the main deficiencies in Sorokin is his lack of attention to social-psychological factors. The role of people in shaping their own future is minimal in Sorokin's system. However, in his emphasis on understanding the interrelationships of social phenomena undergoing change, his assumption of the normality of change, and his insistence on a proper scientific methodology, Sorokin aids us in our quest to understand change.

Endnotes

1. Derk Bodde, "Harmony and Conflict in Chinese Philosophy," in *Studies in Chinese Thought*, ed. Arthur F. Wright (Chicago: American Anthropological Association, 1953), p. 21.
2. Wm. Theodore de Bary, Wing-tsit Chan, and Burton Watson, *Sources of Chinese Tradition* (New York: Columbia University Press, 1960), p. 221.
3. Quoted in Ssu-yu Teng and John K. Fairbank, *China's Response to the West* (New York: Atheneum, 1967), p. 151.
4. For Khaldun's thought, see Ibn Khaldun, *The Muqaddimah: An Introduction to History*, trans. Franz Rosenthal, ed. N. J. Dawood (Princeton: Princeton University Press, 1967); and Charles lssawi, *An Arab Philosophy of History* (London: John Murray, 1950). A clear and concise exposition may be found in Howard Becker and Harry Elmer Barnes, *Social Thought from Lore to Science* (New York: Dover, 1961).
5. Issawi, *An Arab Philosophy of History*, pp. 7-9.
6. Khaldun, *The Muqaddimah*, p. 30.
7. Ibid., p. 45.
8. Ibid.
9. Ibid., p.47.
10. Ibid., p.93.
11. Ibid., p. 94.
12. Ibid., p. 286.
13. Ibid., p. 93.
14. Ibid., pp. 136-42.
15. Toynbee's system is set forth in twelve volumes. An abridgment of most of his *A Study of History* is provided by D. C. Somervell: *A Study of History, Volumes 1-5* (New York: Oxford University Press, 1946) and *A Study of History, Volumes 6-10* (New York: Oxford University Press, 1957). These two abridgments, plus Toynbee's *Reconsiderations* (New York: Oxford University Press, 1961), provide a sufficient account.
16. Somervell, *A Study of History, Volumes 1-5*, p. 49.

17. Ibid., pp. 88-139.
18. Ibid., p. 88.
19. Ibid., p. 214.
20. Ibid., p. 215.
21. Ibid., p. 198.
22. Ibid., p. 242.
23. Ibid., p. 368.
24. Ibid., p. 407.
25. Ibid., p. 548.
26. Somervell, *A Study of History. Volumes 6-10*, p. 338.
27. Toynbee, *Reconsiderations*, p. 256.
28. Sorokin's ideas are fully explicated in his *Social and Cultural Dynamics*, 4 vols. (New York: American Book Company, 1937-1941). Sorokin abridged his own work in a single volume, *Social and Cultural Dynamics* (Boston: Porter Sargent, 1957). Two other sources are his *Society, Culture, and Personality* (New York: Harper & Bros., 1947) and, written in a popular style, *The Crisis of Our Age* (New York: Dutton, 1941).
29. Sorokin, *Social and Cultural Dynamics*, vol. 4, p. 87.
30. Ibid., p. 21.
31. Sorokin, *The Crisis of Our Age*, p. 17.
32. Sorokin, *Social and Cultural Dynamics*, vol. 1, pp. 66-75.
33. Sorokin, *The Crisis of Our Age*, p. 173.
34. Sorokin, *Social and Cultural Dynamics*, vol. 4, p. 141.
35. Ibid., p. 47.
36. Ibid., p. 83.
37. Sorokin, *The Crisis of Our Age*, p. 252.
38. Ibid., p. 253.
39. Sorokin, *Social and Cultural Dynamics*, p. 92.
40. Ibid., pp. 145-146.
41. Ibid., p. 590.
42. Ibid., p. 592.
43. Sorokin, *The Crisis of OurAge*, p. 23.
44. Sorokin, *Social and Cultural Dynamics*, vol. 4, pp. 775-77.
45. Sorokin, *The Crisis of Our Age*, p. 271.
46. Ibid.
47. Sorokin, *Social and Cultural Dynamics*, vol. 4, p. 779.

CHAPTER THREE

Sociohistorical Theories: Developmental

Although the cyclic view of history prevailed among the Chinese, Greeks, and Romans, a number of ancient thinkers saw the course of social change differently—namely, in terms of a linear process. That process might be one either of degeneration or of some kind of progress. Mingled in with Chinese thought about the great cycles, for example, was another perspective that saw the past as a golden age and all history since that time as a process of deterioration. Some thinkers tried to reconcile this with the cyclic view by asserting that they were simply living in the downswing of a cycle.[1]

It has been popular to stress the fact that the notion of progress—one type of linear development—is to be found only as we emerge into the modern era. However, neither the linear concept of history nor its variant of progress as the direction of development was unknown to ancient people. The linear concept of history may be seen in St. Augustine, who wrote in detail about the "rise, progress, and appointed end of the two cities, one of which is God's, the other this world's."[2] The two cities represent, of course, the church and the world outside of the church. History is the process of interaction between the two cities, in which each suffers evil and enjoys good. The two cities have different faiths, different hopes, and different love, and "they must be separated by the last judgment, and each must receive her own end, of which there is no end."[3]

For Augustine, the end for the City of God was unending bliss, while the end for the earthly city was unending damnation, although not all ancient thinkers were as pessimistic about the "earthly city." If progress is conceived not in terms of continuing progress from the remote past into the eternal future but in terms of "human cultural and intellectual advancement over a very long period of time," then both Greek and Roman thinkers held to an idea of progress.[4]

Nevertheless, it is only in the modern West that the notion of progress became the dominant theme, and only in recent centuries that the idea of progress throughout the whole of history has appeared in thought. This latter point was argued by Condorcet, Comte, and Spencer, among others. Condorcet proclaimed the progress of humankind with an almost lyrical enthusiasm. He announced that no limits inhere in the perfectibility of human faculties, "that the perfectibility of man is truly indefinite; that the progress of this perfectibility . . . has no other limit than the duration of the globe on which nature has placed us."[5] He did recognize that the rate of progress might vary, but neither fixation nor regression was possible.

Thus, some developmental theorists have posited a basically evolutionary pattern—human beings and society are more or less slowly, but surely, evolving toward a better state. Others, while sometimes seeing the ultimate outcome as preferable to the present, stress conflict, or a dialectical pattern of development. In this chapter, we will look at a few theorists of both kinds.

Evolutionary Development

• Auguste Comte

In part because he coined the name *sociology,* Auguste Comte (1798-1857) has generally been identified as the "father" of the discipline.[6] Comte's own work was primarily not that of the innovator, however, as much as that of the systematizer; he gathered together much of the thought of certain French thinkers, fashioned it into a system, and christened it *sociology.*

Comte divided sociology into statics and dynamics. The "statical" aspect of sociology is similar to what we would call *structure* today, while the "dynamical" aspect refers to *change. Statical sociology* rests on the philosophical assumption that society is an organism united by consensus, for "there must always be a spontaneous harmony between the whole and the parts of the social system."[7] The study of dynamics is actually more interesting, but we must "contemplate order, that we may perfect it."[8]

Dynamical sociology is the study of the sequence of human development, and each step in that sequence is the necessary consequence of the preceding step. As Leibniz argued, "the present is big with the future."[9] Social science, therefore, has as its task the discovery of the laws that govern the sequence. The discovery of those laws, in turn, provides a rational basis for facilitating the progress of humankind.

One factor that helps us discover the laws of development is their universality. That is, the laws apply to all societies, so that one could study the most advanced of societies and learn about the sequence through which all must pass. For Comte, one of the most advanced societies was his own—the past development and the future direction of France was the model that would apply to all societies.

In his search for the laws of historical sequence, Comte identified three stages of historical development (which corresponded to three stages of development in the human mind). Thus, he posited a "fundamental law" of the development of human intelligence, namely, that it "passes successively through three different theoretical conditions: the theological, or fictitious; the metaphysical, or abstract; and the scientific, or positive."[10] These three stages are both three successive methods of intellectual functioning and three corresponding types of social orders.

In the theological state, intellectual functioning "supposes all phenomena to be produced by the immediate action of supernatural beings."[11] Comte subdivided the theological state into three stages: fetishism, polytheism, and monotheism. The stage of fetishism marked the beginning of the theological era of humankind; in this stage, man "conceives of all external bodies as animated by a life analogous to his own, with differences of mere intensity."[12] Comte goes into great detail showing how this mode of thinking (and all the modes) relates to the social order. In the stage of fetishism, for example, society was characterized by sacerdotal authority, by the beginning of the conquest of nature, and by behavior based more on affect than on the intellect. The family unit emerged, along with a permanence of residence that facilitated the subsequent development of the state.

During the polytheistic period, the city emerged, landed property became a social institution, the caste system appeared, and war was waged as "the only means of rendering the political organism durable and progressive."[13] Finally, in the period of monotheism, a modification of the theological and military character of the theological state began to take place. The Catholic church failed to provide a viable basis for social life. Women and laborers were emancipated. Church and state were ruptured by the universal claims of the church and the local nature of political power. And war shifted from aggressive to defensive action.

Many of the changes and developments of the theological period were a preparation for the positive era of humanity. The worship of Mary, for example, paved the way for the worship of humanity. A transitional period—the metaphysical era—was still necessary, however. The metaphysical state is a modification of the first, the theological, state; the assumption of the mind is not the existence of supernatural beings but of "abstract forces; veritable entities (that is, personified abstractions) inherent in all beings, and capable of producing all phenomena."[14] Nature, rather than God, becomes the basic causal factor of the universe. And natural, abstract laws, rather than divine laws, become the explanatory tools.

In the social order corresponding to this mode of thinking, the theological philosophy and military polity finally reach their "decline and dissolution . . . in preparation for a new and permanent organic state of society."[15] Comte spoke of the analysis of this period as an "irksome task"; the more pleasant task was the consideration of the emerging positive state.

In the positive state, then, the human mind no longer searches for "absolute notions, the origin and destination of the universe, and the causes of phenomena"; instead, it looks for the laws governing phenomena, "that is, their invariable relations of succession and resemblance."[16] Reasoning and observation become the tools of the intellect. The social order that will ultimately emerge from this mode of thinking will be an ideal state in which material, intellectual, and moral factors will be properly combined for the maximum well-being of humanity.

In the positive state, the Religion of Humanity will emerge. Sociologists will be the priests of the new religion, and will guide humankind in a harmonious existence. The priest-sociologists will teach human beings to think positively (i.e., scientifically) and will relate the doctrines of love, order, and progress to the human race. Military power will be replaced by industrial power, and people will live harmoniously as their behavior and social institutions are shaped and directed by their positive mode of thought.

It is obvious, then, that Comte viewed change in terms of progress. Moreover, he saw progress as occurring in every facet of the social order, including the physical, ethical, intellectual, and political realms. Such progress is tied up with scientific development; the latest and most complex of sciences—sociology—will enable humankind to attain the ideal social order. The disorder of his own day, according to Comte, was rooted in the simultaneous existence of the three incompatible philosophies—theological, metaphysical, and positive. Any of the three can create a social order, but their coexistence precludes any sort of order. It is necessary, therefore, to ascertain which of the philosophies must ultimately prevail, and once this is ascertained, "every man, whatever may have been his former views, can not but concur in its triumph."[17] It is the task of sociology to show the inevitable triumph of the positive philosophy, and to teach humankind to accept and utilize it to create the new order.

Progress, in other words, occurs through the exercise of reason in the positive stage of history:

> *It is only through the more and more marked influence of the reason over the general conduct of Man and of society, that the gradual march of our race has attained that regularity and persevering continuity which distinguish it so radically from the desultory and barren expansion of even the highest of the animal orders, which share, and with enhanced strength, the appetites, the passions, and even the sentiments of Man.*[18]

Indeed, "since the birth of philosophy, the history of society has been regarded as governed by the history of the human mind."[19]

We have already seen that the social order that will be created by the positive mind is one of intellectual and moral progress toward benevolence among fellow humans. In fact, Comte's vision of the future does not, in this respect, differ from that of Marx. In the new order, "our characteristic qualities will find their most perfect respective confirmation, their completest mutual harmony, and the freest expansion for each and all."[20] But Comte goes beyond asking about the direction of change, and inquires into the rate. Given the ultimate end of humanity, what factors affect the pace with which we shall reach that end?

There are three factors, according to Comte, that influence the rate of our progress. The first of these is ennui. "Man, like other animals, can not be happy without a sufficient exercise of all his faculties, intense and persistent in proportion to the intrinsic activity of each faculty."[21] Like modern self-actualization theorists, Comte saw a hierarchy of needs in humans; once their lower faculties have been exercised, they will be driven to use the higher. The greater the exercise of the higher faculties, the greater the rate of progress.

A second factor affecting rate is the duration of human life. Comte, like many other thinkers, assumed that age brings with it an increasing conservatism, while youth is characterized by an "innovating instinct." If a human's life span were increased, say tenfold, conservative forces would be considerably more powerful, inhibiting the rate of change. On the other hand, "an ephemeral life would be quite as mischievous as a too protracted one, by giving too much power to the instinct of innovation."[22] There is, therefore, an optimum length of human life for an optimum rate of progress, and any increase or decrease in average life span will affect that rate to some degree.

The third factor affecting rate of change is the demographic one—the natural increase of population. This contributes more than any other factor to the acceleration of progress. By increase, Comte referred not simply to more numbers but to density of population. The higher concentration of humans in a given space will create new wants and new problems, and will therefore generate new means of progress and order "by neutralizing physical inequalities, and affording a growing ascendancy to those intellectual and moral forces which are suppressed among a scanty population."[23] Again, however, Comte was aware that factors influencing the rate of change can be extreme in two directions; not only can too slow a rate of population increase impede progress, but too rapid a rate will do so as well by making the support of human life too difficult and the stability of social phenomena too fragile.

In sum, Comte made a number of contributions to sociology in general and to the study of social change in particular. Among the more important of the latter were his recognitions that change is normal, that the problem for sociological investigation is to identify those factors that affect the rate of change, and that sociologists must be involved in using their knowledge to shape the future of humankind. Thus, Comte answered a question that was raised by Robert Lynd in 1938 and reopened in the 1960s in the form of a vigorous debate: what is the purpose of sociological knowledge? Also, what is the responsibility of the sociologist toward society? Comte's answer was that sociological knowledge will be used to further the progress of society, and the sociologist will be the vehicle through which the knowledge will become effective. To be sure, he perceived the role of the sociologist in somewhat narrow terms. The direction of change is foreordained. All that the sociologist can do is facilitate the development of society toward its predetermined end. The sociologist accomplishes this by education. The individual must be educated so as to reproduce the development of humankind: "In his brief career, he must pass through the three stages which an aggregate of nations has wrought out with infinite comparative slowness; and if any material part of the experience is evaded, his training will be abortive."[24] The primary responsibility of the sociologist is to teach people to think, to function in the positive mode, so as to facilitate the creation of the positive society.

Comte, of course, also took some wrong directions. He was too restrictive in identifying factors that affect rate. He accepted the myth of unidirectionality, assuming that all humankind was becoming like the Western European industrial society he knew. He minimized the power of human beings to shape their own future; the only strategy for effecting change was an educative one, and that would merely remove the barriers to progress into the positive era.

But Comte did have a vision of a more humane social order, and he did acknowledge that humanity could have a part in bringing that order to pass. For that, and for his effort to identify the variables that affect the rate of change, we can credit him with a significant contribution to the study of social change.

• Herbert Spencer

Although he had little formal education, Herbert Spencer (1820-1903) wrote prolifically on subjects covering a wide area of knowledge.[25] His writings include volumes on philosophy, biology, psychology, ethics, and sociology. He was initially interested in biology, then turned to engineering before serving for a time as editor of the *Economist* and, finally, leaving that position to write his work on philosophy. His aim was to unify the totality of human knowledge around the principle of evolution. (It was Spencer, incidentally, rather than Darwin who coined the idea of "survival of the fittest," and he applied it to humans rather than the animal world.)

The principle of evolution that governs all being—the natural world as well as humans and society—involves a passage "from an indefinite, incoherent homogeneity to a definite, coherent heterogeneity."[26] Another way of stating this is to say that evolution is a process of successive differentiation and integration. The meaning of this for social change will become clear below.

First, however, we must note another premise upon which Spencer builds his theory of change, namely, that society is an organism. In other words, there are important analogies between societies and biological organisms and, therefore, a number of reasons for treating society as an organism. First, society experiences continuous growth. As it grows, its parts "become unlike: it exhibits increase of structure."[27] Thus, life—whether of a society or an organism—is a matter of continuing growth and increasing structural complexity. The increasing structural complexity, or differentiation, means an increasing differentiation of functions. Dissimilar parts have differing functions, which are not merely diverse but which must operate together in order for the whole to exist. That is, the parts are mutually dependent on one another. For example, the human body is composed of eyes, arms, hands, ears, blood vessels, various internal organs, and so on. Each is separate, yet each is dependent on the other and must work with the others to form a living whole. In society, the various parts—government, family, economy, and other factors—also are separate but interdependent, and must function together for a viable whole.

Spencer obviously used his knowledge of biology to understand social phenomena. The way in which Spencer used biology, however, has been misunderstood.[28] Spencer did not set forth an evolutionary theory of change in the modern biological sense. Rather, he accepted Lamarck's view of biology—evolution through the inheritance of acquired characteristics. Spencer believed that social change occurs as a result of physical, emotional, and intellectual changes in individuals. The rate of change, therefore, is limited by the rate at which individuals change and pass on those individual modifications to succeeding generations. In essence, "environmental changes create new needs, new needs require new habits, which, in turn, require changes in the physical, emotional, and intellectual traits of individuals. These changed individuals then mold social institutions into corresponding forms."[29]

The extent to which Spencer used biological ideas may be seen in his description of social institutions, which he spoke of in terms of the sustaining, distributing, and regulating systems. With respect to the first, "the parts carrying on alimentation in a living body and the parts carrying on productive industries in the body politic, constitute, in either case, a sustaining system."[30] The distributing system of society is necessitated by the increasing complexity of society; it is a system of transfer among the interdependent parts. Just as an annelid (segmented worm) cannot evolve into a crustacean or insect without the growth of a vascular system, so a medieval society cannot evolve into an industrial society without roads and commercial classes. Finally, the regulating system emerges out of warfare between societies; it develops, in other words, as a means of "dealing with surrounding organisms, individual or social—other animals to be caught or escaped from, hostile societies to be conquered or resisted."[31] In the organism this is represented by the neuromuscular system, and in society by the governmental-military system.

In speaking of social institutions in terms of systems, then, Spencer was not viewing them in a static manner—as the stable structure of an organism. He described them in terms of their own evolution, their appearance as survival mechanisms, and their subsequent course of development. We may trace the evolution of the digestive system of an animal: "The entire alimentary canal becomes adapted in structure and function to the matters, animal or vegetal, brought in contact with its interior."[32] We may also trace the evolution of the industrial or productive system of a society: "It takes on activities and correlative structures, determined by the minerals, animals, and vegetals, with which its workers are in contact."[33] Similarly, the evolution of distributing and regulating systems may be identified, whether those systems are part of an individual or a society.

Since evolution is the basic principle of being, and since societies are organisms, we may understand societal development in terms of human growth: "Societies, like living bodies, begin as germs—originate from masses which are extremely minute in comparison with the masses some of them eventually reach."[34] There are, in fact, numerous parallels between the growths of individual and social organisms. The process in both cases is one of ongoing differentiation and integration; units multiply, enlarging the group, and groups unite, further enhancing group integration. This "compounding and re-compounding" occurs in the vegetable and animal worlds, and also in the social. For example, as a primitive tribe spreads, through an increase in its numbers, it reaches a point where it separates into a number of tribes, which gradually grow distinct from each other. This may be a continuous, repetitive process; but there may also be the formation of a larger society through the uniting of several tribes. This latter occurs "without obliterating the divisions previously caused by separations."[35]

Furthermore, societal growth involves not only the multiplication of groups and the union of groups, but also increasing density or solidarity. The integration that follows differentiation means not merely a "larger mass," but also the "progress of such mass toward that coherence due to closeness of parts."[36] It is clear that the evolutionary principle that Spencer found in the universe as a whole—indefinite, incoherent homogeneity giving way to a definite coherent heterogeneity—is also true of human societies.

Spencer illustrated the societal transition from homogeneity to heterogeneity by contrasting primitive and modern societies. The primitive tribe, he argued, is "alike in all its parts," while the "civilized nation" is "full of structural and functional unlikenesses."[37] Furthermore, along with the increasing heterogeneity goes increasing coherence. The nomadic group is held together by no bonds (an assertion Khaldun would have vigorously denied). The tribe has more coherence, for it is held together by subordination to the leader. This coherence increases until we achieve the civilized nation, which is sufficiently integrated to hold together for "a thousand years or more."

Increasing definiteness also characterizes the process of social growth. The initial social organization is vague; with growth, social arrangements become more precise, customs become laws, laws become more specific, and social institutions separate and become distinct. "Thus in all respects is fulfilled the formula of evolution. There is progress towards greater size, coherence, multiformity, and definiteness."[38]

What is the driving mechanism of this growth? It is the struggle for existence between the various societies. The whole process of compounding and re-compounding, of change from homogeneity (primitivism) to heterogeneity (civilization), would have been impossible without conflict between tribes and between nations—group defense and offense require cooperation among the members of the group. This, in turn, has led to "all kinds of cooperations" that have facilitated the growth of civilization. While admitting the "horrors" resulting from such conflict, Spencer insisted that apart from such conflict "the world would still have been inhabited only by men of feeble types, sheltering in caves and living on wild food."[39]

On the other hand, once civilized society has emerged out of the bloody throes of societal wars, there is no longer a need for conflict between people. War, therefore, will disappear. This leads us to a consideration of the two types of society for which Spencer is known, and which characterize the general pattern of human evolution. In general, societies may be classified as militant or industrial. These are not, however, mutually exclusive types; in theory and in actuality, characteristics of the two types are mingled. Nevertheless, the trend of evolution is from the militant to the industrial.

The militant society is organized on the basis of compulsory cooperation, while the industrial society rests on voluntary cooperation. The militant society has a despotic central power which exercises absolute authority over individual conduct; the industrial society has a democratic or representative type of government that is limited in its political control of personal conduct. In the militant society, then, "the individual is owned by the State."[40] The preservation of the society is the dominant concern; the individual's preservation must be a secondary matter.

There is a necessary relationship between the structure of a society and the personalities of its members. In a militant society, success in warfare is the source of the highest honor, and goodness is equivalent to bravery and strength. People in a militant society are chauvinistic; the "triumph of their society [is] the supreme end of action."[41] People lack initiative; they are utterly subservient to authority, which they regard as inevitable and essential.

In the industrial society, these traits give way to converse ones. The industrial society is one of an enduring peaceful life; the society is organized for production, not for warfare, and the individual member rather than the overall society becomes the focus of concern. Instead of absolute authority governing the relations of the people, there is interaction based on contract. Centralized authority is limited to the negatively regulative; that is, it no longer says both "you shall do this" and "you shall not do that," but only "you shall not do that."

What kind of person will we find in industrial society? The citizenry will be marked by "growing independence, a less-marked loyalty, a small faith in governments, and a more qualified patriotism," as well as by "a growing respect for the individualities of others."[42] Thus, Spencer had a vision of a society in which governmental control was minimal and individuals pursued their own welfare with relative autonomy; like Adam J. Smith, Spencer believed that the ultimate end of a laissez-faire society would be maximum well-being for all.

Spencer was not the optimist that Comte was, however. Unlike Comte, he saw the possibility of societal regression as well as progress. If the general direction of evolution is toward the industrial society, it should be noted that it is possible to revert back to a more militant society. International conflict or the reappearance of defensive and offensive activities may thrust a society back toward the militant type. In addition, Spencer departed from Comte at the point of the role of human action in societal evolution. While admitting that human action was an integral part of the evolutionary process, Spencer denied that such action could in any way accelerate the process. People or governments, by their interference in the social process, might retard the rate of evolution, but they would be unable to increase it: "The processes of growth and development may be, and very often are, hindered or deranged, though they cannot be artificially bettered."[43] There are no shortcuts to utopia; the role of sociology is to identify the process and help people to accept it and calmly await the appearance of the new age. We must "see how comparatively little can be done, and yet to find it worth while to do that little: so uniting philanthropic energy with philosophic calm."[44]

Although Spencer's insistence on the limited role of human action was consistent with his evolutionary perspective, it was not consistent with his value of individualism. As noted above, his ideal society is one in which individuals may freely pursue their own interests. Spencer cherished the autonomy of the individual while at the same time he affirmed the inexorable process of development that transcends the individual. As David Wiltshire points out, Spencer tried to ease out of the apparent contradiction by arguing that the exercise of "free will" by individuals "itself constitutes the motive power of social evolution, even if the direction in which it moves is predetermined."[45] Furthermore, "perfect individuality" is that which is congruent with the evolutionary pattern. "The zenith of individualism, then, is the absolute freedom to conform."[46] We can state confidently, however, that Spencer would see little freedom in conformity in the government-dominated, conflict-ridden world of the twentieth century.

What have we learned from Spencer? Again, we find the emphasis, often abandoned by succeeding generations, on the normality of change. Again we see the emphasis on conflict as a driving mechanism of social change. Spencer also shared the tendency of others (before and since) to be ethnocentric in his vision of utopia; he believed that nineteenth-century England provided the best example of evolution toward the industrial society.

Spencer recognized that societies can experience regression as well as progress. He insisted upon a relationship between the structure of a society and the nature of and behavior of the people in it. For Comte, the social structure was fashioned by humans as a consequence of their mode of thinking; in Spencer, this relationship is changed, and it is the structure that demands a particular mode of thinking and type of personality. While both views are oversimplified, contemporary Westerners are prone to adopt the Comtean perspective and to neglect the powerful influence on thinking and behavior exerted by the social structure.

One final point is the issue raised by both Comte and Spencer regarding the role of sociology and sociologists (and, for that matter, people generally) in social change. This issue has plagued sociology throughout its history and is not yet resolved. Should the sociologist be an academic, or should he or she be involved in effecting social change? Can sociology provide us with tools for effecting change, or does it simply make us aware of how helpless we are? When we deal with strategies of change in the last part of this book, we will assume that Comte had the greater insight at this point—people can shape the future. Whether sociologists ought to be among those who are shaping the future is still being debated. Or, as some would argue (and I agree), by the very nature of their work, social scientists are accumulating knowledge that will be used to shape the future. The question is not whether it shall be used, but on whose behalf it will be used.

• *Emile Durkheim*

Our final example of a development theorist of the evolutionary type is Emile Durkheim (1855-1917).[47] Durkheim was the son of a Jewish rabbi; he studied in both France and Germany, taught philosophy in Paris, and initiated the first course in social science ever given in France.

Nisbet has suggested four major points in Durkheim's theory of change.[48] The first is the problem of origins. What was the original state of the advanced nations of the time? For most nineteenth-century thinkers the answer was plain: contemporary primitive peoples provided the clues to the original condition of civilized nations. Durkheim accepted this perspective. Like Spencer, he searched for human origins among the primitive peoples of the day; comparing those people with the citizens of developed nations would indicate the course of social development.

A second point is Durkheim's description of the stages of development. He shared the interest of his time in identifying stages of evolutionary development, but did not make this the focus of his work. Moreover, he rejected the "reality of developmental continuity in the history of social types. In this he was exceptional in his age."[49] Nevertheless, virtually any student of sociology will connect the name of Durkheim with the two kinds of solidarity—mechanical and organic.

Mechanical solidarity was the early, primitive form of social organization, and could still be seen in existing primitive peoples. Organic solidarity derives from the division of labor accompanying social development. In mechanical solidarity, there is a preponderance of shared ideas and tendencies (rather than individual differences); the social order has great homogeneity. In fact, "the collective conscience completely envelops our whole conscience and coincides in all points with it."[50] Furthermore, this solidarity is maintained by the application of repressive sanctions to those who deviate; such sanctions are the expression of social rage in the face of offenses against "strong and defined states of the collective conscience."[51]

Organic solidarity, by contrast, is rooted in differences rather than likenesses (the similarity with Spencer's evolutionary law of homogeneity-heterogeneity is apparent). The increasing complexity of a society demands that solidarity rest upon differentiation; diverse functions involve the division of labor, which is the essence of organic solidarity. This solidarity is characterized by restitutive sanctions; not punishment but "the return of things as they were, in the reestablishment of troubled relations to their normal state" becomes the purpose of the law.[52]

Durkheim summed up the distinction between mechanical and organic solidarity in three points.[53] The former "binds the individual directly to society without any intermediary," while the latter involves interdependence among individuals. The former is found in a society characterized by shared beliefs and sentiments, while the latter characterizes a differentiated society. The former can be strong only to the extent that individual personalities and rights are relatively indistinguishable from the whole, while the latter demands unique personalities and personal rights.

A third point in Durkheim's theory of change is his identification of the causal factors in change. What leads to the division of labor and the new type of solidarity? He argued that the division of labor varies directly with "the volume and density of societies."[54] Volume and density do not simply facilitate the division of labor; they cause it. In other words, as the number and rate of interactions of the population increase, there is a necessary increase in the division of labor; the latter, in turn, necessarily leads to organic rather than mechanical solidarity. The necessary increase in the division of labor in the denser and more populated societies results from the more acute struggle for existence. That is, the more alike people are, the greater the rivalry between them, for they both struggle for the same scarce resources. Durkheim uses the analogy of a tree upon which 200 species of insects were found. If, he argues, they were all of the same species, it would be impossible for all to survive, for all would feed on the bark, or all on the leaves. Similarly, in the case of human society, people of differing occupations can survive in the same city because they "pursue different objects," and are therefore not impelled to destroy each other. In sum, the division of labor in the denser, more populated society is necessary in order to avoid socially destructive conflict.

More recent empirical work yields mixed results for Durkheim's argument about the relationship between population and the division of labor. Using data from a number of nations, Clarke reported that the division of labor increases with urbanization; however, he found no relationship between size of national populations and changes in the division of labor.[55]

Finally, Durkheim discussed the direction of change. Although he was immersed in an intellectual context that reveled in the progress of the human race, Durkheim's own conclusions fell in with the minority who felt misgivings if not despair about the future of humanity. He pointed to the suicide rate as one indicator of the crisis of modern civilization—that is, as evidence of the lack of integration of society. Moreover, he noted that neither kinship relations nor religion could be an integrating force for human beings in the modern era, and he would not accept the state as a substitute for these older means. The only hope that Durkheim could see for humanity was in occupational organizations. For in the future "our whole social and political organization will have a base exclusively, or almost exclusively, occupational."[56] Occupational organizations had not developed adequately, however, to meet the needs of the social order; the future, therefore, was at best precarious.

Social evolution, then, is the increasing dominance of organic over mechanical solidarity. It is a historical law "that mechanical solidarity which first stands alone, or nearly so, progressively loses ground, and that organic solidarity becomes, little by little, preponderant."[57] When group solidarity changes in form, the social structure changes. The two types of solidarity, therefore, correspond to two different types of societies. Durkheim did not contend, however, that either type of solidarity would be total in any real society. The direction of change is toward organic solidarity and the type of social structure characterized by that solidarity, but remnants of mechanical solidarity will remain.

In sum, Durkheim, like Khaldun, stressed the significance of solidarity. Both considered solidarity necessary for a viable society. Like Comte, Durkheim gave great importance to demographic factors in change—a prime mechanism of change is the increasing density of population. If we compare the three theorists considered in this chapter with respect to the direction of change, we find a continuum: Comte saw increasing advance and progress; Spencer saw a tendency toward progress but also the possibility of regress; and Durkheim painted human future in rather bleak terms. Durkheim was also an early voice of doubt about the attainments of "civilization." He felt that there is probably an inverse relation between the growth of culture and human happiness. Certainly, a "normal savage can be quite as happy as the normal civilized man."[58] Human happiness has probably diminished rather than increased with social development. Durkheim thus reminds us to beware of the fallacy of utopia apprehended; there are flaws in the present, and the salvation of humankind does not consist of helping everyone else to become like us as quickly as possible.

Dialectical Development

As Spencer showed, conflict may be incorporated into evolutionary development. For the evolutionary developmentalists, conflict was not the focal process; at most, it had a subsidiary place in the evolutionary process. For another set of developmental theorists, however, conflict is the central fact of social change. Since we shall deal with conflict in more detail in a later chapter, we shall examine here one particular type of conflict—dialectical development, which is primarily associated with the names of Karl Marx (1818-1883) and Frederick Engels (1820-1895).[59]

Both Marx and Engels were born in Prussia; the former was the son of a Jewish lawyer (who was later converted, with his entire family, to Christianity) and the latter the son of an affluent and conservative manufacturer. They became friends in Paris, and subsequently wrote both in collaboration and singly to produce the foundation works of Marxism.

Two of the pillars upon which Marxist thought rests are the *dialectic* and *materialism*. The dialectic asserts that contradiction is the essence of all things; in both the natural and human worlds, contradiction is the central fact of being. Consequently, we must look to the dialectic for the key to change, which is inextricably bound up with the struggle of opposites.

Although the dialectic has a long history, Hegel's notions were the immediate influence on Marx. Hegel himself, incidentally, rarely used the expressions that are commonly attributed to him to describe the dialectical process—thesis, antithesis, and synthesis. In fact, Hegel called the use of the three terms a "lifeless schema."[60] Hegel did, however, stress such notions as process and contradiction and historical development, and these notions were accepted by Marx. Engels pointed out that the dialectic was not usable in its full Hegelian form, however, for Hegel made an "ideological perversion" out of it. That is, Hegel was an idealist who conceived of the real world as a reflection of the "absolute concept," while Marx and Engels made concepts the reflection of the development of material existence.

The meaning of the dialectic will become clearer as we examine certain basic laws, which were adopted from Hegel and discussed in some detail by Engels in *Anti-Duhring*.[61] First, then, all existence is characterized by the unity and conflict of opposites. In other words, all existence is characterized by contradictions. Such contradictions are inherent in nature as well as in society. For example, says Engels, we find that motion must be measured by its opposite—rest. A stone suspended from a rope represents a certain quantity of mechanical work or motion, and that quantity can be measured by the weight and distance from the ground. Measuring motion by rest in this fashion is a "crying contradiction." In the social realm, contradiction may be seen in such things as the opposition between the forces and relations of production in a capitalist society. Such a contradiction is a unity and conflict of opposites because the two are inextricably united in the same society, yet in conflict with each other. The contradiction, therefore, becomes a driving mechanism of change, for the contradiction cannot be maintained indefinitely. Dialectics, he argued, is "the science of the general laws of motion and development of Nature, human society and thought."[62] Three general laws of dialectics are the unity and conflict of opposites, the change of quantity into quality, and the negation of the negation.

The transformation of quantity into quality may also be illustrated at the natural level and at the social level. The law asserts simply that at a certain point quantitative variations become qualitative variations. Water changes to steam at 100° Celsius; continuing quantitative changes have resulted in a new qualitative state. At the social level, an example is provided by the way in which a "new power" is created by group cooperation; the new power is qualitatively different from the total of individual powers.

The law of the negation of the negation can be illustrated by simple algebra. The quantity *a* can be negated by making it minus *a*. If the minus *a* is multiplied by a minus *a*, the result is a^2, which is the negation of the negation. At the societal level, the law is illustrated by the development of various modes of the economic structure. The capitalist order is the negation of the feudal order, and the socialist order negates the capitalist order—it is the negation of the negation.

Thus, all social development proceeds in accord with dialectical laws. Incidentally, Marx himself never used the terms *historical materialism* (created by Engels) and *dialectical materialism* (created by Plekhanov); nevertheless, he spoke of the materialist basis of his method, and materialism is the second pillar upon which Marxist thought rests. The meaning of materialism is well expressed in a conclusion once reached by Marx which, he said, continued as a "guiding thread" to subsequent work:

> *In the social production which men carry on they enter into definite relations that are indispensable and independent of their will; these relations of production correspond to a definite stage of development of their material powers of production. The totality of these relations of production constitutes the economic structure of society—the real foundation, on which legal and political superstructures arise and to which definite forms of social consciousness correspond. The mode of production of material life determines the general character of the social, political and spiritual processes of life.*[63]

Marxism, then, seeks to bring the study of social life down from the fruitless flights of speculation; that study must deal with "real individuals, their activity and the material conditions under which they live, both those which they find already existing and those produced by their activity."[64]

Proceeding from these premises of the dialectical and materialist essence of all being, Marx and Engels constructed an interpretation of history which may be outlined as follows.

1. People enter into relationships that are independent of their will. We should look for the causes of change in the modes of production

rather than in ideas, in the economic rather than the philosophical aspects of any era. Historical understanding can come only through structural analysis; the effort to gain that understanding from studying human minds will always be frustrated. It is not the way people think, nor what they think about, that shapes history; it is, rather, the manner in which they relate in production and to production. The reason for this will become clearer in the next point.

2. Every society is characterized by an infrastructure—the economic structure—and a superstructure—which includes ideology, law, the polity, the family, and religion. The superstructure arises out of the infrastructure. That is, the material base of a society is the foundation upon which all the rest is built, so that a change in the mode of production leads to a change in all the social relations. In turn, people create "the principles, the ideas, the categories, conformably with their social relations."[65] This is not, however, to assert a simplistic, deterministic relationship. In a letter to Bloch in 1890, Engels pointed out that the productive mode of existence was the "ultimately" determining element, but that the various elements of the superstructure "also exercise their influence upon the course of the historical struggles and in many cases preponderate in determining their *form.*"[66] Thus, the infrastructure provides a framework upon which varied forms of the superstructure exert some influence.

3. Change comes about as a result of the contradiction between the forces and relations of production.[67] In the course of the development of the productive forces, a stage is reached at which these forces become destructive. They are destructive because they contradict existing relationships of production. But what does Marx mean by this contradiction? Raymond Aron has suggested two possible interpretations.[68] One is that as the forces of production develop, they reach a point at which "individual right of ownership represents an impediment to their progress." There is, then, a contradiction between continued expansion of the productive forces and individual right of ownership. But if one considers corporate growth (which precludes individual ownership) an integral part of capitalist development, this contradiction disappears (since individual right of ownership is not an integral part of capitalism).

A second interpretation is that the contradiction is between distribution and production: a capitalistic society is unable to absorb its own production because of capitalist appropriation of social production. As Engels put it, production expands more rapidly than the market, with an inevitable collision which is insoluble "so long as it does not burst the capitalist mode of production itself."[69] Although we have not yet seen nor been able to predict the point at which a capitalist society becomes incapable of absorbing its own production, this second interpretation seems to me the most reasonable.

4. Contradiction is of the essence of the social process. That is, the contradiction does not arise out of external forces or factors that impinge upon the society; the contradiction is an integral part of social development. A capitalist society gives birth to the material conditions that will ultimately destroy the society. Dialectical development means that the contradiction emerges out of the essence of the social process. No external challenge, no external proletariat is required for Marx and Engels; slave, feudal, and capitalist societies carry within them the seeds of self-destruction.

5. The contradiction between the forces and relations of production is manifested in class conflict. "The history of all hitherto existing society is the history of class struggles."[70] This occurs because in the course of the development of the productive forces there is a class that must "bear all the burdens of society without enjoying its advantages, which, ousted from society, is forced into the most decided antagonism to all other classes."[71] One class rules—the bourgeoisie—and lives in affluence at the expense of the other class—the proletariat—which is driven into an increasingly wretched state of existence. Thus, the society becomes polarized into two antagonistic groups. The ruling class derives its power from its control of property, and maintains its power, in part, because the state is its tool.

The ruled class, the proletariat, exists in the agony of increasing impoverishment and alienation. Impoverishment is due to capitalist exploitation. Alienation includes one's estrangement from the products of one's labor, from oneself, from one's "species-being," and from other people.[72] Both poverty and alienation are created by the capitalist mode of production which concentrates property and power in the hands of a minority of individuals.

6. The outcome of the contradiction is a revolution. The contradiction between forces and relations of production, the struggle between the classes, is resolved by revolution. Past revolutions were inadequate because "the mode of activity always remained unscathed and it was only a question of a different distribution of this activity."[73] The communist revolution, on the other hand, is directed against the preceding mode of activity; it does away with labor (as a class) and abolishes classes and the rule of classes. Along with this is the withering away of the state, which was an instrument of control of the ruling class.

If the revolution is to succeed, if there is to be a genuine social revolution as well as a political transformation, there must be a large-scale "alteration of men."[74] The revolution, therefore, must take the form of a practical movement. There is no other way to overthrow the ruling class, and the class overthrowing the ruling elite can only "succeed in ridding itself of all the muck of ages and become fitted to found society anew" in revolution.[75] Only where classes and class antagonisms have been abolished will humanity experience social evolution without political revolution.

7. Beyond the communist revolution is the classless society. The society of the future will have, as noted in point 6, no classes and no state. Without entering into the debate about the possibility of a classless society, we may inquire briefly into the meaning of a stateless society. Is the withering away of the state realistic in a complex, industrial society? If "the state" refers to a centralized decision-making apparatus, the disappearance of the state in an industrial society would seem inconceivable (although the anarchists would strongly disagree). We have noted that Marx identified the state as a tool of the ruling class; it may be, therefore, that the argument about the disappearance of the state really involves the disappearance of the class character of the state. In other words, the withering away of the state need not demand the elimination of any centralized administrative apparatus.

In any case, in the society of the future, the seizure of power by the proletariat ends class differences and class antagonisms. "The government of persons is replaced by the administration of things and the direction of the processes of production."[76] Instead of being dominated by external factors, people will gain control and create a fully human existence. There will be the "abolition of private property, of human self-alienation, and thus, the real appropriation of human nature, through and for man," and, along with this abolition of alienation, there will be a "return of man from religion, the family, the State, etc., to his human, i.e., social life."[77] Ultimately, the social order will evolve (rather than emerge through violent struggle) into a condition where everyone will give according to ability and receive according to needs.

Thus in Marx and Engels we have a portrayal of the social process as dialectical—contradiction inheres in it and becomes the driving mechanism of change. All history may be characterized in terms of stages that exhibited different modes of production. Each mode of production, in turn, was characterized by a particular kind of relationship among the people. Ancient society had slavery; feudal society had serfdom; and bourgeois society has wage earners. The communist revolution, however, ushers in a stage of history in which we have a "community of free individuals, carrying on their work with the means of production in common, in which the labour-power of all the different individuals is consciously applied as the combined labour-power of the community."[78] The agony of history has come to an end. Contradiction has finally been erased from the human scene. Each person can live in peace with self and with others. The leap has finally been made "from the realm of necessity into the realm of freedom."[79]

It would require volumes to take note of the numberless expositions, critiques, and modifications of the Marxist view. For our purposes, it will be sufficient to acknowledge the immense influence of Marxism since the middle of the nineteenth century and to point out certain facets that particularly bear upon social change. In Marxist thought, of course, change is normal; dialectical development proceeds continually until the communist revolution, after which there is a social evolution. We could well ask the question, if conflict is central to social development throughout most of history, how can we conceive of a period in which desirable development occurs without conflict? For contradiction is the basic driving mechanism of development. Certainly all nations that have experienced a communist revolution have also experienced continuing internal conflict to some degree. Mao handled this problem by distinguishing between antagonistic and nonantagonistic contradictions, the former referring to contradictions between "ourselves and our enemies" and the latter referring to contradictions "among the working people."[80] For example, in a new socialist society such as China there are contradictions between the modern and the traditional, between industry and agriculture (there is a need for developments in both, but it may not be possible to pursue both simultaneously), between centralism and democracy, between "red" (political purity) and expert (technical know-how), and others. The contradiction between "red" and expert occurs whenever one procedure seems correct from an ideological point of view and another seems correct from a purely technical point of view. For instance, from a technical point of view, it could be argued that factory efficiency will be maximized when workers are required to submit to the authority of managers. But that would be contrary to Maoist ideology, which argues that democratic processes are always more valuable to social well-being. The point is that there are still contradictions in socialist societies, but the antagonistic and nonantagonistic contradictions demand very different responses; democratic processes are sufficient to deal with the nonantagonistic contradictions.

At first, it might appear that Marx and Engels have given us an unalterable historical sequence for all societies, much as Comte did. Some parts of their writings would support such a notion and would appear to affirm that all societies must pass from feudalism through capitalism to socialism and communism. A closer reading, however, shows this to be a wrong interpretation. In a letter written in 1877, Marx berated a critic because the latter tried to turn his "historical sketch of the genesis of capitalism in Western Europe into a historico-philosophic theory of the general path every people is fated to tread, whatever the historical circumstances."[81] That, said Marx, was a distortion of his views, for he recognized that a different historical context could lead to very different outcomes. What we need are comparative studies of societal development, and not the vulgar application of a superhistorical theory to all societies. In other letters, Marx makes analyses that clearly show that he did not use the development of Western Europe as an inexorable model. Thus, he notes that a revolutionary movement in Italy failed because the peasants were not mobilized, and he felt at one point that the revolution might take hold in underdeveloped Russia rather than on the continent.[82] In some writings, Marx and Engels overstate the case in accord with their polemic purpose. This may make their position appear more inflexible than it actually was. In any case, they did not insist on a unidirectional development for all societies.[83]

One of the contributions of Marxism that has made it attractive to so many people in both the developed and the developing nations of the world is the humanistic vision of the future which it offers, and its emphasis on the role of human action in making that future. Contrary to Spencer, who narrowed the human role to just behaving in such a way as not to impede the slow evolutionary process, and contrary to Comte, who limited the significant efforts at shaping the future to an elite of educators, Marxism places history in the hands of the masses. The point of philosophy, argued Marx, is not merely to understand history, but to change it. He gave the world a philosophy designed to do precisely that. His vision of the future is optimistic, humanistic, and activistic. The Marxist theory of change is not a mere adventure of the mind; it is a directive to action, a tool whereby people can seize control of the historical process in order to gain their freedom.

If people are to gain their freedom, they must be unified through an awareness of the reality in which they are enmeshed. The proletariat must make the transition from being a class "in itself" to one "for itself." The peasants, for example, were not considered a class, in the full sense of the word, by Marx. They lacked class consciousness, and lacking that consciousness they were helpless to effect change. In this, we find echoes of the solidarity that Khaldun said was necessary for any group to triumph.

Another important contribution of Marxist thought is its avoidance of the strict determinism-indeterminism dichotomy. As emphasized earlier, the economic infrastructure is *ultimately* determining; given any specific economic structure, there is some latitude for variation and for interacting effects of the superstructure. In both their correspondence and their actions, Marx and Engels showed themselves to be pragmatic, and to be willing to consider various courses of action whether or not those courses were consistent with previous theoretical statements.[84] History was not considered capricious, but neither was it viewed as so predetermined as to admit of no human action.

Finally, Marxism stresses the crucial significance of the social structure in understanding human behavior. It is not consciousness that shapes reality, but reality that determines consciousness. What one is, how one thinks, and what one believes reflect the structure in which one exists. To the extent that we forget the critical influence of the social structure, we will be prone to accept a myth of utopia apprehended, and we may find ourselves making people culpable (e.g., the poor) for effects of the structure.[85]

Endnotes

1. Derk Bodde, "Harmony and Conflict in Chinese Philosophy," in *Studies in Chinese Thought*, ed. Arthur F. Wright (Chicago: American Anthropological Association, 1953), p. 27.
2. Augustine, *The City of God*, trans. Marcus Dods (New York: Modern Library, 1950), p. 609.
3. Ibid., p. 668.
4. Robert A. Nisbet, *Social Change and History* (New York: Oxford University Press, 1969), p. 47.
5. Quoted in Howard Becker and Harry Elmer Barnes, *Social Thought from Lore to Science*, 3rd ed. (New York: Dover, 1961), p. 474.
6. Comte's thought has been well summarized by Raymond Aron, *Main Currents in Sociological Thought I*, trans. Richard Howard and Helen Weaver (New York: Anchor Books, 1968), pp. 73-143. Selections from Comte's work with extended commentaries on his thought may be found in George Simpson, *Auguste Comte: Sire of Sociology* (New York: Thomas Y. Crowell Company, 1969).
7. Auguste Comte, *The Positive Philosophy*, trans. Harriet Martineau (New York: Calvin Blanchard, 1858), p. 461.
8. Ibid.
9. Ibid., p. 464.
10. Ibid., p. 25.
11. Ibid., p. 26.
12. Ibid., p. 545.
13. Ibid., p. 574.
14. Ibid., p. 26.
15. Ibid., p. 637.
16. Ibid., p. 26.
17. Ibid., p. 36.
18. Ibid., p. 521.

19. Ibid.
20. Ibid., p. 838.
21. Ibid., p. 517.
22. Ibid., pp. 518-19.
23. Ibid., p. 520.
24. Ibid., p. 798.
25. For Spencer's sociological thought, see Herbert Spencer, *Principles of Sociology*, ed. Stanislav Andreski (London: Macmillan, 1969). A good summary may be found in Becker and Barnes, *Social Thought from Lore to Science*, pp. 664-81.
26. Quoted in Becker and Barnes, p. 667.
27. Spencer, *Principles of Sociology*, p. 21.
28. Valerie A. Haines, "Is Spencer's Theory an Evolutionary Theory?" *American Journal of Sociology* 93 (1988): 1200-23.
29. Ibid., p. 1210.
30. Spencer, *Principles of Sociology*, p. 58.
31. Ibid., p. 79.
32. Ibid., p. 64.
33. Ibid.
34. Ibid., p. 23.
35. Ibid., p. 27.
36. Ibid., p. 29.
37. Ibid., p. 154.
38. Ibid., p. 155.
39. Ibid., p. 178.
40. Ibid., p. 503.
41. Ibid, p. 533.
42. Ibid., pp. 570-71.
43. Herbert Spencer, *The Study of Sociology* (New York: D. Appleton & Company, 1874), p. 401.
44. Ibid., p. 403.
45. David Wiltshire, *The Social and Political Thought of Herbert Spencer* (New York: Oxford University Press. 1978)., p. 237.
46. Ibid., p. 239.
47. The main source of Durkheim's theory of change is *The Division of Labor in Society*, trans. George Simpson (New York: Free Press, 1933). An excellent survey and critique of this and other aspects of Durkheim's thought may be found in Robert A. Nisbet, *Emile Durkheim* (Englewood Cliffs: Prentice-Hall, 1965). For a brief discussion of Durkheim's basic orientation toward social change (and, in particular, toward social evolution). See Roscoe C. Hinkle, "Durkheim's Evolutionary Conception of Social Change," *The Sociological Quarterly* 17 (Summer, 1976): 336-46.
48. Nisbet, *Emile Durkheim*, pp. 92-102.
49. Ibid., p. 95.
50. Durkheim, *The Division of Labor in Society*, p. 130.
51. Ibid., p. 80.

52. Ibid., p. 69. For an interesting examination of Durkheim's thesis about the transition from mechanical to organic solidarity, see Ralph H. Turner, "Type of Solidarity in the Reforming of Human Groups," *Pacific Sociological Review* 10 (1967): 60-68. On the basis of a study of reactions to disaster, Turner argues that the two types of solidarity are not exclusive, such that the more we have of one. the less we have of the other. Rather, organic solidarity builds upon mechanical, and the latter must always be the foundation for the former. Thus. in cases of community disaster, organic solidarity is reestablished only after a period in which mechanical solidarity is enacted and the "continuing assurances" upon which organic solidarity rests have been recreated.

53. Ibid., pp. 129-31.

54. Ibid., p. 262. Durkheim posited an interaction between the two variables, however. Thus, there is a cumulative process, with population volume and density increasing the division of labor, which in turn increases the "concentration" of society.

55. Clifford J. Clarke, "The Durkheimian Relationship Between the Division of Labor and Population: Cross-National Historical Evidence," *Sociological Focus* 20 (1987): 13-31.

56. Durkheim, *The Division of Labor in Society*, p. 190.

57. Ibid., p. 174. Actually, there are problems with Durkheim's concept of organic solidarity. He, himself, abandoned it in his later work, and there are some logical grounds for questioning the utility of the concept as he formulated it. See the discussion in Whitney Pope and Barclay D. Johnson, "Inside Organic Solidarity," *American Sociological Review* 48 (1983): 681-92.

58. Ibid., p. 244.

59. The literature on Marx, Engels, and subsequent Marxist thinkers is voluminous. For some of the more important writings of Marx and Engels, along with brief commentary, see Lewis S. Feuer, ed., *Marx & Engels: Basic Writings on Politics and Philosophy* (New York: Anchor Books, 1959) ; and T. B. Bottomore and Maximilien Rubel, eds., *Karl Marx: Selected Writings in Sociology and Social Philosophy* (New York: McGraw-Hill, 1956). A valuable and lucid exposition and critique of Marx may be found in Aron, *Main Currents in Sociological Thought I*, pp. 145-236. For a critique and effort to reformulate Marx, see Ralf Dahrendorf, *Class and Class Conflict in Industrial Society* (Stanford: Stanford University Press, 1959).

60. Gustav E. Mueller, "The Hegel Legend of Thesis-Antithesis-Synthesis," *Journal of the History of Ideas* 19 (1958): 411-14.

61. Frederick Engels, *Anti-Duhring: Herr Eugen Duhring's Revolution in Science*, trans. Emile Burns (New York: International Publishers, 1939), pp. 131-56.

62. Ibid., p. 155.

63. From the Preface to "A Contribution to the Critique of Political Economy," in Bottomore and Rubel, *Karl Marx*, p. 51.

64. Karl Marx and Friedrich Engels, *The German Ideology*, ed. R. Pascal (New York: International Publishers, 1947), p. 7.

65. Karl Marx, *The Poverty of Philosophy,* trans. H. Quelch (Chicago: Charles K. Kerr, 1920), p. 119.

66. Karl Marx and Frederick Engels, *Selected Correspondence* (Moscow: Foreign Languages Publishing House, n.d.), p. 498.

67. By the "forces of production" Marx referred to productive capacity, including instruments, people, and experience and skills. By the "relations of production" Marx meant the mutual relationships that characterize people as they engage in production (including property relations).

68. Aron, *Main Currents in Sociological Thought I,* pp. 200-201.

69. Engels, *Anti-Duhring,* p. 301.

70. From the "Manifesto of the Communist Party," in Feuer, *Marx & Engels,* p. 7.

71. Marx and Engels, *The German Ideology,* p. 69.

72. From the "Economic and Philosophic Manuscripts of 1844," in Robert Freedman, *Marxist Social Thought* (New York: Harcourt, Brace & World, 1968), pp. 71-78.

73. Marx and Engels, *The German Ideology,* p. 69.

74. Ibid.

75. Ibid.

76. Engels, *Anti-Duhring,* p. 307.

77. From the "Economic and Philosophic Manuscripts of 1844," in Bottomore and Rubel, *Karl Marx,* pp. 243-44.

78. From "Capital," in Bottomore and Rubel, *Karl Marx,* p. 250.

79. Engels, *Anti-Duhring,* p. 310.

80. Anne Fremantle, ed., *Mao Tse-tung: An Anthology of His Writings* (New York: Mentor Books, 1954), p. 265.

81. Feuer, ed., *Marx & Engels,* p. 440.

82. See Martin Needleman and Carolyn Needleman, "Marx and the Problem of Causation," *Science and Society* 33 (1969): 331.

83. See Shlomo Avineri, "Marx and Modernization," *Review of Politics* 31 (1969): 172-88.

84. Needleman and Needleman, "Marx and the Problem of Causation," pp. 322-39.

85. For a discussion of the differences between personal and social problems, and the critical consequences of the distinction, see C. Wright Mills, *The Sociological Imagination* (New York: Grove Press, 1959), pp. 8-11, and Robert H. Lauer, *Social Problems and Quality of Life,* 4th edition (Dubuque, Iowa: Wm. C. Brown, 1989), pp. 6-10.

CHAPTER FOUR

Structural-Functional Theories

To step from Marx into structural-functionalism is to enter a totally different world. It is a world that many critics have called static, a world without radical change. However, structural-functionalists have dealt with change, and since they represent a major theoretical perspective in sociology, it is necessary to see how change looks from their vantage point.

First, however, let us briefly characterize this theoretical perspective. Pierre van den Berghe has well summarized the general structural-functional approach in terms of seven elements.

1. Societies must be analyzed as wholes, as "systems of interrelated parts";
2. Cause and effect relationships are "multiple and reciprocal";
3. Social systems exist in a state of "dynamic equilibrium" such that adjustment to forces impinging on the system is made with minimal change within the system;
4. Perfect integration is never realized, so that every social system has strains and deviations, but the latter tend to be neutralized through institutionalization;
5. Change is basically a slow, adaptive process rather than a revolutionary shift;
6. Change is the result of adjustment to changes outside the system, growth by differentiation, and internal innovations; and
7. The system is integrated through shared values.[1]

Many of these points will emerge again as we examine the perspectives of two prominent structural-functionalists: Talcott Parsons and Neil

Smelser. We shall reserve criticism of them, however, for the final section, where we shall ask to what extent structural-functionalism comes to terms with the problem of change.

Systems in Change

• Talcott Parsons

Few men in the history of sociology have been such popular targets of emulation, modification, and attack as Talcott Parsons (1902-1979). One of the most frequent points of attack has been his tortuous style of writing. As we strive to understand his perspective on change in the following paragraphs, we shall stay as close as possible to the confines of his own terminology—as close as is consistent with understanding.

It is important to recognize at the outset that Parsons's views on social change have themselves changed. His initial concern with the nature of social structure and the primacy of structure in sociological analysis gave way to a later concern with social evolution. In order to understand the structural-functionalist approach as advocated by Parsons, we will look at both his early and his later ideas.

Initially, then, Parsons insisted that the study of change must grow out of the prior study of structure. In the study of societal evolution, for example, there is a parallel "between organic and sociocultural evolution: Structural analysis must take a certain priority over the analysis of process and change."[2] In biology, morphology is the "backbone" of the theory of evolution; and in sociology, the identification and sequential ordering of structural types must be the foundation for an understanding of sociocultural evolution.

This, of course, is not to deny the importance of change, as some of Parsons's critics have charged him with doing. In fact, in an early work he asserted that the "theory of action was concerned equally with the conditions of stability and the conditions of change. . . . It is impossible to study one without the other."[3] In studying the mechanisms by which stability is maintained, we must also deal with the forces tending to change. The existence of change is not denied, and the importance of change is not slighted. However, change can be understood only through a prior understanding of structures.

What is the nature of the structure that is the essential basis for the analysis of change? We begin with the social system. In broadest terms, a system is two or more interacting units, and the units may be psychological aspects of people, individuals as wholes, or groups (including entire societies). Every system is "embedded in an environing situation," however, so that whether a particular entity is a unit of a system or a system itself depends upon the focus of analysis.[4] That is, for some purposes an organization such as a university may be viewed as a system itself, while for other purposes it may only be an entity within a larger system.

The social system is a particular kind of system—a group of interacting individuals, each of whom seeks to maximize his or her own gratification within the context of a particular culture. The individuals in a social system basically pursue their own happiness, and the meaning of that happiness and the means available for achieving it will vary from one culture to another. As Parsons himself put it, a *social system* is "a plurality of individual actors interacting with each other in a situation which has at least a physical or environmental aspect, actors who are motivated in terms of a tendency to the 'optimization of gratification' and whose relation to their situations, including each other, is defined and mediated in terms of a system of culturally structured and shared symbols."[5]

The system, therefore, may be defined in terms of its units, its patterns, and its boundaries. The minimum unit of the social system is the role, while various kinds of groupings may form "higher-order" units. The patterns of interaction in the social system are normative; that is, they are culturally defined as appropriate and right (or inappropriate and wrong). The boundaries of the system are maintained to the extent that the system remains integrated through shared values. For example, as long as a social system such as a university continues to function as an educational organization in which all participants behave in accord with a shared value on learning, the boundaries are maintained. Fiscal crises and new educational philosophies may impinge upon the system and cause various kinds of adjustments, but the system's identity remains intact. If, however, a fiscal crisis became so serious at a particular university that all the people involved turned their organization into a profit-making consulting firm, the original boundaries would be replaced by new ones. The organization would still be a system integrated by shared values and maintaining its boundaries, but the values and boundaries would have become part of a different system even though the people were the same. The remote chance of this being a realistic example illustrates the tenacity with which systems tend to maintain their boundaries and the stability that tends to characterize societal values.

Furthermore, every system has four functional imperatives. That is, every system must confront and successfully resolve (if it is to survive) the problems of adaptation, goal-attainment, integration, and latent pattern maintenance. These four imperatives apply to all systems of action—nature, culture, personality, and society. In fact, they apply at the "general action" level, for adaptation is the function of the behavioral organism, goal-attainment is the function of the personality, integration is the function of the social system, and latent pattern maintenance is the function of the culture.[6] At the level of the social system, the functions of adaptation, goal-attainment, integration, and latent pattern maintenance are associated with, respectively, the economy, the polity, law, and the family.[7]

By examining the entities that perform each of the functions, we gain some idea of what Parsons means by each. In brief, *adaptation* involves response to the demands of the environment. If we use an organization—the university—as an example, the problem of adaptation is one of gaining the resources necessary in order to achieve goals. The university must secure adequate funding, competent personnel, and the necessary facilities in order to carry on a program of education. *Goal-attainment* involves the mobilization of resources. The university must make decisions about the way to use its funds, its facilities, and its personnel in order to achieve its educational goals. *Integration* is important for the regulation of subsystems. The various groups and units in the university–departments, schools, research centers, administration, student body, and so forth—must work together with sufficient coherence and solidarity to attain goals. *Latent pattern maintenance* refers to the problem of maintaining the value pattern of the system. The university must socialize personnel into the organizational values and motivate them to perform their various tasks. Thus, two of the functioning imperatives focus on problems internal to the system—latent pattern maintenance and integration—while the other two focus on problems that relate to the environment of the system—adaptation and goal-attainment. Two involve what are basically instrumental actions—adaptation and latent pattern maintenance—while the other two involve what are basically consummatory actions—goal-attainment and integration.

Finally, the four functional imperatives are related to four structural categories (role, collectivities, norms, and values), with each of the structural categories being primarily involved in the fulfillment of one of the functional imperatives. Adaptation is the basic function of the role. Presidents and development officers in universities secure funds; purchasing agents secure supplies; chairpersons and deans recruit personnel; and so forth. Goal-attainment is the work of collectivities. Committees and various administrative units make decisions about such matters as the budget and the appropriate behavior for faculty members. Integration depends upon norms that "regulate the great variety of processes that contribute to the implementation of patterned value commitments."[8] Norms define expectations and thereby govern such university relationships as those between faculty and students, administration and faculty, and physical plant operatives and administration. Latent pattern maintenance is the function of values. A value on liberal education and intellectual activity secures the commitment of academic personnel even during times when salaries are not as high as those they might obtain in industry; the same values motivate them to perform their various duties even when the latter impose inordinate demands on time.

It is important to understand the nature of the functional imperatives, because they are the links between structure and process. When we look at processes in and of social systems, we do so in the light of those four functional imperatives, which are also the structural essence of any social system.

The first point we must make is the distinction between process and change. According to Parsons, all processes involve some kind of change, but we may "distinguish from others the processes which change social structures."[9] He calls those particular kinds of processes "change." Change, in other words, is a particular type of process that involves alteration in social structures. Parsons also distinguishes two kinds of dynamic problems in systems. The first is the problem of processes of equilibrium, which "go on under the assumption that the structural patterns of institutionalized culture are given, i.e., are assumed to remain constant."[10] The second is the problem of structural change, i.e., the problem of processes which involve fundamental alterations in the system.

The distinction between two kinds of dynamic problems does not involve an absolute dichotomy, however. There is a very important "mixed case," which involves structural change in the subsystems but not in the "over-all structural pattern." The most important type of such a process is structural differentiation, which "involves genuine *reorganization* of the system and, therefore, fundamental structural change of various subsystems and their relations to each other."[11] For example, a university's subsystem of adaptation might be altered through a restructuring of authority. Administrative roles might be reduced to advisory functions and to the task of implementing the decisions made by a new unit composed of faculty, students, and parents of students. The adaptive subsystem would undergo structural differentiation, but the overall structural pattern would not necessarily change.

In all, we may identify four types of processes in Parsons's thought: *equilibrium,* which involves processes within the system; *structural change,* which involves fundamental alterations of the system; *structural differentiation,* which involves change in one or more subsystems but not in the overall system; and *evolution,* which is the process describing the developmental pattern of societies over time. These four kinds of processes are not, of course, mutually exclusive or independent. But they are analytically distinguishable, and we shall examine each in turn in a little more detail.

First, equilibrium refers to processes that serve to maintain the boundaries of the system. The equilibrium may be either static or moving. Processes are continual in both types, but in the latter case there is a patterned process of change. An example is the growth of scientific knowledge. This represents, of course, not a fundamental alteration of the system but change in "the cognitive *content* of the relevant part of the culture."[12] The important point to keep in mind here is that equilibrium means neither stagnation nor change. Certainly scientific knowledge has greatly altered the nature of American society, but it has not effected the structural change of our society. Similarly, the introduction of computers into an organization can greatly affect such factors as efficiency, capacity, and work roles in the organization without changing the fundamental character of that organization (in terms of its goals and values).

Equilibrium in social systems may be analyzed in terms of four laws:

1. The *principle of inertia* asserts continuation of rate and direction of a process unless "opposing motivational forces" impinge upon the process;
2. The *principle of action and reaction* asserts that any change of direction of a process will be balanced by another change "which is equal in motivational force and opposite in direction";
3. The *principle of effort* states that changes in the rate of processes are in direct proportion to "the magnitude of the motivational force applied or withdrawn";
4. The *principle of system-integration* states that the fate of "pattern" elements hinges upon their value as integrative factors.[13]

The similarity of the laws of equilibrium to classical mechanics is obvious. The idea of equilibrium is also obvious—it states that strong forces are at work to prevent basic changes in the system. For that reason, Parsons's use of the concept has been strongly attacked. He, however, has said that the criticisms leave him "completely unimpressed" because the concept is absolutely essential to social science. Equilibrium is a concept of "regularity under specific conditions as applied to the internal state of an empirical system relative to its environment."[14] Such regularity is neither rigidly patterned nor unalterable, and the only alternative Parsons sees to it is "sheer randomness."

The second type of process is structural change. Such a change in any social system is, by definition, a change in the system's normative culture. This means change in "the paramount value system" at the highest level of the social system. There will also be changes among the subsystems and in the social roles. The interdependence of units within a system means that fundamental change in any unit is likely to involve some kind of change in other units, and changes at a particular level of the system are likely to effect some kind of change at other levels.

Examples of structural change are provided by the developing nations of the world, in which the primary impetus to change has come from outside the society itself. It is also possible for the source of such change to be internal; this may come about through the work of a charismatic leader. Change that results from a charismatic leader takes place in the religious sphere; that is, the meaning of the individual's life and of the nature of the society are given new definitions.

The third type of process is structural differentiation. As noted earlier, this process involves alterations in the subsystems but not in the overall system's structure. In other words, in structural differentiation, "the institutionalized values will be assumed to remain constant."[15] This is not to say that there are no changes at the value level. The *content* of the values changes as a result of differentiation, but the *pattern* does not. For example, a pattern of "instrumental activism" may continue to underlie different kinds of families in the United States as the family undergoes structural differentiation. The same pattern will underlie "employing-productive units" which have already, earlier in history, differentiated from the family. One pattern, then, may apply to two distinct systems (nuclear family and employing-productive unit) which have emerged by differentiation from an older system (the self-sufficient family of early America). The resulting values must be able to "legitimize the functions of both differentiated units under a single formula which permits it to do what it does and, equally essential, not to do what the other does."[16]

What have we just said? Essentially, the argument is that differentiation is a process that involves those kinds of changes which are congruent with the basic values of the society. Parsons outlines the main stages in this process of differentiation, illustrating them by reference to the family.[17] First, there will be some kind of frustration in goal-attainment. Thus, the family household which performs "occupational" functions as well as those we ordinarily associate with the family may differentiate into two new units—a nuclear family and an employing-productive unit—that separately perform the functions once characteristic of the original unit. The frustration encountered in the initial stage of differentiation may be rooted in the productive or socialization functions, or in both.

The second stage occurs at the boundary between the goal-attainment and other subsystems, and involves problematic relations. In the case of the family, the relations of goal-attainment to markets and to the legitimization of the family's position in society are important. In the third stage, there must be a balance between the two aspects of frustration mentioned above, that is, between "the conditional components of facilities and rewards" and the "normative components of expectation systems."[18] It is, in particular, the building-up of frustrations with the latter, the normative aspects of expectations, that is crucial to differentiation.

The fourth and final type of process that we find in Parsons's work is the evolution of societies. The general direction of societal evolution is toward "the enhancement of adaptive capacity."[19] Parsons analyzes this evolution in terms of a paradigm, which begins with the process of differentiation. In this case, differentiation involves new units "which differ in *both* structure and functional significance for the wider system."[20] If this process has been truly evolutionary in nature, then the new units will perform, or have the adaptive capacity to perform. their functions more effectively than those functions were performed in the original unit. Parsons calls this the "adaptive upgrading aspect" of evolution.

Differentiation raises problems of integration. There is greater complexity to the system; there are more units to coordinate. Adaptive upgrading may demand that ascriptive facets of mobilizing resources be abandoned, and that "otherwise excluded elements" be included in order to achieve integration. In essence, ascribed characteristics (sex, race, kinship) may have to give way to achieved characteristics (expertise, education) as the basis for mobilizing resources.

Finally, the paradigm for the study of evolution includes the problem of values. A value pattern must be effected which is congruent with the nature of the emerging social system. For the value pattern designates the desired type of social system as well as integrating that system. An appropriate new value pattern is therefore necessary for both the legitimatization and the integration of the new social system.

There are a number of "evolutionary universals" that characterize the historical process.[21] These universals are important to the evolutionary process and thus will be likely to exist in any society. Four of the universals are fundamental to all social systems—some form of communication, kinship organization, religion, and technology (which may be primitive). These four basic characteristics permit further evolutionary development, during which the society will gradually be characterized by the other universals: a system of stratification; cultural legitimation for the stratification system; bureaucratic organizations; a system of money and markets; universal norms (expressed in a legal system); and a democratic polity.

Because these various universals appear sequentially, Parsons may be called—in his later works—a developmental theorist. In fact, Parsons has described not only the direction of evolution (enhanced adaptive capacity), but also the major stages of evolution. He identifies three broad levels of evolutionary development—primitive, intermediate, and modern. The crucial factor in the transition from primitive to intermediate levels was language, particularly written language. The latter increased the differentiation between social and cultural systems and made the cultural system far more potent than it had been. The crucial factor in the transition from the intermediate to the modern level was the institutionalization of norms in the form of a legal system. In both instances, in other words, the transition has been marked by "critical developments in the code elements of the normative structures."[22]

One other question that we may ask with respect to Parsons involves the sources of change. It is already obvious that change is highly problematic. The ideas of equilibrium and inertia suggest that forces of considerable magnitude are necessary to overcome the stability of the system. We have also pointed out the endurance of values; structural change involves change in the value system, and the latter is highly resistant to alteration. Furthermore, the equilibrium is maintained by the processes of socialization and social control.

On the other hand, Parsons sees intrinsic potential for change in "the combination of the inherent tendencies to deviation and the imperfections of the integration of value-orientations."[23] Nevertheless, these facets of the social system appear limp in the face of the powerful forces tending to maintain equilibrium. Apart from certain institutionalized processes of change, therefore, "change is never just 'alteration of pattern' but alteration *by the overcoming of resistance*."[24] Considerable effort is required to overcome that resistance.

In fact, "severity of strain is never alone an adequate explanation of change."[25] Strain may be resolved in a way that leaves the structure intact. In addition to an excess of strain, therefore, change is facilitated by four other factors:

1. Mechanisms that are able to overcome the "inevitable resistances of institutionalized structural patterns";

2. A mode of reaction to the strain that includes "adequate constructive possibilities";
3. The existence of a model of the pattern that is to be institutionalized;
4. The use of sanctions to reward behavior that is in accord with the model, and to do so with sufficient consistency so that values and self-interest will be congruent with each other (the "hallmark of institutionalization").[26]

Finally, the factors leading to change may arise either within (endogenous) or without (exogenous) the social system. Exogenous sources of change are those that arise from the other systems—organisms, personalities, cultures—with which the social system interacts. Examples of such sources are genetic changes in populations and changes in the physical environment as these are perceived by people or articulated in technological knowledge. A major source of exogenous change is the other social systems with which a particular system interacts; intersocietal conflict and war or the threat of war may effect change in the social systems involved.

Endogenous changes are those resulting from internal strains, which are disequilibria between inputs and outputs among subsystems. That is, strain means that the relation between two or more subsystems is under pressure to change, and to change in a manner that is incongruous with systemic equilibrium. Such strains may be resolved by the system, may be arrested or isolated, or may result in structural change.

In his later work on evolution, Parsons is less clear about the sources of change. Turner argues that Parsons "apparently views evolution as guided by the cybernetic hierarchy of controls, especially the informational component. . . . Without such informational control, movement to the next stage of development in an evolutionary sequence will be inhibited."[27] To say that information (in the form of language, writing, and such institutionalized sources as law and science) is critical does not yet tell us precisely how that informational control leads to a new stage of evolution or how the system of information itself develops. In other words, Parsons has repeated one of the problems of the early evolutionists by describing the various stages without giving us much help in understanding why the transition occurs.

• *Neil Smelser*

Smelser provides us with a good example of the application of Parsonian theory to the study of change. We shall examine his analysis of the Industrial Revolution after first noting a few general points he makes about theories of change. For Smelser identifies a number of issues that must be dealt with in any theory of change, some of which have not been attended to with any degree of precision.

For example, one essential element of any theory of change is the specification of the dependent variables. What is it that changes? In general, theorists have stated or assumed that change is temporal variation in one or more of the following: "aggregated attributes of the population of a social unit," "rates of behavior in a population over time," "social structure, or patterns of interaction among individuals," "cultural patterns."[28] Examples of each of these would be, respectively, changes in the proportion of age groups in a population, changes in crime rates, changes in authority relations in some social entity, and changes in values.

Specification of the dependent variables, of course, cannot be done properly without a concomitant identification of the independent variables. What are the determinants of change? What is it that causes the changes just noted? According to Smelser, the determinants of change generally are identified as one or more of the following: "the structural setting for change," "the impetus to change," "mobilization for change," "the operation of social controls."[29]

The structural setting involves an examination of the social structure in order to ascertain the implications for change that inhere in that structure. For example, if we wanted to estimate the probability of change through reform in any society, we would search for, among other things, the structural means for the expression of grievances. The greater the number of channels for expressing grievances, the more likely it is that reforms will be implemented.

The impetus to change implies that structural conduciveness alone is not adequate, however. There must also be some kind of force tending toward change. That force may be an internal one—demographic changes that exert pressure for other kinds of changes—or it may be an external one—the threat posed by another society, whether the threat is a military or an economic one.

Mobilization for change is related to the direction of change. The fact that change is facilitated by the structure, and that there is pressure toward change, does not yet indicate what direction such change will take. The direction depends on the manner in which resources are mobilized and how they are used to effect the change. Such mobilization, in turn, is crucially tied up with the leadership involved in the change.

Finally, social controls are always present to offer resistance to change. These social controls may be the established authorities, such as the mass media, governmental officials, and church leaders. They may suppress change, or they may have a significant role in determining the direction change takes.

Smelser performs a useful service in reminding us of the importance of specifying the independent and dependent variables. One of the problems of comparing various theorists is that they do not take the same variables as the focus of analysis. The reader might, in fact, find it interesting to reflect back on the theories we have treated thus far, asking, with respect to each: What is it that changes and what are the determinants of that change?

As Smelser's list of the determinants of change shows, he works within 'the Parsonian perspective; and he has applied that perspective to a historical analysis of the Industrial Revolution. Smelser points out that over time we may observe both short-term adjustments and long-run structural changes. The latter, in contrast to the former, involve changes in the roles of the social system, including the "disappearance, re-creation, and reorganization" of those roles.[30] It is long-term structural change that is the focus of his own study.

Specifically, Smelser investigates structural differentiation, which he says is particularly relevant for a growing social system. Differentiation must be understood in terms of the four functional requisites for any system—adaptation, goal-attainment, integration, and latent pattern maintenance. Further, differentiation implies that there is a definite sequence involved in the change. Smelser identifies seven steps in the sequence:

1. Dissatisfaction deriving from the failure to achieve goals satisfactorily and from the awareness of the possibility of change;
2. Psychic disturbances, taking the form of a variety of emotional reactions and aspirations which are, however, inappropriate in terms of resolving the problems;
3. A more rational use of the energy expended in step 2 in an effort to "realize the implications of the existing value-system";
4. A brain-storming stage, in which ideas are generated in profusion without anyone's being responsible for their implementation or consequences;
5. An effort to specify the particular ideas and institutional patterns to be implemented;
6. The implementation of change by individuals or groups, with their performance subjected to sanctions in accord with the existing system of values;
7. The "routinization" of acceptable changes.[31]

The above are only "empty boxes," says Smelser, and must be filled in by the specific social system under analysis. For the case of industrial change, the filling in results in the following sequence of change:

1. Dissatisfaction deriving from the failure to achieve satisfactory levels of productivity and from the awareness of potential for attaining higher productive levels;
2. Psychic disturbances, which take the form of inappropriate disjunctive emotional reactions and unrealistic aspirations;
3. "A covert handling of these tensions and a mobilization of motivational resources" in an effort to "realize the implications of the existing value-system";
4. Encouragement of the generation of a profusion of ideas without assignment of responsibility for their implementation or consequences;
5. An effort to specify the particular ideas so that entrepreneurs will commit themselves to them;
6. The implementation of change by entrepreneurs, who are rewarded by profits or punished by their financial failure as the consumers respond to their innovations;
7. Routinization through the acceptance of gains "as part of the standard of living and their incorporation into the routine functions of production."[32]

What is the operation of these seven steps in history? They are not to be regarded as discrete stages. That is, dissatisfaction does not vanish with the appearance of psychic disturbances. Various steps may persist, or may disappear and reappear. Furthermore, there may be regression; the attainment of step 5 may be followed by regression to step 2. The sequence may also be "truncated"; minor dissatisfactions may never lead to further steps. Finally, we may expect to find a number of sequences of differentiation operating simultaneously: "the appearance of the factory system concealed several distinct processes of differentiation."[33]

As noted above, this sequence proceeds in the context of the four functional requisites of any social system. The analysis is too complex to be detailed here, but we should note the way in which Smelser makes use of the four functions. For an industry (Smelser's analysis focuses on the English cotton industry from 1770 to 1840), the "functional dimensions" include the "procurement of capital facilities" (the adaptive subsystem), the "control of production" (the goal-attainment subsystem), the "control of industrial organization" (the integrative subsystem), and "technical production" (the latency subsystem).[34] In addition, of course, each of these may be treated as a system in itself with its own four subsystems. Once the boundary interchanges among the resulting sixteen subsystems have been identified, the industrial process has been sufficiently delineated for one to proceed to an analysis of change. The change takes the form of differentiation within the adaptive, goal-attainment, and integrative systems (values remain constant during a sequence of differentiation).

Smelser devotes considerable attention to the family, and we may illustrate his approach by sketching in very broad terms the application of the seven steps outlined above to the family unit affected by the revolution of the English cotton industry. One of the early technological improvements in spinning involved the enlargement of mules (spinning machines) and an increase in the number of mule spindles. Power looms were introduced into weaving in the 1820s. These developments exerted pressure on the traditional family division of labor and became the foci for dissatisfaction. Families felt constrained to differentiate the work of the various members and to separate work roles from other functions of the family unit.

Dissatisfaction, however, is always legitimated by values, in this case the "broad values of personal responsibility, discipline, and the calling."[35] (These values underlay the pleas of moral leaders for people to be industrious, temperate, and rational with regard to their use of time and money.) The combination of this legitimated dissatisfaction with the inflexibility of the family led to various disturbances, including destruction of property, strikes, and a variety of forms of psychic distress. A number of "stop-gap measures" such as police action, public pleas, and some legislative measures were employed to cope with the disturbances (step 3). It was, ultimately, factory legislation that "eased the family economy of the working classes toward a new structure"[36] (steps 3 to 7). That new structure involved the differentiation of the family unit with respect to division of labor and to consumption and savings—the new family was one in which economic roles of adults were segregated from those of children and educational responsibility was shifted out of the family; and a number of innovations, including savings banks and cooperative stores, were developed to ensure the financial welfare of the family.

The Great Debate: Exegesis or Eisegesis?

In the first chapter, we briefly noted that a considerable amount of debate has revolved about the issue of whether the position represented by Parsons and Smelser adequately deals with change. Does a full interpretation of the Parsonian perspective yield a basic concern for understanding change (exegesis), or is the concern for understanding change read into the perspective (eisegesis)? Conflict theorists have insisted that structural-functionalism cannot deal with change. Structural-functionalists have, of course, disagreed. As we have seen, Parsons asserts the importance of understanding change, and both he and Smelser applied the perspective of structural-functionalism to specific analyses of change.

There have been a variety of responses to the debate between conflict theorists and structural-functionalists. Some theorists have attempted to point out the shared assumptions of the two perspectives. These shared assumptions, they have argued, could form the basis for further theoretical development. But nothing has come from such efforts.

A somewhat different approach has been to select those aspects of each perspective which are valid and use them to develop theory. For example, Neal pointed out that conflict theorists emphasize the diverse interests of various groups, whereas structural-functionalists focus on the values that integrate society.[37] She argued that both values and interests are factors and can be used by examining the personality characteristics of decision makers. There are four types of people, who differ in accord with a basic orientation to change or nonchange on the one hand and to values or interests on the other hand. These four types, in turn, are related to Parsons's four functional imperatives. Thus, the value-nonchange-oriented actor seeks to bring about change in accord with values to which he or she is committed, to adapt (respond) to the larger society by articulating the values. The interest-change-oriented actor basically wants approval from those people whom he or she loves, fears, or respects and gains it by pursuing the goals of those people. The value-nonchange-oriented actor essentially wants to maintain the traditional values, while the interest-nonchange-oriented actor focuses on the norms of his or her group and on the ritual adherence to those norms. Neal has shown the applicability of her scheme to Catholic priests. Clagett has shown how it can be utilized to analyze change in education.[38]

Others have tried to show how structural-functionalism can be modified to incorporate the processes of change. An early attempt was that of Bertrand, who developed a stress-strain model of social systems which could, he argued, account for conflict, deviation, and change.[39] Bertrand said that any viable model of social systems must include both conflict and change as ongoing processes (rather than abnormalities) and social organization as a structure that facilitates goal-directed action (rather than a state of equilibrium). The stress-strain model posits the existence of inherent structural problems (stresses) and behavioral manifestations of those problems (strains). In essence, Bertrand argues that socialization can never be total, so that individuals will invariably deviate from values and roles in the society. The result may be conflict, and when the conflict or deviation brings about disorganization, there will be some kind of adjustment or change in the system. Since stresses and strains are part of the very nature of social life, conflict, deviation, and change must also be an intrinsic part of every social system.

More recently, Paul Colomy has acknowledged the difficulties and discussed the ways in which functionalists are trying to rectify them.[40] *Differentiation theory* is the result of the efforts of functionalists to adequately explain social change. Early differentiation theory had three bases. First, it identified a master trend of change—the replacement of multi-functional units in a society with more specialized units (such as the replacement of some of the family's functions by work and educational organizations). Second, it identified the impetus for the change, such as structural strain. And third, it argued that this process of differentiation "increases the effectiveness and efficiency of a social system or sub-system."[41]

Whereas the earlier work focused on the increased efficiency and the reintegration of the system that followed differentiation, more recent theorists maintain that the differentiated units in a society are new bases of interest, and that people will defend those interests against any perceived threats. This defense of vested interests means that the system is not as efficient and effective in dealing with a changing environment. There is conflict as well as integration as a result of the process of differentiation. Moreover, there can be processes of dedifferentiation, in which people reject and even reverse the move towards increasing complexity; uneven differentiation, in which some subsystems change at a different rate and to a different degree than other subsystems; and incomplete or blunted differentiation, in which a process of differentiation begins but is not completed.

The debate and the varied responses to it all underscore the point that the study of social change does not flow naturally out of the structural-functional perspective. Without minimizing the importance of understanding structure, it seems clear that the approach taken in structural-functionalism, with its biological and mechanical modes of thought, tends to make the study of change awkward. Indeed, the efforts of structural-functionalists to understand and analyze change have resulted more from criticisms of the perspective than from any inherent applicability to that approach.

In his later work, Parsons appears to assume the normalcy of change. As we have seen, however, his evolutionary perspective provides more in the way of concepts and categories that describe the characteristics of various stages than a theory of change. In fact, Giddens has criticized Parsons's emphasis on adaptive upgrading on two grounds.[42] First, to the extent that "adaptative success" is an explanatory concept, the stimulus to change is still external. The social system is not evolving because of its own internal dynamics but is, rather, progressing as a result of continual adaptation. In other words, Giddens sees Parsons as reluctant to admit the normalcy of change even in his evolutionary thought. Second, Giddens argues that adaptation is an "ill-conceived" term to apply to the evolution of human societies: "Animals, as Marx pointed out long ago, simply 'adapt' to the environment, accepting its exigencies; where animals produce, they do so mechanically, and their production does not constitute a significant intervention in nature. But human beings actively transform nature, and subordinate it to their own ends."[43]

One additional problem with the notion of enhanced adaptive capacity is that it accepts the myth of unidirectionality and utopia apprehended that we discussed in Chapter 1. As John Wilson has pointed out, "There is a tendency to treat as indices of heightened adaptive capacity only those innovations which stand in the direct line of Western modernization. . . . Who is to say that a higher GNP at the cost of greater inequality is evolutionary?"[44]

Parsons's work on evolution leaves many unanswered questions. We get a sense of somehow missing something of the essence of the process. In general, his conceptual framework seems far more suitable for investigating stability than for investigating change. In fact, the work of the Parsonians is valuable in that it reminds us of the fact of persistence in social life. We must not equate change with total fluidity. There are continuities and stabilities as well as change, and some kinds of change (what Parsons called structural change) are far more consequential for human life than others.

In sum, as initially formulated, Parsons's functionalism carried the message that the highest value is on preservation and survival of the social system, that internal conflicts are evil and threatening, and that "the best social change is no change."[45] Subsequent developments took a different approach, but it seems that the more recent work on differentiation is a reaction to criticism rather than a natural outgrowth of this perspective's utility. There are some useful ideas in structural-functionalism, but its potential for understanding change appears limited.

Endnotes

1. Pierre L. van den Berghe, "Dialectic and Functionalism: Toward a Synthesis," in *System, Change, and Conflict*, ed. N. J. Demerath III and Richard A. Peterson (New York: Free Press, 1967), pp. 294-95.

2. Talcott Parsons, *Societies: Evolutionary and Comparative Perspectives* (Englewood Cliffs: Prentice-Hall, 1966), p. 111.

3. Talcott Parsons and Edward A. Shils, eds., *Toward a General Theory of Action* (New York: Harper & Row, 1951), pp. 230-31.

4. Talcott Parsons, Robert Bales, and Edward Shils, *Working Papers in the Theory of Action* (Glencoe, Ill.: Free Press, 1953), p. 174.

5. Talcott Parsons, *The Social System* (New York: Free Press, 1951), pp. 5-6.

6. Talcott Parsons, Edward Shils. Kaspar D. Naegele, and Jesse R. Pitts, eds., *Theories of Society* (New York: Free Press, 1961), p. 61.

7. Talcott Parsons, *Sociological Theory and Modern Society* (New York: Free Press, 1967), p. 348.

8. Parsons, *Societies*, p. 19.

9. Ibid., p. 21.

10. Parsons, Shils, Naegele, and Pitts, *Theories of Society*, p. 37.

11. Ibid.

12. Parsons, *The Social System*, p. 491.

13. Parsons. Bales, and Shils, *Working Papers on the Theory of Action*, pp. 102-3.

14. Talcott Parsons, "The Point of View of the Author," in *The Social Theories of Talcott Parsons*, ed. Max Black (Englewood Cliffs, N.J.: Prentice-Hall, 1961), p. 337.

15. Talcott Parsons, "A Functional Theory of Change," in *Social Change*, ed. Amitai Etzioni and Eva Etzioni (New York: Basic Books, 1964), p. 89.

16. Ibid., p. 96.

17. Ibid., pp. 89-90.

18. Ibid., p. 90.

19. Parsons, *Societies*, p. 21.

20. Ibid., p. 22.

21. Talcott Parsons, "Evolutionary Universals in Society," *American Sociological Review* 29 (1964): 339-57.

22. Parsons, *Societies*, p. 26.

23. Parsons and Shils, *Toward a General Theory of Action*, p. 231.

24. Parsons, *The Social System*, p. 491.

25. Parsons, Shils, Naegele, and Pitts, *Theories of Society*, p. 75.

26. Ibid., pp. 75-76.

27. Jonathan H. Turner, *The Structure of Sociological Theory* (Homewood, Ill.: Dorsey Press, 1974), p. 45.

28. Neil J. Smelser, *Essays in Sociological Explanation* (Englewood Cliffs, N. J.: Prentice-Hall, 1968), pp. 200-201.

29. Ibid., pp. 205-207.

30. Neil J. Smelser, *Social Change in the Industrial Revolution* (Chicago: University of Chicago Press, 1959), p. 14.
31. Ibid., pp. 15-16.
32. Ibid., p. 29.
33. Ibid., p. 32.
34. Ibid., p. 25.
35. Ibid., p. 210.
36. Ibid., p. 272.
37. Sister Marie Augusta Neal, *Values and Interests in Social Change* (Englewood Cliffs, N.J.: Prentice-Hall, 1965).
38. Arthur F. Clagett, "Role Adjustment Modes of Public School Teachers," *The Journal of Educational Research* 67 (September, 1973): 29-33; and "Ideology, Role Playing and Individual Choice: A Research Perspective," *Quarterly Journal of Ideology* 3 (Summer, 1979): 22-33.
39. Alvin L. Bertrand, "The Stress-Strain Element of Social Systems: A Micro Theory of Conflict and Change," *Social Forces* 42 (October, 1963): 1-9.
40. Paul B. Colomy, "Recent Developments in the Functionalist Approach to Change," *Sociological Focus* 19 (April, 1986): 136-58.
41. Ibid., p. 142.
42. Anthony Giddens, *Studies in Social and Political Theory* (New York: Basic Books, 1977), pp. 120-21.
43. Ibid., p.121.
44. John Wilson, *Social Theory* (Englewood Cliffs, N.J.: Prentice-Hall, 1983), p. 102.
45. George A. Huaco, "Ideology and General Theory: The Case of Sociological Functionalism," *Comparative Study in Society and History* 28 (January, 1986): 50.

CHAPTER FIVE

Social-Psychological Theories

Although some of the theorists we have examined so far have dealt with social-psychological factors in change, they have generally given a minor role to the individual. We have seen the effects of broad historical currents, of great impersonal forces, of the nature of the structure in which people carry on their existence, but we have not encountered an approach that focuses on the individual and his or her personality (Khaldun's theory, it will be remembered, asserted that the personality was a function of the social structure). Even where it is granted that it is people who make history, we are not sure how much latitude those people actually have to shape the direction of change.

Can the actions of individuals alter the direction of development? Is personality a factor in change? Are human beings the pawns of forces that are beyond their control if not their understanding? Can we do no more than, as Spencer insisted, allow free sway to the inevitable evolutionary process? The first two theories we shall study in this chapter attempt to answer such questions, and they answer them by affirming the critical significance of the individual. More specifically, they assert the critical importance of personality in economic development.

A related concern is the attempt to account for the social psychology of modernization. As we shall discuss in Chapter 12, modernization refers to the social and cultural developments that occur along with economic growth. The questions to be discussed in the section following on "the modern individual" are as follows. Is there a "modern" person who holds attitudes and values that are distinct from those of the premodern individual and that are a necessary part of the modernization process? If so, is the modern individual a result of modernization or a necessary cause of modernization?

The Creative Personality: Everett E. Hagen

Hagen is an economist who has attempted to incorporate principles of psychology into a theory of economic development. He argues that economic development, which may be defined in terms of continuing increase in per capita income arising out of technological advances, must be understood in terms of the creative personality.

There are, of course, other explanations of economic growth, and Hagen deals with a number of them in order to show their inadequacy. Theories based on race or climate or particular social, religious, or economic conditions have all failed to explain adequately why certain groups became the cutting edge of technological and economic change. These past theories are not wholly wrong; they are simply insufficient (and in some cases irrelevant).

How, then, does economic growth occur? First of all, we must keep in mind that such growth is gradual, encompassing an extended period of time. For one thing, the innovations required are not simply technoeconomic, but social. We are not talking, therefore, about sudden, radical shifts, but long-term processes. Those processes are intimately linked with creative individuals, who themselves emerge out of a particular kind of social context over time. These individuals are not randomly dispersed throughout the society; rather, innovations that generate economic growth are made "disproportionately by members of some one or more social groups, and not the groups who are in the best position to have contacts abroad or access to new knowledge and to capital."[1]

The task of the theorist, therefore, is to ascertain how the creative personality develops and, specifically, why it develops in certain groups within the society rather than in others or in the society at large. Note that the creative personality *develops*; that is, as we shall see, the traditional individual is not creative. The question is, then: What leads to a generation of innovators? We must understand this, for the growth that is the goal of most people will not occur without the development of creativity in personality: "Social change will not occur without change in personalities."[2]

But if we are going to study personality, we must know what we mean by it. Hagen says that we may describe personality in terms of "needs, values, and cognitive elements of world view, together with intelligence and energy level."[3] If we can identify the types of needs, values, and cognitions that characterize an individual, and combine this with a knowledge of his or her intelligence and energy level, "then no important ambiguity remains concerning how he will act in any given situation."[4]

The needs that comprise one important dimension of personality may be classified according to whether they are manipulative, aggressive, passive, or succorant-nurturant. Manipulative needs include the need to achieve, to gain autonomy, and to secure order. Aggressive needs are illustrated by the need to attack, the need to overcome opposition, and the need to dominate. Passive needs include the need for dependence, for affiliation, and for being guided by others. Succorant-nurturant needs include the needs to both give and receive such things as support, protection, and love.

Using these dimensions, we may distinguish between innovational and authoritarian personalities. The two personality types do not necessarily differ by intelligence or energy level; highly intelligent and highly energetic individuals may be found among both types. However, there are important differences in needs, values, and cognitions. Innovational personalities perceive their social milieu as having a logical order which they are able to comprehend. Furthermore, they believe that their social milieu values them; such valuation, however, may appear to rest upon their achievements, causing them considerable anxiety. Because innovational personalities have a high need for succor and for being assured of their value, they are driven to achieve.

Among other characteristics of innovational personalities are high needs for autonomy and order, self-understanding that enables them to empathize with others, a high need for nurturance, and a concern for the welfare of others as well as for their own well-being.

The above qualities not only fit the innovational personality for the work of economic development, but present a rather stark contrast with authoritarian personalities. The latter perceive the social milieu as lacking in any order that is comprehensible to them. They do not believe that they are valued by their social milieu. They perceive power to be a function of their position rather than of their achievements.

This cognitive view of the world generates, in authoritarian personalities, a considerable amount of rage which must somehow be contained. Consequently, there is a high need for submission-dominance, a low need for succorance-nurturance, and a low need for both autonomy and achievement. Finally, authoritarian personalities, in contrast to innovational personalities, do not give the same weight to the welfare of others as they do to their own well-being.

It is perhaps already evident how these two personality types are said to lead to two different types of behavior. The innovational personality almost by definition engages in behavior that is creative. At least, this person possesses every quality that would facilitate creative behavior. The world must be comprehensible, for example, if one is to make the effort to shape the direction of change. One of the reasons the traditional individual does not innovate, according to Hagen, is that such a person "perceives the world as an arbitrary place rather than an orderly one amenable to analysis and responsive to his initiative."[5]

We would expect, then, to find any economically stagnant society to be pervaded by authoritarian personalities. The whole society, in fact, will be one that has a rigid hierarchy of authority. Relationships will be structured in accord with authority, and any problematic situation will be dealt with by submission to authority. Hagen sees the experiences of childhood as inevitably generating considerable rage, which can be channeled into creative action. But in the traditional society, "rage can be vented by dominating everyone below one in the social hierarchy. . . . It can also be vented in more overt form against outsiders."[6] In every way, then, the traditional society and the authoritarian individual are structured for uncreative behavior.

Nevertheless, change does occur. Economic growth does begin in some societies. Personality types do change. How can we account for such changes? What is it that impels some groups to break out of the strong bonds of tradition and authoritarianism? Hagen has summarized the answer in terms of five laws:

1. The *law of group subordination,* which locates the impetus to change in some group that perceives itself to be subordinated;
2. The *law of rejection of values,* which states that the subordinated group will discard the values of those who dominate it;
3. The *law of social blockage,* which qualifies the above by pointing out that a subordinated group will discard dominant values and engage in deviant behavior only when traditional avenues for advancement have been blocked;
4. The *law of group protection,* which says that individuals engaging in novel behavior gain social support from the subordinated group;
5. The *law of non-alien leadership,* which asserts that economic growth will not occur in the whole society unless the deviant group that has begun the process is accepted and followed.[7]

Let us attempt to follow through the process described by these five laws. Because of the stability of a traditional society, something must happen to alter the personalities of some group within that society. The needs, values, and conditions must change, and that change is effected by "the perception on the part of the members of some social group that their purposes and values in life are not respected by groups in the society whom they respect and whose esteem they value."[8] Hagen calls this the "withdrawal of status respect."

Withdrawal of status respect, in turn, exerts pressure on authoritarian parents, who will respond by structuring a home life that leads to "progressively increasing retreatism over a period of several generations."[9] Eventually, the creative personality will emerge from this. The shift from retreatism to the generation of creative personalities is given impetus by changes in parental personalities. which occur gradually over a period of generations.

Hagen focuses in particular on the personality of the father, which he says varies along two dimensions during the time of increasing retreatism. One dimension is the expectations the father has regarding his position in the family, and the other is the expectations he holds regarding the behavior of his son or sons. He may remain traditional in one set of expectations while becoming untraditional in the other. That is, "a stern father may expect high achievement of his sons, and a weak father may expect only that they learn to behave in the traditional manner."[10]

Thus, the father in the retreatist family has a "transitional" personality. That personality varies along the two dimensions noted; the father may be stern or weak and he may expect either strong achievement or traditional obedience. The various combinations of these dimensions lead to a number of different types of transitional personalities. Hagen selects four for analysis, and says that each of the four will tend to generate creative personalities. The four are as follows:

1. The father who is still relatively authoritarian, but who has high expectations for his son's achievement because of his own guilt over his lack of achievement;
2. The father who is stern and who senses guilt over his failure to achieve and transfers his expectations for achievement to his son, but who nevertheless shows love toward his son;
3. The father who is erratic, who tends to dominate his home, who has few expectations for his son's achievement, but who is sufficiently detached from the home or his son to allow the latter to avoid the threat posed by the father;
4. The father who is weak and who does not impede the "childhood explorations" of his son (although he also does not have high expectations for his son's achievement)."[11]

Thus, over several generations, the withdrawal of status respect leads to retreatism, which ultimately leads to creativity due to modifications in personality. This does not yet tell us, however, the direction of the creative behavior. That is, when will the innovational personality direct behavior toward creative economic and technological activities? This depends on the values that have been incorporated into the innovational personality, and on the social recognition that potentially may be gained through economic innovation. With respect to the latter, it will be remembered that creative efforts on the part of members of a status-deprived group will be directed toward regaining social approval. With respect to the former, a number of values are important for technoeconomic innovation, including merit based upon personal achievements, approval of business, and approval of manual work.

Hagen supports his theory by examining a number of historical examples of economic development, including that which occurred in England prior to the Industrial Revolution and nineteenth- and twentieth-century development in Japan, Colombia, and Burma. He has provided us with an ambitious attempt to account for the importance of the personality in economic growth. There are nevertheless a number of serious problems with the theory.

First, Hagen leaves us with the feeling that economic development is largely a matter of the caprice of history. *If* some group experiences withdrawal of status respect, and *if* that status can be regained through entrepreneurial activity that results in technological and economic innovation, then the society will experience development. Change is neither normal nor continuous, but is more like historical mutation. Hagen does, however, present a theory that reveals change as gratifying rather than traumatic; that is, once growth has begun, the process is presumably one that is physically therapeutic to the status-deprived group.

A second major difficulty with Hagen's theory is one common to any perspective that makes extensive use of psychoanalytic tools, namely, the problem of scientific verification. Many of the concepts Hagen uses, such as the Oedipus complex, various defense mechanisms, rage, guilt, and anxiety, must be inferred from behavior. The inferences seem valid only if one accepts the basic psychoanalytic theory. For example, to say that the apparent friendliness of the Burmese is a mask for their underlying rage and aggression is highly questionable unless one accepts the psychoanalytic framework. Indeed, the interpretation is problematic even if the framework is accepted; Hagen admits that at points his analysis is necessarily "speculative, or, to use the term loosely, intuitive."[12]

A third difficulty with Hagen's theory is that certain ideas are discordant with some empirical evidence. For example, the Oedipus complex, which assumes hostility on the part of boys toward their fathers due to jealousy over the father's role as lover of the boy's mother, does not appear to be as universal as Freud assumed. In fact, the hostility may not be due at all to jealousy over the father's role as lover, but to the father's role as disciplinarian. In Trobriand society, where the mother's lover (father) is not the same as the disciplinarian (uncle), Malinowski found that youthful hostility was directed toward the uncle rather than toward the father.[13]

Hagen also assumes that withdrawal of status respect by the larger society leads to debilitating consequences, at least for some considerable time, for the personalities of members of the deprived group. This assumption is problematic. Rosenberg found that self-esteem depended on experience in the neighborhood rather than on the esteem with which one's group was held by the larger society; his sample of 5,024 New York secondary school students indicated that "the social prestige of a nationality or religious group is generally unrelated to the self-acceptance of its members."[14] What was important was the neighborhood in which the child grew up; if the child had to endure status deprivation there, self-esteem tended to be lowered.

The implications of such findings may not be so clearly in opposition to Hagen's theory as the foregoing brief statements would indicate; nevertheless, the studies cited leave us feeling somewhat uncomfortable with the theory. A Freudian view of humanity has generated an imaginative theory of change, but we are left unconvinced. Hagen's challenge to social change theorists does not lie in the specifics of his theory; rather, it lies in his coming to terms with the role of the individual and various psychological factors involved in change.

The Achievement-Oriented Personality: David C. McClelland

More prominent than Hagen's writings is the work of David McClelland, who also focused upon the personality as a prime mover in change. Like Hagen, McClelland has been interested primarily in a specific kind of change—economic development. Since, according to McClelland, it is the entrepreneurial spirit that impels development, the task of the theorist is to account for the emergence of that spirit. The spirit is exemplified in businessmen, who, contrary to the popular image, are not driven by any profit motive per se, but rather by "a strong desire for achievement, for doing a good job. Profit is simply one measure among several of how well the job has been done, but it is not necessarily the goal itself."[15]

McClelland's basic thesis, then, is that "a society with a generally high level of *n* Achievement will produce more energetic entrepreneurs who, in turn, produce more rapid economic development."[16] The need for achievement (symbolized by *n* Achievement) is one of the basic needs of human beings, and, as with motives in general, it is the result of the social experiences of childhood. Thus, a variety of social factors influence child-rearing practices, which, in turn, either facilitate or impede the development of a need for achievement. That need is also a function of the kinds of reading materials to which the child is exposed. If the need for achievement is strongly developed, the individual will exhibit appropriate behavior, will manifest the entrepreneurial spirit, and will thereby act in such a way as to promote economic development.

This, in brief, is the thesis. A question now arises as to how we may measure the need for achievement. McClelland notes that Freud has taught us that a variety of motives may lead to any particular behavior. Human behavior is not always rational, particularly as an observer might conceive of rationality. Freud showed us how to get at motives through the analysis of dreams and free associations; that is, we may discover irrational motives in fantasy.

Using Freud's insights and the methodology of psychology, McClelland devised a projective technique for measuring the achievement motive. The technique essentially tries to ascertain the extent to which people's thoughts turn naturally to achievement-oriented ideas. For example, if an individual writes a story on the basis of a picture he or she has been shown, we can count the number of ideas in the story that are related to achievement. This simple count may then be used as a score of n Achievement, representing the individual's achievement drive, or the strength of his or her motivation for achievement.

The projective technique just described was part of the initial development of the study of achievement. In the effort to explore more fully the relationship between *n* Achievement and economic development, McClelland and his associates pursued three types of research. First, they sought to get group measures of *n* Achievement and to relate these to indicators of economic development. Second, they obtained "individual measures of motives, interests, values and performance of both mothers and their sons in various countries."[17] Third, they investigated the behavior, including motives, of business entrepreneurs.

The group measures were based on the idea that fantasy could be discerned as readily in literature as it could in stories written by ordinary individuals. Folk tales, stories used in elementary schools, and imaginative literature of the past were utilized to provide a group score of *n* Achievement. Content analysis yielded the extent to which the varied literature reflected high levels of achievement motivation; the literature, in turn, was assumed to influence members of the society and to reveal the "natural" mode of thinking in the society. For example, a children's story might have the theme of children building a boat. In an achievement-oriented society, the emphasis might be on constructing a boat that sails properly. An affiliation-oriented society may prefer the story to stress the enjoyment of shared play in sailing the boat. A power-oriented society might produce a story in which the emphasis was on the way the children organized in order to build the boat.

The second type of research conducted by McClelland and his associates focused on the sources of n Achievement and on its effects among adolescents. Why do some boys acquire high levels of n Achievement, while others remain at very low levels? How does the level of *n* Achievement bear upon vocational interests and performance? Answers to these questions were sought in the context of a cross-national study. In Japan, Germany, Brazil, and India, samples of boys were tested, and (except in India) their mothers were interviewed. The mothers were questioned about their views on independence and mastery training. The boys were tested by two projective techniques: story writing and spontaneous drawings. The boys were also given questionnaires relating to their values.

Finally, the third type of research involved testing of living businessmen to ascertain whether their level of *n* Achievement was higher, and their entrepreneurial activity more extensive, than that of other men their age. This research was also cross-national, involving businessmen and other professionals in the United States, Turkey, Italy, and Poland.

Obviously, McClelland has tried to identify a factor that is not restricted to any particular culture. In fact, he points out that while there may be some cultural differences, there are also basic similarities—people in all societies seem to strive to perform well according to some standard when their level of achievement motivation is high. Do the data support the cross-cultural validity of the achievement motive? After comparing rates of growth of various nations (based upon increases in electrical production) with levels of *n* Achievement and then making historical comparisons between rates of growth and achievement-related stories in children's readers, McClelland concludes that the relationship between *n* Achievement and economic growth is strongly supported. Preponderance of achievement-oriented stories in imaginative literature "is associated in modern times with a more rapid rate of economic development."[18]

This holds true for both Communist and Western nations and for both newly developing and well-developed nations.

Neither stage of development, political structure, nor any other known factor seems to inhibit the relationship; those who have high levels of motivation to achieve will do so: "What people want, they somehow manage to get, in the main and on the average, though as we shall see later other factors can modify the speed with which they get it."[19]

If a high level of achievement motivation can account for economic growth, a low level can explain the lack of such growth. For example, Bernard Rosen asked why Brazil has not maintained the rate of growth necessary to meet the needs of its expanding population. The natural resources are certainly sufficient. Rosen's explanation was that the level of achievement motivation and the kind of achievement values possessed by Brazilians are inadequate to the task. When compared with a sample of Americans, Brazilians showed lower levels of achievement motivation, a lower value on activism, less future orientation, and a lower valuation on such things as work and physical mobility.[20]

The careful reader who is familiar with Max Weber's thesis regarding the Protestant Ethic has probably already discerned some familiar ideas. McClelland himself points out the similarities, suggesting that the historical development of capitalism detailed by Weber may be understood, in its psychological aspect, by the notion of *n* Achievement. For "Weber's description of the kind of personality type which the Protestant Reformation produced is startlingly similar to the picture we have drawn of a person with high achievement motivation."[21] Protestants, according to Weber, worked harder and longer, saved money for future goals, and overtook and outdistanced others in the race for business success. What drove them on? The Calvinist businessmen were prevented by religious convictions from using their success to indulge themselves; consequently, according to Weber, they got little from their wealth except an "irrational sense" of having done their work well; and "this is exactly how we define the achievement motive in coding for it in fantasy."[22] In essence, McClelland says that the effect of the historical factors delineated by Weber was to increase the *n* Achievement in those Calvinists who facilitated the development of capitalism.

What, specifically, are the sources of *n* Achievement? In a general way we may say that the motivation to achieve derives from the values, beliefs, and ideologies held by people. More particularly, the studies indicate that three factors are particularly important in creating high *n* Achievement in boys: "parents' high standards of achievement, warmth and encouragement, and a father who is not dominating and authoritarian."[23]

Thus, the experience of the child is crucial: the need for achievement may be acquired by the time the child is eight or ten years old. One important experience for the child involves "early mastery training," which tends to produce high levels of *n* Achievement. For example, it was found that mothers of boys who had high *n* Achievement "tended to expect 'self-reliant mastery' at earlier ages than mothers of sons with low n Achievement."[24] As long as early mastery training is based upon parental concern rather than authoritarianism or rejection, it is likely to generate high *n* Achievement.

A second important experience, therefore, is the quality of parent-child interaction. It seems to be important for the mother to react with affection whenever the child achieves and for the father to refrain from domination of his son. But the inhibiting nature of paternal authoritarianism does not apply to the mother: "The mothers of the 'highs' also show more authoritarianism towards their sons, just as they showed more 'warmth.' They appeared to be much more actively involved than the mothers of the sons with low *n* Achievement."[25]

Thus, *n* Achievement may be inhibited by a number of factors in the child's experience, including paternal authoritarianism, low parental expectations for achievement, and demands for achievement that come too early in the child's life (as the case of the lower-class children who are expected to care for themselves at a very young age). High levels of *n* Achievement, on the other hand, are most likely to be produced when there are "reasonably high standards of excellence imposed at a time when the sons can attain them, a willingness to let him attain them without interference, and real emotional pleasure in his achievements short of overprotection and indulgence."[26]

Finally, there are certain social background variables that influence the development of the achievement motive. That is, the patterns of child-rearing just described are less likely to be followed in more traditional Catholic groups. The emphasis on a ritual rather than on an individual contact with God does not encourage self-reliance. In addition to religion, McClelland briefly looks at the effects of social class, the individual's physique, family structure, slavery, occupational status, and climate. These latter exercise at most indirect influence, however; the crucial factors are those outlined earlier.

An initial reaction to McClelland might be that he has presented a much stronger case than Hagen. He has operationalized all his variables and provided an abundance of empirical evidence to support his case, but a closer look raises a number of questions. McClelland himself discusses the varied measures that can be employed to indicate economic growth. His own selection of increased electrical production as a particularly useful measure makes his data look far better than would other indicators. For example, if we use annual growth of gross national product per capita as an indicator of economic development, countries with high *n* Achievement do not appear to have always fared very well. The 1925 scores, based on children's readers, showed Ireland, Australia, Canada, and Sweden at the head of the list. Yet, in the period roughly from 1948 to 1960, when the effects of the 1925 stories should have been manifesting themselves, Ireland ranked 44.5 out of 68 countries in annual growth of GNP per capita, while Canada ranked 50 and Sweden ranked 31. The same 1925 data put the Soviet Union at the bottom of the list of 30 countries in *n* Achievement; yet that nation ranked 12 in annual growth of GNP per capita during the decade of the 1950s.

Another problem revolves around the validity of the idea of a group level of *n* Achievement. The need for achievement was conceived of as a personality variable, as individual motivation. What does it mean to speak of a level of achievement motivation for an entire society? Does that make any more sense than, for example, a group level of wrath? Hagen seems more realistic at this point in his identification of small status-deprived groups within a society who account for development. McClelland himself recognizes that not every member of a society engages in entrepreneurial behavior. How, then, does the societal level of *n* Achievement translate itself into an individual level? McClelland does not really give an adequate answer to this question.

Finally, the graphs provided by McClelland raise serious problems with his thesis.[27] We expect a lag between the time children read achievement-oriented stories and the time they engage in entrepreneurial behavior. The graphs give us little confidence that levels of n Achievement are related in any consistent way to subsequent entrepreneurial activity. In ancient Greece, there seems to be a lag of hundreds of years. In other cases, depending on the time lag we allow, achievement motivation and entrepreneurial activity appear to change simultaneously or even inversely. In any case, the historical evidence presented does not allow us to anticipate with any confidence that a high level of *n* Achievement in a nation's literature will result in increased entrepreneurial activity at some more or less specified point in the future.

In sum, both Hagen and McClelland have tried to come to terms with the role of the family, and the consequent personality type developed in children, in economic development. In some cases, their conclusions are similar—authoritarianism inhibits innovational activity, and the irrational facets of human existence are very important in understanding behavior, for example. But two different pictures of the entrepreneur emerge: Hagen's entrepreneur is a somewhat grim creature, driven by anxiety, struggling with a stigmatized identity; McClelland's entrepreneur appears far more emotionally stable and healthy, driven by the desire to achieve but deriving identity from the dominant, approved values of the social milieu.

Neither of the two social-psychological theories, then, is convincing in toto, but both are notable efforts to account for social-psychological variables. That there are individual factors involved in change, both as dependent and independent variables, is undeniable. A particular individual may significantly affect the direction of change.[28] There are also various consequences for the individual who must come to terms with change; as noted in Chapter 1, a high rate of change seems to generate considerable stress in individuals.

The precise relationships between social structure, culture, and the individual have not yet been fully clarified. Hagen and McClelland have directed our attention to the family and personality development; in addition, the former theorist stresses the importance of irrational factors and the latter stresses the importance of motivation. In the next section, we will examine an approach that stresses the interrelations between social structure, cognitive processes, and the modernization of a society.

The Modern Individual

Auguste Comte, as we noted earlier, argued that societal progress is tied up with appropriate cognitive functioning: when individuals in a society think scientifically, they will facilitate the development of a scientific social order. Studies of "individual modernity" or the "modern man" likewise emphasize the importance of cognitive processes in the pattern of change known as modernization. There has been a good deal of controversy surrounding the studies of individual modernity. We will examine some of the research and the controversy, beginning with the foundation works of Joseph Kahl and of Alex Inkeles and David H. Smith.

Kahl's purpose was to examine value orientations used to organize people's careers and, in particular, to "delineate and to measure a set of values that represents a 'modern' view of work and life."[29] His assumption was that a modern society demands a particular kind of person, one who can function within and facilitate the development of that society. By *modern,* Kahl meant that complex of characteristics which has been identified by a number of researchers and which includes such things as a small proportion of workers in agriculture; the application of technology to production; urbanism; a complex, commercial, and industrial economy; a relatively open stratification system; an emphasis on education and communications; and rational, secular values. In other words, a modern society is one like the United States or other developed Western nations. Traditional and modern are, of course, ideal types, and most societies must be characterized as a mixture.

What kind of person is required for a modern society? According to Kahl, there are a number of values that characterize the modern individual, but the "core" is measured by seven scales: activism, low integration with one's relatives, a preference for urban living, individualism, low community stratification, participation in the mass media, and low stratification of life chances. The meaning of modernity as indicated by these scales is summarized by Kahl as follows:

> *A "modern" man is an activist; he attempts to shape his world instead of passively and fatalistically responding to it. He is an individualist, who does not merge his work career with that of relatives or friends. He believes that an independent career is not only desirable but possible, for he perceives both life chances and the local community to be low in ascribed status. He prefers urban life to rural life, and he follows the mass media.*[30]

All of these values were measured by the extent of agreement or disagreement with various statements. For example, activism was measured by responses to seven statements, one of which was "Making plans only brings unhappiness, because the plans are hard to fulfill." Low community stratification was measured by responses to three statements, one of which read: "The control of this city is in the hands of a small group of people, and an ordinary citizen has not got much to say about things." In other words, the scales included the respondents' beliefs about certain matters, their preferences for certain things, and their perceptions of certain situations.

Kahl's samples were in Brazil and Mexico, and his scales were also used on a sample of 503 American housewives. His basic finding was that modernism is strongly associated with socioeconomic level and weakly associated with urban-rural location, and that this is true in all three nations. That is, people at similar socioeconomic levels have similar scores on the modernism scales, whether in Brazil, Mexico, or the United States.

There are some national differences. Brazilians were generally more modern in family matters than Mexicans, while Mexicans were more modern in work attitudes than Brazilians. This illustrates, said

Kahl, the need for more intensive study in order that we may understand "the ways in which modernism spreads in inconsistent and contradictory patterns."[31]

Similar work was carried out somewhat earlier by Inkeles and Smith with samples of respondents in Argentina, Chile, East Pakistan, India, Israel, and Nigeria.[32] Like Kahl, they see the modern individual as essential for a functioning modern society. As developing nations become more modern in their institutions, more and more of their people will possess the kind of personality defined as modern. In fact, Inkeles and Smith argue that changed attitudes and values are "one of the most essential preconditions for substantial and effective functioning of those modern institutions which most of the more 'practical' programs for development hope to establish."[33] Furthermore, like Kahl, they found that the modern individual possesses similar characteristics cross-nationally. Wherever found, the modern individual is "an informed participant citizen; he has a marked sense of personal efficacy; he is highly independent and autonomous in his relations to traditional sources of influence, especially when he is making basic decisions about how to conduct his personal affairs; and he is ready for new experiences and ideas, that is, he is relatively open-minded and cognitively flexible."[34]

Such modern qualities of personality, the authors asserted, are likely to come from participating in modern modes of production such as the factory. More, such qualities of personality may be demanded of participants if the factory is to be effective and efficient.

In order to gather data about the modern individual, Inkeles and Smith constructed the "OM scale" as a measure of overall individual modernity.[35] Initially, they defined thirty areas (such as political activism, extended kinship obligations, and technical skill valuation) that seemed pertinent to modernity. Information on these areas was gathered by constructing a large number of statements designed to measure attitudes. The scale was refined through testing. The ultimate basic finding was that overall modernity is strongly associated with education, exposure to the mass media, and occupational experience. In fact, these three variables accounted for roughly 90 percent of the variance in modernity scores.

Education was the most important variable in modernity scores. This conclusion was supported by a study in Brazil that used a form of the OM scale.[36] In the study, Donald Holsinger tested three groups of elementary school children with varying amounts of schooling. He found that the greater the exposure to school, the higher the modernity score. One group of children who were tested on two different occasions were found to increase in their modernity scores between the first few months of school and a second test near the end of the school year. Thus, the longer the schooling, the higher the modernity score. This is congruent with the conclusion of Inkeles and Smith: "In all six countries, education emerged as unmistakably the most powerful force in shaping a man's modernity score. Indeed, judged by the number of points on the OM scale a man gained for each additional year of schooling, education was generally two or even three times as powerful as any other single input."[37]

Second in importance, after education, in high levels of modernity was factory experience. However, some nonindustrial workers (cab drivers, barbers, and others) also had relatively high modernity scores. Apparently, there are some kinds of nonindustrial work that tend to be a "school" for modernity, although in general the urban nonindustrial employees were less modern than industrial workers.

One factor that Inkeles and Smith found *not* important in individual modernity was the city. Neither size nor relative cosmopolitanism of differing urban areas made a difference in modernity scores. Other variables that have sometimes been associated with modernism, or the lack of modernism, were also not significant: ethnic origin, religion, and school quality.

In sum, in the work both of Kahl and of Inkeles and Smith, a set of modern characteristics of the individual is said to arise from and to facilitate the development of a modern society. In neither case is unidirectional causality suggested; no claim is made that the modern individual causes the development of a modern society or vice versa. Rather, there is interaction, with individual modernity facilitating societal modernity and, in turn, societal modernization generating greater numbers of modern individuals.

There are a number of similarities in the two studies. The definitions of a modern society and a modern individual are similar. In both cases, the modern society is said to demand modern individuals for its functioning and further development. Both found the modern individual in all societies studied. Both found education closely related to modernity (in Kahl's work, education was one of three variables used to determine socioeconomic level). Both stressed the importance of the mass media and of occupation (again, Kahl's measure of socioeconomic level included occupation as one of the variables).

One apparent difference was Kahl's finding that urban location is related to modernity and Inkeles and Smith's finding that neither quantity nor quality of urban experience was related to modernity score. The difference is only apparent. Kahl compared people in metropolitan areas, including life-long residents and migrants, and people in small towns. Inkeles and Smith, on the other hand, studied "urban experience" in terms of number of years spent in the city, the relative size and cosmopolitanism of the city, and the location of the individual's place of work in the city. In other words, residents of small towns were not included in their samples. In any case, however, the intrinsic role of the city in making individuals modern is small. Inkeles and Smith found that two farm cooperatives they studied were also effective in developing individual modernity. Kahl also pointed out that location (urban or rural) explained only about 7 percent of the variance in modernism.

Other scales, in addition to those of Kahl and of Inkeles and Smith, have been constructed. All are based on the assumption that individual modernity contributes to the modernization of a society. Some subsequent studies have questioned this assumption, however. A number of researchers have found little correlation between individual modernity and certain kinds of modern behavior (such as contraceptive use, listening to the radio, joining organizations, and others).[38] As Michael Armer and Larry Isaac conclude from their survey of Costa Rican men, "psychological modernity (a) is important in determining only a limited number of behaviors examined, and (b) generally adds little to explaining behavioral variations beyond objective background characteristics."[39]

We should not conclude, nevertheless, that individual modernity is a useless concept. For one thing, past studies are possibly marred by methodological problems. There is a question about whether the various scales are valid and, if valid, whether the scales are equivalent measures of modernity.[40] Furthermore, there is a serious shortcoming in that the studies have been cross-sectional rather than longitudinal. In order to assess the extent to which individual and societal modernity co-vary, we need studies over time. Indeed, there has been virtually no correlation of individual and societal modernity. The studies have identified a complex of characteristics of individuals (modernity), and have shown that that complex is closely associated with such things as education, occupation, participation in the mass media, and, to a lesser and even uncertain extent, urbanism. The essential notion, however, that individual modernity is a necessary correlate of the modern society remains an assumption rather than a conclusion of empirical studies. The researchers have yet to demonstrate that a modernizing society requires individual modernity in at least a segment of its population. If this can be shown, then we need to inquire further into how extensive the individual modernity must be and what the consequences of more or less individual modernity in a society are.

Endnotes

1. Everett E. Hagen, *On the Theory of Social Change* (Homewood, Ill.: Dorsey Press, 1962), p. 35.

2. Ibid., p. 86. In a later publication, Hagen backs away from this somewhat by saying that change in personality is not "the only possible or important cause" of innovation. It is, however, the only one with which he is concerned, and he seems to give it major prominence in historical cases of economic growth. For the disclaimer, however, see Everett E. Hagen, "British Personality and the Industrial Revolution: The Historical Evidence," in *Social Theory and Economic Growth,* ed. Tom Burns and S. B. Saul (London: Tavistock Publications, 1967), p. 35.

3. Hagen, *On the Theory of Social Change,* p. 101.

4. Ibid.

5. Ibid., p. 98.

6. Ibid., p. 57.

7. Everett E. Hagen, "How Economic Growth Begins: A General Theory Applied to Japan," *Public Opinion Quarterly* 22 (1958): 380-82.

8. Hagen, *On the Theory of Social Change,* p. 185.

9. Ibid., p. 200.

10. Ibid., p. 217.

11. Ibid., pp. 219-20.

12. Ibid., p. 201.

13. Bronislaw Malinowski, *Crime and Custom in Savage Society* (Totowa, N.J.: Littlefield, Adams & Co., 1967), pp. 100-111.

14. Morris Rosenberg, *Society and the Adolescent Self-Image* (Princeton: Princeton University Press, 1965), p. 61.

15. David C. McClelland, "Business Drive and National Achievement," in *Social Change,* ed. Amitai Etzioni and Eva Etzioni (New York: Basic Books, 1964), p. 166.

16. David C. McClelland, *The Achieving Society* (New York: Free Press, 1961), p. 205.

17. Ibid., p. 57.

18. Ibid., p. 105.

19. Ibid.

20. Bernard C. Rosen, "Achievement and Economic Growth in Brazil," *Social Forces* 42 (1964): 341-54.

21. McClelland, *The Achieving Society,* p. 47.

22. Ibid.

23. McClelland, "Business Drive and National Achievement," p. 176.

24. McClelland, *The Achieving Society,* p. 342.

25. Ibid., p. 352.

26. Ibid., p. 356.

27. Ibid., pp. 120, 132, 139, 150, and 155.

28. This has been persuasively argued with respect to Lenin's role in the Russian revolution by Sidney Hook, *The Hero in History* (Boston: Beacon Press, 1955), pp. 184-228.

29. Joseph A. Kahl, *The Measurement of Modernism* (Austin: University of Texas Press, 1968), p. 4.
30. Ibid., p. 37.
31. Ibid., p. 146.
32. Alex Inkeles and David Horton Smith, *Becoming Modern* (Cambridge: Harvard University Press, 1974).
33. Ibid., p. 313.
34. Ibid., p. 290.
35. David Horton Smith and Alex Inkeles, "The OM Scale: A Comparative Socio-Psychological Measure of Individual Modernity," *Sociometry* 29 (1966): 353-77.
36. Donald B. Holsinger, "The Elementary School as Modernizer: A Brazilian Study," *International Journal of Comparative Sociology* 14 (1973): 180-202.
37. Inkeles and Smith, *Becoming Modern*, p. 304.
38. See Alejandro Portes and Jose A. Cobas, "Modernism and Behavior: The Predictive Value of Subjective versus Objective Factors in a Developing Country," *International Review of Modern Sociology* 6 (Autumn, 1976): 253-66; and Michael Armer and Larry Isaac, "Determinants and Behavioral Consequences of Psychological Modernity: Empirical Evidence from Costa Rica," *American Sociological Review* 43 (June, 1978): 316-34.
39. Armer and Isaac, "Determinants and Consequences of Psychological Modernity," p. 331.
40. Michael Armer and Allan Schnaiberg, "Measuring Individual Modernity: A Near Myth," *American Sociological Review* 37 (June, 1972): 301-16; Jere Cohen and Amnon Till, "Another Look at Modernity Scales: Reanalysis of the Convergent and Discriminant Validities of the Armer, Kahl, Smith and Inkeles, and Schnaiberg Scales," *American Sociological Review* 42 (April, 1977): 373-78; and Michael Armer and Allan Schnaiberg, "Reply to Cohen and Till," *American Sociological Review* 42 (April, 1977). Another issue that has been raised about the scales is whether they are invalid because the researchers have assumed that individual modernity is unidimensional, whereas it is actually a multidimensional construct. That is, the values subsumed under individual modernity are diverse components of a multidimensional value system. They do not necessary co-vary, therefore, but may change independently of each other. See R. Kenneth Godwin, "The Relationship Between Scores on Individual Modernity Scales and Societal Modernization," *The Journal of Developing Areas* 9 (1975): 415-32; and William C. Rau, "The Tacit Conventions of the Modernity School: An Analysis of Key Assumptions," *American Sociological Review* 45 (April, 1980): 244-60.

CHAPTER SIX

Confrontation: The Analysis and Development of Theory

Most of the theories we have discussed fall into the category of "classic," since most are part of long-standing sociological tradition and/or have become widely known efforts to explain change. At this point, they may seem to represent a mass of varied explanations that offer a confusing diversity of answers to important questions about change. A first task in this chapter, therefore, will be to allow a confrontation of the theories, in the sense of comparing and contrasting what they have to say about social change. We will see some common elements among the theories as well as some diversity.

Although theorizing about social change has not stopped, it has not been prominent in the last few decades. In the second section of this chapter, we will examine briefly some of the contemporary directions of social change theory. As in the past, sociologists have utilized theoretical developments in, and analytical tools of, other disciplines in an effort to understand social reality. In addition, there has been renewed interest in some older theoretical approaches, particularly evolutionary and dialectical perspectives.

Theory Revisited: Contrast and Comparison

As I have indicated in the past few chapters, each theory has something to offer us in the way of understanding social change. Each is a valid theory in the sense that it fulfills the explanatory function (whether or not one actually agrees with the explanation offered).

Each is also valid in that it can be put to an empirical test. The empirical test will vary, however, with most of the theories demanding the use of historical materials, some allowing the use of survey and statistical data, and some allowing the use of both types. For example, Toynbee's theory can only be tested by broad historical materials. If we wanted to narrow the scope of research and still remain within Toynbee's theory, we could study something like the functioning of a particular kind of elite during the period of cultural disintegration. Or we could test the hypothesis that a period of cultural disintegration will be marked by an increased sense of sin among people. The theory is more suited to broad historical study than to the formulation and testing of hypotheses. On the other hand, a study of individual modernity could utilize historical materials to show the development of modern individuals during industrialization, as well as statistical data and survey research to test the relationship between societal and individual modernity in the present. Thus, while all of the theories can generate testable hypotheses for further research, some of the theories and the derived hypotheses will be too broad for the tastes of most sociologists.

A broad theory is not a worthless theory—the fact that the theory does not readily yield hypotheses for testing does not make it of no value. Toynbee, for example, has stressed the role of elites throughout the process of change. Even if we reject his overall theory, we must still consider the role of elites, and perhaps we can examine that role in some of the terms that he suggested.

In sum, the various theories are all valid in the sense that all offer us explanations of social change; all stimulate our thinking about change; all demand that we attend to certain aspects of social reality in our thinking about change; and all provide answers—implicitly or explicitly—to important questions about change. In the remainder of this section, we shall discuss the latter point, beginning with a question raised in the first pages of this book: What do we mean by social change?

• The Meaning of Change

Change was defined in Chapter 1 as an inclusive concept that refers to alterations in social phenomena at various levels from the individual to the global. We also noted that significant change at one level is not necessarily significant at another level, and that we can choose to study change at one or more of a number of different levels. Each of the theorists we have dealt with would affirm change, at least in the long run, at all levels. For the most part, social change theorists reject the myth of deviance and affirm the normality of change (structural-functionalism is a notable exception, and the social-psychological theorists tend to leave the question open).

Nevertheless, there is generally a focal point of interest. The theories tend to focus on a particular level or levels, in some cases explaining and in others leaving open the question of how changes at other levels follow from the ones that occur at the focal point of interest. With the cyclic theories, the focal point of interest is the civilization. Khaldun wanted to explain the cycles of conquest in Arab civilization; Toynbee was interested in the rise and decline of world civilizations; and Sorokin focused on the oscillating sociocultural patterns of human history. Each of these theorists also identified change at other levels, but all such changes were used to illustrate the nature of the focal interest—the cyclic variations in whole civilizations.

The developmental theorists, on the other hand, focused on the societal level, and they generally believed that all societies would follow the particular line of development that they identified. In each case, the change that is the focal point of interest is the pattern of development of an entire society. Comte, Spencer, and Marx all saw societal development as leading to a more humane social order, while Durkheim had a pessimistic vision of the outcome of societal evolution. Again, each saw change occurring at other levels, and in the case of Marx, institutional (economic) change was viewed as crucial to the process of societal development. Nevertheless, the major interest for each was the pattern of development of the whole society. Each defined that pattern differently (theological to scientific for Comte, militant to industrial for Spencer, mechanical to organic solidarity for Durkheim, and ancient to communist for Marx). The question that inevitably is raised by such efforts (and that is underscored by modernization studies, as we noted in Chapter 1) is whether there is indeed a similar end for most or all societies. We have already rejected the myth of unidirectionality and utopia apprehended. This, however, is not to deny certain common features that may characterize, for example, industrial societies. Industrial societies could all be defined by such considerations as status by achievement, mobility possibilities, a money economy, and others, while still differing in important aspects. One need only compare a typical factory in Japan, Yugoslavia, and the United States to see a number of striking differences in the working situation of these three industrial countries. Paternalism persists in Japan, while workers control the factories in Yugoslavia (though constrained to some extent by the government). To be a factory worker means something different in the three situations, even though all are societies in which there is status by achievement, mobility possibilities, a money economy, and so forth.

In sum, the developmental theorists, like the cyclic, see change occurring at all levels, though they focus attention at the societal level. Like the cyclic theorists, they see change as normal and immanent. Change occurs by the very nature of things, by the very nature of social life. Furthermore, change is patterned rather than capricious or random. We can anticipate the kind of change occurring and, according to some (Comte and Marx), accelerate the rate of change to the more humane society of the future.

In contrast, structural-functionalists give priority to structure over change. Structures tend to be stable. Change in the form of certain societal processes occurs continually, but actual structural change is uncommon and must normally be the result of external forces that impinge upon the social system. The focal points of interest are the society and culture. Structural change means a change in the basic values by which the system is integrated. Concurrently, there are changes at other levels, but these can occur without structural change. For example, structural differentiation may occur in an institution such as the family or economy without structural change occurring in the society. Furthermore, although we have called these processes at subsocietal levels *change,* there are technically only two kinds of processes that Parsons identifies as social change: structural change and societal evolution. Social change means an alteration in the social system itself (in the basic values that integrate the system). Thus, alterations in attitudes or patterns of interaction, community stratification systems, and so forth are not technically social change. Such alterations may occur as a result of social change, but they do not in and of themselves constitute that change.

In contrast to the other theories, then, structural-functionalism narrows the definition of change to a particular kind of process. It does not deny the alterations that occur at various levels, but insists that social change refers to alterations in the social system, which means a change of culture (values) and of the structure (societal roles).

Finally, the social-psychological theories examine a particular kind of change: modernization and economic development. Hagen, McClelland, and the studies of individual modernity are all concerned with the role of the individual in a developing (modernizing and economically expanding) society. The assumption is that a developing society requires a particular kind of individual, an individual defined by Hagen as a creative personality, by McClelland as an achievement-oriented personality, and by Kahl and Inkeles and Smith as a modern man. There is no implicit or explicit argument that all kinds of change require particular kinds of people. Rather, there is interest in a particular level of change—the institutional—and the kind of individual who facilitates institutional modernization and economic growth.

Thus, in terms of levels of change, the meaning varies from individual (changing attitudes and beliefs) to civilizational change. Most of the theorists we have studied, however, are macrosociologists, focusing on the civilizational and societal levels. Most either leave the question open or accept the normality of change, and most would affirm the fact that change occurs at all levels of social reality. It is interesting that cyclic theorists have centered their analyses around the civilizational level of change, while the focal level has been society for developmental theorists, society and culture for structural-functionalists, and institutions for much of the social-psychological work. These linkages are not necessary. We have previously noted, for example, that cyclic phenomena occur at all levels of social reality. The classic perspectives have had macrolevel approaches. In Part III we will study some approaches to social change that are theoretical but tend to be less global. In typical sociological terms, they are middle-range theoretical approaches in contrast to the grand-theory type that has dominated Part II. The classic perspectives took social change as a pervasive and large-scale phenomenon, but theory must deal with lower levels of social reality as well as the higher.

• *Direction of Change*

We have already touched upon this issue in noting that the developmental theorists offered us specific directions for the course of societal change. Early sociologists such as Comte had little doubt about the progressive nature of the direction of change or about our ability to specify in some detail the characteristics of the various stages. On the contemporary scene, futurists (whom we shall discuss further later) are busily at work constructing scenarios, some of which are horrendous, some neutral, and some thoroughly optimistic.[1] All have one common characteristic—an assumption that the future direction of societies can be specified, or at least a probable set of directions can be specified. On the other hand, it has been argued that change is not substantively directional.[2] The argument is not that we are unable to predict the direction, but that there is no such direction. Thus, the issue of the directionality of change is still with us.

What do our theorists have to say about the matter? The cyclic theorists all affirm direction in only a limited sense—all civilizations rise and fall, the history of humankind is a history of the flowering and wilting of successive civilizations. The developmental theorists, in contrast, have portrayed the beginnings and the ultimate end for human societies, and in some cases the stages in between. They differ in their vision of the end, but all are able to offer us at least some sketchy notions about the ultimate social order. Structural-functionalism has little to offer, except Parsons's notion of an enhanced adaptive capacity of evolving societies. The theory itself does not require any particular direction (or, indeed, that there be any substantive direction at all).

The social-psychological theorists of modernization necessarily focus on a particular direction. They define modernization in terms that make a modern society an essentially Western one and then proceed to identify the kind of individual necessary for such a society. They do not imply, however, that all societies must modernize in that sense.

In sum, most of the theorists either have specified a particular direction of change or have only investigated a particular direction. Furthermore, the direction has been considered more or less inevitable (more or less in the sense that progress can be retarded according to some theorists and that there can be deviant cases). In the next section, we will look at some more contemporary efforts to specify the direction of change when we examine the futurists.

• *Human Nature*

As the above has shown, the majority of the theorists we have examined have proceeded on the basis of two assumptions: (1) that change is normal and pervasive, and (2) that the direction of change can be specified. A third assumption that underlies theories in general and social change theories in particular involves human nature. All theories explicitly or implicitly have an image of the nature of human beings. In fact, as Shibutani points out, there is a "model of man" in every social order: "In one society men are thought to be rational by nature; in another, animals enslaved by passions; in another, creatures made in the image of God."[3] Our assumptions about the nature of human beings are not always made explicit, but they always underlie our thinking about human behavior.

What, then, is the image of human beings that is found in social change theories? First, all of our theorists view humans as social creatures. All see humans as creatures who require group life and who are the products of their social milieus rather than as creatures who are solely determined by genetics. Beyond this, there are a number of points of agreement and disagreement in the views about the basic nature of humans. We will look at the various theories in terms of three elements of the image of human nature. First, is there anything that is innate to humans per se? Second, are humans basically free or determined in their behavior? Third, what is the basic motivation for humans?

With respect to anything innate to humans, Khaldun posited aggressiveness. Like Hobbes, therefore, Khaldun believed that people must have a strong authority over them in order to control their aggressiveness. Khaldun also stressed the impact of the social structure upon the personality of individuals. Similarly, other theorists have stressed the manner in which the individual is a product of his or her social milieu. Spencer linked personality to the prevailing type of social order. Marx argued that individuals reflect the material circumstances of their existence. The students of individual modernity insist upon the necessity of a particular kind of personality in a modern society. In other words, most theorists imply that humans are plastic creatures who are shaped by their social environment, and that there is little if anything that is innate to humans and also significant to our understanding of social change.

This is not to say that humans are nothing more than reflections of their environments, however. The individual also reacts back upon the social order, affecting the social order, as we shall discuss below. Nevertheless, in terms of understanding social change, there are no innate characteristics of humans that merit attention. Humans do have certain basic needs, as implied or specified by all of the theorists. However, to say that people have organic needs, moral needs, economic needs, the need for achievement, the need for social recognition, and so forth is different from saying that humans are innately evil or aggressive or good or cooperative. Needs themselves are a result of social definitions rather than genetic makeup—one has a need for achievement because one's social milieu tended to create that need, not because of one's genes.

Not all humans have the same needs. Moreover, those who have a similar need may define it differently. For example, fundamentalist Protestants may define the gratification of economic needs in terms of satisfaction with what one gets and with giving at least a tenth of what one gets to the church; others in the same society may define the gratification of economic needs in terms of maximizing income and broadening one's consumption pattern. Thus, defining humans as creatures with certain basic needs allows far more diversity and far more impact to the social environment than does defining humans as having certain innate characteristics. The theorists of social change see humans as plastic creatures who are significantly shaped by the social environment. Social change theorists assume that plasticity and the need for social interaction are the primary innate characteristics of humans.

With respect to the second element, the issue of determinism, we should first be aware that we are treading on hotly disputed and difficult ground. There are disagreements about the meaning of freedom and determinism, and about whether or not certain theorists are deterministic. The latter issue is compounded by the fact that theorists may not be consistent in their writings. We already noted this in our discussion of Sorokin, who made the individual a vehicle through which vast, impersonal forces effected change yet also asserted the possibility of change occurring through the initiative of humans. Sociologists not only have been inconsistent in their writings, but have also sometimes used deterministic notions in a selective way to advance particular causes.[4] For example, the behavior of criminals might be treated with the assumption that criminals are the victims of the system, while the behavior of police would be treated under the assumption that the police are personally accountable for every act. In other words, some behavior is treated as determined while other behavior is treated as the result of free will.

All of these considerations make it difficult to deal with the issue of determinism. Nevertheless, the issue is an important one, for it involves the question of whether we can effect change by our own actions or whether, on the contrary, we can only learn to adapt to those changes that are determined by forces beyond our control. The cyclic and developmental theorists all allow for limited human action. That is, the overall direction of change follows a particular pattern, but there is room for variation within the pattern. Khaldun's portrait of the ruler stressed the importance of the type of relationship established with the people. The ruler cannot alter the cycles of growth and decay, but the ruler can accelerate or delay a particular cycle. Likewise, Toynbee, Sorokin, Comte, Spencer, and Durkheim all pointed to, or suggested the possibility of, the role of the individual or individuals in altering the rate of change within an overall pattern which is determined by factors beyond the individual. This is similar to Marx's notion of human freedom (which was borrowed from Hegel)—freedom is the recognition of necessity. That is, humans make history, but the history they make follows a necessary course that they cannot alter. They become free when they recognize, or become conscious of, the course of history and act so as to facilitate it.

In structural-functionalism the notion of individual freedom is complicated by the fact that the role rather than the biological individual is the unit of analysis. Nevertheless, as shown by Smelser's analysis of the Industrial Revolution in England, there is some scope for individual action as strains impinge differently upon different groups and as individuals opt for various modes of response to the internal disturbances created by strains in the social system. Parsons himself identified personalities as one of the possible exogenous sources of change.

Of course, there are limitations to the kind of change that can be effected. People are not free to choose and create any kind of social system they desire, for any system must fulfill the four basic functions, and the effort to change some aspect of, for example, the goal-attainment subsystem will inevitably result in alterations in the other subsystems.

The social-psychological theorists all imply a considerable amount of freedom. Humans are not determined by external forces, but are free to follow modern or traditional ways, to strive for economic development, or to pursue some other interest. Again, the possibilities are not infinite. One cannot create a modern society while retaining traditional values and relationships. One cannot spur a society to grow economically without a generally high level of the need for achievement. Overall, the social-psychological approach affirms the greatest amount of freedom to humans in that humans can act so as to create various alternative futures. It is not merely a matter of accelerating or delaying a particular kind of future, but of choosing between various futures and then creating the one chosen.

In sum, all of the theorists treat humans as creatures who are capable of voluntary behavior that can effect change. The extent to which humans can affect the course of history varies considerably, from affecting the rate of a predetermined direction to affecting the nature of the future social order. In no case, however, are humans treated as wholly determined. Implicitly or explicitly, some scope is always given to the effects of human action. Of course, some might object that the kind of freedom represented by the recognition of necessity is no freedom at all. It must be remembered, however, that most developmental theorists who espoused such freedom also argued that the direction of change was beneficial for humanity. To participate in a necessary process, it could be argued, is to participate in the acquisition of one's own maximum well-being. Whatever else freedom may or may not be, it must not be something that is contrary to individual well-being.

The final element of human nature is the question of basic motivation. Is there a universal motivation that drives all people and that finds expression in efforts at change? As noted above, Khaldun posited an innate aggressiveness that drives people, but the other theorists do not ascribe any innate quality to humans that could serve as a basic motivation (not even an innate rationality). If people are aggressive, it is because their social environment has created such aggressiveness. If people have a need to achieve, it is because they have learned to value achievement in the socialization process. How is this compatible with the notion of freedom of action we have just discussed? If even the motivations to act are a product of the social environment, is not the individual really determined in all his or her behavior? Perhaps the best answer to the apparent dilemma is provided, ironically enough, by Durkheim, who is sometimes thought to make the individual nothing more than a reflection of society. Actually, however, Durkheim asserted that humans have a dual nature—they are both biological and social creatures. Robert Nisbet, in his excellent discussion of Durkheim's views on individualism, said that "not all individuals assimilate and internalize society's codes in the same way. Conflicts among norms can result in tensions within individuals. Different values are set by society on individuals, and the consequence of this is a tension between individualism and the moral authority of society that is eternal."[5]

Imperfect socialization, combined with the fact that humans are biological as well as social creatures, means that individuals will react differently in the same situation and that individuals are never solely the reflection of their social environments. Humans must deal with conflicting impulses and ideas, so that human behavior is a creation and not merely a reaction or reflection of something external. Whether or not the various theorists would put the matter in these terms, the fact is that their perspectives demand that we acknowledge and account for both the social shaping of the individual and the individual's freedom to act and to affect to some extent the rate and/or kind of change that occurs.

• *The Mechanism of Change*

Part III deals with a great variety of mechanisms of change. By mechanism, I mean the primary and proximate cause, not the *only* cause. To identify technology as the cause of a particular change in social relationships, for example, should not obscure the fact that the technology itself was the result of certain causes and that other factors may have facilitated or supported the effects of the technology on social relationships. The question we are asking here, therefore, is as follows: What do our theorists see as the driving mechanism of change, as the primary factor in change? Even if the direction of change is predetermined, something must be moving the social order along its path. The question of mechanism, therefore, is a legitimate one to pose to all of the theorists.

Khaldun identified conflict as the basic mechanism of change, and in this he was joined by Spencer. Toynbee identified challenges and the human responses to those challenges. Sorokin presents us with a problem, for he stressed immanent change—any sociocultural system changes by virtue of the activities within the system. Even if the environment did not change at all, the system would change because of internal processes. Sorokin also allowed for some external factors to cause change in a system. His main emphasis, however, is on the lack of any particular cause; in general, sociocultural systems change in accord with a law and logic of their own: "in the fundamental transformation of culture from Sensate to Ideational or *vice versa*, none of the cultural variables are either causes or effects, either leaders, laggards, or led. All are parts of one system that has its own immanent law and logic of change."[6] In essence, Sorokin denies that there is a driving mechanism of change other than the inherent nature of social life. This is not a satisfactory answer, and it is not entirely consistent with some other statements of Sorokin. Nevertheless, it represents his dominant thought on the subject.

For Comte, intellectual evolution is the driving mechanism for social evolution. As people acquire new modes of thinking, they help create social orders that correspond to these modes. As we noted before, ennui, longevity, and population growth can affect the rate of change, but the primary factor is the mode of thinking. Marx took the opposite stand: the primary factor is material rather than idealistic. The driving mechanism of change is the material conditions of existence and, in particular, the contradiction between the forces and relations of production. For Durkheim, the transition from mechanical to organic solidarity was the result of the division of labor, which was, in turn, a consequence of increasing number and density of population.

In structural-functionalism, the lack of emphasis on change is reflected in a lack of specificity about mechanisms of change. Parsons offered both internal and external causes of change. Language and the institutionalization of norms in the form of a legal system are the two crucial factors in the broad span of societal evolution, but any number of factors can account for structural change in a particular society. For Parsons, there is no particular mechanism that is predominant.

Finally, the social-psychological theorists posit various internal states of individuals as the mechanism of change. Change occurs because of the actions of individuals who are driven by internal conditions, such as anxiety, the need for achievement, or a value on economic development.

All of the factors that I shall discuss in more detail in the next part have been identified as mechanisms of change by the theorists. Materialistic factors, idealistic factors, interactional mechanisms, and structural sources have been presented in the thinking of theorists analyzed in this part. These factors are not mutually exclusive, of course. For example, Marx did not deny the importance of ideas; he only denied that ideas have an independent force of their own unrelated to material conditions. According to Marx, when material conditions create ideas that reflect the real needs of people, those people are then motivated to enter into conflict with other people in order to change the social order. We should not be misled, therefore, by this effort to identify the driving mechanism of change in the various theorists. No theorist was so simplistic as to ignore the importance of multiple factors in change. Rather, just as they tended to focus on a particular level of change while recognizing the general pervasiveness of change, so they tended to stress a particular mechanism while recognizing that other causal factors are also at work.

• Conclusions

Much of the previous discussion is summarized in Table 6-1. Obviously, the various theorists have provided us with considerable diversity. To some extent, the diversity reflects contradictory assumptions and positions. For example, although Marx affirmed the importance of ideas, his position still contradicts that of Comte, who also affirmed the importance of ideas. Comte made ideas crucial in the development of the social order, whereas Marx made the social order crucial in the development of ideas. The diversity also reflects the complexity of social life, however, and the fact that analysts must necessarily focus on limited facets of that social life. Thus, the fact that developmental theorists had little or nothing to say about the internal states of individuals does not mean that they considered those states irrelevant. No theorist or researcher can focus on all of the relevant variables at once. He or she selects, from the multitude of variables that are operative, those that interest him or her and that seem to be significant. The various theorists I have examined to this point have different emphases, and make differing contributions to our understanding of change. None offers a completely satisfactory analysis, but none is completely useless. Acceptable answers to all questions are not given, but the theorists have raised the important questions and have provided us with a variety of reasonable and heuristic answers.

Contemporary Directions in Social Change Theory

Francis Bacon once observed that if a man begins with certainties, he will end up with doubts; but if he begins with doubts, he will end up with certainties. The study of social change from Comte to the early work of Parsons reflects the former—a beginning with certainty that ends up in doubt. Comte's certainty about the nature and direction of

Table 6-1 • Comparative Characteristics of Change Theories

Characteristic	Type of Theory			
	Cyclic	Develop-mental	Structural-Functional	Social-Psychlogical
1. Change is normal	Yes	Yes	No	*
2. Focal level of change	Civilizations	Societies	Society and culture	Institutions
3. Change has an identifiable direction or pattern	Yes	Yes	*	*
4. Change is effected by human action	Limited to rate	Limited to rate	Yes	Yes
5. Mechanism of change	Conflict (Khaldun) Challenges (Toynbee) Immanent (Sorokin)	Conflict (Spencer) Ideas (Comte) Demographic (Durkheim) Material contradiction (Marx)	Various factors, both internal and external to the social system	Internal states of individuals

* Not answered in the statements or logic of the theory.

change contrasts sharply with Parsons's assertion that "the present state of knowledge" disallows the development of a general theory of change.[7] Nevertheless, there has been a resurgence of interest in social change in the last few decades, an interest that initially took the form of a critique of the inadequacies of structural-functionalism. Some efforts have been directed toward reconciling structural-functionalism with a conflict or dialectical perspective, while others have focused upon the development of new theory or the resurrection of abandoned theory. In particular, contemporary developments include work in six areas: conflict and dialectical theory, evolutionary theory, social-psychological theories, general systems theory, mathematical and quasi-mathematical models, and futuristics. We will discuss conflict and dialectical theory in chapters 9 and 12 (world system theory). The most extensive social-psychological theory is that of Martindale, which will be discussed in Chapter 11. Here, we will look at each of the other areas in turn.

• *Evolutionary Theory*

We have already noted Parsons's effort to use evolution to explain long-term social development. A number of sociologists and other social scientists have produced works on evolution. We will look at some anthropological efforts, as well as the work of the sociologist Gerhard Lenski and that of the economist Kenneth Boulding.

In anthropology, evolutionary thought has had a checkered career. Early anthropologists were infatuated with the idea of evolution. It was almost fanatically rejected by a succeeding generation, to be cautiously rediscovered by a still later group. During the course of all this, some rather diverse meanings have been attached to the notion of evolution.

In the latter part of the nineteenth century, social anthropologists identified evolution in terms of a pattern of development from lower to higher forms of cultural life. This pattern was marked by a series of successive stages, and the task of the anthropologist was to identify the stages. For example, Lewis H. Morgan, who first applied the notion of evolution to actual social development, traced the evolution of human culture through the successive stages of savagery, barbarism, and civilization. His basic concern was with categorizing societies according to "distinguishing social characteristics that people shared at certain levels of social organization" and with "noting the sequences in the development of these types."[8] Unlike some others, Morgan realized that a diffusion of elements from other cultures may intrude upon the sequence and alter it. In brief, Morgan argued that culture advanced along with technological developments. As people improve control over their lives through new technology, culture develops. In the beginning, humans were little more than beasts. Through the mechanism of speech, and with the invention of various tools and weapons, there was cultural progress from savagery to civilization.

This early, unilinear idea of evolution broke down as the twentieth century dawned, however. It was attacked at a number of points, most of which involved the disparity between the theory and the accumulating knowledge of primitive societies. Some, if not most, of the studies upon which the theory was based were inadequate and inaccurate, and the theorists themselves did not generally engage in intensive field studies. Furthermore, evolutionary theory tended to minimize the importance of cultural borrowing, and the new anthropologists tended to see that borrowing as of crucial importance. Finally, unilinear evolution reinforced ethnocentric attitudes and led to the disparagement of the "less advanced" societies.

The new evolutionary thought lacks the myth of unidirectionality. It is an effort to synthesize some of the insights of the early evolutionists with the later diffusionist and functionalist thought. Diffusionist thought emphasized the mobility of various cultural traits and tried to ascertain how the traits that comprise any given culture came together. Functionalist thought stressed the interdependence of traits, the linkage of traits into a meaningful whole; this perspective, like sociological functionalism, seems incapable of adequately treating the problem of change.

The new evolutionism includes diverse ideas, however. Some contemporary anthropologists equate evolution with change, while others conceive of it as growth, development, or progress. E. R. Wolf conceives of evolution in terms of cumulative development that is both quantitative and qualitative.[9] The quantitative aspect implies a ranking along a numerical scale; cultures might be differentiated, for example, according to the amount of energy harnessed or demographic characteristics or intensity of communication. The qualitative aspect means "the emergence of new cultural components which subsume and integrate preexisting components in a new way."[10] Most inventions are the integration in a new way of previously existing parts. The state is a social invention that results in a qualitative change in organization of the culture. A major qualitative change has been the transition from unspecialized cultures to those that function on the basis of specialization of parts, that is, the transition from hunting-and-gathering societies to more complex forms.

A number of anthropologists have paid more detailed attention to developing evolutionary thought. We shall examine briefly three of them: Leslie White, Julian Steward, and the team of Marshall Sahlins and Elman Service. Each represents a modern variant of evolutionary thought, and each presents us with a distinctive approach.

Leslie White claims to deal with culture as a whole rather than with particular cultures.[11] Like Durkheim, White rejects the role of psychological factors and the "great man" theory of development. Human behavior must be understood in terms of culture. If humans are competitive, for example, it is not because they are by nature that way, but because they exist in a competitive culture. How, then, can we account for culture?

According to White, culture must be understood in terms of three layers: the technological layer is lowest, the sociological is next, and the philosophical is the highest. That is, technology is the most basic facet and the prime mover of the cultural process. Technology and technological developments shape the social system, and philosophies reflect both the social system and the underlying technology. Technology, then, determines the kind of social system that exists, and technology and society work together to determine the nature of philosophy. There are some reciprocal influences at work among the three layers, but the basic causal direction is from technology to society to philosophy.

Furthermore, culture is "a symbolic, continuous, cumulative, and progressive process."[12] It is symbolic in the sense that a human is an animal who uses symbols (and, especially, an animal who uses language). It is continuous because the symbolic nature of culture enables it to be easily transmitted from one individual to another and one generation to another. It is cumulative in that new elements are constantly being added. It is progressive in the sense of attaining increasing control over nature and more security of life for humans.

In other words, culture is a self-generating phenomenon that enfolds the existence of every individual and, thereby, explains all of human behavior.

White's argument is clear in his treatment of invention. No invention or innovation (and, consequently, no change) will emerge until cultural development has reached a point that will admit a novel element. More importantly, when the development of culture has reached that point, the novel element will emerge independently of people's desires. A primary support for this latter argument is the occurrence throughout history of simultaneous and independent discoveries or inventions. Indeed, the list of such inventions and discoveries is impressive, and includes, among others, technological inventions such as the telegraph, mathematical breakthroughs such as calculus, and the formulation of scientific laws such as those pertaining to the behavior of gases. In some cases, two people made the discovery or invention. The law of inverse squares was formulated by Newton in 1666 and independently by Halley in 1684, and the kinetic theory of gases was set forth in 1850 by both Clausius and Rankine. In other cases, three or more people made a discovery or created an invention independently of one another. The laryngoscope was invented by Babington in 1829, by Liston in 1837, and by Garcia in 1855. The solution to the problem of respiration was discovered in 1777 by Priestley, by Scheele, by Levoisier, by Spallanzani, and by Davy. The development of culture, in other words, is a self-sustaining process that is independent of particular individuals, including those individuals we think of as creative. For the appearance of an innovation does not depend upon any particular individual.

Thus, while people have remained basically the same in terms of intelligence and biological makeup, culture has grown at an exponential rate. This growth must be understood in terms of the nature of culture itself, not in terms of the activities of particular people. Cultural evolution is a phenomenon *sui generis*. It is like an overarching process that engulfs us and carries us along, willingly or unwillingly, into the future.

A different approach to evolution is offered by Julian Steward, who created the idea of multilinear evolution. According to Steward, there have been three main approaches to understanding cultural development. One was the early evolutionists' theory of unilinear evolution. The second was that of the cultural relativists, who saw development as "essentially divergent," and who tried to identify characteristics that distinguished societies from one another. The third approach is multilinear evolution.[13]

Multilinear evolution is "an affirmation that significant cross-cultural regularities exist but a denial that such regularities must pertain to all human societies."[14] Culture has evolved along a number of different lines; we might picture it as a branching tree. At the same time, there are some cross-culturual regularities, or parallels in cultural history. These parallels arise from the fact that cultural change results from adaptation to environment; similar adaptive processes in similar environments result in the cross-cultural regularities.

Steward calls the process of adaptation "cultural ecology." The problem presented to us by cultural ecology is the determination of "whether the adjustments of human societies to their environments require particular modes of behavior or whether they permit latitude for a certain range of possible behavior patterns."[15] This, of course, requires ascertaining the extent to which behavior is determined by environmental factors. The method of cultural ecology involves: (1) an analysis of the interrelationship of technology and environment; (2) analysis of "behavior patterns involved in the exploitation of a particular area by means of a particular technology"; and (3) determination of the extent to which those behavior patterns affect various other facets of the culture.[16]

In comparing cultures, in searching for cross-cultural regularities, the analysis focuses on "cultural cores," which are the facets of the cultures involved in subsistence activities and economic patterns. The societies whose cultural cores are being compared must be at the same level of sociocultural integration and be of the same cultural type. Even when we find regularities, they will pertain to limited aspects of the cultures rather than to each culture as a whole; we could expect to find cross-cultural kinship types, religious types, or government types, for example.

Thus, Steward has tried to avoid the mistakes of the early evolutionists and provide a theory of evolution that incorporates both the generalizing and the historical approach to social anthropology. Unfortunately, he makes very modest claims for a rather complex theory and method, and we are not encouraged to regard his work as more than an interesting effort to affirm evolution while discarding the mistakes of the early evolutionists.

The third anthropological approach is that of Sahlins and Service, who give the basic pattern of evolution as the inverse of inorganic evolution (increasing disorder that ends in homogeneity): cultural evolution is marked by an "increase in organization, higher energy concentration, and ... increased heterogeneity."[17] Furthermore, that evolution involves both advance and divergence, progress and variation. These two facets are called general evolution and specific evolution.

In other words, evolution is a process marked by simultaneous movement in two directions: "On one side, it creates diversity through adaptive modification: new forms differentiate from old. On the other side, evolution generates progress: higher forms arise from, and surpass, lower."[18] Although the two processes occur simultaneously, it is important to recognize that cultural change must be viewed from one or the other of the two perspectives; we can analyze change *either* in terms of adaptation or in terms of general progress.

For from the perspective of adaptation, the two authors argue, "we are cultural relativists." Adaptive advances are relative, each being suited to its own situation and none being any better than any in other cultures. The authors acknowledge their indebtedness to Steward for his pioneer work in adaptation. They argue that there is also general progress in culture which "can be absolutely, objectively, and nonmoralistically ascertained."[19] This general cultural evolution involves the successive appearance of new levels of "all-round development."

An example of general evolutionary analysis is provided by the authors with respect to warfare. In terms of specific evolution, we would try to explain differing types of warfare practiced by diverse groups, such as the Plains Indians and the Iroquois. It would be found that the types are adaptive forms to specific contexts. From the perspective of general evolution, we would search for stages in the overall development of warfare. We would then discover increases in the scale of war, in the number of people fighting and dying, in the duration of the war, and in the consequences of warfare for human societies. As the authors point out, then, "progress" is not to be equated with "good" but with development.

To sum up the distinction between the two aspects: "General cultural evolution ... is passage from less to greater energy transformation, lower to higher levels of integration, and less to greater all-round adaptability. Specific evolution is the phylogenetic, ramifying, historic passage of culture along its many lines, the adaptive modification of particular cultures."[20] Sahlins and Service make a number of additional points about their theory, such as the "phylogenetic discontinuity of progress," which says that advanced forms of culture do not usually generate the next stage of advance; adaptation at one stage tends to mean the inability to be adaptive at a higher stage.

We need not delve into the details of the thoughts of any of the above theorists in order to see that they clearly are trying to reaffirm evolution and just as clearly are rejecting the unilinear type. Stages of evolution can be identified for culture as a whole. Specific cultures, however, show diverse lines of development. The new evolutionists recognize the errors of their intellectual forebears, but they continue the search for patterns of development that can be scientifically identified and analyzed.

In sociology, one of the more elaborate analyses of the evolution of societies is that of Gerhard Lenski.[21] Lenski points out that there are certain similarities between organic and sociocultural evolution. Thus, symbol systems are roughly analogous to genetic systems; societies are roughly analogous to species; both kinds of evolution involve processes of continuity, innovation, and extinction; and both kinds of evolution are long-term complex processes "characterized by the progressive emergence of organizations which possess ever greater capacities for the mobilization of energy and information."[22] There are also important differences, particularly the conscious and deliberate aspects of sociocultural evolution and the transmission of acquired characteristics in that evolution (the inheritance of acquired characteristics is a discredited notion in organic evolution).

Continuity, innovation, and extinction are basic aspects of the evolutionary process. Although continuity appears to contradict the notion of change that is implicit in evolution, we must recognize that evolution refers to a particular kind of change, namely, cumulative change. In other words, evolution involves the cumulative acquisition of new elements to an existing base, so that both continuity and innovation are integral parts of the process. Continuity is particularly evident in the habits and customs of societies, and is largely maintained because of the socialization process.

Innovation results from both internal and external factors. Inventions, discoveries, alterations of existing cultural elements, and diffusion from one society to another are the basic forms of innovation. One important aspect of innovation is the great variation in rate from one society to another and from one age to another. Such variations are due to: differing amounts of information available to societies (only within the last few hundred years have individuals stopped trying to write in a single effort all of the knowledge of humankind); differing population size (the more minds available for problem solving, the more quickly a solution is likely to be found); the amount of contact among societies; the relative stability or instability of the environment; the extent to which inventions and discoveries are fundamental (the steam engine is more fundamental than the can opener); and societal attitudes about innovation. These various factors are not independent of one another, but tend to support one another, work in conjunction, and therefore multiply the overall effects. As this suggests, there has been a historical trend toward an accelerating rate of innovation.

The third aspect of the evolutionary process is extinction. One kind of extinction, which Lenski says is relatively unimportant, is the unintentional loss of important cultural elements. Another kind is the process of selection. Within societies, people can choose from alternatives, and such choices mean that both innovation and extinction may occur. Extinction can also occur with respect to whole societies, which may be extinguished through war, cultural conquest, disease, or internal conflict. The people themselves, of course, are not necessarily killed, but the society as an identifiable entity no longer exists—it may be literally killed through the death of its inhabitants or extinguished through absorption into another society.

Through continuity, innovation, and extinction, then, there is an evolutionary process in human history. This process may be characterized by the twofold trend of diversity and progress.[23] By diversity, Lenski refers to the fact that "the number and variety of societies have increased greatly, and the adaptive patterns of mankind have grown more and more varied."[24] In the contemporary world, diversity is manifested in the differences between simple societies, between simple and complex societies, and within complex, industrial societies.

The second trend, progress, does not refer to increased happiness or morality but to technological development and to the organizational and ideological changes that occur along with that development. Technology is a crucial aspect of sociocultural evolution: it is more likely than any other cultural element to be an autogenous source of change. Progress, therefore, simply refers to the fact that evolution is characterized by continuing technological developments, which are primarily responsible for changes in other aspects of the society, including social organizations and ideology. Lenski is careful to disassociate himself from a technological determinism, however. Evolution is probabilistic, he argues, not deterministic. A society's technology is only one force out of many that are operative. Basic subsistence technology is "the most powerful single force in the field, not with respect to the determination of every single characteristic, but rather with respect to the total constellation of characteristics."[25]

How have these various processes and trends manifested themselves in terms of the kinds of societies that have appeared in human history? Basing his typology in good part upon the earlier work of Goldschmidt, an anthropologist, Lenski distinguishes among a number of societies that differ in terms of their level of technological development. First, there is the simple hunting-and-gathering society, in which only a very rudimentary technology is employed and hunting and gathering are the means of subsistence. In the advanced hunting-and-gathering society, there is also the spear and the bow and arrow, and these developments greatly enhance the group's ability to secure food.

Horticultural and agrarian societies represent a new mode of subsistence—namely, plant cultivation. In an advanced horticultural society, there are, in addition to the plant cultivation of the simple horticultural society, metal tools and weapons. With the addition of a plow for cultivation we have the simple agrarian society, and with the further addition of iron tools and weapons we have an advanced agrarian society. There are also fishing, herding, and maritime societies, which are roughly at the same levels of development as the horticultural and agrarian societies, but which specialize in terms of the kind of subsistence technology used.[26]

Finally, there is the industrial society, which is distinguished from the others by the development of new sources of energy—coal, petroleum, natural gas, hydroelectric power, and atomic power. With the development and use of such power, agriculture gives way to industry as the primary source of societal wealth.

The previous discussion is simplified, of course. As Lenski points out, he has used the minimum criteria—in most cases, a single criterion—to distinguish the various societies. Nevertheless, the typology gives us a general portrait of the historical appearance of various kinds of societies. The hunting-and-gathering societies are the oldest, and existed as the dominant type for the greater part of human history. Advanced hunting-and-gathering societies appeared about thirty-five thousand years ago. It was another twenty-five thousand years before a new type emerged, and the first new type was probably the fishing society. Simple horticultural societies may be traced to the Middle East of about 7000 B.C., and about three thousand years later metal tools and weapons were sufficiently common to identify advanced horticultural societies.

The Middle East was also the site of the invention of the plow, which was in use in simple agrarian societies by 3000 B.C. Advanced agrarian societies did not emerge until about 1000 B.C. Finally, about twenty-eight hundred years later in the nineteenth century A.D., Britain developed into an industrial society.

Lenski's approach highlights the significance of technology in change, showing how technology has been a prime factor throughout human history and not merely in the last few centuries. A different emphasis is offered by the noted economist Kenneth Boulding, who stresses the role of knowledge in social evolution.[27] Boulding contrasts *biogenetic process* and *noogenetic process*. The former "is the process whereby the know-how by which biological organisms are made is encoded in the DNA and the genes. Change in the biogenetic structure takes place through mutation in its own patterns in the genes."[28] The noogenetic process emerges after a sufficiently complex nervous system has evolved from the biogenetic process; it is the process whereby learned behavior is transmitted from one generation to another. For humans, noogenetics is the dominant process. In fact, human history could be described as the "noogenetic evolution of human artifacts," with "artifacts" including everything from language to technology to social organizations and institutions.

Societal evolution, Boulding argues, is characterized by the same basic processes as biological evolution—replication, recombination, redefinition, realization, and selection.[29] In biological evolution, replication refers to the process by which DNA molecules reproduce exact copies of themselves. In societal evolution, replication is the ability (through language, writing, and varied forms of communication) to transmit knowledge both within and between generations. Biologically, recombination refers to the continual rearrangement of chromosomes and genomes out of the existing genes. Socially, recombination is the process of bringing together diverse artifacts into some new combination (Boulding gives the example of the automobile, which was produced by combining a great many different kinds of artifacts). Redefinition is mutation, an essential process for biological evolution. Socially, it refers to invention and discovery and is, therefore, essential to societal evolution. Biologically, "realization" is known as epigenesis; similarly, socially, realization refers to the process of organized communication whereby the necessary instructions are sent for the full development of some phenomenon. Finally, selection is a well-known aspect of biological evolution, involving the survival of some phenomena and the extinction of others. The same selective process characterizes societal evolution, as some inventions and discoveries find a "niche" and others do not.

In spite of the above similarities, there are certain important differences between societal and biological evolution, and the human brain is the essential element in those differences. As Boulding puts it, "It is this extraordinary capacity of the human brain for making images not only of the world outside it. which it sees as reality, but also, in fantasy, of innumerable worlds of the imagination, which distinguishes it from even the highest brains of nonhuman animals."[30]

The human brain enables us to develop what was the "first major artifact" of society—language. It enables us to construct complicated images of the future, which, in turn, lead to the creation of more artifacts. It enables us to alter our images in the light of further information that we receive. It has enabled us to develop science, which is the highest stage of the evolution of knowledge. Thus, "the great difference between biological and societal evolution is that, whereas prehuman organisms occupy niches and expand to fill them, the human organism is a niche-expander creating the niches into which it will expand."[31]

Finally, societal evolution is distinctive in possessing certain kinds of "social organizers," types of interpersonal relationships that form the basis for organizations. In particular, Boulding says that three types of relationships act as organizers: threat, exchange, and integrative or love. The threat system is exemplified in international relationships, in such matters as the arms race, though it can also be seen sometimes in homes, schools, factories, and elsewhere. The exchange system characterizes economic relationships. The integrative system ultimately dominates the others; it is diverse, including all those relationships of "love and hate, pity and envy, sociability and misanthropy, assent and dissent, legitimacy and illegitimacy, dominance and subordination, equality and inequality, identity and alienation."[32] While analytically we may distinguish the three systems, empirically all relationships involve some combination of the social organizers.

As indicated above, all evolutionary thinkers address the question of the extent of the parallelism between biological and social evolution. The question has been argued both ways. Some have insisted that social evolutionists need to minimize or eliminate the biological connotations, while others argue that social evolutionists need to follow the biological model more closely.[33] The most extreme use of the biological model is found in sociobiology, a perspective that emerged in 1975 with the publication of Edward Wilson's book on the topic.[34] Wilson claimed that sociobiology could incorporate all social phenomena and explain them in terms of a neoDarwinian synthetic theory of evolution. According to the sociobiologists, there is a biological and evolutionary basis for everything from aggression to altruism to taboos to forms of social organization such as the family.

Sociobiologists have been criticized on a number of grounds, including the circularity of their arguments. For instance, they use the evolutionary concepts "fitness" and "adaptation." Behavior is selected on the basis of fitness and adaptiveness. If the behavior exists, therefore, it is by definition fit and adaptive. This circularity has been noted by Jill Quadagno, who sums up her critique of the theory by pointing out that sociobiology has "a preconceived notion of change leading to a necessarily adaptive order in which progress is economically calculated in terms of gene survival."[35] In terms of both its logic and its method, therefore, Quadagno concludes that the theory is not useful for studying social behavior.

With respect to the less biologically oriented approaches, such as that of Lenski and others, there is still some question of their usefulness. Evolutionary theory is most useful in understanding largescale, long-term trends of change. But we are still left with the problem of explaining significant differences among societies at the same level of evolutionary development. Evolutionary theory provides insight into the broad sweep of history, but does not appear to cast much light on numerous other questions that arise about social change.

• *General Systems Theory*

General systems theory arose out of developments in biology and mathematics. In particular, two modern developments are an integral part of the theory. One is *cybernetics,* which "showed how the life-likeness of living and social, as well as mechanical, systems depended on feedback."[36] Feedback is actually a familiar process—the thermostat in most homes is a feedback mechanism, "telling" the furnace or air conditioner when the temperature needs adjusting. The other development was *information theory,* and particularly the idea that information is a central part of the organization of any system, increasing the order of that system. Living systems survive and grow through the input and use of information.

When general systems theory is used in sociological analysis, the social system is treated as an ongoing process in which feedback allows for adaptation to the environment. In other words, in contrast to the stable equilibrium stressed in structural-functionalism, the society of the general systems theory is an open system, a changing system, a continually adapting system. The theory is, of course, far more complicated than this suggests. Our purpose here is simply to provide a background for an intricate and sophisticated theory of societal change that employs the basic ideas of general systems theory—Amitai Etzioni's *Active Society.*[37]

The "active society" is one that is marked by continuing change, but change that is directed so as to be a response to the needs of individuals who comprise that society. The active society is an option which has been opened up in the "postmodern" age, rather than an actual society in the contemporary world. How can such a society be realized? How can humans build a society in which there is responsiveness to the needs of the citizenry and, consequently, a turning away from the alienation that is said to characterize modern societies? In an active society, in other words, people will be able to experience an "authentic" life, as the existentialists would term it, or "self-actualization," as humanistic psychologists would term it.

A number of characteristics of the active society relate to what Etzioni called "societal guidance," or the capacity of a society to direct itself so that its members can experience an authentic or self-actualizing existence. First, societal guidance demands that knowledge be gathered and utilized. Knowledge is a "propellant of transformation." Thus, increasing investments in research and development have enabled the developed nations to continue their economic growth in the face of predictions of collapse by some economists.

Knowledge can, of course, be used in various ways. The same knowledge can be used to create an atom bomb or an atomic energy power plant. In the active society, knowledge will be used by elites to make effective decisions. The decision-making process will involve feedback from various societal units as part of the knowledge base. Furthermore, power will be used to control societal processes in a nonalienating manner. Social control is an integral part of any society, including the active society. In the latter, however, control involves the specification of preferred conditions and the revision of processes so as to achieve those conditions. Control, therefore, demands the exercise of power, and decision makers are faced with the problem of choosing the kind of power needed. For the exercise of power is not only inevitable but also costly: "The exercise of power has a societal cost, a distorting effect which curtails activation. Power may assure that 'things get done' but often may not insure that the resulting world will be responsive to those who live in it."[38]

What kind of power will minimize the costs—that is, secure the desired societal directions without alienating the people involved? Etzioni answers the question by reference to his well-known typology of power and compliance. Simply put, compliance may be achieved by coercive power, which employs force; utilitarian power, which employs material sanctions; or normative power, which employs symbolic sanctions. Coercive power generates high alienation. The remuneration used in utilitarian power involves less alienation. The lowest alienation occurs with the use of normative power, which involves commitment on the part of the people over whom the power is exercised.

Another important characteristic of the active society is the building of a consensus that is an authentic expression of the preferences of people and the consequence of their participation in societal processes. Societal guidance depends upon the ability of people to ascertain jointly their shared needs and to formulate new needs. People must not be manipulated into consensus, but must create that consensus out of their own joint efforts.

This is not to say that the people act without any centralized authority or control. For the government is a crucial factor in societal guidance. It is a decision-making center, the hub of a communication network that spans the society, and an integral part of the feedback system that keeps the society moving in the desired direction.

Obviously, social control and the building of consensus are two important aspects of societal guidance. Etzioni uses these two aspects to suggest four types of societies. First, passive societies are low in both control and consensus-building; the underdeveloped nations of the world are similar to such societies. Second, there are overmanaged societies, similar to the totalitarian nations, in which there is high control but low consensus-building. Third, there are drifting societies, which are high in consensus but low in control; this type is approximated by capitalistic democratic societies. Finally, the active society is high in both social control and consensus-building. It is the society of the future.

Etzioni devoted over 650 pages to discussing, elaborating, and answering possible objections to these and other ideas. Obviously, then, we have only skimmed over some of the more important ideas. The relationship to general systems theory is evident—the stress on feedback and information pervades *The Active Society.* Moreover, Etzioni has provided us with not only a theory of societal and political processes, but a portrait of an ideal society. For our purposes, his portrait is as interesting for its emphasis on change as for anything else. Many of the utopian visions (and utopian societies as well) have had little general appeal because they have been stagnant, as H. G. Wells once observed. Utopia must incorporate change, for change is the essence of human life. Etzioni has the insight to recognize that an ideal society cannot be one that lacks change. Perfect social stability is death, not utopia.

• *Mathematical Models*

Mathematical models provide any discipline with the aura of hard-nosed science. Most sociologists are probably skeptical about the extent to which the complexities of social life can ever be adequately compressed into mathematical equations. Nevertheless, there are some processes that can be fairly well described in mathematical terms. For example, Hornell Hart has shown how aspects of culture have changed over time in accordance with two patterns that he calls *cultural acceleration* and *logistic surges*.[39] In the former, human ability to control the environment has been enhanced at an accelerating rate, and the rate of acceleration itself has accelerated. Thus, if we plot such things as world speed records, cutting tool efficiency, and expectation of life over time (generally, over thousands or even hundreds of thousands of years), we get a curve that rises up at an increasing rate. Obviously, the process cannot completely described by such a curve, for otherwise we would have to posit infinite speed, infinite efficiency, and eternal life at some point in time. Nevertheless, the curves do describe the pattern of change within certain temporal boundaries, and that pattern is one of an accelerating rate.

The logistic surge, on the other hand, refers to changes that begin slowly, speed up quickly, then slow again or even stop. Examples of this kind of change are developments of particular inventions, such as birth control clinics, and the growth of particular social entities, such as the British Empire. Thus, cultural acceleration tends to characterize "the long-time development of basic capacities (such as the use of power, speed in travel, expectation of life, and power of destruction)," whereas the logistic surge tends to characterize particular inventions or social organizations.[40]

A number of studies have shown, or have attempted to show, the utility of a mathematical study of change. The work of Hamblin, Jacobsen, and Miller is rather convincing, because they marshal data that fit their equations fairly well as they analyze the processes of adaptation, diffusion, and innovation.[41] We may illustrate their approach by the use of a particular example—namely, the mathematical analysis of the diffusion of innovations. Figure 6-1 is a graph of the diffusion of a new drug among physicians as described by James Coleman. Curve *A* shows the rate of adoption among "integrated" physicians, and curve *B* represents the process among isolated physicians. As shown, physicians who were more integrated into their local medical communities adopted the new drug much more quickly and to a greater extent than those who tended to be isolated with respect to the medical community. The process of diffusion differed somewhat in terms of rate and extensiveness depending upon the social characteristics of the potential adopters.

The two curves can be represented mathematically by logistic and decaying exponential equations. Thus, there are two types of diffusion processes, each of which can be represented by a mathematical equa-

Figure 6-1 • Adoption of New Drug by Integrated (Curve A) and Isolated (Curve B) Physicians

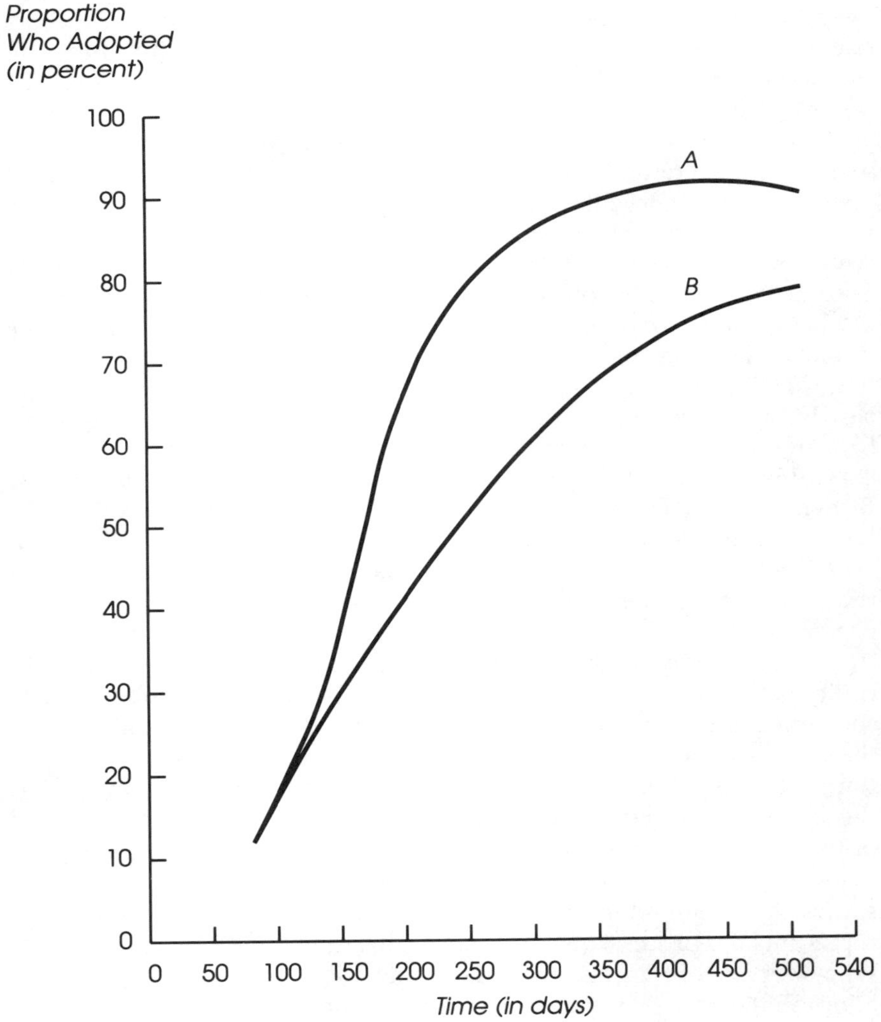

tion. The authors make a number of tentative conclusions on the basis of their data and some reasonable inferences. First, both processes of diffusion are characterized by four conditions:

1. There is a delimited population that may adopt the innovation. (The population may consist of individuals or groups.)
2. There are shared values in the population, especially a value on the positive aspects of adopting the innovation.
3. Adoption of the innovation must provide some reinforcement if diffusion is to occur.
4. The innovation must be introduced by an external stimulation such as advertising.

What determines whether a diffusion process will follow the logistic or the decaying exponential pattern? The process will be a logistic one (curve *A*) if there is continual, random interaction among those in the population—if, that is, "there is persuasive communication among the adopting units about the innovation and its reinforcing consequences."[42] On the other hand, the decaying exponential equation (curve *B*) will characterize a process of diffusion in which the potential adopters are relatively isolated and thereby influenced only by some external communication.

Finally, there is one further condition that can affect the two processes. Namely, both will proceed at a faster rate as the level of reinforcement increases.

As these conclusions indicate, mathematical approaches do not have to operate purely at an abstract, quantitative level. Moreover, to say that a process follows a mathematical law is not to say that it follows a single, rigid path. Innovations were found to diffuse in two different manners among physicians, depending upon the factors noted above. Nevertheless, mathematical sociology is only one approach to social change, and its usefulness in studying a broad range of change phenomena is questionable. I would doubt that the study of change can ever be an essentially mathematical affair, but mathematical models can certainly illuminate the nature of some processes of change for us.

• *Sociology of the Future*

The study of the future has become a serious affair. A deluge of books and articles about the future has inundated the bookstores and journals.[43] As to the source of this interest, Victor Ferkiss has suggested that the requirements of the military during the Cold War era provided the impetus for the development of a science of the future.[44] Systems analysis and the study of the future were born together amidst the efforts of the military and civilian think tanks to ascertain future developments as a framework for making present decisions. Future technology had to be somehow anticipated in the present lest the nation find itself engaged in the production of obsolete materials and obsolete strategies.

In addition to the military imperatives, John McHale has pointed out that two aspects of contemporary change have generated a concern for the future.[45] One is the enormous growth in human ability to manipulate natural environmental processes, and the other is the lag in our conceptualization of that ability and of social change processes. In other words, there is a survival imperative facing humankind, and the awareness of that imperative has generated our interest in the future.

Most futurists are not as interested in working out a theory of change as they are in specifying one or more scenarios of the future. There have been many efforts to identify broad trends and to lay out general characteristics that can be subsumed under notions such as *post-industrial* or *post-affluent*.[46] For example, Daniel Bell has argued that Western society is becoming post-industrial. In brief, there are five dimensions to post-industrialism:

1. Economic sector: the change from a goods-producing to a service economy;
2. Occupational distribution: the preeminence of the professional and technical class;
3. Axial principle: the centrality of theoretical knowledge as the source of innovation and of policy formulation for the society;
4. Future orientation: the control of technology and technological assessment;
5. Decision making: the creation of a new "intellectual technology."[47]

Thus, in the post-industrial society, science, scientists, universities, and others who produce and manage knowledge will be preeminent.

One factor that Bell and most other futurists ignore is the possibility of radical shifts in the direction of change due to scarce resources. Typically, the future is portrayed in terms of increasing affluence and well-being and of a continuing and successful assault on those problems that have oppressed humankind. But there is some question about the practicality of the dreams of the futurists in the light of what we know about the earth's resources (see Chapter 12). Furthermore, forecasts made in the 1960s do not give us much confidence in the ability of futurists to accurately portray the direction of change. As a 1979 assessment of the work of futurists pointed out, futurists almost universally failed to foresee the major upheavals that affected the 1970s.[48] Among other things, they did not foresee the Vietnam War, the dramatic shift in the rate of population growth, the rise in inflation, and the surge of women into the labor force. Moreover, there were some real blunders in forecasting as well as some missing observations. A 1973 study said that China would not deal with multinational corporations or engage in significant trade with the United States; that Iran was an anchor of stability in the turbulent Third World; and that Egypt would continue to be hostile to the West.

Some of these problems of forecasting are due to the fact that futurists try to extrapolate from trends rather than work from theory. There are, however, a few proponents of the study of the future who have developed theories of change in which the image of the future is a crucial variable. One of these is the extensive, pioneering work of Fred Polak, which we shall discuss in Chapter 8. Another useful effort is that of Bell and Mau, who developed a cybernetic-decisional model of social change in which the image of the future is a central variable.[49] The model involves a change process that can be described as "a feedback cycle resulting in a spiral of progressive interaction between information and action. Motivated individuals, . . . their images of the future, and their resultant behaviors are the key elements that keep the system moving and bring a future into being in the present."[50] The behavior of those individuals (who may act either as individuals or as members of some group) follows from a decision about which alternative future to pursue.

Bell and Mau allow for a number of variables to enter into the overall process, including various beliefs, human biology, aspects of social organization, values, and so forth. Let us, however, confine ourselves to the meaning of the "image of the future" in their model. In essence, "an image of the future is an expectation about the state of things to come at some future time. We may think most usefully of such expectations as a range of differentially probable possibilities rather than as a single point on a continuum."[51]

Images of the future can vary along a number of dimensions. They may be optimistic or pessimistic. They may contain the assumption that a particular future is inevitable or only attainable through appropriate human action. They may demand the destruction of aspects of the present or portray the future as an extrapolation of the present. In other words, images of the future can be as varied as the imaginations of humans. One may conceive of any number of various futures, and to the extent that a particular image is shared by a significant number of people, the direction of change may follow in accord with that image.

Social change, then, is the result of human action, and human action is directed by an image of the future. Those images are themselves the result of a great number of other variables. Bell and Mau do not suggest that the construction of future images is purely an exercise of unrestrained imagination. Images will be congruent with group values and may reflect group interests. They will reflect in some ways, in other words, the social structure in which they arise. Furthermore, the future is shaped by more than human action based on a particular image. Various groups with diverse or contradictory images may be striving to shape the future. Also, natural disasters such as earthquakes or epidemics may intrude upon the process of change.

Thus, there are many variables to take into account. Change is not a simplistic consequence of the image of the future. Rather, the latter is a central part of a cybernetic system, and the images themselves are subject to change:

> *As the future becomes the present, an opportunity occurs to assess the adequacy of beliefs about the past, present, and social causation, and the desirability of goals and their relevance to basic values. Old images of the future and beliefs may be revised. In this way, a cycle is closed, but an element of feedback is introduced that keeps the system dynamic. Information is processed and changes occur. At every stage, between every element in the model, it is assumed that there is room for innovation and creativity.*[52]

Another way to deal with the problem of forecasting is to suggest a variety of possible scenarios for the future. An interesting example are the five scenarios for the year 2000 suggested by the Italian sociologist Ferrarotti.[53] The first possibility suggested by Ferrarotti is the "Anthill Society," which is a world of increasing population growth, urbanization, and inequality. In the Anthill Society, there is a loss of individuality, a widening gap between the rich and the poor, and increasing problems of underdevelopment and hunger.

A second possibility is the "Polycentric Society." In contrast to the Anthill Society, the Polycentric Society involves decentralization. Cities spread out. A few people will make fortunes in the competition for wealth and status. Most, however, will not achieve high wealth, leaving an alienated majority.

"Differentiated Gigantism" is the third possibility. It is a society devoted to technology. Automation, cybernation, the use of robots, and the dominance of information characterize this society. But it is the means rather than the ends that are stressed, so that the third scenario involves a lack of a sense of direction.

Fourth, there is the "Corporate Society," one in which power is concentrated in the hands of corporate leaders. Like the Anthill Society, the Corporate Society involves a widening gap between the rich and the poor, shrinking the middle class significantly. The political structure is weak and cannot represent the interests of the underdogs, who continue to plod along with little meaning in their lives.

Finally, there is the "Multivalent, Multidimensional Society," which Ferrarotti himself considers the best option. It is decentralized, integrated, and conducive to individual growth and fulfillment. The print media, including books, will become less important than oral communication between people, which includes communication via electronic means.

Ferrarotti's scenarios are but one set of numerous possibilities that have been proposed. The scenarios are useful in reminding us of the fact that we always have alternatives. Clearly, some of the alternatives are more possible or more probable than others. And some would be defined as more desirable than others. Thus, the futurists remind us that we need to strive for the alternatives deemed most desirable and to avoid those that would take humankind in unwanted directions.

Endnotes

1. For a sampling of futuristic views, see Alvin Toffler, *The Futurists* (New York: Random House, 1972).
2. Robert Nisbet, *Social Change* (New York: Harper & Row, 1972), pp. 40-45.
3. Tamotsu Shibutani, *Society and Personality* (Englewood Cliffs, N.J.: Prentice-Hall, 1961), p. 393.
4. For an interesting discussion of these points, see Paul Hollander, "Sociology, Selective Determinism, and the Rise of Expectations," *The American Sociologist* 8 (1973): 147-53.
5. Robert A. Nisbet, *Emile Durkheim* (Englewood Cliffs, N.J.: Prentice-Hall, 1965), p. 51.
6. From a statement Sorokin wrote to explain his position, in Howard Becker and Harry Elmer Barnes, *Social Thought from Lore to Science*, vol. 2 (New York: Dover), p. 786.
7. Talcott Parsons, *The Social System* (New York: Free Press), p. 486.
8. Melville Jacobs and Bernhard J. Stern, *General Anthropology* (New York: Barnes & Noble, 1952), p. 122.
9. E. R. Wolf, "The Study of Evolution," in *Readings in Social Evolution and Development*, ed. S. N. Eisenstadt (Oxford: Pergamon Press, 1970), pp. 181-90.
10. Ibid., pp. 182-83.
11. White's thought may be found in two books: Leslie A. White, *The Science of Culture* (New York: Farrar, Straus & Giroux, 1949); and *The Evolution of Culture* (New York: McGraw-Hill, 1959).
12. White, *The Science of Culture*, p. 140.

13. Julian H. Steward, *Theory of Culture Change: The Methodology of Multilinear Evolution* (Urbana: University of Illinois Press, 1955), p. 4.
14. Ibid., p. 5.
15. Ibid., p. 36.
16. Ibid., pp. 40-42.
17. Marshall D. Sahlins and Elman R. Service, eds., *Evolution and Culture* (Ann Arbor: University of Michigan Press, 1960), p. 8.
18. Ibid., pp. 12-13.
19. Ibid., p. 27.
20. Ibid., p. 38.
21. Gerhard Lenski, *Human Societies* (New York: McGraw-Hill, 1970).
22. Ibid., p. 61.
23. There are a number of other patterns besides these two, according to Lenski, including cyclical change; technostasis, or the lack of technological development; and regression. Diversification and progress are the "master" trends.
24. Lenski, *Human Societies*, p. 95.
25. Ibid., p. 142.
26. Lenski also notes that there have been "hybrid" societies, in which there are two or more modes of subsistence. Such societies cannot be placed in any of the single categories. They also illustrate the difficulty of creating a typology and remind us not to forget the complexity of human societies in the midst of our efforts to define neat categories.
27. Kenneth E. Boulding, *Ecodynamics: A New Theory of Societal Evolution* (Beverly Hills. Calif.: Sage Publications, 1978).
28. Ibid., pp. 122-23.
29. Ibid., pp. 124-26.
30. Ibid., p. 127.
31. Ibid., p. 136.
32. Ibid., p. 189.
33. See, for example, Szymon Chodak, *Societal Development* (New York: Oxford University Press, 1973), p. 40; and Marion Blute, "Sociocultural Evolutionism: An Untried Theory," *Behavioral Science* 24 (1979): 46-59.
34. Edward O. Wilson, *Sociobiology: The New Synthesis* (Cambridge, Mass.: Belknap, 1975).
35. Jill S. Quadagno, "Paradigms in Evolutionary Theory: The Sociobiological Model of Natural Selection," *American Sociological Review* 44 (February, 1979): 108.
36. Orrin E. Klapp, *Models of Social Order* (Palo Alto: National Press Books, 1973), p. 287.
37. Amitai Etzioni, *The Active Society* (New York: Free Press, 1968). A brief, lucid summary of main points of the theory may be found in Amitai Etzioni. "Toward a Macrosociology," in James S. Coleman, Amitai Etzioni, and John Porter, *Macrosociology: Research and Theory* (Boston: Allyn and Bacon, 1970), pp. 107-43.
38. Etzioni, *The Active Society*, p. 342.

39. Hornell Hart, "Social Theory and Social Change," in *Symposium on Sociological Theory,* ed. Llewellyn Gross (Evanston, Ill.: Row, Peterson, 1959), p. 201.

40. Ibid., pp. 218-19.

41. Robert L. Hamblin, R. Brooke Jacobsen, and Jerry L. Miller, *A Mathematical Theory of Social Change* (New York: Wiley, 1973). A more detailed discussion of the diffusion of innovations will be offered in the next chapter.

42. Ibid., pp. 63-64.

43. See Bettina J. Huber, "A Selected and Annotated Bibliography," in *The Sociology of the Future,* ed. Wendell Bell and James A. Mau (New York: Russell Sage Foundation, 1971), pp. 339-454.

44. Victor C. Ferkiss, *Technological Man: The Myth and the Reality* (New York: George Braziller, 1969), p. 12.

45. John McHale, *The Future of the Future* (New York: George Braziller, 1969), p. 62.

46. See Gary Gappert, *Post-Affluent America: The Social Economy of the Future* (New York: New Viewpoints, 1979), for a good summary of both his own and others' perspectives on the nature of the future.

47. Daniel Bell, *The Coming of Post-Industrial Society* (New York: Basic Books, 1973), p. 14.

48. James Traub, "Futurology: The Rise of the Predicting Profession," *Saturday Review,* December, 1979, pp. 24-32.

49. Wendell Bell and James J. Mau, eds., *The Sociology of the Future* (New York: Russell Sage Foundation, 1971), pp. 6-44.

50. Ibid., p. 18.

51. Ibid., p. 23.

52. Ibid., p. 27.

53. Franco Ferrarotti, *Five Scenarios for the Year 2000* (Westport, Conn.: Greenwood Press, 1986).

PART THREE

Mechanisms of Change

One question that all theories seek to answer is the nature of the driving mechanism of change. As we have seen, a great variety of answers have been given. Change has been conceived of as being the result of conflict, of creative elites, of new modes of thinking, of external forces, of individual motivation to achieve, and of a number of other causes.

We have already argued in the first chapter that change should be viewed as normal. In this part, we shall examine in greater detail the mechanisms that may help explain the direction and rate of that change. Some of these mechanisms have already been identified by the theorists we examined in Part II. Now we shall examine them without restricting their influence to a particular theoretical framework. If, for example, we look at technology and try to see its effects in the light of a number of empirical studies that have been made, what conclusions can we draw about technology as a driving mechanism of change? Such an analysis provides materials out of which new theories can be constructed to advance our understanding.

CHAPTER SEVEN

The Materialistic Perspective

Marx succinctly captured the materialistic perspective on mechanisms of change in his well-known statement: "The windmill gives you society with the feudal lord; the steam-mill, society with the industrial capitalist."[1] As Marx himself recognized, the relationship between technology and social change is more complex than a simple reading of the above statement would indicate. In this chapter, we shall try to clarify the relationship. First, many writers have stressed the primacy of technology in change; Thorstein Veblen and William F. Ogburn have done so in a way that merits some attention, and we shall begin by examining their ideas. Then we shall note certain inadequate ideas about the relationship between technology and change, ideas that lead one into an intellectual cul-de-sac. A third step will be to examine empirical studies and to try, in the light of those studies, to specify the relationship between technology and change. Fourth, we will discuss one of the major approaches to the study of technology and change—the diffusion and adoption of innovations. Finally, we shall look at what has become a burgeoning concern: the potential impact of technology on our future.

The Technocratic Vision: Veblen and Ogburn

Thorstein Veblen (1857-1929) lived a life of detachment and protest. Both his private and professional life were highly unconventional; his writings portray a man who stood aloof and used a merciless scalpel of criticism on the diseased social order of his day. Veblen, who was greatly influenced by Marx and by evolutionary thinking saw the social order as crucially shaped by technology:

> *The machine process pervades the modern life and dominates it in a mechanical sense. . . . The machine has become the master of the man who works with it and an arbiter in the cultural fortunes of the community into whose life it has entered. . . . The machine is a leveller, a vulgarizer, whose end seems to be the extirpation of all that is respectable, noble, and dignified in human intercourse and ideals.*[2]

In other words, Veblen was particularly concerned with the effects of technology on patterns of thought and behavior. He argued that human beliefs and conduct are primarily shaped by the way in which one earns one's living and gains one's wealth, which, in turn, is a function of technology.

The ineluctable link between technology and economic factors on the one hand and social change on the other is seen in Veblen's account of social evolution.[3] That evolution involved the change from savage, neolithic society to "barbarism" in its initial phases. The former society was characterized by smallness, peace, cooperative relations, and industriousness. Property was communally owned for the most part and was shared by the members of the group. Men and women were regarded as equals.

As the population grew, various groups with diverse ways came into contact with one another. The stage of barbarism emerged, in which the relationships between groups were competitive and warlike. Furthermore, people became oriented toward private gain rather than toward communal ends. Veblen saw the same type of social order as present in his own time; for that reason, he declared that modern society is little more than a latter-day barbarism.

A crucial step in the process of social evolution, according to Veblen, was the emergence of private ownership. With private ownership, the "leisure class" came into being. The first form of ownership was the ownership of women by the stronger men of the community, who captured the women in war. Technological developments in the areas of handicraft and agriculture gave a productive value to the female captives, who initially were taken because of "their usefulness as trophies."[4] The victors found it profitable to marry the women, for they could then receive not only prestige in the eyes of their peers, but also the fruit of the women's work.

Man had evolved to a new point. He now acted not simply on the basis of the instincts of workmanship, idle curiosity, and parental concern but in accord with the "quasi-instinct" of pecuniary emulation. His possessions had come to mean his "prepotence" over other members of his community. Property became the basis both for esteem in the eyes of others and for one's own self-respect. In such a situation, men were driven by the quasi-instinct of pecuniary emulation; that is, they struggled to outdo one another in the acquisition of wealth.

The question emerges of how, in an expanding society, to demonstrate one's wealth. Women did most of the work in the period of early barbarism, so that labor was a mark of inferiority. "Conspicuous leisure" therefore became the symbol of the achievement of wealth and the attainment of status. With the continuing development of society, however, conspicuous leisure as a means of displaying status became more difficult to maintain; conspicuous consumption and conspicuous waste became the common means of demonstrating one's position in society. Moreover, the leisure class that employed these means to the fullest (even the poorest engaged in some degree of conspicuous consumption) set the standards of what was right, good, and beautiful. Those standards were all pecuniary in nature. Things are right, good, and beautiful in terms of their relationship to money. The gloss on a gentleman's hat has no more intrinsic beauty than the gloss of worn pants; but the former is beautiful because of its cost, while the latter is repugnant because it indicates lack of wealth.

As may be evident, Veblen did not conceive of change as leading inevitably to a better social order. In fact, he thought that it was easier for a society to regress than to make progress. Furthermore, in the course of change there are always conflicts and contradictions. Specifically, Veblen argued that patterns of thought, which have been created by processes in the past, are never capable of meeting the demands of the present. Habits of thought are appropriate for past circumstances and are "never in full accord with the requirements of the present. . . . This process of selective adaptation can never catch up with the progressively changing situation in which the community finds itself at any given time."[5] In other words, institutions, including habits of thought, are created by processes in the past, persist into the present, but are inappropriate to the present situation. Consequently, there is conflict between the habits of thought necessary for the new material conditions and the habits and institutions that tend to persist from the past.

Thus, Veblen argued that human thinking and behavior reflect technological and economic factors. Veblen was not a technological determinist, as some have claimed. He did not see technological change as leading ineluctably to particular kinds of social change. However, he did consider technological developments a crucial aspect of the direction of change. Moreover, Veblen advocated the idea of the technologically minded—the engineers and technicians—becoming the leaders in a new social order. In his earlier work, Veblen asserted that workers would be the agents of change, but he came to believe that the industrial values of the engineers would make them the creators of the new social order.[6] The new order would be a kind of self-governing industrial organization, with an emphasis on efficiency and productivity and a consequent maximizing of the well-being of all. Such ideas found expression in the technocracy movement in the United States, which sought to replace capitalism with a system in which production and distribution would be controlled by technicians.

There are similarities between Veblen's thought and that of William F. Ogburn (1886-1959). Ogburn also gave primacy to technological developments, and he developed and became famous for an idea that pervades Veblen's work—the lag and inevitable adjustment of cultural factors vis-à-vis technology. The theory of cultural lag involves the identification of at least two variables that can be shown to have been in adjustment at one time. One of the variables is then shown to have changed before, or to a greater extent than, the other because of a discovery or invention. In other words, whenever the rates of change of the interdependent parts of a culture are unequal, we have a condition of cultural lag, and the consequent adjustment is "less satisfactory" than that which existed initially.[7]

Even a casual observer can find examples that support the notion of cultural lag. Take, for example, the two variables of family size and religious doctrine. The doctrine may make sacred the large family. Then, with modernization or new techniques of birth control, or both, family size may shrink. The religious doctrine, however, may oppose this trend and the use of birth control methods, causing maladjustment between church and family.

Ogburn himself provided the example of workers' compensation for accidents as support for his theory. In an agricultural society, he pointed out, accidents occurred much less frequently during work. Individual liability for such accidents was an acceptable mode of adjustment. The law of negligence involved an identification of the individual whose neglect of duty resulted in the accident and required that individual to pay damages. But the common law was not adequate for the situation created by the development of industry. There was a maladjustment because of the rapid rise in number of accidents and the inadequacy of the law to deal with the situation. Employers had developed a number of defenses against the law of negligence. One was the notion that the employee assumes ordinary risks when accepting a job. A second defense was that the employee himself (or herself) may have contributed to the accident and, therefore, to any injuries resulting from the accident. A third defense was the idea of "common employment," which asserted that employers were not liable for any accident that resulted from negligence on the part of the employee's coworkers. Under any of these three conditions, the employer was legally protected from liability. Therefore, during the time when industrial expansion was occurring and the common law of negligence still governed accidents, workers suffered from the maladjustment in the culture. Only when workers' compensation laws were passed was there the necessary readjustment to a just situation for the worker.

As the above suggests, the maladjustment identified by Ogburn has consequences for the quality of human life. In fact, he argued that social adjustment is of two types: that among various parts of culture and that between culture and human beings. The human problems of adjustment may be seen in various kinds of stress and deprivation, and in the nervousness, insanity, crime, prostitution, and other social problems that are indications of maladjustment in social life.

The theory of cultural lag is only one aspect of Ogburn's thought on change, however. His explanation of cultural evolution focuses on four factors: invention, accumulation, diffusion, and adjustment.[8] Of these, invention stands out as a prime factor, analogous in importance to mutation in biological evolution. Invention refers not only to mechanical inventions but also to social inventions (e.g., international organizations) and cultural innovations (e.g., new religious rituals). Scientific developments are also included, and much of the work of Ogburn and his students has centered on showing the consequences of new technology to the social order.

The second factor, accumulation, results from a greater number of new elements being added to a culture than old elements being lost from it. Diffusion, the third factor, simply refers to the spread of inventions from the area of their origin to other areas. Adjustment, the final factor, refers to problems arising from the interdependence of all aspects of a culture. For example, inventions in the economy will inevitably affect government in some way; the government is constrained to adjust to the new situation posed by the changed economy. Or new technology will have repercussions on the family, compelling it to adjust to a changed environment, even though the technological innovations were not directly related to the family.

Material invention, then, is the main source of progress. The nonmaterial aspects of the culture must adjust to material developments, and the gaps between the two will be areas of social problems. Technology is the driving mechanism of change, according to Ogburn; people seem to be forever gasping to keep up and adapt to the world that technology is ever creating anew.

Technology and the Intellectual Cul-de-Sac

Because technology is so prominent and potent in the modern world, there is a tendency for some people to take extreme positions, positions that lead into an intellectual cul-de-sac. The result is a blockage of further thought regarding the complexities of change. Veblen and Ogburn make a valuable contribution in demonstrating the compelling effects of technology and the manner in which technological changes create human problems. But has the case been overstated? Can too much be claimed for technology? A number of positions that have been taken on the subject of technology and change seem one-sided and self-defeating: they lead into a cul-de-sac.

One cul-de-sac is the view of technology as *the* prepotent factor in change. This position, represented more by Ogburn than by Veblen, seeks to explain change solely in terms of technology as the driving force. However, change can also result from political, economic, and social factors independent of technological developments. As Stanislaw Andrzejewski has pointed out, there are numerous examples of fundamental changes that have occurred without any significant technological developments.[9] There was little improvement in production methods during the ancient Greek commercial expansion or during the growth and subsequent decline of capitalism in classical antiquity. Consider also the rise and fall of dynasties in the Arab world that formed the basis for Ibn Khaldun's theory; such changes occurred without any technological developments. The position that technology is the prime mechanism of change, therefore, seems refuted by considerable historical evidence.

A second cul-de-sac is the view of technology as an inexorable force in change. As Marshall McLuhan put it: "Any technology gradually creates a totally new human environment."[10] According to this view, technology is an irresistible force in change as well as an overwhelming one (in the sense of effecting massive changes). We need to distinguish between change that did, and that which *had* to, result from technology. We also need to distinguish between changes that technology made possible and those that it compelled. As we have just pointed out, some change occurs without any particular technological development. Another example of this is provided by William Whyte's account of the considerable changes that occurred in the social organization of a glass-making factory along with very little technological change.[11] The source of the changes was the influx of a new generation of glassworkers of different ethnic origin from the initial group.

Furthermore, even when there is technological change, it does not necessarily lead to other changes. An interesting example of this is provided by a study of two South Indian villages in an area where an irrigation scheme had been introduced twenty-five years previously.[12] One of the villages changed from dry to wet cultivation, since it was in the center of the irrigated area. The other village, however, remained dry. The social order of the wet village was virtually unchanged in spite of the technological change and the new economic opportunities and affluence. The traditional kinship and hereditary nature of politics continued as before.

The dry village, by contrast, experienced considerable change. There was a diversification of the economy; new job opportunities and entrepreneurial activities opened up for the villagers. Hereditary politics did not completely vanish from the village, but heredity was displaced as the basis for political behavior.

In sum, a technological change resulted in considerable economic, social, and political change in one village. What happened in the other village refutes the idea of the inexorable force of technology to create massive changes; its social and political life remained essentially as it was prior to the technological change.

A third cul-de-sac is the view of technology as the Savior. Americans have been particularly prone to be awed in the face of technology: "The Big Technology has been for Americans what the Cross was for the Emperor Constantine. *In hoc signo vinces.*"[13] This perspective was not created by Americans; it has historical roots. The saving power of technology stems from such ideas as the Baconian notion that knowledge is power. Auguste Comte gave impetus to the viewpoint by equating social progress with the development of a scientific mode of thinking. Pragmatic American thought seized the notion with relish and enshrined it. Today, its devotees range from scientists to militarists.[14] Whatever differences those devotees may have among themselves, they have one thing in common: the conviction that the development and application of technology can resolve all the varied problems of humankind.

There is abundant evidence that technology creates as many problems as it solves and that technological innovations may generate considerable stress in people. For some people, for example, technological developments mean new opportunities; for others—those displaced by automation—they mean economic and psychological crisis. The invention of the steam locomotive brought prosperity and importance to a community studied by Cottrell; the invention of the diesel made that same community obsolescent, and its stable and comfortable world was shattered.[15]

The same shattering effect has been experienced by many primitive societies into which modern technology has been introduced.[16] Furthermore, modern technology may be of little use to an underdeveloped society, particularly in terms of the human costs of that technology. That is, in an underdeveloped society it is not necessarily better to use machines rather than personpower. A tractor may be of less value than an ox if the problem is one of enormous underemployment. In addition, if the cost of labor is low, the use of technology may yield no greater net profit than the use of personpower, and the former compounds the problem of unemployment as well as failing to increase profits.[17]

A fourth cul-de-sac is the idea of technology as the Antichrist. This view carries the previous one to the opposite extreme; technology is the source of human ills, a modern despot before whom human beings fawn in helpless adoration. This conception derives in part from thinkers such as Rousseau and Thoreau and their ideas of naturalism and in part from the various socialist criticisms of the capitalistic misuse of technology.[18]

Some of the more disturbing critiques of the technologically dominated society have been made in the literary anti-utopias such as Orwell's *1984.* At a more realistic level, thinkers such as Jacques Ellul and Theodore Roszak have made trenchant criticisms of technocracy. Ellul sees modern human beings losing control over their own destiny to a rampant technology. The totality of human life is increasingly shaped by technique: "Our civilization is constructed *by* technique . . . , *for* technique (in that everything in this civilization must serve a technical end), and *is* exclusively technique (in that it excludes whatever is not technique or reduces it to technical forrm)."[19] Thus, people have become enslaved to that which they thought was their servant. Humanity has created a monstrosity and is devoured by its own creation. In the process, human patterns of thought and behavior have become phenomena that are shaped in their totality by technology.

Roszak also paints a grim picture of technology's role in the modern world. He argues that American youth have perceived the fact that the central struggle of the modern world is not with some of the more obvious injustices such as poverty and war but with the more subtle and insidious enemy called *technocracy.* Technocracy is "that social form in which an industrial society reaches the peak of its organizational integration. It is the ideal men usually have in mind when they speak of modernizing, up-dating, rationalizing, planning."[20] In a technocracy, the leaders justify their behavior by citing the technical experts who have, in turn, justified themselves by appealing to scientific thought. And, of course, the appeal to science leaves no room for argument. In such a society, Roszak sees the rebellion of youth as the hope for a new and better world.

A less strident critique is offered by William Catton in his discussion of "homo colossus" and the "technological turn-around" that has occurred in human history.[21] Through much of human history, Catton argues, technology has been a means of adaptation between humans and their environment. But that relationship has now been reversed. Our appetite for energy is voracious. We consume ever-increasing quantities of the world's resources. Hunting and gathering societies consumed about 3,000 kilocalories of energy per person per day; the number for those in modern industrial societies is around 210,000 kilocalories, an increase of seventy times. Even comparing Americans in the 1980s with those in the early days of the Republic (1790), we find that energy use per person has increased nineteenfold. The increased energy use, of course, is a function of our advanced technology. In effect, our technology requires decreasing the number of humans on the earth.

We must distinguish, of course, between technology, itself, as a progenitor of social ills and people's willingness to subject themselves to technology's apparent demands or their unwillingness to rationally control its use. In his critique, Catton calls social scientists to recognize what is happening in the world and to take action. Indeed, what we do with our technology is a matter of choice and commitment rather than of the irresistible demands of technology itself.

In other words, technology is no more the Antichrist than it is the Savior. To the extent that people exalt technology and willingly enslave themselves to it, the technocracy becomes a frightening reality. On the other hand, few of those who have enjoyed the fruits of modern technology will wish to join a "back-to-nature" movement. We do well to recognize the potential disjunctive consequences of technology; we would also do well not to forget that modern science and technology have given us new freedom by delivering us "from the bondage of material poverty" and opening up "a great area of choice where vision and will can operate."[22]

How Technology Causes Change

With the above caveats in mind, we may now look at the impressive evidence that shows technology to be a mechanism of social change and, specifically, at the way in which technology impels that change. There are two approaches which may be, and have been, taken in demonstrating the force of technology: either we may identify specific changes and try to trace them back to technological changes, or we may take a specific technological innovation and try to trace its ramifications. In either case, the consequences of technological change for social change are seen to be extensive.

The former approach was taken by William Ogburn and Myer Nimkoff in their effort to account for various changes in the family.[23] The social changes in the family were first identified by using a panel of experts, and then eight major changes were selected out of the lists supplied by the experts. The eight major familial changes were a growing emphasis on romance, earlier marriages, smaller families, fewer functions for the family, a greater number of working wives, diminished parental authority, more emphasis on the children, and a greater amount of separation and divorce.

These changes were then traced back to technological innovations. For example, how can we account for the weakening of kinship ties in the modern family? First, there are the effects of rural-urban migration, which causes a spatial and, therefore, social and psychological separation. Such migration is possible only because of innovations in transportation such as the railroad; and the railroad was made possible by the invention of the steam engine. Thus, through the process of sequential causation, we arrive at the steam engine as a causal factor in weakened kinship ties.

The other approach, tracing the consequences of innovation, can be illustrated by a variety of studies. All of them dramatize the extent to which a single innovation can have manifold consequences. For example, the printing press affected all social institutions.[24] It facilitated the Protestant Reformation by making the Bible available to large numbers of people for the first time in history. The wide distribution of books, only possible with the printing press, affected governments by opening the doors of knowledge to masses of people. Governments were aware of the potential threat of books; in the late 1600s the British government imposed strict laws on colonial printers. "The government allowed itself to pick who was to be a printer, how often they printed, and what they printed in colonial America."[25] It proved to be a disastrous policy; printed materials had already stimulated the drive for freedom, and the people would not take such restrictions lightly. By facilitating the rapid spread of knowledge, the printing press also opened the possibility of mass education. The economy, likewise, was afftected by the creating of a new industry and its impact on the efficiency and effectiveness of other industries.

We have, of course, only touched upon the innumerable consequences of printing. Consider what life would be like without books, newspapers, magazines, and printed documents such as contracts and governmental regulations, and it becomes clear that printing has an impact on most aspects of our lives. Indeed, it is not an exaggeration to say that the printing press is inextricably linked with the rise of modern civilization.[26]

It is difficult to even identify all of the consequences of innovations such as the printing press, the automobile, and the computer. It is somewhat easier to trace the consequences of a new technology in a primitive society. A classic effort is Linton's study of the Betsileo, a Madagascan tribe that moved from dry to wet rice culture.[27] This simple technological innovation, the irrigation of crops, led to significant changes in tribal life. As irrigation was more widely adopted, there was no longer a need for the joint family groups that effectively cultivated the dry fields. A single household could care for the irrigated field. Some households moved away into the jungle as land suitable for the wet rice cultivation became unavailable near the village. This mobility led to the formation of new villages.

The new villages, in turn, required some kind of organization for maintenance and defense. Furthermore, although the joint family no longer had an economic function, it still retained religious significance. Since the joint family was scattered throughout a number of villages, people came together from various villages for religious functions. There were also intervillage marriages. These factors facilitated the development of a sense of tribal identity between villages.

Ultimately, as the sense of identity grew and the demands for defense increased, the tribal democracy of old was replaced by a monarchy. The people now had a king. In place of democracy, a caste system emerged, with king, nobles, commoners, and slaves. In sum, the whole of life was radically altered as a consequence of the new technology. Nevertheless, it is important to keep in mind, as we shall discuss below, that the new technology gave the people alternatives that they did not have before. The new patterns of tribal life were perhaps not feasible or at least not as adaptable to the old conditions of dry rice cultivation. This does not mean, however, that the new patterns were inevitable. We always need to distinguish between changes that are required by technology and those that are made possible as new alternatives.

The logic of this approach of tracing the consequences of new technology is easily followed and, therefore, may be deceptive in its results. Consider the logical and similar effects of such technological developments as the automobile, improved refrigeration. and television.[28] With respect to the automobile, a first effect is that extensive travel is facilitated, which means that people are able to travel a greater distance to purchase commodities. This reduces the frequency of contact within the community; an area becomes a mass of strangers who live in relative isolation from one another. People are therefore forced to satisfy psychic needs within the family, and if family members are incapable of meeting such needs there may be sufficient frustration within the family to result in a divorce.

A similar sequence may be traced with respect to improved refrigeration and television. The former means that food can be kept in the home for a greater length of time, while the latter means that a novel and appealing source of entertainment has entered the home. Consequently, people remain at home more because there is less need to go out for either supplies or entertainment. This means greater isolation; the members of the community are strangers to one another. The family bears the brunt of satisfying psychic needs, and the same consequences result. In other words, all three inventions can be shown (at least logically) to contribute to the breakdown of community life.

As reasonable as the above appears, a little thought will show that there are alternatives that are just as reasonable. The same automobile that takes people out of their community can take them to visit other people as well as to shop; the auto can help maintain kinship ties or friendships, thus helping psychic needs to be fulfilled outside of the immediate family. The refrigerator that makes trips to the store less frequent can also mean more time for cultivating interpersonal relationships. And so on. This is not to say that the former interpretation is wrong and the latter right, but only that we must be cautious of accepting arguments that are reasonable but that lack empirical support. Anyone familiar with early nineteenth-century America would be highly skeptical of any contemporary breakdown of community that has resulted from technological developments. That is, there is little historical evidence that there was any "community" to break down under the impact of the automobile, refrigerator, and television.

Nevertheless, the role of technology in change has been enormous. To exercise some skepticism about some of the statements that have been made regarding the impact of technology is not to deny the potency of that impact. How can we account for the potency of technology? How does technology effect change? There are a number of factors involved.

First, technology increases our alternatives. New technology may bring previously unattainable ideals within the realm of possibility, and it may alter the relative difficulty or ease of realizing differing values. Thus, technological innovation means that a society faces a greater range of alternatives, and when it opts for a new alternative it may set off extensive changes in numerous areas.

Even minor technological change may have manifold consequences in this way. Although once again the case is overstated, White has shown that medieval technical inventions had significant consequences both economically and socially in Europe.[29] He argues that the invention of the stirrup, which reached northern Europe by the eighth century A.D., led to a restructuring of medieval society. The stirrup changed warfare; foot soldiers fighting in close order were rendered impotent by the mounted knight. The stirrup enabled the knight to carry his lance rather than to merely throw or thrust it. The knight, horse, and lance became a new entity—a single and powerful weapon.

Considerable capital was required to maintain a knight. A reorganization of land tenure resulted, with each unit of tenure supporting a number of knights. The feudal system, with its knightly class endowed with fiefs and holding numerous rights and obligations, thus emerged as an alternative that was created by a new military technology.

The stirrup created new alternatives. Once a new alternative is chosen, there are likely to be changes throughout the society. Some of those changes will be defined as negative by at least some people. For example, Lane has traced the extensive changes in British merchant shipping since the mid-1950s.[30] Until the mid-fifties, British ships carried a significant amount of the world's trade and British shipping companies ran prestigious passenger lines. Ports throughout the world had waterfront districts that catered to the seamen's desire for alcohol and women. But all of this changed. The passenger liners died as a result of air travel. The waterfront districts lost their trade with the emergence of container ports, which take the cargo from the ships in a matter of hours rather than the days that used to be spent in port. For some old seamen, and for those who made a living from the shore leave of the seamen, the passing of the old way has been distressing. New and better technology has made the old way of life obsolete. Of course, we should keep in mind that many people define the changes as positive, including those who prefer quicker travel and those who have found new economic opportunities in the container ports.

A second way in which technology effects change is by the alteration of interaction patterns. Once the technological innovation is adopted, there may be certain necessary shifts in interaction patterns, shifts that are demanded by the technology itself. This is most clearly seen in industrial organizations, although we could again refer to changed patterns resulting from the automobile and other innovations that have affected mobility. The latter, however, do not represent a *necessary* shift; in the case of the industrial organization, the changes in interaction are inevitable.

An example of the inexorable changes in interaction patterns is the introduction of automation into an automobile plant.[31] A number of factors affect the frequency as well as the kind of interaction patterns on the job, including the amount of attention demanded by the job, spatial patterns of the workers, amount of control over the pace of the work, amount of noise, and the number of tasks that involve teamwork. Automation had considerable effect upon these variables and, therefore, upon interaction.

In the automated plant, closer and continual attention is required of the worker. The spatial patterns are altered so that there is greater distance between workers. The worker tends to have less control over the pace of work. The automated machines are perceived by many workers to be noisier than the nonautomated ones. Finally, fewer tasks require teamwork in the automated plant. As a result, social interaction within groups of workers is less frequent after automation. Furthermore, the interaction involves fewer workers, and the quality of the interaction is altered. There is little sense of teamwork; many workers are social isolates on the automated production line.

Automation also changed supervisor-worker relationships. Because of the closer attention required on the automated line, and because the worker on that line controls a greater proportion of the production process, the worker is subjected to a greater amount of supervision. There is, therefore, an increased frequency of interaction with superiors. Unfortunately, because of the changed role of the supervisor in an automated plant, this interaction is perceived in more negative terms than the superordinate-subordinate relations in the nonautomated factory.

Interaction between workers is also affected by the introduction of computers and robots into the workplace. When computers were brought into an insurance company, clerks found themselves spending a great deal more time alone, working with machines rather than with other people.[32] Similarly, a researcher who studied a machine plant ten weeks before and after the installation of a robot found that the new technology was a mixed blessing:

> *The mill job changed from handling metal to handling the robot control panel. The workers were unanimous in praising the robot for eliminating fatigue and physical strain from their work. But they complained of more subtle kinds of stress. Where once a worker could joke, sing, or daydream as he loaded the milling machine, the robot demands his full attention. As one worker said, "I don't have time to talk with anyone. I don't want them breaking my concentration."*[33]

Technology can also change interaction patterns in intimate relationships. One of the problems with home computers, for example, is that some people become addicted to them. In one study of twenty families, the researcher found that two husbands, one wife, and two teenage sons developed an obsession with their computers, devoting themselves to working on the machines and neglecting their relationships with other family members.[34]

The changes we have discussed so far would be defined generally as undesirable. But technology can also lead to changed interaction patterns that people define as desirable. For example, the introduction of various kinds of microtechnology (radios, bicycles, clocks, and contraceptives) into rural Buganda resulted in four kinds of change:

1. The economy has been made more efficient in terms of both production and distribution, and new consumption aspirations have been created.
2. Community events and activities have increased in number and duration.
3. There is new content for individual identities.
4. The level of information and the amount of certainty and security possessed by the individual have changed.[35]

The above changes include some that would be defined by the participants as very desirable. For instance, bicycles have made the transportation of people and of goods more efficient. They have also enhanced interpersonal relationships because the bicycle owner can transport neighbors and friends, or their goods. New relationships are possible because of the increased mobility of people. Moreover, the bicycle owner acquires an enhanced self-concept by gaining new status in the community. Some new problems are created, of course, but the point is that the introduction of a technological innovation into a community does not have only negative consequences for the people. Some desirable, as well as undesirable, alterations can occur in interaction patterns.

A third way in which technology effects change lies in the tendency for technological developments to create new social problems. These problems elicit some kind of response, which may result in a variety of changes to resolve the problem. For example, in a subsistence economy, poverty may not be defined as a social problem because human life is perceived to hang precariously by the thread of capricious fate. In an affluent, technologically sophisticated society, poverty becomes a compelling problem because human life is a function of the use and misuse of resources. In a primitive society, individual health may rest on the whimsy of the gods or the efficacy of the actions of the witch doctor. In a modern society, individual health becomes a matter of public concern and, to some extent, responsibility. When population density is sparse and the need for sons to help earn a living is great, birth control may be both religiously and pragmatically taboo. When population threatens to crush every hope for enhanced human well-being, birth control becomes a matter of public concern and responsibility.

In other words, technology has helped to create a highly complex world with numerous new problems, problems that were once either nonexistent (because they were not defined as problems or because they really did not exist) or insoluble. These problems must often be dealt with by the application of technology or the development of new technology (e.g., control of pollution). That means that we are resolving problems by the use of that which has created the problem in the first place—technology. In using technology to resolve the problems, we are creating new problems. Industrialization resolved for many people the problem of survival; now it has revived the problem in terms of the pollution of the environment. The problems created by the development and use of sophisticated technology for pollution control await us in the future.

A good example of a problem created by technology is provided by John Burke's study of the steam engine.[36] Burke argues that the regulatory agencies of the federal government, which are not set up in the Constitution but that are so familiar to the present scene, arose in the context of a significant change in attitudes in early nineteenth-century America. That change was greatly facilitated by the steam engine, or at least by the application of the steam engine to river traffic. The use of the steam engine on boats enabled Americans to use the extensive network of rivers for cheap transportation, but also led to a hazardous situation.

The first steamboats were relatively safe, for they used low-pressure engines. When high-pressure engines began to be used, problems quickly developed. The engines were subject to boiler explosions, and that made them hazardous to the people using, and working around, the boats. By the middle of 1817, four explosions had taken five lives in the East and twenty-five more lives on the Ohio and Mississippi rivers. In 1824, a boiler burst in New York harbor, killing thirteen people and injuring many more. The New York explosion finally impressed the seriousness of the situation upon Congress. Some Congressmen became convinced that legislation was needed to prohibit high-pressure engines. Nevertheless, the legislation was not soon forthcoming. Some segments of the public were also concerned about the problem; the Franklin Institute of Philadelphia (which was established to study and promote applied science) made an extensive study of boiler explosions. Between 1825 and 1830, forty-two more explosions occurred, killing about 273 people. Finally, in 1852, an effective bill was passed. It addressed the problem by governing the maximum allowable pressure and establishing agencies to take action against those who broke the regulations.

Thus, a combination of public reaction and congressional action established a formal mechanism for regulating a sector of private industry by the government. This was a reversal of the decentralizing tendencies of the latter part of the eighteenth century, and was part of a new wave of governmental incursion into the private sector. Thus, the application of a technological innovation created a social problem, and the efforts to resolve that problem led to significant change in the relationship between government and industry.

It is the combination of the existence of the problems and of the potential for coping with them that creates the pressure for change. The problems may remain insoluble apart from changes in the polity, or changes in the relative domains of the public and the private, or changes in our hierarchy of values.

Consider medical technology and the health of the aged as an illustration. Developments in medical technology have made good health for the aged feasible. At the same time, the costs involved are so high that the health of the aged is problematic and a matter of public issue. The result, in America, has been a continuing struggle involving changes in governmental programs (the initiation of Medicare and Medicaid in 1965) and public debate over the extent of collective responsibility for the health of the citizenry. One aspect of the public debate is the question of whether there should be some kind of national health insurance.

A fourth way in which technology brings about change is through what I would call the *domino effect,* the tendency for any change or innovation to set off a chain of other developments so that change becomes self-perpetuating. The domino effect may occur in at least two different ways. First, any particular technological innovation will tend to have a number of different applications. In some cases, the applications may involve what seem to be completely different phenomena. For example, the automated organ that was popular at the end of the seventeenth century was used to solve an important problem in the production of woven silk fabrics.[37] The son of an organ maker, Basile Bouchon, applied the principle of the pegged cylinder to the silk loom, thereby automating what had been a manual job handled by boys (sometimes with disastrous results when they pulled the wrong strings while a design was being woven). Centuries later, in the United States, technological developments useful for manufacturing firearms were applied to the production of sewing machines, and the technology of manufacturing sewing machines and bicycles facilitated the later production of automobiles. Most technological developments have a "spin-off," a variety of applications other than that for which they were first developed.

A second way in which the domino effect occurs is by serendipity, the accidental discovery of something while looking for something else. That is, in the course of developing a particular technology, other innovations may be accidentally produced. There are numerous cases in the history of science of serendipity, including Galvani's discovery of electric current, Roentgen's discovery of X-rays, and Fleming's discovery of the antibiotic effect of penicillin. When people are convinced of the value of new technology and are committed to technological development, the domino effect is inevitable.

The domino effect is intensified by the global competition of the modern world, the worldwide demand for new products, and the development of *venture capital*.[38] In essence, venture capital means that the time between development and application of new technologies has been shortened dramatically. In the past, banks would become interested in innovations only after they were at the application stage and the bankers could see the possibility of a return on their investment. Venture, or risk, capital, however, is an investment by people who are willing to gamble on technological developments even at the stage of exploration of an idea. Venture capitalists believe that a certain number of the investments will not pay off, but that some will and those that yield a return will more than compensate for those that do not. Thus, with money to proceed at a more rapid pace, it no longer takes twenty years or more for an idea or an innovation to become a commercial product. The microprocessor appeared in many different electronic products within five years of its invention.

The Diffusion and Adoption of Innovations

We have previously noted that people do not necessarily accept changes that outsiders define as helpful or desirable for them. Innovations such as fertilizer, hybrid seed, the technique of boiling contaminated water, and various other techniques for improving the economy and people's health have been rejected by substantial numbers. Furthermore, when an innovation *is* accepted, it tends to follow the pattern described in the last chapter (Figure 6-1). That is, not everyone accepts it immediately, and there is often a minority that never accepts it.

The above indicates some of the issues raised in the study of the diffusion and adoption of innovations. Why are innovations accepted or rejected? What factors enter into various rates of acceptance? What kinds of roles are involved in the processes of diffusion and adoption?

What sociocultural factors affect those processes? If we accept the notion that technological innovation is a crucial factor in social change, then the diffusion and adoption of innovations are processes of obvious importance for us to study.

There has been a long tradition of interest in diffusion in anthropology and sociology. In anthropological approaches, diffusion refers to the spread of elements or traits from one culture to another. Some anthropologists would dispute this, however; Bronislaw Malinowski argued that diffusion cannot even be studied unless we take organized systems or institutions as the units that are diffused rather than traits or even trait complexes.[39] A more general definition, then, would assert that diffusion is the spread of some facet of one culture to another.

The theory of diffusion arose as an alternative to evolution. Some of the early diffusionists were as extravagant in their claims as were the early evolutionists. During the 1920s, G. Elliott Smith and W. J. Perry claimed that all the early civilizations arose as a result of diffusion from Egypt. A flowering of culture had occurred in Egypt about 3000 B.C., with developments in such fields as agriculture, mathematics, technology, and the polity. These innovations spread throughout the Mediterranean and, eventually, throughout the world.

This theory was supported by such evidence as cultural similarities between the early Egyptians and peoples in the Western hemisphere. Even the totemism of the Australian aborigines was said to have been a degenerate form of culture that derived from Egypt. In other words, these diffusionists were able to support their theory by arguing that the diffused culture was altered in the course of its spread. On that basis, however, one could argue that virtually anything came from anywhere else; for if, as Smith argued, the pyramid-shaped sacrificial altars of the Mayans derived from the Egyptian habit of constructing pyramids for their mummified dead, it would seem possible to link all sorts of cultural features by the exercise of one's imagination. In addition to the impossible connections between cultures that the theory entails, it also falls before the fact of multiple, simultaneous invention of similar ideas and techniques.

Nevertheless, the diffusionists provided a necessary corrective to the evolutionists. The pattern of cultural development could not be understood as a series of stages through which each culture passed as though it existed in isolation. Cultures interacted, and that interaction was of critical importance for change.

Later anthropologists laid great stress on the importance of diffusion as a pattern of change. As A. L. Kroeber put it, "whatever else diffusion does or does not involve, it does always involve change for the receiving culture. The total part played by diffusion in human culture is almost incredibly great."[40] This, argued Kroeber, is clear in part because of the "retarded" nature of marginal cultures. That is, those cultures that were farthest from the "higher centers" of civilization, and consequently less likely to benefit from diffusion, fell further and further behind in terms of development. Societies that are relatively isolated are never as culturally rich and complex as those that interact with other societies.

Some anthropologists would argue that as much as 90 percent of known cultures is the result of diffusion. This is perhaps most evident in modern, complex societies. In a famed and often quoted passage, Ralph Linton detailed the foreign origin of innumerable facets of the average American life: pajamas, soap, umbrellas, money, coffee, the pattern of one's bed, and so forth. Linton concludes that if the American is a conservative, he will "thank a Hebrew deity in an Indo-European language that he is 100 percent American."[41]

The process of diffusion clearly affects primitive peoples also. Kroeber offers the example of pipe smoking.[42] Smoking originated in tropical America, where tobacco is an indigenous plant. It spread by diffusion throughout Central and North America, with both cigar and pipe smoking appearing among various peoples. The Eskimos apparently did not smoke until recent centuries. They borrowed the habit from traders who came across the Bering Strait. The traders had acquired it from the diffusion across Europe and Asia; the source of that diffusion was Spain, where it had arrived as a result of contact by Spanish explorers with the Indians of tropical America. In other words, pipe smoking reached the Eskimos after a process of diffusion around the entire world.

Obviously, diffusion is an important pattern of change. The problem, then, becomes one of how to use the concept as an analytical tool. That is, what are the problems of theory and method involved in the study of diffusion? One problem, of course, is how to determine whether a particular aspect of culture is the result of diffusion or of innovation within the culture. Some facets of culture are easier to trace back than others. The problem is compounded by the fact that diffusion very often involves modification as well as transfer.

Let us look at two examples of the modification that typically occurs in the process of diffusion, one in a traditional and the other in a modernizing society. First, consider the introduction of iron implements to the traditional Maori.[43] Captain James Cook first made contact with the Maori in the seventeenth century. He reported that at first they had no interest in iron implements. But they soon recognized their value and began to ask for them. For the next two centuries, the Maori particularly wanted such things as axes, hatchets, and any large pieces of iron they could get. Intitially, they used the iron to replace their stone and bone implements (chisels and axes). Later, they substituted iron for wooden implements, such as spades and hoes.

There are two important points to be made about the Maori adoption of iron. First, the new technology was not inherently valued by the Maori. They had no interest in it until they saw how it could be useful to them in terms of their own way of life. Second, the new technology was used by them in accord with their own culture. They used short-handled hoes and spades, for instance, because they preferred to work in a squatting rather than a stooping or standing position. They used nails as chisels and to score trees for felling. In other words, they used the implements in different ways and for different purposes than the Europeans used them. The iron did make a difference in Maori culture, but the new technology was modified in the process of adopting it.

Similarly, the Japanese are noted for their willingness to borrow freely from other cultures and also to give their borrowings a distinctive Japanese cast. When Japan began to modernize in the late nineteenth century, they borrowed from the West, among other things, three institutions—the police, the postal service, and newspapers.[44] In each case, the Japanese modified the institution in accord with their own needs. They used the French model for their police system because it had both police and administrative functions, was highly centralized, and was used for political surveillance and control. Those characteristics seemed important to the leaders of the newly modernizing nation. But the Japanese went beyond the French model. Among other things, they created the world's first Police Academy in 1885.

The postal system was modeled after that of England, though the Japanese did not use all aspects of the British system. By the end of the nineteenth century, the Japanese system "ranked with the best in the world."[45] But their system was not a carbon copy of the British system; it was modified to suit their own peculiar needs. Finally, the Japanese instituted newspapers, an idea that they got from the West but which they, again, modified to suit their own needs. In fact, Japanese newsmen were quite innovative, using formats and advertising that would increase circulation. By the first decade of the twentieth century, Japan had six newspapers with a combined daily circulation of more than 100,000. They freely borrowed and freely modified, and thereby they greatly facilitated the modernizing process.

One final point that is made in anthropological discussions of diffusion is that the process is often a reciprocal affair. We have already noted that much of American culture is the result of diffusion from other cultures. Few people may be aware of the extent to which Americans and others have been influenced by the country's original inhabitants, the American Indians (who, of course, have also been influenced by European culture). As Alan Beals has outlined it:

> *Plants domesticated by American Indians furnish almost half of the world's food supply. . . . A few of the better known plants include "Irish" potatoes, corn, beans, squash, and sweet potatoes. Among drugs and stimulants tobacco is the most widely diffused of the plants borrowed from the American Indian. Of the many Native American drugs which are found in modern pharmacology, the best known are coca in cocaine and novocaine, curare in anesthetics, cinchona bark as the source of quinine, ephedra in ephedrine for clearing sinuses and nasal passages, datura in pain-relievers, and cascara in laxatives.... The commercial cottons used today are derived principally from the species cultivated by American Indians. . . . American Indian music had a decisive influence on some American composers. . . . A number of composers visited Western reservations, gathering and arranging melodies and borrowing themes.*[46]

Finally, Indians influenced the content of American literature, as witnessed by such classic works as Longfellow's *Hiawatha* and Cooper's *Leatherstocking Tales.* Diffusion is rarely a one-way process, even when the two cultures involved are at different stages of economic development and one is relatively powerless with respect to the other. Few people will reject a good idea or a useful innovation merely because it is associated with foreigners, and no culture has a monopoly on good ideas and useful innovations.

In sociology, the forefather of diffusion studies is generally acknowledged to be the Frenchman Gabriel Tarde, who wrote a work on "imitation" in 1890. An English version appeared in 1903. Tarde was the first to suggest such ideas as a curvilinear pattern of adoption of new ideas, and cosmopolitanism as a characteristic of innovators. By imitation Tarde meant the process of adoption of innovations, and he sought to identify the laws governing that process.

A pioneering effort in the study of diffusion and adoption is Everett Rogers's study, based on a review of over 500 publications.[47] The innovations included in his study range from new drugs to new hand tools to new educational programs to hybrid corn. In other words, innovation is a broad concept as defined by Rogers—it is any idea that is *perceived* as new by an individual. The idea may have actually existed in other places or among other people, but that does not alter its effects upon the individual who encounters it and perceives it as new.

According to Rogers, there are four crucial elements in the process of diffusion and adoption: the innovation itself, the communication of the innovation, the social system in which the process occurs, and certain temporal aspects. The innovation, as we noted above, is any new idea. Thus, an innovation might be a fad of some kind, a social movement, a new form of dancing, a new gadget, or a technological development. Most of the innovations that form the basis for Rogers's discussion are technological, but he stresses the point that we must not restrict the notion of innovation to the technological.

The second element is communication. "The essence of the diffusion process is the human interaction in which one person communicates a new idea to another person."[48] Without communication, of course, the innovation cannot spread. The communication of an innovation occurs in a social system, which is the third element of importance and which is defined as "a population of individuals who are functionally differentiated and engaged in collective problem-solving behavior."[49] This definition means that a social system might be anything from a primitive tribe to the farmers in a particular area to the physicians in a particular community. Within any social system, there are norms, various statuses, and opinion leaders, all of which are important in understanding the fate of innovations in that system.

Diffusion and adoption occur over time, of course. If, therefore, one individual communicates a new idea to another individual in the context of a particular social system, there will be either an adoption or a rejection by the second individual. If the second individual adopts, he or she will normally pass through five stages: awareness, interest, evaluation, trial, and, finally, adoption. Thus, adoption involves the acceptance and use of an innovation by individuals, while diffusion involves the spread of the innovation within the social system.

The processes are complex and involve numerous variables. Rogers summarized his conclusions in fifty-two generalizations. A few of these will give the flavor of his work:

- *Innovativeness of individuals is related to a modern rather than a traditional orientation.*
- *An individual's innovativeness varies directly with the norms of his social system on innovativeness.*
- *Relatively later adopters are more likely to discontinue innovations than are earlier adopters. . . .*
- *Awareness occurs at a more rapid rate than does adoption. . . .*
- *The relative advantage of a new idea, as perceived by members of a social system, affects its rate of adoption. . . .*

- *Earlier adopters have more opinion leadership than later adopters. . . .*
- *Change agents have more communication with higher-status than with lower-status members of a social system.*[50]

Rather than examining all of the generalizations, let us follow the four basic elements identified by Rogers and note some of the conclusions that have been reached in the research.

• *Innovations*

With respect to the innovations themselves, Rogers has identified five characteristics, as perceived by potential adopters, that affect the rate of adoption. One is the relative advantage of the innovation. Obviously, the more people perceive the innovation to enhance their advantage relative to the existing situation, the more they will tend to adopt the innovation. The obverse is also true—relative disadvantage, or lack of advantage, will inhibit adoption.

In an interesting study of the diffusion and adoption of the telephone in the United States in the early part of the century, Fischer has shown the importance of perceived advantage.[51] In 1900, fewer than 5 percent of American farm households had telephones. By 1920, nearly 40 percent had them, a rate of adoption that was greater than that occurring among the more affluent urban dwellers. Moreover, the greater rate occurred in the face of industry marketing efforts that were concentrated in the urban areas. Rural dwellers perceived both business and social advantages to the telephone. For business, it saved time and money by giving the farmer the opportunity to place orders and to call ahead for provisions and compare prices. Socially, it saved lives by being used to get help for medical or fire emergencies. More importantly, perhaps, it alleviated loneliness; farmers' wives were able to keep in touch with each other in a way never before possible. Ironically, then, in the urban areas the vendors worked hard to invent uses for the telephone in order to sell it, while in the rural areas the farmers worked hard to get the new technology, perceiving it to have important business and social advantages for them and their families.

A second perceived characteristic of innovations is their compatibility with existing values and needs. Thus, a new method of birth control may diffuse through a system where there is a value on family limitation, but is unlikely to diffuse where religious values condemn artificial birth control. Professionals as well as lay people may resist an innovation that is incompatible with their values (as opposed to rejection on technical grounds). For example, professional therapists in a

Massachusetts study were found to be less accepting than lay people of a community-mental-health ideology.[52] The ideology was no doubt contrary to some of their own ideologies of therapy, but it was also contrary to their self-interests.

Third, the rate of adoption of innovations will be affected by their perceived complexity. Some innovations will be perceived to be very difficult to understand and utilize, and will therefore be adopted more slowly or even rejected. Rogers argues that complexity is the reason the rhythm method of birth control has been much less successfully introduced in India than has the IUD. The latter demands little attention from users, while the former requires learning and a fair amount of attention. Similarly, a study of the adoption of agricultural conservation technologies by some American farmers concluded that one of the factors affecting the likelihood of adoption was the perceived complexity of the technology.[53]

Fourth, innovations are more or less adopted on the basis of their "trialability," the extent to which it is possible to institute them on a trial basis . "New ideas which can be tried on the installment plan will generally be adopted more quickly than innovations which are not divisible for trial."[54] Farmers are unlikely to adopt a new variety of seed unless they can sow it in a small portion of their acreage. In a study of California farmers, Steven Polgar and his associates found that a mosquito eradication program was rejected because it could not be instituted gradually.[55]

Finally, the rate of adoption is affected by the communicability of the innovation. The more a potential adopter can observe the effects of the innovation, the more likely he or she is to adopt it. The more an innovation can be easily explained or demonstrated, the more likely it is to be adopted. In some cases, sheer physical distance may inhibit adoption. Thus, in his study of birth control, Frederick Jaffe found that the most important variable affecting the acceptance of family planning was the accessibility of services.[56]

• *Communication Channels*

There are various ways of communicating an innovation to a target population, and the particular way chosen will affect the rate of adoption. Rogers argues that both the purpose of the communication and the nature of the target population must be considered in selecting a channel. If the purpose is to inform, the mass media may be the best channel, for the media allow us to reach a large population both rapidly and efficiently. If the purpose is to persuade, interpersonal channels will be more effective; an individual is more likely to be persuaded by another person than by a newspaper or radio or TV report.

This argument is not wholly valid, because different kinds of communication have been found to influence different kinds of adopters. The mass media are effective in reaching early adopters, while interpersonal channels are more effective in reaching late adopters.[57]

The importance of the mass media and of official kinds of interpersonal influence is highlighted in a study by Harjit Sandhu and Donald Allen of farm modernization in Punjab, India.[58] The researchers administered questionnaires to 495 farmers in 93 villages. Two individual factors were found to be important in the extent to which farmers adopted modern farming technology (use of improved seeds, fertilizers, pesticides, and various kinds of agricultural equipment and tools)—education and land size. Even more important were certain village characteristics, particularly agency help and communication.

Agency help referred to the availability of financial aid and technical advice. The former could be secured through banks, cooperatives, and private sources. The latter came from the Department of Agriculture. Communication was measured by the extent to which farmers did such things as visit agencies, secure agency advice, listen to radio programs about farming, view a film, attend lectures, and read newspapers. There was a strong correlation between participation in these channels of communication and the adoption of innovations. As may be evident, both kinds of channels were used—the mass media and the interpersonal in the form of official personnel. Indeed, it would seem that when rapid diffusion and adoption of innovations is desired, all channels must be used simultaneously and continuously.

• The Social System

As noted above, there are a number of facets of the social system that have been identified as important. We shall look at three: norms, opinion leaders, and change agents. Norms influence the individual's reaction to innovations, and have been found to be even more important than certain individual characteristics. Thus, in a study of modern versus traditional norms m Wisconsin townships, Anne Van den Ban found that township norms were more important in determining whether farmers adopted new ideas than were such factors as the farmers' wealth and education. A farmer in a traditional township was less likely to adopt innovations than one in a modern township, even if the former had higher a level of education and wealth than the latter.[59]

Opinion leaders are another important aspect of the social system that bears upon the fate of innovations. Opinion leaders are able to influence others because of their competence, their conformity to norms, and their status. In other words, opinion leaders have influence independent of their relationship to a particular innovation. When they promote an innovation, therefore, it is more likely to be adopted.

Opinion leaders are not necessarily those who initially adopt an innovation. In one study, farmers indicated that they generally did *not* seek the advice of those who had first adopted a particular innovation. Rather, they spoke with those whose advice they respected on the matter.[60] Moreover, an individual who is an opinion leader in one area is not necessarily a leader in a different area. Rogers pointed out that any individual opinion leader is considered expert in only a few areas. Finally, opinion leaders are more likely than others in the social system to utilize a broad variety of sources of information, to be cosmopolitan in orientation, to have higher levels of social participation, to have higher status, and to be more innovative (although they are not necessarily the innovators).

As the above suggests, opinion leaders can either stimulate or retard the diffusion of an innovation. Much of the research shows how opinion leaders stimulate diffusion. But a study of dentists demonstrated the power of opinion leaders to retard diffusion.[61] The research focused on the diffusion of alloys as gold substitutes in dental restoration. The utility of the alloys was somewhat controversial. The researcher found the rate of adoption in Boston lower than that in the rest of the country. Interestingly, an expert who opposed the use of the alloys lived in Boston. That expert apparently functioned as a "negative" opinion leader, inhibiting the diffusion of the innovation in his area.

The third aspect of the social system we will discuss is the change agent. In contrast to the opinion leader, who is a member of the social system into which the innovation is introduced, the change agent is a professional who attempts to exert the kind of influence defined as desirable by a change agency. The change agent may use an opinion leader within a system in order to facilitate his or her work. Normally, the most intensive efforts of the change agent occur in the early stages of adoption, when the rate of adoption is low.

Rogers provides a good example of effective work by a change agent in his description of aphid control in a Greek village.[62] The case demonstrates some of the important considerations of the agent, including the norms of the system, the people's needs for change, the use of opinion leaders, and the possible consequences of implementing the innovation. In the case, a Greek student was sent by the government to introduce new agricultural ideas in a village. He met the village school teacher on the train, and was introduced by the teacher to other villagers when they arrived at their destination. The student felt that the other villagers were not particularly happy to see him.

One of the first things that struck the student's attention was the large number of aphids on the crops. He asked about them and was told that they were sent by God and were therefore to be accepted. He said nothing more at the time. Eventually he discovered that the teacher was somewhat isolated from most other villagers, so the student struck up a conversation with a shopkeeper. The man had a watermelon patch and was interested in destroying the aphids. As shopkeeper, he was also an opinion leader, and when the application of insecticide solved his problem, he told others to look at his crop. The student let the shopkeeper take over at that point and persuade his fellow villagers to consider using the insecticide. Within a few days, the student was deluged with orders for insecticide.

As Rogers notes, the quick success of the student is a rare phenomenon among change agents. Nevertheless, the principles he employed must be used in any effort to introduce a technological innovation—rapport must be developed with the people; their way of life must be understood and respected; and local leaders must be used when possible (those who are leaders in the true sense of the word, of course, and not merely those who possess power).

• *Time*

Diffusion and adoption are processes. They occur over time. That means, among other things, that different people adopt an innovation at different times. How can we account for this? Rogers classifies adopters into a number of categories: innovators, early adopters, early majority, late majority, and laggards or late adopters.[63] These various categories can be further distinguished along a number of lines.

First, with respect to attitudes, we move from the "scientific and venturesome" attitudes of the innovators to increasingly more conservative attitudes. The late adopters are likely to possess beliefs in magic and folklore. The categories also differ according to educational level, with innovators having the highest level of education as well as the capacity to deal with abstract ideas. Innovators are more cosmopolitan than others, have traveled more widely, and are leaders in organizations. Innovators have a high social status, though some of their own practices may not be generally accepted. Finally, innovators gain their information from technical and scientific sources, and may be scientists themselves. This contrasts with the early adopters, who get information from change agents and written sources; early majority, who get information from farm magazines and friends and neighbors; and late majority and late adopters, who rely primarily on friends and neighbors.

How many people are we talking about in each of these categories? Rogers defines the first 2.5 percent of adopters as innovators, the next 13.5 percent as early adopters, the next 34 percent as early majority and another 34 percent as late majority, and the last 16 percent as laggards or late adopters. The term *laggard* is probably an unfortunate choice, incidentally. Rogers himself recognizes that not every innovation, not even every innovation that is adopted, is beneficial for people. In some cases, then, the laggards may be the only people who are pursuing a healthy course. As we noted earlier, technology is not the Savior, and every technological innovation is not beneficial per se for all people.

• Advances and Modifications

Many of Rogers's propositions, as some of the studies cited indicate, have been supported by subsequent research. There have also been some modifications and advances, however. In particular, researchers have tried to specify more precisely the variables that are important in understanding why an innovation does or does not diffuse through a population.

Dewees and Hawkes, for example, examined technical innovation in the Pacific Coast Trawl Fishery.[64] They note that there is intense competition among commercial fishermen, so that decisions about adopting or rejecting innovations that can affect the size of one's catch may be critical. On the basis of their study, the researchers proposed a model of adoption that includes three sets of variables: personal characteristics, attitudes, and perceived attributes of the innovation. Personal characteristics include age, years of experience and education, size of firm, kinship ties, access to information, degree of cosmopolitanism, and proportion of income gained from fishing. Attitudes include those toward current and anticipated fishing conditions, aversion to risk, difficulty of getting a loan, and financial commitment to fishing. Perceived attributes of the innovation include economic advantage, simplicity, prestige, perceived risk, compatibility, trialability, plasticity, and others.

In addition to specifying the variables, the researchers argue that the variables that are crucial will differ depending on the particular innovation under consideration. To test this, they looked at six technical innovations. As expected, the effects of the variables are different depending on the innovation. For example, cosmopolitanism was positively associated with adoption of two of the innovations, but unrelated to the other four. Perceived prestige of the innovation was positively related to two of the innovations, negatively related to one, and unrelated to the other three. The negative relationship was with a chromoscope, a color video depth recorder that locates fish. The researchers speculate that the fishermen might have been reluctant to adopt the chromoscope in spite of its prestige because its use may have lessened the prestige that they gained from applying their own experience and skill to their trade.

It is important to know whether these results will generalize to other kinds of innovations; that is, whether there is a unique subset of variables that apply to differing innovations. It is also important to continue to search for critical variables. Another personal characteristic, discovered in research on some Western farmers, is skill.[65] The farmers who adopted a conservation innovation were more likely to have the higher degree of mechanical skill that the innovation seemed to require.

Finally, a considerable amount of diffusion research has involved the study of consumer products. A review of this research shows both support of Rogers's work and some advances.[66] For example, with regard to the adoption process, consumer researchers note that the process can take one of two forms: (1) hierarchy of effects model—awareness, knowledge, attitude formation, trial, and adoption; or (2) low-involvement model—awareness, trial, attitude formation, and adoption.

The hierarchy of effects model is more likely to occur where there are high learning requirements on the part of consumers (you may need some training in order to use your new personal computer); high adoption costs (you have to buy software along with your personal computer), and a multiperson adoption decision (the entire family may have to agree that the cost of the personal computer is worth its benefits). The low-involvement adoption model is likely to occur where there is little learning on the part of consumers (you need only turn your new portable, handheld television on and off) and low adoption costs (the television requires no additional equipment).

With regard to personal influence and opinion leadership, consumer researchers have found that personal influence is more likely to occur in the hierarchy of effects process. Negative personal influence (don't buy it) has greater impact on others than positive influence (you should get one of these). Opinion leaders have influence over a limited number of products; that is, different people serve as opinion leaders for different products. The traits that are important in opinion leaders also vary depending on the type of product involved.

With regard to the social system, consumer researchers find that diffusion depends on changes in the society. As norms change over time, the possibility of new products diffusing becomes greater or lesser. For example, women in Europe have come to value time more in recent decades, so that new markets have opened up for time-saving devices. Products will diffuse more rapidly and more completely in a society that is relatively homogeneous.

The diffusion process of products tends to take one of two patterns—the sigmoid (an S-shaped pattern similar to that of Figure 6-1) or the exponential. The exponential pattern is more likely to occur in the low-involvement process described above, along with minimal personal influence, low adoption costs, and low uncertainty about the nature of the innovation. Marketing can affect the rate and maximum penetration of the innovation, but not the pattern.

Consumer researchers have also looked at the personal characteristics of innovators (that is, those who adopt early). Many of the same variables identified by Rogers are important—high income, high education, younger age, greater social mobility, and more willingness to risk. Innovators are also more prone to use information from the mass media.

Finally, with regard to perceived characteristics of the innovation, consumer researchers again find that those identified by Rogers are crucial. In addition, innovations will diffuse more rapidly among those who already have some related knowledge or experience. For example, people who use video games and programmable calculators are quicker to purchase a personal computer.

In sum, our knowledge of the diffusion and adoption of innovations is probably as thorough and valid as any that we have in sociology. There are, however, a number of unanswered questions and problem areas. For example, we need to take more account of conflict and contradictions within social systems. A system does not simply have norms that favor innovation or norms that favor the status quo; systems may contain diverse and contradictory norms because they have diverse groups with contradictory interests. Greater account needs to be taken of social structure in studies of diffusion and adoption. In her study of the rate of adoption of innovative agricultural practices in five villages in India, Sylvia Hale found village power relations crucial.[67] There were considerable differences in the rate of adoption depending upon such factors as caste, size of land holdings, and political affiliation. Similarly, we noted earlier that the telephone diffused more rapidly among rural than urban people in the United States. But it did not diffuse equally among all rural people. Independent, well-to-do farmers adopted it readily, but tenant farmers were slow to adopt.[68] It is not clear why tenant farmers were slower. Perhaps they had different norms, or perhaps the economic or social advantages were not as pertinent to them. In any case, the point is that there are social structural factors, other than the ones typically studied, that are quite significant for understanding rates of diffusion.[69] These factors often involve conflicting interests, so that the innovation that will be advantageous to some will be disadvantageous to others. The same computer that enhances efficiency, profits, and, thereby, the satisfaction and well-being of an executive may enhance the anxiety and isolation of a number of workers. Social systems always contain contradictory elements, and innovations are therefore seldom unmixed blessings.

Contemporary Prepotent Technologies

In this final section, we shall briefly examine three contemporary technologies that are "prepotent,"[70] and we shall point out some of the implications for change in these technologies. The three are *cybernation, social engineering,* and *biological engineering.* The challenge pointed out earlier in this chapter—for people to seize control of technology rather than to allow themselves to become subservient to it—becomes particularly acute in the light of the potential changes that could come about through these three technologies.

Cybernation is the use of technology, particularly computers, to duplicate human functions. Cybernation means that "whole blocks of activity become unnecessary and new ones arise."[71] With cybernation, there is an enormous increase in social alternatives, many of which force us to confront our values. The decisions that must be made are not simply business or engineering but moral decisions. Let us look at just a few examples.

It is now technologically possible to develop a central data storage facility that would provide public access to a wide range of specialized and general information. This could lead to: a greater degree of education taking place in the home; an increased tension between traditional teaching techniques and the technique of programmed instruction; the commercialization of information, with extensive changes in business practices; more sophisticated and powerful techniques for combatting crime; an enhancement of private proficiency in such areas as law and medicine; and so on. On the other hand, the same technology could obviously be used for a different purpose—to create an Orwellian spy system, in which the activities of all citizens were recorded for a centralized enforcement agency.

Cybernation involves many other exciting and challenging as well as threatening possibilities. Artificial intelligence enables us to use computers for medical diagnosis, chemical analysis, various kinds of business problem-solving. Developments in fiber optics mean that your entire financial history can be placed in the small magnetic strip on the back of your bank credit card.[72]

We do not yet know the full impact of something like the computer, but an interesting observation has been made by Sherry Turkle on their effects on the way we think.[73] In her study, Turkle found that the computer is forcing us to rethink the meaning of thinking, feeling, and, indeed, of being human. She found that children who use computers begin to define themselves in different terms from people of previous generations:

> *Before the computer, the animals, mortal though not sentient, seemed our nearest neighbors in the known universe. Computers, with their interactivity, their psychology, with whatever fragments of intelligence they have, now bid for this place. We met children who seemed ready to give it to them. These children defined themselves not with respect to their differences from animals, but by how they differ from computers. Where we once were rational animals, now we are feeling computers, emotional machines.*[74]

The long-term consequences of this development are unknown. But it would appear that the computer is affecting us in ways more subtle than we have realized.

Social engineering, the second of the prepotent technologies, refers to "the systematic application of knowledge and theory about men and institutions to the guidance-transformation-manipulation of men and institutions."[75] Potential for exercising social control could hardly be more clearly stated. In fact, as Karl Mannheim pointed out long ago, the development of our capacity for social engineering requires us to redefine the meaning of human freedom.[76] Mannheim identified three stages in the development of social techniques and said that freedom means something different in each one. In the stage of chance discovery, freedom may be defined in terms of restrictions on responding to stimuli in the environment; individuals are restricted in their freedom when something intrudes upon their response to environmental stimuli. In the stage of invention, humans are involved in conscious modification and direction toward goals, and freedom means the ability to influence the aims of collective action. In the third stage, which Mannheim felt was imminent, humanity will be engaged in conscious planning of relationships, and freedom will consist of free zones within a planned structure.

But even if we are willing to redefine freedom to include only free zones, we are faced with the possible loss of even that bit of liberty by the potential of social engineering. It is possible, of course, that new methods of behavior manipulation will greatly enhance human capacities and performance; it also is possible that they will greatly encourage dehumanizing totalitarian systems. One way of manipulating human behavior is through chemical and electrical technologies. Drugs may be developed that will produce specific personality changes in individuals. Control is also possible via radio stimulation of the brain. These developments could lead to a new hedonism, or new capacities for learning, or control of criminal behavior and deviance, or the creation of socially desirable attitudes and needs. But what is criminal behavior and deviance? What are socially desirable attitudes and needs? Such questions thrust before us the grim possibility of a tyrannical elite performing a social lobotomy in order to create a servile population.

If the above sounds like an updated version of a prophecy of doom, we might reflect upon the subtle ways in which social engineering has already been utilized. For example, an organization may be restructured to achieve higher productivity and better interpersonal relationships.[77] While such goals may seem laudable on the surface, there is a thin line between aiding human growth and manipulating people for other ends—increased productivity, for example. Another way in which social engineering has been employed is in the field of motivation research. Social scientists who work in this area teach their clientele how to sell their products or market their services in the face of apathy or resistance. Closely related is the use of the mass media to create an image of the good life and the meaning of manhood and womanhood and the values we ought to affirm.

Behavioral technology may be at its most effective on a one-to-one or small-group basis. Advocates of neuro-linguistic programming claim that they can cure phobias, resolve lifelong traumas, greatly enhance the power of business people to influence others, and enable lawyers to sway juries and salespeople to sell just about anything to anyone.[78] In essence, neuro-linguistic programming uses psychological principles, including those employed in clinical hypnosis, to "get in sync" with others and thereby influence them. Of course, the influence is unrecognized by the others. And while few would object to using the principles for therapy, is it ethical to use them to sway juries or to sell products or to enhance one's power in the organization?

The last prepotent technology is biological engineering, which is an effort to control the biological self and environment. Advances in biological engineering have raised difficult technical, legal, and ethical questions. For example, plant engineering is an important part of biological engineering. There are some exciting possibilities that can emerge, including disease- and drought-resistant plants. But from a technical point of view, what are the consequences of developing such plants? The way to develop more disease-resistant plants, for example, is to develop higher levels of natural toxins. But those toxins may be carcinogenic to humans, and may, therefore, increase the incidence of cancer. I say "may," because we do not know at this point. It is a difficult technical question, and experts do not agree on the answer.

One of the more dramatic areas of biological engineering involves research on recombinant DNA, which is a way of manipulating the genetic material of individual cells. Recombinant DNA is involved in plant engineering. But it can also be used in animals and humans. It holds the promise of finding cures for a number of chronic diseases and for the various human disabilities that have a genetic basis (such as cystic fibrosis). Some day, gene transplantation may enable parents to free a child of an inherited, debilitating disease. Gene manipulation, however, also raises the possibility of choosing characteristics in our children. Would this result in a new power elite composed of those who could afford to utilize the technology and produce superior offspring? And might a government some day decide to construct particular kinds of people who would be particularly suited for certain social roles? The possibilities boggle the mind.

While some of these possibilities are yet to be realized, there are problems with what we can already do. In fact, Robert Blank argues that the new technologies are forcing us to either confront our health care policies or face a major crisis.[79] He notes that such things as organ transplantation, the treatment of disabled infants, and the use of new reproductive technologies, among others, all pose dilemmas of individual versus social claims. For instance, we can transplant a heart into an adult individual and give that person some more years of life. The cost of the transplant, however, is enormous. Should that individual receive such care in view of the fact that the same amount of money could provide prenantal care to a great many pregnant women who would then give birth to healthier babies? A substantial amount of the health care dollars in this country go to those who are in the later years of their lives. Should some of that money be used instead for prenatal and child care?

The ethical and legal dilemmas of biological engineering have come into public prominence primarily in the area of reproductive technologies. The use of artificial insemination, in vitro fertilization, and surrogate mothers has made the news in a number of cases. One of the well-publicized cases involved "Baby M," who was born after a couple contracted with a young woman in 1985 to conceive a child for them through artificial insemination. The woman was paid $10,000 plus all medical expenses. She had two children of her own and claimed that she wanted to help a childless couple. But after the child was born, the young woman said she had made a terrible mistake and that she would keep the child. Subsequently, court battles and flight by the young woman to another state took place. One problem was that there were no legal or ethical precedents to follow in making a decision.

Less well-publicized, but quite as difficult, are problems surrounding premature births. In the 1960s, only about half of infants born who weighed between 2 pounds, 2 ounces and 3 pounds, 3 ounces survived; by the 1980s, more than 80 percent were surviving.[80] For those between 1.5 pounds and 2 pounds, 2 ounces, the survival rate was less than 10 percent in the 1960s and about 50 percent in the 1980s. The technology enables doctors to save an increasing number of babies who would have died only a few decades ago. But there are some unanticipated problems. A number of the infants go on to have problems such as epilepsy, cerebral palsy, blindness, mental retardation, learning disabilities, and poor motor coordination. To some extent, the problems may be due to the very technology that enabled the babies to survive.

Clearly, biological engineering is raising many difficult questions, and future developments will continue to raise them. Consider, for example, one other possibility—population growth. If such developments as genetic control and creation of artificial organs lead to a superior human, relatively free of disease and enjoying increased longevity, what are the consequences for an already overcrowded earth? The moral and social implications of this prepotent technology are complex and compelling. We have only touched upon the numerous problems it raises.

Although we have been discussing them individually, the three kinds of technology are not mutually exclusive. For example, cybernetic techniques may be employed in social engineering. In one such effort, a computer has been used in psychotherapy.[81] In this experiment, at the University of Wisconsin Medical Center, the computer was used to interview patients by asking them various questions to which they would type out answers on keyboards. The answers were then fed back into the computer. For example, the computer might question the patient (on a small television screen): "Are you feeling anxious, frustrated, tense or nervous?" Patients were also asked to list one or more of their major problems. While the whole process seems to support the notion that our world is increasingly impersonal, the experiment may have benefited some of the patients. At least, in some cases they gave information to the computer that they had not given to human interviewers.

Finally, all three technologies, as much of the above implies, can have both positive and negative consequences. All hold out the promise of better lives. But all can also contribute to human stress. Computerized workplaces can make a business more efficient and effective. But people who work all day at a terminal are likely to have physical discomfort and a certain amount of stress and mental strain.[82] Or consider the distress of someone who learns that his or her biological father was an unknown man who simply contributed his sperm. One woman said that she "felt betrayed, as if her entire life had been some sort of fiction."[83] And what of those who receive organ transplants? Many patients have psychological problems after a transplant, ranging from mild concerns and anxieties to psychotic breaks.[84] The same technologies that heal and give life may also leave a good deal of trauma in their wake. That trauma, in turn, may lead people to make further changes in their lives and their societies.

Technology, then, has always been an important mechanism of change. The wheel, the stirrup, the splitting of the atom, the computer—all have had great impact upon society. Indeed, it is questionable whether the computer has had any greater effects upon the social order of our day than the wheel did upon the social order of antiquity. But there is at least one important difference today: developments are proceeding at an accelerating rate. The pace of technological change leaves us breathless, and the future promises to be even more demanding than the present. Technology will be an increasingly important factor in change and will require numerous agonizing decisions. It will be used to address contradictions in the social order, and will create new contradictions in its wake. It will continue to present us with both the hope of utopia and the threat of devastation. As such, it demands our studied attention.

Endnotes

1. Karl Marx, *The Poverty of Philosophy,* trans. H. Quelch (Chicago: Charles H. Kerr, 1920), p. 119.

2. Thorstein Veblen, *The Theory of Business Enterprise* (New York: Scribner's, 1904), pp. 306, 323, 358.

3. Thorstein Veblen, *The Theory of the Leisure Class* (New York: Mentor Books, 1953), contains the essential elements of his theory of social evolution.

4. Ibid., p. 34.

5. Ibid., p. 133.

6. Don R. Stabile, "Veblen and the Political Economy of Technocracy: The Herald of Technological Revolution Developed an Ideology of 'Scientific' Collectivism," *American Journal of Economics and Sociology* 46 (January, 1987): 35-48.

7. William Fielding Ogburn, *Social Change: With Respect to Culture and Original Nature* (New York: Viking, 1938), pp. 200-201.

8. William Fielding Ogburn, *On Culture and Social Change*, ed. and with an introduction by Otis Dudley Duncan (Chicago: University of Chicago Press, 1964), p. 89.

9. Stanislaw Andrzejewski, "Are Ideas Social Forces?" *American Sociological Review* 14 (1949): 758-63.

10. Marshall McLuhan, *Understanding Media: The Extensions of Man* (New York: Signet Books, 1964), p. viii.

11. William Foote Whyte, *Organizational Behavior: Theory and Application* (Homewood, Ill.: Irwin-Dorsey, 1969), pp. 253-54.

12. T. Scarlett Epstein, *Economic Development and Social Change in South India* (New York: Humanities Press, 1962).

13. Max Lerner, *America as a Civilization* (New York: Simon & Schuster, 1957), p. 227.

14. Emmanuel G. Mesthene, *Technological Change: Its Impact on Man and Society* (Cambridge, Mass.: Harvard University Press, 1970), p. 16.

15. W. F. Cottrell, "Death by Dieselization: A Case Study in the Reaction to Technological Change," *American Sociological Review* 16 (1951): 358-65.

16. See the various case studies in Edward H. Spicer, ed., *Human Problems in Technological Change* (New York: Russell Sage Foundation, 1952).

17. Guy Hunter, *Modernizing Peasant Societies* (New York: Oxford University Press, 1969), p. 145.

18. Mesthene, *Technological Change*, p. 17.

19. Jacques Ellul, *The Technological Society* (New York: Knopf, 1964), p. 128.

20. Theodore Roszak, *The Making of a Counter Culture* (Garden City, N.Y.: Anchor Books, 1969), p. 5.

21. William R. Catton, Jr., "Homo Colossus and the Technological Turn-Around," *Sociological Spectrum* 6 (1986): 121-47.

22. Barbara Ward, *The Rich Nations and the Poor Nations* (New York: Norton, 1962), p. 155.

23 William Fielding Ogburn and Myer F. Nimkoff, *Technology and the Changing Family* (Boston: Houghton Mifflin, 1955).

24. Don Steele and Robert Burchfield, "The Printing Press and Its Consequences, in Paul A. Alcorn, *Social Issues In Technology* (Englewood Cliffs, N.J.: Prentice-Hall, 1986), pp. 35-43.

25. Ibid., p. 38.

26. For a similar example of the manifold ramifications of a new technology, see Francis Allen's discussion of the automobile, in *Technology and Social Change*, ed. Francis R. Allen et al. (New York: Appleton-Century-Crofts, 1957), pp. 107-32.

27. Ralph Linton, "The Tanala of Madagascar," in *The Individual and His Society*, ed. Abram Kardiner (New York: Columbia University Press, 1939), pp. 282-90.

28. See "The Effects of Technology" in *The Futurist*, vol. 5 (December, 1971): 228-29.

29. Lynn White, Jr., *Medieval Technology and Social Change* (New York: Oxford University Press, 1962).
30. Tony Lane, *Grey Dawn Breaking: British Merchant Seafarers in the Late Twentieth Century* (Manchester: Manchester University Press, 1986).
31. William A. Faunce. "Automation in the Automobile Industry: Some Consequences for In-Plant Social Structure," *American Sociological Review* 23 (1958): 401-407.
32. Thomas L. Whisler, *Information Technology and Organizational Change* (Belmont, Calif.: Wadsworth, 1970).
33. Daniel Goleman, "The Electronic Rorschach," *Psychology Today*, February, 1983, p. 41.
34. Reported in *Time*, October 15, 1984, p. 109.
35. Michael C. Robbins and Philip L. Kilbride, "Microtechnology in Rural Buganda," in *Technology and Social Change*, ed. H. Russell Bernard and Pertti Pelto (New York: Macmillan, 1972), p. 203.
36. John G. Burke, "Bursting Boilers and the Federal Power," *Technology and Culture* 7 (1966): 1-23.
37. James Burke, *Connections* (Boston: Little, Brown, 1978), pp. 108-111.
38. William F. Miller, "Emerging Technologies and Their Implications For America," *USA Today*, November, 1986, pp. 61-65.
39. Bronislaw Malinowski, *The Dynamics of Culture Change*, ed. Phyllis M. Kaberry (New Haven: Yale University Press, 1945), p. 19.
40. A. L. Kroeber, *Anthropology* (New York: Harcourt, Brace & Co., 1948), p. 412.
41. Ralph Linton, *The Study of Man* (New York: Appleton-Century Co., 1936), p. 327.
42. Kroeber, *Anthropology*, pp. 478-80.
43. William C. Schaniel, "New Technology and Culture Change in Traditional Societies," *Journal of Economic Issues* 22 (June, 1988): 493-98.
44. D. Eleanor Westney, *Imitation and Innovation: The Transfer of Western Organizational Patterns to Meiji Japan* (Cambridge, Mass.: Harvard University Press, 1987).
45. Ibid., p. 102.
46. Alan R. Beals, *Culture in Process* (New York: Holt, Rinehart & Winston, 1967), p. 215.
47. Everett M. Rogers, *Diffusion of Innovations* (New York: Free Press, 1962). A brief exposition of the major ideas may be found in Everett M. Rogers and Rabel J. Burdge, *Social Change in Rural Societies*, 2nd ed. (New York: Appleton-Century-Crofts, 1972), pp. 349-75.
48. Rogers, *Diffusion of Innovations*, p. 13.
49. Ibid., p. 14.
50. Ibid., pp. 311-14.
51. Claude S. Fischer, "The Revolution in Rural Telephone, 1900-1920," *Journal of Social History* 21 (Fall, 1987): 5-26.
52. Frank Baker and Herbert C. Schulberg, "Community Mental Health Ideology, Dogmatism and Political-Economic Conservatism," *Community Mental Health Journal* 5 (1969): 433-36.

53. Peter J. Nowak, "The Adoption of Agricultural Conservation Technologies; Economic and Diffusion Explanations," *Rural Sociology* 52 (Summer, 1987): 208-20.

54. Rogers and Burdge, *Social Change in Rural Societies,* pp. 353-54.

55. Steven Polgar, Howard Dunphy, and Bruce Cox, "Diffusion and Farming Advice: A Test of Some Current Notions," *Social Forces* 42 (1963): 104-11.

56. Frederick S. Jaffe, "A Strategy for Implementing Family Planning in the United States," *American Journal of Public Health* 58 (1968): 713-25.

57. Jack Rothman, *Planning and Organizing for Social Change* (New York: Columbia University Press, 1974), p. 448.

58. Harjit S. Sandhu and Donald E. Allen, "The Village Influence on Punjabi Farm Modernization," *American Journal of Sociology* 79 (1974): 967-79.

59. Anne Willem Van den Ban, "Locality Group Differences in the Adoption of New Farm Practices," *Rural Sociology* 25 (1960): 308-20.

60. Herbert F. Lionberger and Joe DeFrancis, "Views Held of Innovator and Influence Referents as Sources or Farm Information in a Missouri Community," *Rural Sociology* 34 (1969): 197-211.

61. Dorothy Leonard-Barton, "Experts As Negative Opinion Leaders In the Diffusion of a Technological Innovation," *Journal of Consumer Research* 11 (March, 1985): 914-26.

62. Rogers and Burdge, *Social Change in Rural Societies,* pp. 367-69.

63. This discussion follows the table on page 358 in Rogers and Burdge, *Social Change in Rural Societies.*

64. Christopher M. Dewees and Glenn R. Hawkes, "Technical Innovation in the Pacific Coast Trawl Fishery: The Effects of Fishermen's Characteristics and Perceptions on Adoption Behavior," *Human Organization* 47 (Fall, 1988): 224-34.

65. John E. Carlson and Don A. Dillman, "The Influence of Farmers' Mechanical Skill On the Development and Adoption of a New Agricultural Practice," *Rural Sociology* 53 (Summer, 1988): 235-45.

66. Hubert Gatignon and Thomas S. Robertson, "A Propositional Inventory for New Diffusion Research," *Journal of Consumer Research* 11 (March, 1985): 849-67.

67. Sylvia M. Hale, "Barriers to Free Choice in Development," *Centro Sociale* 22 (Winter, 1975): 89-122.

68. Claude S. Fischer and Glenn R. Carroll, "Telephone and Automobile Diffusion in the United States, 1902-1937," *American Journal of Sociology* 93 (March, 1988): 1153-78.

69. Studies of the diffusion and adoption of innovations in organizations have helped correct this deficiency by demonstrating the importance of such organizational characteristics as size and complexity. See J. Victor Baldridge and Robert A. Burnham, "Organizational Innovation: Individual, Organizational, and Environmental Impacts," *Administrative Science Quarterly* 20 (June, 1975): 165-76.

70. Donald N. Michael, *The Unprepared Society: Planning for a Precarious Future* (New York: Harper & Row, 1968), pp. 37-65.

71. Ibid., p. 42.
72. Miller, "Emerging Technologies," p. 63.
73. Sherry Turkle, *The Second Self: Computers and the Human Spirit* (New York: Simon & Schuster, 1984).
74. Ibid., p. 313.
75. Michael, *The Unprepared Society*, p. 51.
76. Karl Mannheim, *Man and Society in an Age of Reconstruction* (New York: Harcourt, Brace & Co., 1940), pp. 370-81.
77. Rensis Likert, *The Human Organization: Its Management and Value* (New York: McGraw-Hill, 1967).
78. Flo Conway and Jim Siegelman, "The Awesome Power of the Mind-Probers," *Science Digest*, September, 1983, pp. 72-75, 91.
79. Robert H. Blank, *Rationing Medicine* (New York: Columbia University Press, 1988).
80. Edwin Chen, "The Story of Matt," *Los Angeles Times Magazine*, December 7, 1986, pp. 12-14.
81. Reported in *Human Behavior*, March, 1974, pp. 31-32.
82. Gunn Johansson and Gunnar Aronsson, "Stress Reactions in Computerized Administrative Work," *Journal of Occupational Behavior* 5 (July, 1984): 159-81.
83. Lori B. Andrews, "Yours, Mine and Theirs," *Psychology Today*, December, 1984, p. 22.
84. Joann Rodgers, "Life On the Cutting Edge," *Psychology Today*, October, 1984, pp. 58-67.

CHAPTER EIGHT

The Idealistic Perspective

In contrast to the materialistic perspective, the idealistic approach is reflected in Alfred North Whitehead's observation that "a general idea is always a danger to the existing order."[1] Whitehead tried to support his thesis by examining the idea of freedom and showing how that idea has been a historical force for change. Not all ideas, of course, are equally effective. It is particularly the ethical ideals of people that have been "the supreme example of consciously formulated ideas acting as a driving force effecting transitions from social state to social state."[2]

Some theorists, then, have stressed the role of ideas, ideologies, or values in effecting change. This does not necessarily mean that the role of material factors is denied. Nor did the treatment of material factors in the last chapter imply that ideas are of no import. The relationship among material factors, ideas, and social change has been variously conceived, but few, if any, theorists would argue that *either* material factors *or* ideas are wholly the driving mechanisms of change. Our first topic in this chapter, therefore, will be an exploration of the various views on the relationship between materialistic and idealistic forces in change. We shall then examine the way in which ideas effect or affect change, and shall conclude with a look at a few modern prepotent ideologies.

The Materialistic versus the Idealistic Perspective

Are material factors or are ideas more potent in effecting social change? Most thinkers have made neither of these factors completely subservient to the other, but rather have recognized the importance of both. They have, however, emphasized each of the factors differently. Generally, four different positions have been taken: the Marxist, the idealist, the interactionist, and the position of concomitant variation. These positions differ according to the causal weight they give to the two factors.

The Marxist position stresses the ultimate force of material factors. It is important here to emphasize "ultimate," for the Marxist does not neglect the role of ideas. There are many thinkers who battle against "an *imaginary* Marxism, urging against it always the importance of ideological factors that no serious thinker has ever denied."[3] The Marxist method involves the study of human reality, and that study "leads back to thought" when the point of departure has been material factors, whereas one is driven to "social and economic reality when one has begun with the history of ideas."[4] Ideas are important, but the ultimately determining factors of human history are material.

Ideologies are legitimizations of a particular order; they arise out of that order, and they tend to perpetuate it by adorning it with legitimacy. The ideology, then, is part of the superstructure that is erected upon the material base of the society. Nevertheless, as Engels pointed out in one of his letters, elements of the superstructure can react back upon the economic base and thereby influence the course of historical development. Ideas thus acquire, within certain limits, a certain autonomy "and a possibility of reacting . . . on the functioning of the economic base. Man's creative thought, inventing ever more perfect instruments of production, transforms, gradually and indirectly, the general economic structure, all social relations, and, as a result, the whole of human reality."[5]

In essence, the Marxist position is that ideas arise out of social processes but may then become important in further social development. Ideas become potent when they reflect the real needs and interests of the people. Those real needs are rooted in the social and economic conditions in which people live. Thus, ideas arise out of particular social and economic conditions and are necessary to motivate people either to defend or to change those conditions. As Lenin argued, there can be no revolution without a revolutionary theory. In addition, ideas are able to be communicated through space and over time, so that they may influence other societies and the material conditions of those societies.

The idealist position gives ideas a dominant place in change. We have already noted that the "father" of sociology, Auguste Comte, maintained that human history must be understood in terms of "the history of the human mind." Comte, then, was basically an idealist in his approach to change, stressing the achievement of a more humane society through the increasing use of reason.

A modern philosophical approach is that of Whitehead, who tried to show how ideas impel men to change their social order. Whitehead argued that Christianity has provided Western man with a set of ideals that have been of enormous importance in the development of Western civilization. In fact, we may understand human progress in terms of the continual changes effected by human beings in their effort to make the ideals of Christianity practicable for all. But Whitehead also recognized that we are dealing with a case of more-or-less rather than of either-or. For "ideas arise as explanations of customs and they end by founding novel methods and novel institutions."[6] Civilization did not originate in a social contract; people did not come together and agree upon ideas that then shaped the course of history. Rather, the first "effort was the slow introduction of ideas explanatory of modes of behaviour and of inrushes of emotion which already dominated their lives."[7] Ideas did, of course, shape behavior; but practice precedes thought. Thus, Whitehead acknowledged the existential source of ideas but gave primacy to the force of ideas in the evolution of civilization.

Perhaps the most influential advocate and exemplar of the idealist position was Hegel, who conceived of history as the development of Spirit in time. Spirit, according to Hegel, represents the absolute; Spirit is the central principle of all existence. Furthermore, Spirit is a process; its development proceeds by the dialectical process from the "in-itself" of the unconscious stage to the "for-itself" of the conscious stage. This dialectical process involves the continual creation and overcoming of contradictions. An entity creates its opposite and enters into conflict with it. The outcome of the conflict is the partial destruction of both entities, and the creation of a new entity that is larger and more differentiated than the original two, and that incorporates into its own being whatever aspects of the original two had a future.

Thus, in the Hegelian dialectic, contradiction is of the essence. Contradiction is "implicitly present in the original products of Understanding, it becomes explicit when these products break down, and start passing into their complements, or being referred to their correlatives, or growing into more 'concrete' forms, and it is 'preserved' in the result of all such processes."[8]

Furthermore, Hegel held that the dialectic is a universal characteristic of reality. In the *Lesser Logic* he wrote that the dialectic is "the principle of all the movement and of all the activity we find in reality. . . . Everything that surrounds us can be treated as an instance of Dialectic."[9] Hegel understood the dialectic both as a method of inquiry and as a pattern of all being. The dialectic is a mode of thinking and the essence of reality, including our experience of reality.

How does this dialectical development of the Spirit in time relate to concrete history? In simplest terms, individuals and nations become instruments of the Spirit. Spirit comes into being in nature and history; history is "Spirit externalized and emptied into Time."[10] Of particular importance in this process is the state, which is the manifestation of the Divine Idea on Earth. The continuing changes in the state result in progress, for the World Spirit is increasingly incarnate in the activities and organization of the state.

This would imply a justification of the existing state, and Hegel was explicit in arguing the point: "The nation to which is ascribed a moment of the Idea in the form of a natural principle is entrusted with giving complete effect to it in the advance of the self-developing self-consciousness of the world mind."[11] This nation would be dominant, because it was the instrument of the Spirit during a particular epoch. Thus, Hegel's objective idealism merges into a worship of the state. Change is the result of the activity of the Spirit in people and nations and, in particular, in the state; the individual finds fulfillment through participation in that state. Few writers have made humans any more subservient to an intangible despot than Hegel did in his portrait of the dialectical evolution of Spirit.

The third position on the relationship between material and ideal factors is the interactionist. This position argues that there is interaction between ideas and material factors and gives more or less equal weight to each. It is the latter aspect that distinguishes this position from the first two, which also acknowledged interaction, but which gave ultimate or dominant consideration to either material or ideal factors.

An example of an interactionist analysis is David Zaret's study of the rise of liberal-democratic ideology in seventeenth-century England.[12] In contrast to those who have argued that liberal-democratic thought grew naturally out of Protestantism, Zaret shows that liberal-democratic ideas were actually a response to perceived failures in Protestantism. Religious ideology led the Puritans to strive for control of the nation. They gained that control in the revolutionary period of 1640 to 1660, seizing control of Parliament and the army and destroying the authority of the established church.

Once in control, however, the Puritans were plagued by divisions and sectarianism as various groups tried to gain dominance for their own particular version of utopia. The power struggle among the groups created anxiety over doctrines, with the various groups all claiming total allegiance to the one, true, biblically-based faith but differing on their interpretations of that faith. One way that people learned to cope with doctrinal anxiety was by developing greater tolerance for divergent viewpoints. Tolerance, in turn, was supported by a renewed emphasis on reason (where reason means thinking based on secular knowledge). Pluralism and tolerance soon became the underpinnings of a liberal-democratic ideology, which developed as a solution to the problems that had been created by those who wanted to make politics subservient to religion.

Thus, the problems that resulted when people tried to apply their religious ideologies to the governance of the nation led to the emergence of a new ideology. The new ideology gave new directions to people. It created its own problems, of course; the interaction between ideas and material factors is endless.

The fourth position is that of concomitant variation. That is, ideas and material factors change together (though not necessarily simultaneously), and it is not possible to identify any causal relationship. This seems to be Crane Brinton's position with respect to revolution.[13] He notes that ideas are always a part of the prerevolutionary situation. Without ideas, there is no revolution. Nevertheless, this does not mean that the ideas cause the revolution or that a revolution might be nipped in the bud through censorship of ideas. It simply means that ideas are always a part of the set of variables involved in revolutions.

In the prerevolutionary situation, there are always a number of discontents about economic, political, and social conditions. These discontents are sharpened through the articulation of ideals and of means of realizing those ideals. Thus, the uniformity in revolutions is the "*expression* of ideas, rather than particular ideas—which may vary enormously in different revolutions."[14]

This latter point suggests why ideas must be considered in the study of change. Ideas, as Brinton notes, are *always* expressed in the prerevolutionary situation. Whether one takes one or the other of the four positions we have outlined, it is clear that ideas always form a part of the variables involved in change. It is not difficult to understand why. Humans are creatures who must make sense out of the world. All myths, all religion, all science, all ideologies function to make the world meaningful. The primitive may explain an accident by reference to a demon inhabiting the stone over which one tripped, while the modern will explain it by reference to one's inadequate perception of the environment; but both the myth and the science serve the same purpose of making whatever happens have meaning.

It may well be true, therefore, that diverse ideologies may accompany similar patterns of change. This does not mean that ideologies are dispensable elements of change. The fundamental question becomes one of sequence: Does the effort to make sense always follow the behavior, or can the behavior itself be shaped by the effort to make reality meaningful? Unless one accepts the position that ideas and material conditions are only matters of concomitant variation, the sequence of the two factors is a basic problem.

How Ideologies Affect Change

Advocates of each of the four positions outlined above agree that ideas are factors in change. In this section, we shall examine evidence that shows that ideas—or, more particularly, ideologies—are independent variables in change. Although this evidence may not prove any of the four positions discussed, it does show clearly that ideas influence the course of change. However much we may argue about the dominance of ideas as mechanisms of change, we cannot deny that people do act on the basis of ideas.

An interesting illustration of the difference in behavior that results from differing ideologies is provided by Joseph Spengler.[15] He notes that the inhabitants of Lisbon responded in diverse fashion to the catastrophic earthquake of 1775. The king's minister threw himself into the task of rebuilding. Scientists tried to determine natural causes of the disaster. Many of the clergy saw it as divine judgment upon an evil city; they resisted the efforts of the king's minister and tried to use the disaster to herd the people more closely into the realm of clerical authority. In other words, there were differing responses based upon differing ideas about the nature of reality. As Max Lerner put it, "ideas are weapons," and either people may possess the ideas in order to understand and control their existence, or the ideas may possess people "as evil spirits were once said to have entered into witches and possessed them and made them do their bidding."[16]

Granted that ideas or ideologies may be independent variables in change, precisely how do they affect that change? We asked this question with respect to technology and found a variety of ways in which technology affects the course of change. We shall find the same with respect to ideologies. Broadly, ideologies act by preventing, impeding, facilitating, or directing change.

• Ideologies as Impediments or Barriers

Karl Mannheim defined ideologies as those systems of ideas that result in behavior that maintains the existing order. The concept of ideology, he said, reflects the idea that "ruling groups can in their thinking become so intensively interest-bound to a situation that they are simply no longer able to see certain facts which would undermine their sense of domination."[17] We need not restrict ideology to such a definition in order to see the truth of Mannheim's statement.

In particular, a number of religious ideologies have impeded or quelled change. In China, Confucian thought acted as a barrier to change, for it idealized the past. Indeed, it went further and set forth ways to emulate the past in concrete terms and considerable detail. Mencius wrote about the feudal hierarchy and various facets of economic and political institutions that existed in the golden days of old. This meant that the Chinese golden age was different from the Western myth of Eden. For the latter may have provided innocence and peace, but not a viable social structure. The Chinese image of the past was potentially replicable in the present. Unlike the early Christians, the Chinese could do more than decry a lost innocence; they could work to preserve and restore the past.

This is not to suggest, however, that Christianity has generally been a goad to change in the West. On the contrary, Christian thought as often as not has impeded change. During the Middle Ages, the clergy employed religious ideology as a tool to acquire greater power and thereby inhibited certain changes from occurring.[18] Economic progress was retarded by the designation of usury as sinful. Whatever surplus wealth developed tended to be channeled into jewels, courtly activities, and the building of religious edifices and palaces. People focused their energies and their resources on expiating their guilt through the building of religious monuments. In other words, rather than being invested in trade or commercial development, surplus wealth was sucked into nonproductive religious activities that were believed to bring about the favor of God. One result was that by the late Middle Ages techniques for supplying water and sanitation (which had been developed by the Romans) were still not being used. The towns and cities were a conglomerate of numerous, and often lavish, religious buildings, filthy, unplanned streets, and haphazardly built structures that combined to facilitate both religious devotion and disease.

Some would argue that religion is as much a victim as a culprit in this business of impeding change. For example, while women throughout the world have been pressing for equal rights, their progress in Islamic nations is much slower than in other nations. However, "Islam itself does not impose any particular restrictions on labor force activity by women (the Prophet Mohammed's wife was a successful trader), but tradition has tended to impose itself in many Islamic nations."[19] In other words, men in Islamic nations use the religious ideology to keep women in a subservient position. One measure of such subservience is the ratio of girls to boys enrolled in secondary schools. In Islamic nations, the ratio in the 1980s was 58 girls per 100 boys, compared with 83 girls per 100 boys in non-Islamic developing nations and 101 girls per 100 boys in developed nations.[20]

Similarly, while many Muslims venerated the Ayatollah Khomeini, who established Iran as an Islamic state in 1979 and ruled until his death in 1989, others view Khomeini's rule as a corruption of Islam. In an effort to solidify his Islamic state and prevent any deviation, Khomeini ordered the execution of thousands of political opponents, including children. As a prosecutor pointed out, citing Khomeini as his authority: "A nine-year-old girl is considered an adult in Islam. So such a girl is responsible for her acts and can be executed if she tries to war on Allah."[21] "Warring on Allah," of course, simply meant opposing the policies of Khomeini. Prisoners were tortured as well as slain. Strict punishments, such as flogging, amputation, and stoning to death, were established for such crimes against the Islamic state as adultery, alcohol consumption, and theft. Iran became a nation beset by a general campaign of terror. Khomeini himself considered the repressive measures a "necessary surgery" that was needed "to purify Iran," and he called on his followers, especially children, "to watch the activities of everyone around them so that they may become spies of Allah. The country was thus brought under authoritarian rule imposed by violence and maintained by degradation and terror."[22]

Many people, including many Muslims, believed that the Khomeini regime was a corruption rather than a fulfillment of Islam. Nevertheless, the point is that a religious ideology was used to justify a reign of terror that prevented any deviation from the status quo.

One other way in which religious ideology inhibits change is through thought control. The Inquisition, the heresy trials, the insistence on pushing all knowledge into an orthodox framework—these are examples of stringent efforts to control the way people think. The history of science abounds in conflicts with the religious authorities. From the trial of Galileo to the trial of Scopes in Tennessee to more recent court battles over the teaching of evolution in the schools, we may trace a continuing line of struggle.

Thought control has not been confined to religious ideologies. Communists have also worked zealously at the task of reshaping human thought. In Russia, developments in biology lagged behind those of the rest of the world because Soviet biology was dominated by Lysenko from the 1940s to the early 1960s. This Russian biologist convinced political leaders that Lamarckian rather than Mendelian genetics was congruent with Marx's thought. At least one of Russia's world-renowned biologists was banished to Siberia, and Mendelian genetics was labeled as nothing more than a capitalistic myth. The effort to pursue science only within ideologically legitimate bounds led to the atrophy rather than the development of science.

Thus, not only religious ideologies, but ideologies generally, may inhibit change. In the United States, according to some observers, the ideology of equality of opportunity minimizes the development of class consciousness and class antagonisms. To the extent that this is true, the ideology will impede the change that would result from class antagonisms and class conflict.

Certainly, ideologies have developed to impede changes in race relationships. This has been true from the earliest days, when the white settlers of the United States believed themselves superior people (and definitely superior to the natives whom they found in this country). Similarly, when the English first encountered the Africans, they thought that the latter were "puzzling" creatures and they tried to explain why people could be black. One of the explanations was that Negroes were descended from Ham, whom, according to the Bible, God had cursed. In any case, Negroes were clearly different, and just as clearly, to the English, the difference was one that made Negroes inferior.

The caste position of blacks in this country following the Civil War was legitimated (and tended to be perpetuated) by an ideology that contained the themes of blacks as children and as beasts. As John R. Howard puts it:

> *The black-as-child theme suggested that blacks were immature, impulsive, and irresponsible, but nevertheless lovable "in their place." They needed the strong hand of the white to keep them in line as a child needs the authority of the parent. The black-as-beast theme suggested that blacks were brutish, insolent, and lust-ridden and needed the billy club of the sheriff to keep them from continual bouts of drunken violence and the lyncher's rope to keep them from being a threat to whites.*[23]

As Howard notes, these two themes are contradictory. An ideology designed to impede change need not be internally consistent in order to be fully believable to those in power. The theme can be chosen to fit the occasion. If one wishes to resist a law that would give blacks equal employment or educational opportunities, one may draw upon the black-as-child theme. If one wishes to resist a law that would break down segregated housing patterns, one may draw upon the black-as-beast theme. The important thing is not to be consistent but to have ideas available that can justify the existing order and argue against change.

• Ideologies as Facilitators

One might conclude from the above that ideologies in general—and religious ideologies in particular—serve only to retard necessary change. Such a conclusion would be false. Ideologies, including religious ideologies, may also facilitate change. This was Weber's thesis in his study of the Protestant Ethic and the spirit of capitalism.[24]

According to Weber, the development of capitalism was greatly facilitated by a particular strain on Protestant thought. That thought shaped the personalities of the entrepreneurs whose activities were responsible for the flowering of capitalism. We may see this by first understanding what is meant by the "spirit of capitalism": "that attitude which seeks profit rationally and systematically" in a way that is exemplified in the writings of Benjamin Franklin.[25] How did Protestantism, and particularly Calvinism, contribute to this attitude?

Weber pointed to Christian asceticism as the source of the rational, systematic approach that impelled capitalism. A basic element of modern capitalism, "rational conduct on the basis of the idea of the calling," was begotten by Christian asceticism.[26] For in Christian asceticism, the individual is driven by a concern for his or her own spiritual well-being, and can assure himself or herself of a state of grace through ascetic action. Faith was the gift of God, but one was able to prove that one possessed that gift through concrete results—namely, Christian conduct that served to increase the glory of God. Works never enable one to gain salvation, but they are indispensable for demonstrating one's possession of that salvation.

The Christian ascetics, therefore, systematically and rationally ordered their moral life. They agreed that the waste of time was a deadly sin. They avoided any kind of spontaneous enjoyment or self-indulgence. They saw the achievement of wealth as the result of their labor and their labor as the consequence of their calling from God; success was the sign of God's blessing. "When the limitation of consumption is combined with this release of acquisitive activity, the inevitable practical result is obvious: accumulation of capital through ascetic compulsion to save."[27] As John Wesley observed, religion necessarily produces industry and frugality, which, in turn, necessarily produce wealth.

In sum, Christian asceticism produced precisely those character traits that were conducive to the development of capitalism. Economic growth proceeded as a consequence of the pursuit of assurance of salvation. People were motivated to behave in particular ways that happened to be the ways needed for the growth of capitalist economy.

Given the kind of Protestant thought described above, will people invariably behave in a way that leads to economic development? The answer must be "no," because we know of instances where Calvinism did not result in the kind of economic behavior that characterized the Europeans studied by Weber. In his analysis of Afrikaner Calvinism in South Africa, Randall Stokes has shown that the social context in which religion operates is of critical importance.[28] An ideology, in other words, does not have an automatic impact on any social situation. Rather, we must understand the way in which a particular ideology intersects with a particular social context.

Thus, although the Afrikaner Calvinism was virtually identical to the eighteenth-century European Calvinism, the effects of religion in South Africa were the opposite of those in Europe. Afrikaner Calvinism was a conservative rather than an innovative economic force. Stokes explains this in terms of the particular social context in South Africa.

For one thing, the Afrikaners came to regard themselves as a kind of "Chosen People" because of their self-identification with the ancient Israelites and their repeated confrontations with the native black population. This led them to regard themselves as collectively (rather than individually) elect and as compromising a sacred society. In a sacred society, traditional ways are upheld with passion and innovations are always suspect. Consequently, the Afrikaners did not exploit new economic opportunities or accept more modern techniques. Finally, because they regarded themselves as collectively elect, the Afrikaners did not suffer the anxiety about salvation that plagued the Europeans and drove them to achieve success as a mark of their salvation.

Thus, the social context in which Calvinism operated in South Africa led to some modifications. The religious beliefs interacted with the social situation and led to results that were the opposite of the results of the European Calvinism. The same religion can have different effects in differing social contexts.

As it is true that the same religion can have contrary results in different situations, it is also true that different religions can have the same results in different situations. The Protestant Ethic is not peculiar to Protestantism, as it turns out. Elements of that ethic have been found in other religions and the same kind of results attributed to them. Robert Bellah has shown that the Tokugawa religion contained the same elements Weber described in the Protestant Ethic, including admonitions to work hard, to avoid wasting time, and to be thrifty and honest.[29] The Tokugawa era preceded the Meiji Restoration, which led to the rapid modernization of Japan. Bellah argues that Tokugawa religion was an important factor in that modernization, for the religion facilitated rational behavior in the economy and polity by securing commitment to core values of the society, motivating and legitimating political innovations, and promoting an ethic of "inner-worldly asceticism" with an emphasis on diligence and economy.

There are other ways in which religious ideologies have facilitated change. While Confucianism was a conservative force in China, Taoism and Buddhism provided the ideological foundation for many of the peasant revolts that marked Chinese history. In contrast to Confucianism, Taoism stressed spontaneity; Laotzu had "no final faith in any authority but the authority of the heart," and he asserted that those who governed human affairs should "act on instinct and conscience."[30] Buddhism and Christianity were also linked with revolutionary action in China (the latter in the Taiping Rebellion). All three religions were employed to fill the void in human spirits left by Orthodox Confucianism and to justify the rebellion which that same Confucianism found abhorrent. Thus, "history shows ample evidence of the persistent role of religion in political struggles against ruling dynasties."[31]

Finally, although it is true that religious activities have frequently diverted resources that might have been used to enhance the material well-being of people, there is another side to the story. Von Der Mehden has pointed out a number of ways in which religious ideologies in Southeast Asia have led people to act in ways that have resulted in material as well as spiritual benefits.[32]

First, the demand to meet religious obligations encourages an entrepreneurial spirit among some people. "There is evidence that some elements of the population are encouraged to increase their income in order to be able to expand their religious giving and that the high costs of some religious observances lead to pressure to produce new income."[33] In addition, people can use feasts and other religious activities to broaden their contacts beyond the local area and enhance their economic and social status.

Second, religious leaders do not confine their activities to the purely spiritual. The mosque, wat, and church are used for community purposes. Particularly in Thailand and the Philippines, an increasing number of religious leaders have gotten involved in community development projects. The leaders see such activity as a natural extension of their spiritual commitment.

Third, religious symbols can be powerful tools for mobilizing people. Religious nationalism has been used to gain mass support against colonial governments. Once nations gained their independence, political leaders used religious themes to encourage development. The people were told that they were living out and protecting their religious faiths through economic development of the nation.

At this point, the question of religious ideology and social change may appear confusing. We have seen that a particular religion can impede some kinds of change and impel others. How can these divergent effects of religious ideologies be explained? In his examination of the relationship between religious orientation and civil rights militancy, Gary Marx found the same disparity and suggested an answer to it. He notes that the net effect of religion was to inhibit change by minimizing protest attitudes; at the same time, he found many religious people to be militant. Marx suggests that this can be understood in terms of the multiplicity of themes of any religious perspective, some of which are in tension if not contradiction. One strand of Christianity is the afterlife and acceptance of one's lot in this life, but another strand is the realization of religious values in this life.[34]

Recent study of other religions supports this idea of multiple strands of thought that offer people diverse ideological positions and diverse patterns of behavior. Within Hinduism, for example, there are a number of value systems; a comparison of Brahmans and the other castes will reveal a good deal of difference in values.

In addition to the multiple strands of thought in all religions. we may briefly note three other reasons why religion facilitates or impedes change. One is that some directions of change are congruent with the existing religious ideology—a number of scholars have argued that Christianity provided the value basis upon which modern science developed (in spite of the numerous historical conflicts between the two). A second reason is that religion changes over time; the relationship between religious ideology and a particular kind of change may be dialectical. Change, then, proceeds out of the context of ongoing resolution of the contradictions between religious ideology and social reality.

Finally, there is the reason articulated by Stokes in his study of Afrikaner Calvinism—the effects of religious beliefs will vary depending upon the social context. People construct their behavior on the basis of the interaction between their beliefs and their social situation. Consequently, religious beliefs that facilitate innovative behavior in one situation will facilitate traditional, conservative behavior in another situation.

Religious ideologies are not, of course, the only kind of ideologies that facilitate change. Economic and political ideologies are also important, perhaps more so than religion in the contemporary world. In particular, the ideology of nationalism is of central significance in the contemporary world. We will reserve discussion of this ideology, however, for the last section of the chapter. Here, we will briefly note the way in which ideology worked hand-in-hand with technological change in the United States during the nineteenth-century.[35] In the early part of the century, there was a growing emphasis on democracy and a firm belief in progress. The ideology of progress through democracy also included the notion that science and technology would enable us to construct a more democratic society and, thereby, to facilitate progress.

There are a number of examples of individuals who used this ideology to gain support for their work. For instance, Robert Fulton sought government support for his canal plans and for certain military innovations. He argued that the canals would make the nation an economic and social unity and would enhance and secure the benefits of republican institutions. He also argued that his new military weapons—the submarine and torpedoes—would enable us both to defend and to extend our democratic way of government.

It was argued by others that not only do science and technology lead to democracy and progress, but the latter are necessary for development of the former. We cannot make technological progress, it was said, unless we have the equality and liberty of a democratic society. Consequently, the ideology facilitated the rapid advances in nineteenth-century technology. This occurred in the face of serious problems and conflict in Europe that resulted from the introduction of new technology. Americans heard of strikes, of riots against the machines, and of the wretchedness of life for the factory workers—men, women, and children. The ideology, however, convinced Americans that those problems would not occur in this country. Rather, they believed that technology would enable them to strengthen and spread their democratic way of life, with its attendant blessings and progress. Technological progress was rapid, therefore, even in the face of evidence from Europe that there could be extremely undesirable results. The ideology facilitated the unhindered development of mechanical technology.

At this point, we shall look a little further into the ways ideology can facilitate change. We have seen evidence that it does facilitate change, but precisely how does it affect the direction of change? There are at least five ways.

First, ideology may legitimate the new direction. It does this both by disrupting the old order and by explaining and validating the emerging new order. In other words, the ideology endows the new order with authority. In the United States, the generation of businessmen known as the "robber barons" legitimated their activity through the ideology of social Darwinism. This suggests that an ideology may promote authority to the extent of justifying vicious behavior. As Lewis Coser has pointed out, when people engage in conflict as the representatives of groups and battle for the ideals of those groups rather than for self-interest, the conflict is "likely to be more radical and merciless than those that are fought for personal reasons."[36] We need only remind ourselves of the Nazi effort to purge Germany of every "undesirable" and inferior element to understand the truth of this statement.

An interesting illustration of the way in which ideology legitimates a new direction is provided by David Swift in his study of the ideology of progressive education. One problem confronting the public school is autonomy; the problem was significant by 1920, when a variety of changes in the nation led to the possibility of greater public interference in the schools. Public interference could mean action contrary to the wishes of school administrators. To counter this threat, the schools adopted techniques that had spread throughout the business world—methods of human relations. Certain administrators devoted considerable time to public relations in order to gain public support for policies and financial needs without losing autonomy. Progressive education ideology included an emphasis on community-centered education, resulting in considerable school-community communication. Thus, "public relations did not have to remain a marginal activity, operating in the shadows, but instead became a legitimate and even mandatory aspect of the school's program."[37] The public could be not only informed, but propagandized; and all was legitimate because of the ideology of progressive education.

A second way in which ideology facilitates change is by legitimating or directing behavior that leads to unanticipated change. This was the character of the Protestant Ethic in the development of capitalism. Economic growth was an unanticipated result of religious devotion. A similar effect of ideology has been pointed out by Philip Selznick in his study of the Tennessee Valley Authority. The TVA was set up to implement a grass-roots ideology; the administration was to have freedom to make decisions independent of centralized control, and the people of the area were to participate in the decision-making process. The ideology made administrative discretion a legitimate activity; but the administrative discretion, as Selznick shows, led to some unanticipated changes in the character of the organization.[38]

A third way in which ideology facilitates change is by providing a basis for solidarity. Ideologies can be integrative mechanisms, neutralizing the conflicting strains that are found in most societies, indeed in most groups of any size. Certainly, Islam provided such a basis for solidarity in Khomeini's Iran, leading to massive support for the regime in spite of its terrorist policies. On a smaller scale, ideology has been the basis of solidarity in many of the utopian groups established throughout history. Utopian groups have generally faced severe economic challenges and frequently have encountered opposition from the larger society. Why do people stay in such groups in the face of such pressures? The ideologies help create a sense of solidarity and purpose that enables them to withstand the pressures. For example, one of the largest American utopian groups was the Shakers, who arrived in this country just before the Revolutionary War. The Shakers were initially greeted with considerable suspicion and opposition because of their celibacy (which was considered unnatural) and their pacifism (which was considered unpatriotic). But the Shaker ideology told the members that they alone followed the way of Christ, and that they must endure in order to achieve salvation. Many not only endured, but found their lives extremely meaningful. "Again and again, individual writers exulted in the virtues of celibacy and the glory of the Shaker way of life. When one was asked whether he found Shaker life monotonous, he replied: 'Nay, it is peaceful and we are bound together by brotherly and sisterly love. This is an earthly heaven. I could live here forever.'"[39]

A fourth way that ideology facilitates change is through its power to motivate individuals. A common problem of the developing nations of the world involves convincing the masses that development is possible, that there is purpose to human existence, and that self-sacrifice is a small price to pay for the rewards that shall be theirs in the future. Ideology enters at this point and becomes a tool of the modernizing elite, but this function of ideology is not limited to the developing nations. Those who participate in social movements in the developed nations are also motivated by ideology. The ideology of a movement often "includes a concept of personal power and control over one's own destiny or the destiny of the world."[40] To the extent that ideology can infuse members of a movement with the passion to believe and act, the ideology is likely to facilitate the change that is the aim of the movement. And when the movement cannot succeed in spite of all efforts, an ideology can motivate members to such extreme forms of behavior as mass suicide. In the late seventeenth and early eighteenth centuries, tens of thousands of "Old Believers" in Russia committed suicide. In 1978, 911 followers of the American minister Jim Jones committed suicide in Jonestown. In both cases, the believers had problems dealing with the tension between a desire to violently confront what they regarded as a demonic state and a wish to create a communal refuge where they could live out the tenets of their faith.[41] And in both cases, the power of ideology to motivate was demonstrated with gory drama.

The fifth and final way in which ideology facilitates change is by confronting a society with a contradiction. As mentioned above with respect to religious ideologies, there can be a clear contradiction between ideology and reality that impels people to act in order to resolve the contradiction. One of the problems of the developing nations is the fact that ideology has often surged too far ahead of reality. There is, for example, often a commitment to universal education, which is unrealistic in terms of economic resources and limited need for a highly educated citizenry. The gap between the ideology—the right of all people to be educated—and the reality—the underdeveloped economy—can create a revolutionary situation.

Of course all societies have their gaps between reality and ideology. The gap may be rationalized or explained away—particularly by those who have everything to gain by keeping things as they are. If we glance briefly at social movements again, however, we find that movement ideologies will generally reject this gap as illegitimate. The ideology of the social movement refuses to allow the society to ignore the gap between the societal ideology and reality. Movement ideology is a relentless message of judgment against the larger society, and, thereby, a continual prod to action for movement members.

• *Ideologies as Directing Mechanisms*

One other way in which ideology affects change is by giving direction, derived from the specifics or logic of the ideology, to that change. Many of the developments in the United States can be related to the ideology that technology will resolve all problems. Rather than in prayer or magic or dependence upon charismatic leaders, Americans have been prone to seek their social salvation in technology. Thus, the way to deal with the problem of war and peace is to ensure our superiority in military technology. The American commitment to this technology has resulted in the arms race that all past history indicates can only end in war; but to many Americans, it is a guarantee of peace. The pursuit of military technology leaves few resources or energies available for considering alternative solutions to the problem of war and peace.

Of course, it is not only in the United States that the ideology of military technology prevails. Global military spending in the 1980s amounted to hundreds of billions of dollars, more than four times the amount that was being spent at the end of World War II.[42] Tens of millions of people, including about 20 percent of the world's scientists and engineers, did work related in some way to the military. And among the twenty countries with the largest foreign debt, arms imports accounted for 20 percent or more of their increase in debt. Clearly, ideologies have the power to motivate and to legitimate specific kinds of behavior.

On a broader scale, Fred Polak has argued extensively that the image of the future that prevails in any society will direct the course of change in that society. A similar point was made earlier by Mannheim. As noted above, Mannheim defined ideology as a system of ideas that maintains the existing order, but he recognized that a system of ideas can also initiate change in the existing order. He called the latter utopia rather than ideology, and said that utopian thinking is "incongruous with the state of reality within which it occurs" and tends "to bust the bonds of the existing order."[43]

According to Polak, the future may be shown to be the cause of present behavior in both a positive and a negative sense. In the positive sense, the image of the future functions to direct present behavior in accord with specific values. That is, members of a society are "magnetically *pulled* towards a future fulfillment of their own preceding and prevailing, idealistic images of the future, as well as being pushed from behind by their own realistic past ."[44] In a negative sense, the lack of an image of the future implies, in Spengler's terms, happened history rather than willed history.

Polak argues that there is a modern aversion to images of the future, with the result that humans are left "standing at the edge of a bottomless abyss, facing death, destruction, chaos."[45] Those who speak about the decline of our culture, he argues, have failed to identify the "torn and still" images of the future that characterize our age. These broken and rejected images are the "gaping wound from which the lifeblood of the culture is draining away."[46]

Polak devotes considerable attention to delineating various images of the future—those of ancient Greece, ancient Israel, ancient Christianity, modern socialism and Marxism, numerous utopian writers, and others—and relating these images of the future to directions of change. With respect to Israel, for example, we must ask how that particular, small group of nomadic people, who were only a minute part of the Arabian Bedouin tribes, attained such great importance in history. The answer is to be found in Israel's "immortal" image of the future. Israel's image has an imperishable quality to it, involving "the full flowering of human dignity and an indirect *influence-optimism* [as] the common features of all the variations of the *one basic image of the future: the image of a salvation to come through Israel, to Israel, and out of Israel.*"[47]

One of the more striking examples of ideology-directed change in the contemporary world is China. Ideology was employed to mobilize the people during the Great Leap Forward of 1958-1960. This was an effort to attain quick and massive economic growth by decentralizing and mobilizing the masses in intensive work. It was clearly a case of "ideological economics"; the direction of change attempted (decentralization, development of communes in urban as well as rural areas, and the commitment of the masses to the effort) flowed from the logic of Maoist ideology.[48]

Likewise, the changes effected by the Great Proletarian Cultural Revolution in the late 1960s were directed by ideology. In fact, the revolution was defined by the Central Committee of the Communist Party as an ideological struggle:

> *Although the bourgeoisie has been overthrown, it is still trying to use the old ideas, culture, customs and habits of the exploiting classes to corrupt the masses, capture their minds and endeavour to stage a comeback. The proletariat must do the exact opposite: it must meet head-on every challenge of the bourgeoisie in the ideological field and use the new ideas, culture, customs and habits of the proletariat to change the mental outlook of the whole of society. . . . The aim of the Great Proletarian Cultural Revolution is to revolutionize people's ideology and as a consequence to achieve greater, faster, better and more economical results in all fields of work.*[49]

Maoist ideology directed the revolt against the bureaucratic tendencies and bourgeois thinking that had crept into Chinese life. Art, education, and other aspects of Chinese society were brought into greater accord with the thought of Mao.

The importance of ideology in directing change in China is also demonstrated in Lee's study of technical innovation in Chinese industry from 1949 to 1971.[50] Lee points out that while technical innovation is normally a function of technical and managerial elites in the industrial nations, it is a responsibility of the workers in China. Mao's ideology stresses worker participation, and makes technology, along with everything else, subservient to political considerations. In particular, argues Lee, there are three assumptions in the ideology that facilitate this approach. First, it is assumed that the relationships of the factory were totally altered by the 1949 communist assumption of power. From that point on, workers became the masters rather than the slaves of their machines. Second, valid scientific theories are rooted in practical experience, and particularly in experience in the productive process. Third, it is assumed that China must follow its own unique path of development rather than try to imitate others, including both the capitalist nations and the Soviet Union.

Within a few years after the communist takeover, then, workers were being encouraged to be innovators, to come up with ideas for technical improvement. As masters of their machines, workers must accept some of the responsibility for technical innovation. By early 1955, this ideology had not yielded the expected results. It was set aside temporarily and a new policy was laid down—namely, the Chinese would try to learn from the Soviet experience, utilize their own practices where proven effective, and seek help from the masses in rationalizing production. The latter point showed that Mao's emphasis on worker participation was not entirely abandoned. However, the desired contribution at this point was largely of a nontechnical nature.

In the Great Leap Forward, there was a return to the principle of worker participation in technical innovation. Foreign (i.e., Soviet) technology would no longer be accepted uncritically as good for China. Rather, China would have to walk on two legs—she would have to make use both of foreign and of indigenous methods in attaining the desired industrial growth. Unfortunately, the Great Leap Forward soon appeared to be an economic disaster, and there was another retreat from emphasizing mass participation in the industrial process. The retreat did not last long. By 1964, Mao was calling for a great movement of the masses in order to revolutionize industrial work. Technicians were ordered to plunge into the actual work process, to identify with the workers, to study closely various experiences with production, and to validate all of their plans by their actual consequences. Thus, Mao's "mass line" and his insistence that theory must be rooted in praxis guided technical and industrial processes. Throughout the period, politics was in command, which is to say that ideology directed the nature of technical and industrial planning.

That ideology continued to be an important directing mechanism in post-Maoist China, and that the Chinese leaders continued to consciously use it as such, is illustrated by a 1986 article by Liu Wusheng in which he reviewed statements of the Communist Party's Central Committee on matters of culture, ideology, and development.[51] The Party consistently affirmed that culture and ideology permeate and promote each other. "Ideological education in the Party is the main pillar of the building of culture and ideology in the whole society, and Party members should, first of all, play an exemplary role ideologically and morally."[52] Economic development is crucial, but it is also crucial, according to the leaders, that economic development be guided by the correct ideology.

Modern Prepotent Ideologies

What are the ideologies that are exercising the greatest influence in the contemporary world? In the past, religious ideologies, the ideology of progress, and various political and economic ideologies have been important. In the contemporary world, the most potent ideologies are nationalism, various types of socialism and communism, and some religious ideologies, particularly Islam. This is not to say that others are unimportant. In the United States, the ideology of "free enterprise" is a factor in the ongoing conflict over the resolution of various social problems. But the ideologies most commonly used to promote and direct change are nationalism, socialism, Marxism, and Islam and other religions. As we shall see, these are not independent ideologies. Nationalism is often linked with one of the other ideologies in various Third World countries. The primary concern of Third World leaders following independence "has been to find political paths and ideologies that are appropriate for their countries," and religion has frequently served as a support for nationalism.[53] In essence, leaders have used socialist, Marxist, and religious ideas to secure national independence and to mobilize the citizenry in the work of nation-building.

Nationalism is a relatively modern phenomenon. The first truly nationalistic movements were the American and French revolutions of the eighteenth century. For in essence, by nationalism we mean "an ideological movement to attain and maintain an autonomy and individuality for a group conceived by some of its members to constitute an actual or potential nation, a movement with a specific doctrine and unique vision of the world, a movement based upon a myth of historical renewal and communal self-discovery."[54] As such, nationalism has been the ideology at the basis of numerous modern revolutions.

Nationalism has been important to all industrializing nations. One of the first great issues in Meiji Japan was that of national unification. The slogan, "Revere the Emperor, Oust the Barbarian" typified the nationalistic hue that characterized the modernization of Japan. In most of the developing nations today, nationalism is linked with some form of socialism. Contemporary ideologies tend to be politico-economic in nature, stressing an indigenous form of economic development that avoids the deficiencies of both the American and the Soviet patterns. With few exceptions, nationalist leaders reject the capitalist and the communist methods of development (as represented by the United States and the Soviet Union).

The content of modern nationalistic ideologies varies greatly. Perhaps the only common element is the idea of "the establishment of a fully secular area of life regulated by a social institution before which all men are at least in certain public senses equal."[55] This rather abstract core allows for considerable diversity in content. In fact, rightist as well as leftist ideologies have been linked with nationalism. Fascist movements such as Nazism have had nationalist aspects in their ideologies, and have played upon nationalist sentiment to gain support.

Thus, nationalism can give a vitality to movements of contradictory political orientations. Nationalism per se demands no particular political orientation other than the unification of a people.

As we noted earlier, one way in which ideology facilitates change is by creating solidarity. The nationalistic ideologies have the creation of an integrated society as one of their most important functions. Developing nations may proceed by divergent paths, but certain tools and resources seem necessary to any path. Among others, one prerequisite for development is the "ideological integration of leaders and followers."[56] Nationalism facilitates that integration, for it tends to generate solidarity and to legitimate the centralization of power.

When nationalism is linked with religion, its power to generate solidarity and to legitimate power is even greater. The power of religion to unify and direct a people is particularly evident in those nations that have officially declared Islam to be the guide for government policy and for law and order.

It is important to keep the resurgence of Islam in historical perspective. That is, during the time of colonial occupation "the Muslim identity was explicitly under assault. Whether their countries were protectorates or full colonies, Muslims were generally reduced to second-class citizenship, pushed off arable land for foreign settlement programs and denied access to educational opportunity."[57] Thus, literacy in North Africa during the 1950s ranged from 4 percent in Algeria to 13 percent in Morocco and Tunisia. The French forbade the natives in their colonies to gather without permission or even to travel freely within the country. And for years, Muslims could not gain full French citizenship without renouncing their faith.

In this context of oppression, Islam was a ready tool to be used against the colonial masters. Religion became a unifying symbol in the struggle for independence. Revolution was defined as a holy war against infidels. Muslim traditions, such as the veiling of women, were reaffirmed in some nations where the colonial masters had tried to eradicate the practice. For example, the French attempted to unveil the women in Algeria. During the revolution of 1954, Algerian men attempted to remove their women from contact with the French. After the revolution, the veiled woman remained as a symbol of Algerian national autonomy.[58] Unfortunately, that meant that Algerian women lost some of the economic, educational, and family rights that the French had tried to give them.

In the 1970s, Islamic activity intensified and Islam "displaced nationalism and socialism as the dominant factor in the ideology and politics of Middle East regimes and opposition movements."[59] The Islamic activists of the 1970s and 1980s operated in the context of five core beliefs:[60]

1. Islam is a total way of life, a guide for all political, legal, and social activity in society;
2. Muslim nations have failed by abandoning their commitment to Islam as a total way of life and by trying to imitate Western ways;
3. Renewal demands a revolution guided by the Koran;
4. To reestablish the rule of God, it is necessary to replace Western-type laws with Islamic law;
5. Although Western society is to be condemned, modernization is acceptable, though even science and technology must always be subservient to Islam.

Wherever these principles have been followed, the resulting state has been patriarchal. As in Algeria, women have been subordinated to men in spite of the worldwide Women's Movement. Iran serves as a dramatic example following the 1979 revolution that removed the Shah and established the Islamic state.[61] The Family Protection Act of 1975, which had attempted to protect women from arbitrary divorce and polygamy, was nullified. Woman's role, the new leaders declared, was to raise her family and be a "pillar" in the Muslim home. The minimum age for legal marriage for women was reduced from 16 to 13. Schools and beaches were segregated by sex. Women singers were banned from the radio. Women judges were removed. All women who worked were required to dress modestly.

Similar restrictions have been imposed on women in other countries where Islam became the guide for national law and policies. In the mid-1970s, for instance, only 11 percent of Algerian and 9 percent of Saudi Arabian females of secondary school age were enrolled in schools. The participation rate of females in the labor force in a number of Middle Eastern countries is less than 3 percent of the adult female population. This low participation rate requires the import of foreign workers in order to provide essential services for these nations.

In sum, Islam is a powerful ideology in the contemporary world. Those who advocate it as a total way of life are engaged in activities designed to transform whole nations. Extremists in some predominantly Muslim nations, such as Egypt, have repeatedly sought to overthrow the government and establish an Islamic state similar to that created by Khomeini in Iran in 1979, even though the current governments pay at least token homage to Islam. For the extremist, token homage is akin to betrayal. The true believer, the person who is thoroughly committed to a particular ideology, will pursue a course of action dictated by that ideology with fervor, and will attempt to mold the world into a new image.

Endnotes

1. Alfred North Whitehead, *Adventures of Ideas* (New York: Mentor Books, 1933), p. 22.
2. Ibid., p. 25.
3. Lucien Goldman, *The Human Sciences & Philosophy*, trans. Hayden V. White and Robert Anchor (London: Jonathan Cape, 1969), pp. 86-87.
4. Ibid., p. 62.
5. A. Schaff, 'The Marxist Theory of Social Development," in *Readings in Social Evolution and Development*, ed. S. N. Eisenstadt (Oxford: Pergamon Press, 1970), p.82.
6. Whitehead, *Adventures of Ideas*, p. 106.
7. Ibid., p. 114.
8. J. N. Findlay, *Hegel: A Re-Examination* (London: George Allen and Unwin, 1958), p. 63.
9. Quoted in Ibid., p. 65.
10. G. W. F. Hegel, *The Phenomenology of Mind*, trans. J. B. Baillie (New York: Harper & Row, 1967), p. 807.
11. G. W. F. Hegel, *Philosophy of Right*, trans. T. M. Knox (London: Oxford University Press, 1953), p. 217.
12. David Zaret, "Religion and the Rise of Liberal-Democratic Ideology in 17th-Century England," *American Sociological Review* 54 (April, 1989): 163-79.
13. Crane Brinton, *The Anatomy of Revolution* (New York: Prentice-Hall, 1952), p. 53.
14. Ibid.
15. Joseph J. Spengler, "Theory, Ideology, Non-Economic Values, and Politico-Economic Development," in *Tradition, Values, and Socio-Economic Development*, ed. Ralph Braibanti and Joseph Spengler (Durham, N.C.: Duke University Press, 1961), pp. 7-8.
16. Max Lerner, *Ideas Are Weapons* (New York: Viking, 1939), p. 3.
17. Karl Mannheim, *Ideology and Utopia*, trans. Louis Wirth and Edward Shils (New York: Harcourt, Brace & World, 1936), p. 40.
18. This paragraph follows Richard T. LaPiere, *Social Change* (New York: McGraw-Hill, 1965), pp. 305-306.
19. John R. Weeks, "The Demography of Islamic Nations," *Population Bulletin* 43 (December, 1988): 26.
20. Ibid., p. 26.
21. Quoted in Alan R. Taylor, *The Islamic Question In Middle East Politics* (Boulder, Colo.: Westview Press, 1988), p. 106.
22. Ibid., p. 107.

23. John R. Howard, *The Cutting Edge* (Philadelphia: Lippincott, 1974), p. 20.

24. Weber's thesis has been subjected to considerable debate. See S. N. Eisenstadt, ed., *The Protestant Ethic and Modernization* (New York: Basic Books, 1968).

25. Max Weber, *The Protestant Ethic and the Spirit of Capitalism*, trans. Talcott Parsons (New York: Scribner's, 1958), p. 64.

26. Ibid., p. 180.

27. Ibid., p. 172.

28. Randall G. Stokes, "Afrikaner Calvinism and Economic Action: The Weberian Thesis in South Africa," *American Journal of Sociology* 81 (1975): 62-81.

29. Robert N. Bellah, *Tokugawa Religion* (New York: Free Press, 1957).

30. Witter Bynner, *The Way of Life According to Laotzu* (New York: John Day Co., 1944), p. 19.

31. C. K. Yang, *Religion in Chinese Society* (Berkeley: University of California Press, 1961), p. 218.

32. Fred R. Von Der Mehden, *Religion and Modernization in Southeast Asia* (Syracuse, N.Y.: Syracuse University Press, 1986).

33. Ibid., p. 200.

34. Gary T. Marx, *Protest and Prejudice* (New York: Harper & Row, 1967), p. 104. See pp. 94-105.

35. Hugo A. Meier, "The Ideology of Technology," in *Technology and Social Change in America*, ed. Edwin T. Layton, Jr. (New York: Harper & Row, 1973), pp. 79-97.

36. Lewis Coser, *The Functions of Social Conflict* (New York: Free Press, 1956), p. 118.

37. David W. Swift, *Ideology and Change in the Public Schools* (Columbus, Ohio: Charles E. Merrill, 1971), p. 123.

38. Philip Selznick, *TVA and the Grass Roots* (New York: Harper & Row, 1966), pp. 262-64.

39. Robert H. Lauer and Jeanette C. Lauer, *The Spirit and the Flesh: Sex in Utopian Communities* (Metuchen, N.J.: Scarecrow Press, 1983), p. 181.

40. Luther P. Gerlach and Virginia H. Hine, *People, Power, Change: Movements of Social Transformation* (Indianapolis: Bobbs-Merrill, 1970), p. 163.

41. Thomas Robbins, "Religious Mass Suicide Before Jonestown: The Russian Old Believers," *Sociological Analysis* 47 (Spring, 1986): 1-20.

42. The figures in this paragraph are from "Perspective," *U N Chronicle* 22 (1985): v.

43. Mannheim, *Ideology and Utopia*, pp. 192, 193.

44. Fred L. Polak, *The Image of the Future*, vol. 1 (New York: Oceana Publications, 1961), p. 15.

45. Ibid., vol. 2, p. 14.

46. Ibid.

47. Ibid., vol. 1, p. 132.

48. A brief description of the Great Leap Forward may be found in Franz Schurmann and Orville Schell, eds., *Communist China* (New York: Vintage Books, 1967), pp. 401-16.

49. From the August 8, 1966 "Decision of the Central Committee of The Chinese Communist Party Concerning the Great Proletarian Cultural Revolution," in Joan Robinson, *The Cultural Revolution in China* (London: Penguin, 1970), pp. 85, 95. This book is a good and brief summary of the Revolution.

50. Rensselaer W. Lee, III, "Ideology and Technical Innovation in Chinese Industry, 1949-1971," *Asian Survey* 12 (1972): 647-61.

51. Liu Wusheng, "'Socialist Culture & Ideology': Its Development," *Beijing Review*, November 10, 1986, pp. 17-18.

52. Ibid., p. 17.

53. Jacqueline A. Braneboy-Wagner, *Interpreting the Third World* (New York: Praeger, 1986), p. 40.

54. Anthony D. Smith, "Nationalism: A Trend Report and Bibliography," *Current Sociology* 21 (1973): 104.

55. K. M. Silvert, ed., *Expectant Peoples: Nationalism and Development* (New York: Random House, 1963), p. 19.

56. Leonard Binder, "Ideology and Political Development," in *Modernization: The Dynamics of Growth*, ed. Myron Weiner (New York: Basic Books, 1966), p. 204.

57. Susan E. Marshall, "Paradoxes of Change: Culture Crisis, Islamic Revival, and the Reactivation of Patriarchy," *Journal of Asian and African Studies* 19 (Nos. 1-2, 1984): 4.

58. Peter R. Knauss, *The Persistence of Patriarchy: Class, Gender, and Ideology in Twentieth-Century Algeria* (New York: Praeger, 1987).

59. John L. Esposito, "Islam in the Politics of the Middle East," *Current History* 85 (February, 1986): 55.

60. Ibid., p. 54.

61. These two paragraphs follow Marshall, "Paradoxes of Change," pp. 8-9.

CHAPTER NINE

Conflict: From Competition to Violence

People make history, but we never act in a vacuum; the history we make always occurs in the context of interaction with other people. Homo sapiens is a social animal, whose existence is fashioned in the matrix of social interaction. Many thinkers, therefore, have looked to social interaction as the driving mechanism of change and, in particular, to a specific kind of interaction—conflict. Like Khaldun and Marx, numerous thinkers have seen the course of history as prodded forward by human conflict.

In this chapter we shall examine the conflict perspective. To what extent are competition, conflict, and the extreme forms of conflict—violence and war—responsible for change? Does conflict always result in change? What kind of change follows when people enter into conflict? Can change occur without conflict? These are some of the questions to which the following sections are addressed.

Competition and Conflict: Pervasive Forces

• Conflict: Thought and Theory

Throughout recorded history, humans have probed into the nature of reality and found conflict there. Human concern with conflict is reflected in ancient religious literature. Weber has pointed out that the ancient war gods not only protected the "undoubted values of everyday routine" but also "had to fight other gods like themselves, just as their communities fought, and they had to prove their divine powers in this very struggle."[1] Greek mythology had Ares, god of war, who was hated by the other divinities because of his savage nature. His sister, Eris, was goddess of strife and delighted in discord and warfare. Their Roman counterparts were Mars and Discordia.

Among the Babylonians, conflict was an eternal, cosmic struggle. The god Marduk had an annual battle against the powers of chaos, represented by the goddess Tiamat. It was an endless extension of the struggle that took place before the creation of the world.

None of the world's great religions omit the theme. In Buddhism, it is primarily an intra-individual struggle with desire. The Hindu classic, *Bhagavad-Gita,* deals with the problem of war and the goals for which humans must struggle upon Earth. In Islam, warfare was ordained by Allah, and whoever battled the infidel was to be richly rewarded. As we have already seen, in the Christian tradition there is, among others, the work of Augustine on the conflict between the City of God and the earthly city, a conflict that characterizes the whole of human history.

In addition to being present in religious thought, concern with conflict is deeply rooted in the thinking of those actively engaged in political and social affairs. As Don Martindale notes, "conflict theory is the creation of men of affairs."[2] Heraclitus, whose family had political and priestly claims, saw conflict inextricably woven into the structure of the universe: "All things come into being and pass away through strife."[3] The Indian statesman Kautilya delineated a theory of warfare and diplomacy that makes Machiavelli sound gentle; Kautilya wrote his work around 300 B.C. The Chinese critic and essayist Han Fei (died 233 B.C.) taught that war is the arbiter of nations, for human nature demands the exercise of power.

Numerous other political and social observers stressed the importance of conflict in human affairs, among them the Greek historian Polybius, Khaldun, Machiavelli, the French publicist Jean Bodin, and Thomas Hobbes. By the eighteenth century, thinkers in economics and biology were making conflict central to their theories. The conflict of self-interest and social interest pervades the work of Adam Smith. Thomas Malthus portrayed the struggle for existence in grim terms. It was while reading Malthus that Charles Darwin was struck by the insight that the struggle for existence and the survival of the fittest are crucial to evolution.

Darwin's ideas were applied to the social order in the ideology of social Darwinism, the first phase of which was represented by Herbert Spencer and William Graham Sumner. They gave what was purported to be a scientific justification for the ruthless business tactics of the captains of industry of the nineteenth century. The business leaders were the "fittest" members of society, and the underprivileged, the "unfit," had to accept their fate in the name of the well-being of society. How could such ideas be accepted and promoted? Richard Hofstadter suggested that "the answer is that American society saw its own image in the tooth-and-claw version of natural selection, and that its dominant groups were thus able to dramatize this vision of competition as a thing good in itself."[4]

Thus, social evolution was conceived of in terms analogous to those of biological evolution. Those who survived thereby proved that they were the fittest. In the United States in the nineteenth century, the captains of industry were the fittest, the victors in the harsh struggle for existence in the business world. "

A series of sociologists in Europe and the United States, working primarily in the latter half of the nineteenth century and the first quarter of the twentieth century, rapidly developed conflict theory and used it to explain certain kinds of change. The major European sociologists include Ludwig Gumplowicz, who argued that social and cultural evolution is totally the result of group conflict. Intergroup war is the social analogy of the struggle for existence and survival of the fittest. An inherent and deadly hatred prevails between diverse groups, people, and races, making conflict inevitable. Thus, "conquest and the satisfaction of needs through the labor of the conquered . . . is the great theme of human history."[5]

Another European, Vilfredo Pareto, characterized history in terms of "an interminable struggle for control."[6] The dominating group seeks to maintain and defend its position; force is the most important factor in maintaining stability. Violence may be necessary to restore social equilibrium when that equilibrium is upset. Such violence needs no moral justification, because it has the quality of regeneration, freeing people to follow the irrational dictates of their own natures.

Among the Americans, conflict was of central concern, and as Lewis Coser says, any view of social change "that did not include concern with conflict phenomena appeared to them seriously deficient."[7] Among these Americans was William Graham Sumner, whose social Darwinism modified as his thought developed. He veered away from his explicit bias in favor of the triumphant businessman. In *Folkways*, he saw the struggle for existence as "a process in which an individual and nature are the parties. . . . In the competition of life the parties are men and other organisms. . . . The competition of life is the rivalry, antagonism, and mutual displacement in which the individual is involved with other organisms by his efforts to carry on the struggle for existence for himself."[8]

Albion Small and Lester Ward also stressed the role of conflict. The latter developed a theory similar to that of Gumplowicz. Ward asserted that every kind of structure, whether inorganic, organic, or social, is created by the interaction of antagonistic forces. Such interaction is a universal law, and the law means that structures continually change, passing from "a primordial stage of great simplicity into a more complex secondary stage."[9]

Unlike Gumplowicz, Ward does not attribute intergroup conflict to inherent hatred, but rather to inevitable encroachments by one group upon the rights and territory of the other. Out of intergroup conflict the state arises, and "to conflict between states is due the march forward to greater social efficiency and higher civilization."[10]

Some more recent efforts to link conflict and change have attempted to reconcile or synthesize conflict and functionalist theories.[11] As Jonathan Turner has pointed out, the debate between theorists in the two camps has gone through a cycle from an initial mild criticism to stringent attacks to attempted reconciliations to questions about the value of the whole debate for the development of theory.[12] Both the debates and the attempted reconciliations have tended to proceed by identifying the assumptions of the two theories. Turner suggests that we do not need any more attempts to reconcile or synthesize on the basis of assumptions. Rather, he argues, we should ask where we can find "points of divergence and convergence" in the propositions of the two perspectives. Turner himself compares propositions developed by a functionalist theorist, Lewis Coser, and a conflict theorist, Ralf Dahrendorf (see below), along four lines: (1) the causes of conflict, (2) the intensity and violence of conflict, (3) the duration of conflict (which is not dealt with by Dahrendorf), and (4) the consequences of conflict.

It is the last point, the consequences or outcomes of conflict, which is of interest here. A comparison of the two theorists in these terms is illuminating in light of my previous argument that structural-functionalists generally shed little light on change. As Turner summed up the matter:

> *For Dahrendorf, the only outcome of conflict is social change, with only the amount and the rate of such change visualized as varying. In contrast, Coser has developed propositions on integrative and adaptive outcomes of conflict for both the parties to a conflict and the social whole within which the conflict occurs. . . . Conflict can cause a shoring up of group boundaries, centralization of decision-making, ideological solidarity, and increased social control.*[13]

Turner is undoubtedly correct when he says that each theorist is one-sided and could benefit from what the other says. And it may be that the best way to advance theory is to identify and reconcile propositions rather than to debate assumptions. But at this point neither approach has yielded a generally accepted and useful theory that combines the insights of the conflict and functionalist perspectives. Furthermore, whether the synthesizer proceeds by identifying assumptions or by listing propositions, the conflict perspective provides the insights about social change while the functionalist perspective provides other kinds of insights. Let us therefore turn to the work of two modern conflict theorists, Ralf Dahrendorf and Raymond Aron, and see how they link conflict with change.[14]

As Turner pointed out, Dahrendorf argues that change and conflict are inextricably linked: "I would suggest . . . that all that is creativity, innovation, and development in the life of the individual, his group, and his society is due, to no small extent, to the operation of conflicts between group and group, individual and individual, emotion and emotion within one individual."[15] Dahrendorf argues that social conflict has a structural origin—namely, the dominance relations that prevail in all social organization. In other words, group conflict is to be seen in terms of conflict over the legitimacy of authority relations.

Dahrendorf's perspective is more intricate than this brief examination can show, but the essence of his thought is contained in four propositions:

1. Every society is at every point subject to processes of change; social change is ubiquitous.
2. Every society displays at every point dissents and conflict; social conflict is ubiquitous.
3. Every element in a society renders a contribution to its disintegration and change.
4. Every society is based on the coercion of some of its members by others.[16]

In sum, Dahrendorf argues that class conflict (conflict over or arising out of authority relations) leads to structure change (change in values or institutions). Such conflict is pervasive because authority relationships are pervasive. Consequently, change is ubiquitous.

Dahrendorf's theory is applicable to more than just the societal level. He himself provides an example of its application at the organizational level—in an industrial enterprise.[17] First, he points out, the industrial enterprise is an "imperatively coordinated" group, for it has a hierarchy of authority characterized by the workers at the bottom (lowest level of authority) and various levels of management above them. Management's authority is legitimate and is maintained through various sanctions (demotion, firing, and so forth). Consequently, there is an inherent conflict of interests between the managers and the workers.

Until the two groups are organized, they have a latent conflict of interests and are called "quasi-groups" by Dahrendorf. Interest groups emerge out of the quasi-groups under the proper conditions, which include intragroup communication, freedom to organize, leadership, and an appropriate ideology. In the case of the industrial enterprise, the interest groups are employers' associations and workers' unions. These enter into varying degrees of conflict (depending upon the mechanisms available for regulating conflict), and the conflict results in structural change in the industrial organizations and in the relative positions of the two groups.

While the above is a familiar process, Dahrendorf argues, it is a useful illustration of the theory. Furthermore, two points must be kept in mind, both of which follow from the theory. One is that the conflict will occur regardless of the nature of management—whether, that is, management is composed of owners, stockholders, elected officials, or representatives of the government. It is not the type of ownership that is crucial, but the fact of authority relationships and the inherent conflict of interests. The other point is that no mechanism of regulating the conflict will eliminate it. Regulation may diminish the intensity of conflict. Mediation, for example, can lead to arguments rather than to violent confrontations and strikes. Nevertheless, the conflict is inherent in dominance relations, which means that change is also inherent. Whether the unit of analysis is an organization or an entire society, authority relations guarantee conflict and change.

In a later work, Dahrendorf attempts to fill in some of the gaps. The most obvious gap, he says, is that his work has tended to be "highly formal and little is said about either the substance of conflict or the direction of change."[18] He attempts to rectify this by using the concept of "life chances." Social conflict revolves about life chances, which may be defined as

> *the crystallized probability of finding satisfaction for interests, wants and needs, thus the probability of the occurrence of events which bring about such satisfaction. The interests, needs and wants in question may be of many kinds: supply of goods, a pension, the acquisition or exchange of commodities, affiliation to an estate, a preferential social position, a position of power, indeed rebirth and the hope for a new future.*[19]

In essence, Dahrendorf has linked not merely conflict and change, but conflict, change, and the stratification system. His previous "authority relationships" and "inherent conflict of interests" have become a struggle between unequal groups for the acquisition of socially valued goods and honors. Social conflict occurs as some groups strive to increase their share while other groups try to defend theirs. To some extent, it is a zero-sum game: whatever one group gets is lost to other groups. The outcome of the struggle to maximize life chances is social change.

The work of Dahrendorf is the best-known and most complete attempt to develop a theory of conflict and change. Although Dahrendorf takes Marx as his point of departure, he has not developed a dialectical theory.

Many sociologists believe that the dialectic is a foundation point for a theory of change. Social life is rife with contradictions at all levels, and these contradictions can become the driving force of change. There are, for example, contradictions between social reality and the ideology that explains reality. Such contradictions have fueled the Civil Rights and Women's movements in this country as minorities have insisted that the nation confront the discrepancy between the ideology of equal opportunity and the reality of minority opportunities.

Some contradictions arise out of contrary developments in the social structure. In part, the race problem reflects the development of the American economy to the point where there is little demand for unskilled and semi-skilled labor, a situation that has affected blacks more than most other groups. The contradiction between the skill structure of black Americans and the skill demands of the American economy was particularly acute when educational opportunities were minimal for blacks, but the contradiction continues to afflict a greater proportion of blacks than whites.

Still other contradictions inhere in social organization and remain, therefore, as inevitable dilemmas of social life. A number of these have been identified by analysts of complex organizations. For example, there is the dilemma of democracy versus action. In brief, a hierarchical form of organization facilitates action, but a democratic form of organization facilitates creativity (and may also reflect the values of the people). Thus, people may come up with more creative solutions to problems when they are organized democratically. However, that very democratic form of organization may impede the translation of those potential solutions into action, for democratic groups tend toward splintering and dissent rather than coordinated action.

As this discussion has already indicated, a second point about the dialectic and change is that the contradictions are diverse. I am suggesting that both a dialectical materialism and a dialectical idealism are deficient. Marx identified contradictions in the material world. Hegel taught an idealistic dialectic. We could also talk about contradictions between the material and the ideal. All three are correct. The contradictions may be in the realm of ideas, as change emerges from the clash of values. Change can also emerge from material contradictions and from contradictions between the real and the ideal. And, finally, there are contradictions that occur between various levels of social reality. As a number of social scientists have observed, there are always contradictions between the perceived needs and desires of individuals and the social order, and these contradictions can motivate individuals to act in ways that bring about change in the social order.[20]

Sociologists have found dialectical thought useful for diverse kinds of analyses, including: the development of a theory of organizations;[21] speculations on new directions for the study of social change;[22] the analysis of charisma;[23] the explication of interpersonal relationships;[24] the understanding of social movements;[25]and the analysis of social structure.[26] Other than by the dialectical materialists, however, little has been done to apply systematically a dialectical perspective to the analysis of change. We will note two exceptions to this neglect.

One exception is the work of the French sociologist Raymond Aron.[27] According to Aron, there are three basic themes in modern societies. First, modern industrial societies are egalitarian with respect to the aspirations of people but are hierarchical in terms of the organization of the society. This results in the *dialectic of equality*. In other words, there is a contradiction between, on the one hand, the belief in the right of all individuals to such things as equal dignity, happiness, and citizenship and, on the other hand, the hierarchical organization of production in order to maximize output. Industrial societies are organized in such a way as to make inevitable inequality of wealth and power, while at the same time they contain the general belief in egalitarianism. The outcome is group conflict, as various socioeconomic strata, groups of differential political power, and ethnic minorities struggle for the egalitarian ideal.

A second theme involves the *contradictions of socialization*. Each individual aspires to be precisely that—an individual rather than a nameless, faceless member of the mass. It requires a certain level of affluence to attain individuality, but that same affluence demands that the individual submit to the system of production in order that economic growth may not be abated. As Aron put it: "Industrial civilization subjects individuals to a strict discipline in their work and to the influence of a public opinion that is diffuse, unwieldy, and elusive, expressed through the constant pressures of the communications media; and yet it claims to have a philosophy of freedom, a philosophy of personality."[28] The outcome of this contradiction is a tendency for the individual to become depersonalized and to suffer from alienation or anomie or both.

Third, there is the theme of the *dialectic of universality.* This theme involves the notion of "one world"—all nations aspire to the wealth and power that the West and Japan have gained through industrialization. There is an obvious gap between the nations, so that the world has contradictory tendencies toward both unity and division. Technological developments, including, of course, the methods of communication and travel, give the world a unifying tendency. This unifying tendency also finds expression in such phenomena as the United Nations and the efforts of virtually all nations to effect economic development. Nevertheless, the inequalities between nations are obvious, and involve both wealth and power and all the other desirable things that go with wealth and power.

Each of these themes is dialectical, according to Aron, because each involves a contradiction between the real and the ideal, or between various aspects of reality and various ideals. As a result, human life is characterized by intergroup conflict, problems of alienation and anomie, and international tension. Thus, Aron offers us a dialectical theory that identifies contradictions between the real and the ideal as the driving mechanism of change. The contradictions generate conflict, and the outcome of intergroup conflict is social change. Aron's dialectic, then, is neither Hegelian nor Marxist, but contains elements of both. The contradictions he identifies are confined neither to the realm of ideas nor to the material world; rather, they involve both ideas and material reality. They are applicable to more than modern societies, because contradictions between reality and ideals can be found in all societies. These contradictions may differ from the three contradictions that Aron says characterize modern societies, but the same dialectical perspective can be used.

The second exception to the lack of dialectical analyses is the more recent and provocative work of Della Fave.[29] Using social inequality to illustrate his thesis, Della Fave shows how norms and counternorms arise in a society to create a dialectical tension that leads to change. How can norms support inequality? Essentially, we are all impressed by those who seem able to control the world, and we make the assumption that those who have achieved great power, status, and/or money have demonstrated their ability to control. They have reaped the benefits of their own abilities. Thus, while the world is not a place of *equality,* it is a place of *equity.* That is, people get out of it what they put into it, and those who invest the most in terms of their own abilities and resources will reap the most in terms of money, status, and power.

But this legitimation of the existing order is countered by a second process, one "based on the principle of equality, which takes the form of ethical criticism and is delegitimating. The two forces exist in varying degrees of tension with one another."[30] Delegitimating norms are facilitated by various ideologies. Religion provides one such ideology. Religion claims to have more power than any secular source, and it exerts enormous emotional influence over people. Early Christianity stressed communistic egalitarianism and rejected any secular authority over behavior sanctioned by religious principles. This historical base provided a natural source of a norm of equality and, therefore, of opposition to any system of inequality.

The principle of equality was also facilitated, ironically, by the rise of the bourgeoisie as capitalism developed in the West. The bourgeois ideology "struck a blow against the notion of inherited privilege and status and became the ideological foundation of republican government, under which the freedom of the market was promoted."[31] To be sure, the bourgeoisie and the new governments they supported placed limits on equality. Only those with property could vote or hold political office. But at the same time the bourgeoisie had overthrown the principle of hereditary privilege, had challenged the inherent authority of the old elites, and had planted the seeds of the legitimacy of equality. Ultimately, the labor movement would arise and press the notion of equality further than the bourgeoisie had ever intended.

Thus, both norms and counternorms in the society have institutional supports. The normative contradictions are not illogical, but are the natural outgrowth of diverse processes in the social order. And since both norms and counternorms are firmly rooted in social institutions, both are strong and form a dialectical tension in the social order that inevitably results in change.

Many thinkers, then, have affirmed the fact that conflict is a pervasive fact of social life and that conflict is the central driving force of social change. In addition to what we have already noted, there is abundant evidence on the relationship between conflict and change. Let us examine some of it more closely (including the relationship between competition, which I view as a form of conflict, and change).

• Competition, Conflict, and Change

Competition does not characterize all societies, but it is a prominent feature of most developed nations, particularly the capitalist nations. What are the effects of that competition? This section makes no pretense of being a complete study of competition and its effects. Various scholars have argued that cooperation is more natural than competition, competition is dehumanizing, competition within an organization may lower productivity, and competition may diminish satisfaction with group participation. One question is raised here: Can competition (which I am assuming is a variant of conflict) lead to change? The answer is yes. This is not to say that competition always leads to change, nor that it leads to desired change, but only that change can result. The precise conditions under which competition produces change, and the kind of change that results, are matters for future investigation.

There is little doubt that competition may lead to social change. In their study of change in organizations, Jerald Hage and Michael Aiken identified competition as one factor that led to a high rate of program change. They defined program change "as the addition of new services or products."[32] They point out that in our society complex organizations of many kinds—universities, hospitals, schools, and profit-making organizations—are in the competitive arena. Universities, for example, compete with one another for quality instructors. Competition compels an organization toward a "dynamic style," forcing the organization to increase its rate of program change and its degree of complexity. These changes, in turn, ultimately lead to change in various other characteristics of the organization.

Competition is also a factor in creativity and innovation. In his extensive study of innovation, H. G. Barnett identified competition as a "potent incentive when mutually desirable rewards are allocated on the basis of performance."[33] In other words, competition is a potent force for innovation when individuals or groups share a desire for certain rewards and must outdo one another in order to maximize their share of those rewards. This potency is exemplified by the difference in scientific productivity in medicine in the United States, England, France, and Germany during the nineteenth century.[34] Joseph Ben-David used the number of scientific discoveries and the number of scientists making the discoveries as measures of productivity. He found that the number of discoveries continued to rise in the United States during the latter part of the century and in Germany during the middle part. During the same period, scientific medical creativity in England and

France declined rather consistently. He also found "relatively smaller fluctuations" in the number of individuals entering scientific careers in Germany and in the United States as compared to other countries.

What accounted for these differences? Why did the science of medicine make its greatest advances in Germany and the United States from the middle of the century on, whereas England and France had shown clear leadership in the earlier part of the century? Ben-David argues that the difference must be sought in the organization of science in the various nations. The situation faced by the medical sciences at the beginning of the nineteenth century required the French and Germans to discover appropriate measures of evaluation and adequate support. Crucial decisions had to be made about scientific facilities, scientific roles, and scientific training, and the Germans made all the right decisions. This was not due to the peculiar insight of individuals; rather, it resulted from the organization of science in the two nations.

Specifically, the German academic system was decentralized as a result of the "political dismemberment" of the Germans. The French possessed a unified academic system, with the greater part of it located in Paris. This decentralization in Germany seems to account for the difference in scientific productivity in the two nations, for it created academic competition, "and competition forced upon the individual institutions decisions which would not have been made otherwise, or at least not made at that time."[35]

Similarly, competition in the United States stimulated creative efforts and led to decisions that facilitated those efforts. In both the United States and Germany during their creative periods, valued rewards awaited the successful scientist. The success of some stimulated others to pursue scientific careers. There was also pressure to expand facilities and training and to abandon outmoded techniques and structures. Increased opportunities for careers in research attracted increasing numbers of students (the number entering such careers in France and Britain fluctuated over the period). Underlying and prodding the whole development was competition among the varied segments of the medical world. The field of medicine was changing rapidly, and the driving mechanism of the change was competition.

The quest for money and prestige has kept competition at the center of scientific and technological developments. Nations, universities, industrial organizations, and individuals all compete with each other to gain the rewards that come from scientific and technological advances. At the individual level, the rewards in the physical sciences include the coveted Nobel Prize. A number of books have detailed the way in which scientists, contrary to the notions of collegiality and the selfless quest for knowledge, have viciously competed with each other as each sought to be the first to attain some goal. For instance, the 1977 Nobel Prize in Physiology or Medicine was awarded to three researchers, two of whom were bitter enemies.[36] The two had originally been colleagues, but they had split to form two separate research teams. Each was determined to be the first to identify and characterize hormones used by the brain to control such bodily functions as temperature, reproduction, and growth.

In their competition for the prize, the two researchers violated many of the norms of the scientific world. For example, credit is usually given to other scientists working in the same area, but each avoided as much as possible acknowledging the work of the other. They also refused to share their progress with each other, working in secret rather than cooperatively. In the end, they both achieved the coveted prize, though both lost the effort to win a victory over the other.

You could argue that the methods each used were counterproductive, and that the breakthrough would have been achieved even earlier had they cooperated instead of competed. But the goal may have proved more elusive without their competition, for both scientists and their teams worked feverishly in their efforts to be first. Their search was not a leisurely pursuit of scientific knowledge. As in this case, the intense competition for rewards generally facilitates scientific and technological change.

It is equally clear that conflict leads to change. In his study of state formation in sixteenth- and seventeenth-century England and France, Lachmann identified conflict among three elites—the clergy, the monarchs and their officials, and lay landlords—as the "critical dynamic" that explains the developments in the two countries.[37] Before the establishment of the absolutist monarchies, various aristocrats, clerics, and others with hereditary rights exercised power over people. Each elite group attempted to protect itself from the other elites as well as from resistance by the peasants over their obligations to the various elites. Thus, in 1500 England and France were not simply divided by the contrary interests of elites and peasants but were lands in which the interests of diverse elites clashed as well. The conflict was resolved somewhat differently in each of the two nations, but in both cases an absolute monarchy was established and in both cases the conflict among elite groups led toward absolutism and away from the multiplicity of power centers that had existed earlier.

Numerous other scholars have linked conflict with change, including creative change. Martindale described societal creativity that lasted for centuries, but the creative age was neither stable nor peaceful. Rather, such an age was generally experienced by the participants as one of unrest and tension.[38] The Renaissance stands out as a period of striking and creative change in contrast to the bleak age that preceded it. Will Durant has identified conflict as a factor in the flowering of creativity in Florence.[39] Finally, Lewis Coser points out that innovation was discouraged by the medieval guild system; individuals were not allowed to employ methods that gave them a productive advantage over others. By contrast, technological change in the modern West is rooted in the institutionalization of science as a tool for shaping existence, and the continual invention and technological change we now experience "was made possible with the gradual emergence of a pluralistic and hence conflict-charged structure of human relations."[40]

Clearly, conflict is a driving mechanism of change. It is effective at all levels of social reality. Individuals strive to change when they perceive contradictions between different attitudes or between attitudes and behavior."[41] Some psychologists argue that children develop logical intelligence more quickly when stimulated by cognitive conflict. At the organizational level, Paul Lawrence and Jay Lorsch discovered that the most effective of six organizations in a plastics industry also had the most serious problem of integration and a high degree of conflict.[42] Effectiveness was defined in terms of sales, profits, and—more importantly for our purposes—new products. They argue that the way in which conflict is resolved is crucial to effectiveness. The effective firms had formalized mechanisms such as departments and individuals who acted as "integrators." Such mechanisms did not suppress or minimize conflict, however; they merely resolved it as it occurred.

Conflict is such an integral part of organizational creativity and change that some have even argued that it is appropriate at times to deliberately stimulate conflict within the organization.[43] Under certain conditions, escalating rather than suppressing conflict can lead not only to desired change but to greater cohesion of the group and higher levels of effectiveness. Of course, conflict can be destructive to a group also, but if it is managed properly it can be an important stimulus to creative, positive change.

Conflict is also an integral part of social movements. A movement may arise out of social conflicts.[44] For example, Roberts and Kloss have argued that there are three master social trends that are oppressive, giving rise to three types of movements.[45] The social trends are bureaucratization, cultural imperialization (including racism, colonialism, and economic exploitation), and industrialization. Antibureaucratic, nativistic and nationalistic, and egalitarian movements arise to oppose and negate the oppressiveness of the master trends.

Once having emerged, of course, the movement continues to engage in conflict with outsiders. And out of that conflict social change may occur. Studies of social movements have tended to focus more on such matters as movement structure and mobilization of members and ideology than on actual outcomes of movement action. Nevertheless, it is clear that various kinds of change emerge from the activities of social movements, including changes

> *in the legal sphere, in various institutions, in patterns of interaction, and so forth. The changes may occur primarily in individuals. Movement members, for example, may develop an enhanced self-concept and a stronger capacity for coping with various frustrations as a result of participating in an expressive movement. Or the changes may occur primarily in the social structure. Widespread alterations occurred in the stratification system, the family, the economy, and other areas in China following the Communist revolution.*[46]

The Civil Rights Movement has been surrounded by conflict of diverse kinds and varying degrees of intensity. It has also resulted in a great many changes, including political and legal developments, improvements in the economic situation of minorities, and new educational programs.[47] Sometimes the particular changes have been intended, and sometimes they have been unintended. But there can be no question but that many changes have emerged out of the matrix of conflict between a social movement and the larger society.

There is another way in which conflict relates to the outcome of a social movement. Contrary to what one might expect, internal conflict in social movements may be a positive rather than a negative factor, as studies both by Luther Gerlach and Virginia Hine and by William Anderson and Russell Dynes have shown.[48] The former argue, on the basis of their studies of the Pentecostal and Black Power movements, that "internecine dogfighting" is functional where both rapid growth of the movement and social change in the larger society are goals of a movement. Conflict is the result of divergent ideas within a movement about such issues as how to organize and how to achieve goals. In both the Pentecostal and Black Power movements, a variety of ways of organizing and of achieving goals may be found. There is experimentation—a kind of trial-and-error approach that would be absent if the movements were characterized by consensus and conformity among the membership. For instance, black power groups have experimented with a variety of ways of communicating the need for change, including use of the mass media, establishment of small groups, and use of established organizations such as the churches. Some groups try methods that other groups reject or disdain, but multiple and diverse efforts are necessary in order to find the most effective ways of implementing change. Thus, conflict within the movement can facilitate rather than impede change.

Similarly, Anderson and Dynes studied a labor movement in Curaçao, and concluded that internal conflict was adaptive for the movement during an uprising in May, 1969. Prior to that time, the island had appeared to be quaint and peaceful to outsiders. Actually, discontent had been rife among workers for some time, and it erupted on May 30, 1969, into a riot that involved thousands of people. The outcome was millions of dollars of property damage, the overthrow of the Antillean government, the creation of new political parties, a new concern for the problems of labor in the government, a strengthening of the police and other means of social control, growth of union membership, and other changes related to the position and well-being of the workers in the society.

Not all of the changes were defined by the workers as desirable, but many were. Anderson and Dynes make the point that even the desirable changes might not have occurred if it had not been for conflict within the labor movement between radical and moderate leaders. To understand this, we must review the events leading up to the riot. Near the end of May, there was a strike at a company doing contract work for Royal Dutch Shell. The strike occurred because outsiders were paid more than native Antillean workers, and because all employees at the company got less pay than those at Shell who did the same kind of work. When no settlement was reached, a number of employees at other companies went out on a sympathy strike or held demonstrations in support of the strikers. The moderate union leaders of the Shell workers were put under considerable pressure to call for a strike of Shell, and this pressure was largely due to the activities of the radical leaders. The moderate leaders appeared to face the choice of joining the growing strike movement or losing their leadership positions. The moderates preferred negotiation and would have accommodated themselves to the companies. They were rendered powerless by the work of the radicals, who received considerable sympathy from the workers for a more militant approach. Thus, the internal conflict in the movement meant that at a critical point the will of the moderate leadership was overruled. Contrary to the desire of the latter, the strike became widespread. The riot was triggered by the shooting of a radical leader during a mass march on the government buildings. After the riot, various groups began to try to restore order. Labor leaders demanded the resignation of the government and new elections, which occurred in June and September, respectively. As noted above, other changes followed that benefited the workers, but all might have been different if the labor movement had been characterized by consensus among workers and union leaders.

The relationship between conflict and change tends to be a self-sustaining process, for change may lead to conflict that leads to further change *ad infinitum*. An example of this is provided by the so-called green revolution in Asia. In India, David Freeman has shown, the green revolution has produced conflict, which has led to further pressures toward change.[49] The green revolution changed agriculture in India with the introduction of new varieties of grains, along with water, fertilizer, and pesticides. In some cases, double and even triple yields of crops resulted. In fact, India more than tripled its wheat harvest between 1965, when the green revolution began, and 1983.[50] There was little increase in output through the rest of the 1980s, however.

While the green revolution increased India's crops to the extent that the nation became an exporter of grains, millions of Indians still faced the problem of hunger and even starvation.[51] Clearly, not everyone has benefited from the revolution. The new technology has had consequences other than improved agriculture. The large farmer, with greater access to land, capital, and credit, profited rather than the small farmer. The disadvantage of the latter was rooted in the fact that a farmer might need to invest as much as ten times the cost for traditional methods in order to take advantage of the new technology. The resulting profit would of course more than compensate for the additional investment. The small farmer, limited by financial resources and even by such things as illiteracy, was unable to share in the green revolution. In addition, because of the greater potential yield of the land, in many cases the small farmer found that the value of the land increased and that rent, therefore, was raised. With the greater yields, the supply of crops increased and tended to cause prices to fall. Thus, for the small farmer it was not merely a matter of failing to benefit from the new technology, but of actually being in a worse condition than before.

The small farmers in India, then, confronted a grim future. In some cases they were evicted from their plots of land by the owners, who wished to take full advantage of the new technology. Even when they were able to continue to farm as before, however, they faced a situation of smaller profits, greater impoverishment, and less economic and social security. The outcome was an intensification of the traditional cleavages between landowners and tenants. These cleavages were manifested in a number of "land grab" movements and violent confrontations between landlords and displaced farmers. This, in turn, has been a source of pressure for additional change. Thus, the initial change, the introduction of innovations in agricultural technology, led to conflict which resulted in pressure for further change.

The change resulting from conflict is not always desirable from the point of view of those subjected to it. This is obvious in the case where one group in the conflict prevails over the other by bringing about changes the other had opposed. But there are also situations where both parties lose, in terms of their own goals. For example, a good many of the communitarian societies established in the nineteenth century in the United States, including Oneida, phalanxes of the Fourierists, and the Ruskin Cooperative Community, collapsed primarily or at least in part because of internal conflict. Similarly, the demise of the New Left in the early 1970s was largely caused by conflict among members. As Irwin Unger puts it, the student left of the 1960s "committed suicide" by its factionalism.[52] The Students for a Democratic Society, for example, was splintered by conflict with the leftist Progressive Labor element in its midst, by ideological differences, and by discord over appropriate strategies. We pointed out above that conflict may lead to an attainment of goals by a social movement, but that is not a uniform outcome. When the cleavages are deep and involve fundamental issues, and when various ideological positions are held by intransigent groups, conflict may lead to self-destruction of the group.

In addition to noting that conflict may bring about undesired change, we may note two additional points about the relationships between conflict and change. First, conflict may impede change as well as impel it; second, some change may occur without conflict. The first point is made by S. N. Eisenstadt, who notes a number of cases of "breakdown of modernization"—in Indonesia, Pakistan, Burma, and Sudan, among others.[53] Specifically, constitutional governments seemed unable to cope with the problems and demands of the modern era, and they yielded to autocratic, authoritarian, or semiauthoritarian regimes. One "basic characteristic" in each case of the breakdown of modernization was the emergence of continuing intergroup conflict marked by intense antagonism. The groups involved were unable to create any continuing and viable patterns of accommodation to one another so that the conflict stifled development toward a modern, constitutional state.

The other point, that change can occur without conflict, is documented by Robert and Barbara Anderson in their study of a Danish village.[54] The village had been a harbor community for two centuries. Then it changed rapidly and pervasively. There were few aspects of village culture, the Andersons note, that escaped significant alterations. The change was both extensive, in terms of affecting virtually the totality of life in the village, and intensive, in terms of occurring very rapidly. Perhaps most striking of all was the fact that as the village moved from being a maritime community to an annex of the urban area, the people adjusted to the change and accepted it almost without any conflict! This, of course, is an interesting instance of support for a point made earlier: while all change involves contradictions, it does not necessarily involve intergroup conflict.

The Andersons attribute the lack of conflict to a number of factors. Initially, technological developments affected the village's industry, making that industry obsolete and creating an economic crisis. The same technological progress resolved the problem, for the village was soon a suburb of Copenhagen. The population grew as workers from Copenhagen settled in the village. Transportation facilities developed to allow these new residents to commute; they also allowed native villagers to find employment in Copenhagen. Within a single generation, the village experienced a social and cultural revolution.

One factor that allowed this change to occur without conflict was the nature of the change; cultural patterns were not rooted up and discarded, but the new patterns were either created out of or conjoined with the old ones. A second factor was the absence of cultural lag; for example, the economic crisis created by the obsolescence of traditional village work was quickly resolved by opportunities for employment in Copenhagen.

A third factor was the absence of groups committed to "the exclusive adoption of either the old or the new cultural forms as symbols of a superior evaluation of culture choice."[55] Finally, the change that occurred involved an increase in prestige. Socially and economically, the prestige of the village was greatly enhanced through its new attachment with Copenhagen.

Thus, while conflict is a most important incentive to change, change may occur without conflict. When conflict does lead to change, that change may not be defined as desirable by those experiencing it. The exact conditions under which conflict impels or impedes change, and those under which it impels change in a socially desirable direction, have yet to be specified.

Gun Barrel Change: The Effects of Violence

"Anything can grow out of the barrel of a gun." So goes a well-known saying of Chairman Mao. There are those who would amend it slightly to say, "Any meaningful change must grow out of the barrel of a gun." And while most Americans would not mean literally that guns must be used, a substantial number approve of violence under various conditions. At an interpersonal level, some justify violence in order to keep the other person "in line" or to get the other person to "shape up." In other words, violence must be used to guide the direction of the other's development and the pattern of the other's behavior. In a study of dating relationships, researchers even found that a number of the victims of violence accepted it as necessary![56] And in a national sample of the attitudes of American men, researchers found that about 20 percent of the respondents agreed that protests involving personal injuries and some property damage are necessary for change.[57]

Can violence bring about meaningful change? What are the consequences of violence? What evidence do we have to enable us to appraise intelligently the relationship between violence and change! Before looking at the evidence and attempting a general appraisal, let us look at the diverse thinking about violence and change.

• *Violence in Thought and Theory*

Some thinkers have argued that violence does little if anything to effect change, and that the change it does bring about is not the kind desired or anticipated. A survey of violence associated with the American labor movement concluded: "'The effect of labor violence was almost always harmful to the union. There is little evidence that violence succeeded in gaining advantages for strikers."[58] One of the most effective tactics used by the workers during the 1930s was the sit-down strike. The sit-down strikes were an effort to avoid rather than precipitate violence, although management defined them as the use of "illegal force."

Furthermore, in many cases violence has been employed to maintain the status quo and has seemed to be more effective for that purpose than for effecting change. For instance, there is a long history of violence by whites against blacks in order to maintain the subordinate status of the latter. The violence has not kept blacks from implementing considerable change over time, but at least in the short run such violence often proved effective. In Wilmington, North Carolina, blacks were making considerable progress in the latter part of the nineteenth century.[59] Poor whites grew hostile at the threat of blacks taking over their jobs and competing with them in the labor market. A vigilante group called the Red Shirts was formed, and many of the poor whites became members. During the 1898 election, newspaper articles overstated the amount of black political power that existed in an effort to gain votes for the Democratic party. After the election, whites were called on to overturn "rule by Negroes" and to take away jobs held by blacks. A riot soon followed, and nineteen blacks were killed. The violence terrorized the black community, which retreated into a passive, subordinate condition for more than a generation.

Sometimes, then, violence can, at least in the short run, maintain the status quo. On the other hand, those who use violence to maintain the status quo may find their efforts to be counterproductive. In the American labor movement, employers used more violence than the workers did, and employer violence served only to arouse sympathy for workers and, ultimately, the legitimization of the union. Young members of the New Left in the 1960s were aware of the potential value of being the objects of violence, and often tried deliberately to provoke the authorities into violent action in order to secure sympathy and, ultimately, to radicalize others. The tactic worked on some college campuses; students otherwise liberal or neutral were radicalized, or at least joined with radicals in militant tactics, in the face of official violence against the radical students.

Finally, it has been argued that violence is but one alternative for effecting change. Granted, the change may have come about through the agony of violence, but it could have been effected by other means. In his study of agrarian reform in Colombia, Albert Hirschman pointed out that sporadic and decentralized violence rather than revolution was sufficient to gain the reforms. Contrary to Latin American practice, wholesale revolution was not necessary to bring about the change.[60]

This general perspective on the relationship between violence and change has been well summed up by Henry Bienen, who reviewed the literature and offers us three propositions:

> *(1) Most social and political change does not result from violent revolution. (2) Where violent revolutions have occurred they constitute much more of a watershed in a slower process than an immediate and radical reordering of society. Moreover, watersheds can be found in nonrevolutionary societies too. . . . (3) Large-scale violence can be associated with "the more things change, the more they remain the same," as Mosca pointed out with reference to violence in the Italian communes and the Greek states.*[61]

A different argument is advanced by other thinkers, who see violence as a chief means of social reform. In the United States, violence has been associated with the race problem from the days of slave insurrection to the present civil rights struggle; violence has also characterized the labor and women's suffrage movements. In each case, according to St. Clair Drake, "it is clear that violence has been an important factor in accelerating the movement toward goals."[62] He argues that the goals could not have been achieved by any less violent means.

A similar point has been made with reference to problems of change in countries with feudal-type social structures. Edmundo Flores, for example, has written that we must accept the need for revolutionary change in Latin America, and that sometimes the change must be violent. For a "harsh fact" of political action in Latin America is that "would-be reformers have faced the determined opposition of the landed elite, the armed forces, and the Catholic Church, as well as . . . the almost inevitable and generally decisive interference of the United States on the side of all three."[63] Even Hofstadter conceded that violence may successfully implement needed change in the special case of "backward" people who have been exploited by colonialism and who have a "firm territorial base."

This last point emphasizes the fact that the utility of violence depends upon the context. None of the thinkers we are discussing have a moral commitment to violence per se. Those who assert the need for violence do so out of their hatred of oppression rather than from love of violence. They do so because they see no other way to effect change.

As we have seen, Marx made this point in his theory of change. Revolution, he argued, is necessary both to shatter the existing irrational social order and to cleanse those who have been oppressed by that order. Violence may be abhorrent to those who are comfortable and satisfied, but to those who have been oppressed, violence is the hammer that shatters their chains. We should note, however, that not all Marxists agree that violent revolution is necessary. At least some use the term "violent" in a metaphorical rather than literal sense, and some even speak of peaceful evolution. An example of the latter is a Chinese thinker who has argued that capitalism has now entered a third phase of "social capitalism," which involves various welfare measures and a greater amount of equality rather than the severe exploitation of early capitalism.[64] This stage involves a time of peace and progress, with capitalism and socialism coexisting and competing peacefully. Socialism will still come to dominate the world, but it will not rise out of the ruins of capitalism. "Instead, developed capitalism will gradually evolve socialist factors and bring the transition to socialism. It is likely to complete this process through peaceful means."[65]

To return to those who believe that violence is necessary and/or inevitable, there is a modified argument that asserts that the threat or fear of violence may be sufficient to bring about change. This, of course, probably demands at least occasional actual violence, but it also means that violence itself is not always necessary. For example, the threat of violence posed by White Citizens Councils in the American South "strengthened the hand of southern moderates in trying to restrain civil rights action from Washington," but the threat posed by the Black Muslims and CORE "strengthens the position of the NAACP in seeking concessions from Southern Whites and action by the Justice Department."[66]

A concrete example is provided by the black struggle for equal public accommodations in Maryland in the early 1960s. Public facilities were segregated in 1960, and nothing seemed able to move the legislature to enact a public accommodation bill. Then groups of blacks led by CORE and a local civil rights group began a series of sit-ins, wade-ins at beaches, marches, and picketing of offices of officials. In this case, violence came from those opposing the blacks and elicited sympathy for their cause. By 1963, Baltimore and the state of Maryland had passed the public accommodation bills. The success of the effort seemed to stem from something other than its own power (relatively few people were ever involved). One factor, in addition to the broader base of support the blacks gained through being the objects of violence, was the fear of violence and civil disorder that was based upon other situations (including the state's own example at Cambridge).[67]

Thus, we have concrete examples of how the fear or threat of violence can effect change. Let us turn now to some of the evidence about the effects of violence itself. Then we shall try to draw some general conclusions about the relation of violence to change.

• Violence and Change

As with conflict, if we ask whether violence can effect change, the answer is clearly yes. It can do so in more than the counterproductive sense noted above. Violence brings about changes desired by those who employ it as well as changes that the violence was designed to quell. Many revolutions have been nothing more than a "change of the palace guard," but many revolutions have effected radical change in the social structure and social life of nations. The Mexican Revolution of 1910 shattered the old social order and marked the beginning of Mexico's emergence into the modern era. In the ensuing years, land reform, new educational opportunities, economic growth, and significant changes in the stratification system were among the altered aspects of Mexican society.[68]

We could delineate similar effects of the revolutions in such countries as Bolivia, Cuba, and China. The extent to which revolution effects change in a nation varies enormously, of course. The point is that revolution is one form of violence that clearly can effect radical change. The change may be minimal—the American Revolution was little more than a minor political change—or it may be massive. The Communist Revolution in China radically changed that nation. In fact, it is impossible to fully capture the nature of the change in a few paragraphs, but

Edgar Snow has expressed for us something of the spirit of the new China:

> *Collective life in new China was above all change and movement. Elements carried over from the past were engaged in dynamic combination and recombination, with new elements of the time-present which was itself always becoming a future something-else. . . . China was not simply a different country; its obsessive haste to catch up with history and to become the world's greatest nation . . . was positively awesome to those who could remember a passive China in which time meant nothing.*[69]

Terrorism is a form of violence that aims at revolution. Terrorist activities reached a peak in the 1960s, then declined, but continue to exist in various parts of the world.[70] Terrorism tends to flourish wherever the intelligentsia are alienated politically from both the authorities and the masses of people. The authorities are oppressive, but the masses are silent and submissive; in frustration, some of the intelligentsia resort to terrorism as a way to stimulate a revolution against a repressive regime. Terrorism seems to be the only alternative because they cannot work through the existing political system, the mass media are inaccessible and supportive of the status quo, and the masses are blind to their oppression or at least to the possibility of change. They use violence in the form of terrorism, then, to show that the government has weaknesses, to raise the consciousness of the masses, and to gain support for the cause of revolution.

Obviously, one objection to terrorism is the death of innocent people, including some of the very masses in whose interests the terrorists purportedly act. But the death of a few innocents is viewed as a small price to pay for the massive overhaul of society; individuals are expendable when one is fighting for a just cause for humankind as a whole.

Generally, terrorism is more likely to obstruct than to foment a social revolution. But under some conditions, terrorism can be effective in producing a national liberation movement. The terrorists who were trying to liberate the Balkans from Hapsburg control and who assassinated Austria's Archduke Ferdinand at Sarajevo in June, 1914, are one example. Algeria provides another example. In 1960, terrorist acts resulted in an overreaction by the French government. The French reaction, in turn, raised the consciousness of the Algerian masses. Soon the resistance to the French became armed, widespread, and nationalistic. Eventually, the Algerians won their independence from French domination.

More frequently, however, terrorism has failed or has even been counterproductive. It is most likely to be effective in those situations where "a nonterrorist army, supported by a broad-based coalition, waits in the wings while terrorists and counterterrorists play out their prologue."[71] In other kinds of situations, terrorism is more apt to simply add to the sum total of human misery in the world and to fail at any meaningful change.

Revolution and terrorism are not the only ways in which violence can effect change. War and the threat of war between nations has historically been a stimulant to technological change. From Archimedes's work on trajectories and machines to repulse the Roman attack on Syracuse to the American scientists' fashioning of the atomic bomb in order to conquer Japan to the microelectronic developments of the present for use in missiles and other weapons, technological developments have been spurred on by international violence or the threat of such violence.

There is also a strong correlation between violence within a nation and the level of socioeconomic development. The relationship seems to be curvilinear. That is, as the nation begins to develop, internal conflict increases. But as the nation attains full modernization, defined in terms of near-universal adult literacy, and as the gross national product (GNP) per capita rises well above subsistence level, internal conflict subsides.[72] This, however, does not tell us about any causal relation. It is an open question as to what extent the development is impelled by the internal violence of the modernizing nations.

Finally, violence may effect change in the context of social movements within a nation. As noted earlier, this is disputed by some, but there seems to be clear evidence that violence has enabled various movements to attain at least some of their goals. William Gamson studied fifty-three "challenging groups" that existed in American society between 1800 and 1945.[73] The groups had goals ranging from minor reform to wholesale revolution. One of the questions Gamson raised in his study was whether violence pays off in collective protest action. He found that those who used violence had a significantly greater likelihood of gaining new advantages than did the nonusers. Two qualifications must be made. First, only eight of the groups engaged in violence. He actually found, then, that six of the eight violence-users gained new advantages, whereas only twenty out of thirty-eight nonusers gained new advantages. (There were seven groups defined as "violence recipients," and none of them gained new advantages.) Thus, the sample of violence-users was small. Furthermore, the groups that used violence did not necessarily initiate the violence. In some cases (Gamson does not say how many) they were responding to an attack.

Gamson makes these points and notes that he cannot say that violence works on the basis of his sample. He does argue that his data show that when violence is associated with success, the violence comes from the weakness of the target and the strength of the protesting groups rather than from any weakness in the protestors. He concludes that violence leads to successful change when "it grows out of confidence and strength and their attendant impatience with the pace of change. It is, in this sense, as much a symptom of success as a cause."[74] Gamson also points out that the successful groups did not use violence as their *primary* tactic. We might add that even if the violence itself does not lead directly to change, it may produce the fear or threat that stimulates change in another situation.

Violence may have certain important social-psychological functions for members of a movement. For one thing, violence can create internal solidarity. This may sound as if it contradicts our previous statement that internal conflict can facilitate the achievement of goals, but two points must be kept in mind. First, there is a useful function for both conflict and solidarity. In the labor movement in Curaçao, described earlier, there was solidarity during the strike, and that solidarity resulted from the prior conflict between radical and moderate factions. The conflict was necessary for the direction taken by the movement, and the solidarity was necessary for the strike to be effective. Furthermore, there was solidarity in the crucial days after the violent riot. This solidarity was important in attaining the various changes that occurred, and it was secured because of the violence of the day. The shooting of a radical leader by the police helped secure the solidarity, but, as we shall indicate below, the mere fact of participating in a violent episode can ensure commitment to a movement. Second, there can be conflict and solidarity in the movement at the same time—the two are not necessarily incompatible. There may be conflict over methods or tactics while there is solidarity in terms of goals and in the face of the external adversary. A group that is truly split by intense conflict over fundamental issues will be ineffective, as exemplified by the demise of the New Left. Apart from such extreme cases, however, solidarity and conflict can coexist quite well and can facilitate goal attainment.

In addition to creating solidarity, violence can also seal the commitment of members to a movement. Commitment to the Black Power Movement was found to involve "bridge-burning" acts, acts of violence that ensured as well as symbolized the individual's commitment to the movement.[75] Since commitment of members is indispensable to the success of a movement, the violence was an important factor in securing change.

What conclusions can we draw about the relation of violence to change? The first is obvious: violence can effect change. Numerous studies indicate that change follows both directly and indirectly in the wake of violence. This bold conclusion must be qualified, however. In their extensive study of collective violence in Europe, Charles, Louise, and Richard Tilly make a number of suggestions.[76] For one, they argue that collective violence is the expression of a struggle for power, and not the result of social breakdown, material deprivation, or irrational action. Second, they argue that we cannot make a sharp distinction between violent and nonviolent action; rather, we must speak of collective action that has a greater or lesser probability of becoming violent. Third, if collective action does become violent, there are a number of considerations with respect to the effectiveness of the action:

1. Collective action with a low probability of erupting into violence is more effective in the short run.
2. Powerless groups are more likely to benefit from violence than are the powerful. (Recall the point above that being the object of violence can broaden a movement's base of support and may enable the movement to gain legitimacy.)
3. In competitive action (where one group attacks the resources of the other, including people and property, and the other may or may not fight back), there is little more than slight readjustments of the power positions of the groups.
4. In reactive action (where a group resists the claim to its resources, which is made by another group), there is likely to be a short-run successful retention of established rights but a long-term loss. (The fact that violence erupted indicates that the institutionalized means of expressing grievances were not working.)
5. In proactive action (where a group claims resources that it previously did not control and is resisted by another group), there is likely to be a short-run failure but long-term success.[77]

In general, the Tillys conclude, violence often works. The collective action that led to the violence in Europe often resulted in the achievement of at least some of the goals of the participants. This was most true for limited and specific goals such as getting rid of an official or gaining an increase in wages. As the goals become more broad and abstract—the kinds of goals that must be achieved in the long rather than short run—violence is less important in success than such factors as the group's organizing ability and its access to resources. In any case, it is the collective action that may result in violence, rather than the violence itself, that is most crucial.

A second conclusion is to qualify further the above by noting the cases of violence without change or without much significant change. The American and French revolutions effected certain political changes, but had little consequence for the social and cultural life of the masses of people in those nations. Such revolutions have been of practically no effect in comparison with the mercantile and industrial revolutions. That is, changes generated by technological developments may have far greater consequences for the lives of most people than those that follow from violence. In a developed nation such as the United States, the major effect of violence on change may be either the indirect effect (producing fear or threat and gaining commitment of individuals to a movement) or the counterproductive effect (producing precisely the opposite of what those who employed it desired).

As noted earlier, violence in the form of terrorism may simply add some anguish to people's lives without bringing about any kind of change desired by the terrorists. For one thing, terrorists are not effective unless they have verbal skills in proclaiming their ideology as well as their willingness to act violently.[78] Terrorism is, after all, an attempt at persuasion, and unless terrorists are at some point effective in ideological persuasion, their violence will not bring about change. Furthermore, most governments are stronger than any terrorist group, and strong action by governments, such as imprisoning their members, has frequently quelled terrorist groups.[79] In Italy, the Red Brigades were eventually neutralized by a combination of some political reform, infiltration of the terrorist ranks, and offers of reduced prison terms to penitents. While there was some political change involved, it was not the kind of change desired by the terrorists.

Overall, there is an ironical aspect to terrorist activities in democratic nations. As expressed by Walter Laqueur:

> *A dialectical process seems to dictate the policy of democratic societies toward terrorists. As long as terrorism is no more than a nuisance, a democracy will rightly resist any attempt to curtail its traditional freedoms. Once terrorism becomes more than a nuisance, once the normal functioning of society is affected, there will be overwhelming pressure on the government to defeat the threat by all available means. Hence the paradoxical conclusion that the more successful the terrorists, the nearer their ultimate defeat. There are exceptions to every rule, but in this case they are few and far between.*[80]

Third, not only is there violence without change, but there is also change without violence. This was Hofstadter's point about violence in the United States. Social reforms in the United States, he argued, are primarily the result of intensive and long-term campaigns of reformers, who make much use of education and propaganda but little, if any, use of violence: "The entire apparatus of the welfare state, from child labor laws, wage-hour regulation, industrial safety laws, and workmen's compensation to legally regulated collective bargaining, social security, and medical care for the aged is the achievement of active minorities which, while sometimes militant and always persistent, were also patient and nonviolent."[81]

Fourth, violence may be one alternative among others for effecting any specific kind of change. As the Tillys pointed out, it is the collective action rather than the violence that is critical to the historical process. Thus, to recognize that certain changes followed from the exercise of violence is not to say that the change could not have occurred without the violence. The work of Gandhi, Martin Luther King, Jr., the Rev. Jesse Jackson, and others illustrates how change may be effected in the context of an insistence on nonviolence. For nonviolence does not mean lack of force. On the contrary, the method of Satyagraha developed by Gandhi involved "the Force which is born of Truth and Love."[82] The "force" is applied by a series of increasingly stronger means of gaining one's objective, ranging from an initial effort to persuade through reason to nonviolent coercion, which involves such tactics as refusal to cooperate and civil disobedience.

In other words, violence is not the only behavior that fits into the category of "coercive." Another tactic that has been employed is disruption of services, in an effort to alter national priorities by intensifying tension in urban areas.[83] Rent strikes and the organizing of the poor to claim welfare benefits are among the other tactics that have been used. The effects of these tactics have yet to be determined, but national concern with the problem of welfare in the 1970s indicates that at least the political leaders were compelled to examine the situation. Many of those political leaders spoke about the need to reorder national priorities.

A fifth conclusion is that violence may be counterproductive. This is a difficult point, for how does one assess the consequences of violent versus nonviolent approaches? How does one determine when violence pays off in terms of meaningful change, and when the costs of violence are greater than any benefits that may be gained? We cannot decide this simply on the basis of the cost of the violence, for we must also take into account the cost of not changing (assuming that violence is necessary to effect the change). For example, Barrington Moore notes that a reasonable estimate of those who died as a result of revolutionary repression in France would be 35,000 to 40,000; but he also points out that in all probability the "death rate of the *ancien régime* from such factors as preventable starvation and injustice" would have been at least as high if not higher.[84]

In other words, the use of violence is risky in terms of costs and benefits, but so is the willingness to tolerate a repressive status quo. Furthermore, as we have shown above, the use of violence may impede the change desired or even lead to the opposite of that which is desired. In May, 1886, the movement to gain an eight-hour day for workers was reaching its peak, and many people were optimistic about the outcome. Then a bomb was thrown in Haymarket Square in Chicago on May 4, killing seven policemen and wounding dozens more. The eight-hour day movement was brought to a screeching halt. Gatherings of strikers were broken up by the police, who claimed to have discovered anarchist plots. Workers themselves were confused and divided about the violence. Many people, including some writing in the press, connected the bombing with the agitation for the eight-hour day.

The events of the time have not yet been completely untangled, but one thing is clear. Two social movements intersected in Chicago, and the violence of the one killed the hopes of the other: "As a mass movement, eight-hour agitation was stopped in its tracks."[85]

One final conclusion that comes from our examination of violence and change is that whether violence is necessary seems to depend on whether there are structural means for effecting change. That is, the very rigid social structure that exercises a feudal type of control over people may be broken by nothing less than violent revolution. One could seriously doubt that China or the Latin American nations that have begun to develop would have progressed without revolution. The only nation in Spanish America to escape civil war during the eighteenth and nineteenth centuries was Paraguay. The cost of this stability was despotism. One of the despots, Francisco Lopez, was responsible for leading his nation into a disastrous war with Argentina, Brazil, and Uruguay. It was the "most savage and sanguinary war in all the records of Latin America," and for Paraguay it meant "virtual extinction. Cautious estimate suggests her population was reduced from 525,000 in 1865 to 221,000 in 1871," and only 28,746 men were among those surviving the havoc.[86] A rigid social structure culminated in greater violence for the nation than any civil war would have been likely to produce.

Thus, violence does produce change. Change occurs without violence, and violence occurs without change. In some cases, violence may be necessary in order to break down a rigid social order. For the most part, violence seems to be only one alternative among others for effecting particular change. It is an alternative that is increasingly perilous. As Martin Luther King, Jr., has eloquently written, "If we assume that mankind has a right to survive then we must find an alternative to war and destruction. In a day when sputniks dash through outer space and guided ballistic missiles are carving highways of death through the stratosphere, nobody can win a war. The choice today is no longer between violence and nonviolence. It is either nonviolence or nonexistence."[87]

Endnotes

1. Max Weber, *From Max Weber: Essays in Sociology,* trans. and ed. H. H. Gerth and C. Wright Mills (New York: Oxford University Press, 1958), p. 333.

2. Don Martindale, *The Nature and Types of Sociological Theory* (Boston: Houghton Mifflin, 1960), p. 142.

3. Quoted in Howard Becker and Harry Elmer Barnes, *Social Thought from Lore to Science,* vol. 2, 3rd ed. (New York: Dover, 1961), p. 705.

4. Richard Hofstadter, *Social Darwinism in American Thought: 1860-1915* (Philadelphia: University of Pennsylvania Press, 1944), p. 174.

5. Ludwig Gumplowicz, *Outlines of Sociology,* ed. Irving L. Horowitz (New York: Paine-Whitman, 1963), p. 203.

6. James H. Meisel, ed., *Pareto & Mosca* (Englewood Cliffs, N.J.: Prentice-Hall, 1965), p. 13.

7. Lewis A. Coser, *The Functions of Social Conflict* (Glencoe, Ill.: Free Press, 1956), p. 18.

8. William Graham Sumner, *Folkways* (Boston: Ginn & Co., 1906), p. 16.

9. Becker and Barnes, *Social Thought from Lore to Science,* p. 719.

10. Ibid., p. 721.

11. See, e.g., Pierre van de Berghe, "Dialectic and Functionalism: Toward a Theoretical Synthesis," *American Sociological Review* 28 (October, 1963): 695-705; Robert Cole, "Structural-Functional Theory, the Dialectic and Social Change," *Sociological Quarterly* 7 (Winter, 1966): 39-58; and Percy S. Cohen, *Modern Social Theory* (New York: Basic Books, 1968), pp. 166-72.

12. Jonathan H. Turner, *The Structure of Sociological Theory* (Homewood. Ill.: Dorsey Press, 1974), p. 121.

13. Jonathan H. Turner, "A Strategy for Reformulating the Dialectical and Functional Theories of Conflict," *Social Forces* 53 (March, 1975): 440.

14. One of the most elaborate and useful theories of conflict has been offered by Randall Collins, *Conflict Sociology: Toward an Explanatory Science* (New York: Academic Press, 1975). Unfortunately, Collins has very little to say about the relationship between conflict and social change.

15. Ralf Dahrendorf, *Class and Class Conflict in Industrial Society* (Stanford: Stanford University Press, 1959), p. 208.

16. Ibid., p. 162.

17. Ralf Dahrendorf, "Toward a Theory of Social Conflict," *Journal of Conflict Resolution* 2 (1958): 180.

18. Ralf Dahrendorf, *Life Chances* (London: Weidenfeld and Nicolson, 1979), p. 61.

19. Ibid., p. 73.

20. See Jay Meddin, "Human Nature and the Dialectics of Immanent Sociocultural Change," *Social Forces* 55 (December, 1976): 382-93.

21. E. N. Grosof et al., "Anchorage in Organization: A Dialectical Theory," *Social Forces* 49 (1970): 81-90.

22. Louis Schneider, "Dialectic in Sociology," *American Sociological Review* 36 (1971): 667-78; and M. Joseph Smucker and Anton C. Zijderveld, "Structure and Meaning: Implications for the Analysis of Social Change," *British Journal of Sociology* 21 (1970): 375-89.

23. Robert S. Perinbanayagam, "The Dialectics of Charisma," *The Sociological Quarterly* 12 (1971): 387-402.

24. Peter M. Blau, *Exchange and Power in Social Life* (New York: Wiley, 1964).

25. Ron E. Roberts and Robert Marsh Kloss, *Social Movements* (St. Louis: C. V. Mosby, 1974); and Michael Useem, *Protest Movements in America* (Indianapolis: Bobbs-Merrill, 1975), p. 28.

26. Susan Lovegren Bosworth and Gary A. Kreps, "Structure As Process: Organization and Role," *American Sociological Review* 51 (October, 1986): 699-716.

27. Raymond Aron, *Progress and Disillusion* (New York: Praeger, 1968).

28. Ibid., p. 64.

29. See L. Richard Della Fave, "The Meek Shall Not Inherit the Earth," *American Sociological Review* 45 (1980): 955-71 and "The Dialectics of Legitimation and Counternorms," *Sociological Perspectives* 29 (1986): 435-60.

30. Della Fave, "The Dialectics of Legitimation and Counternorms," p. 442.

31. Ibid., p. 449.

32. Jerald Hage and Michael Aiken, *Social Change in Complex Organizations* (New York: Random House, 1970), p. 13.

33. H. G. Barnett, *Innovation: The Basis of Cultural Change* (New York: McGraw-Hill, 1953), p. 72.

34. Joseph Ben-David, "Scientific Productivity and Academic Organization in Nineteenth-Century Medicine," in *Comparative Perspectives on Formal Organization*, ed. Henry A. Landsberger (Boston: Little, Brown, 1970), pp. 195-214.

35. Ibid., p. 206. See also Donald C. Pelz and Frank M. Andrews, *Scientists in Organizations* (New York: Wiley, 1966), pp. 7, 151, 240-60. The authors provide evidence that scientists in organizations are more effective under conditions of competition and intellectual rivalry.

36. Nicholas Wade, *The Nobel Duel: Two Scientists' 21-Year Race to Win the World's Most Coveted Research Prize* (New York: Anchor Press, 1981).

37. Richard Lachmann, "Elite Conflict and State Formation in 16th- and 17th-Century England and France," *American Sociological Review* 54 (1989): 141-62.

38. Don Martindale, *Social Life and Cultural Change* (Princeton: Van Nostrand, 1962), pp. 71-72.

39. Will Durant, *The Renaissance* (New York: Simon & Schuster, 1953), p. 73.

40. Lewis A. Coser, "Social Conflict and the Theory of Social Change," *The British Journal of Sociology* 8 (1957): 199.

41. Robert H. Lauer and Warren H. Handel, *Social Psychology: The Theory and Application of Symbolic Interactionism*, 2nd ed. (Englewood Cliffs, N.J.: Prentice-Hall, 1983), p. 10.

42. Paul R. Lawrence and Jay W. Lorsch, *Organization and Environment* (Boston: Harvard University Press, 1967).

43. Evert Van de Vliert, "Escalative Intervention in Small-Group Conflicts," *Journal of Applied Behavioral Science* 21 (1985): 19-36.

44. See Anthony Oberschall, *Social Conflict and Social Movements* (Englewood Cliffs, N.J.: Prentice-Hall, 1973).

45. Roberts and Kloss, *Social Movements.*

46. Robert H. Lauer, ed., *Social Movements and Social Change* (Carbondale: Southern Illinois University Press, 1976), p. xxiii.

47. Maurice Jackson, "The Civil Rights Movement and Social Change," *American Behavioral Scientist* 12 (March-April, 1969): 8-17.

48. Luther P. Gerlach and Virginia H. Hine, *People, Power, Change: Movements of Social Transformation* (Indianapolis: Bobbs-Merrill, 1970); and William A. Anderson and Russell R. Dynes, *Social Movements, Violence, and Change* (Columbus: Ohio State University Press, 1975).

49. David M. Freeman, *Technology and Society: Issues in Assessment, Conflict, and Choice* (Chicago: Rand-McNally, 1974), pp. 89-90.

50. Keith Schneider, "The Green Revolution: How Much Farther Can It Go?" *The New York Times*, August 21, 1981.

51. Tony Barnett, *Social and Economic Development* (New York: Guilford Press, 1989), p. 123.

52. Irwin Unger, *The Movement: A History of the American New Left, 1959-1972* (New York: Dodd, Mead, 1974), p. 191.

53. S. N. Eisenstadt, "Breakdowns of Modernization," in *Readings in Social Evolution and Development*, ed. S. N. Eisenstadt (Oxford: Pergamon Press, 1970). Eisenstadt wrote this paper in 1962-1963.

54. Robert T. Anderson and Barbara Gallatin Anderson, *The Vanishing Village: A Danish Maritime Community* (Seattle: University of Washington Press, 1964).

55. Ibid., p. 143.

56. June Henton, Rodney Cate, James Koval, Sally Lloyd, and Scott Christopher, "Romance and Violence in Dating Relationships," *Journal of Family Issues* 4 (1983): 467-82.

57. Monica D. Blumenthal, Robert L. Kahn, Frank M. Andrews, and Kendra B. Head, *Justifying Violence: Attitudes of American Men* (Ann Arbor: University of Michigan Press, 1972).

58. Philip Taft and Philip Ross, "American Labor Violence: Its Causes, Character, and Outcome," in *The History of Violence in America,* ed. Hugh Davis Graham and Ted Robert Gurr (New York: Bantam, 1969), p. 382.

59. June Nash, "The Cost of Violence," *Journal of Black Studies* 4 (1973): 153-83.

60. Albert O. Hirschman, "Revolution by Stealth! The Case for Sequential Reforms," in *Economic Development: Evolution or Revolution?* ed. Laura Randall (Boston: D. C. Heath, 1964), pp. 76-106.

61. Henry Bienen, *Violence and Social Change* (Chicago: University of Chicago Press, 1968), p. 78.

62. St. Clair Drake, "Urban Violence and American Social Movements," in *Urban Riots: Violence and Social Change* (New York: Random House, 1968), p. 23.

63. Edmundo Flores, "Land Reform and the Alliance for Progress," in Randall, *Economic Development,* p. 42.

64. Lu Congming, "Modern Capitalism Reassessed," *Beijing Review,* January 9-15, 1989, pp. 24-27.

65. Ibid., p. 26.

66. H. L. Nieburg, "The Threat of Violence and Social Change," *American Political Science Review* 56 (1962): 872.

67. Donald Von Eschen, Jerome Kirk, and Maurice Pinard, "The Conditions of Direct Action in a Democratic Society," *The Western Political Quarterly* 22 (1969): 309-25.

68. See, for example, Joseph A. Kahl, *Comparative Perspectives on Stratification: Mexico, Great Britain, Japan* (Boston: Little, Brown, 1968), pp. 1-30.

69. Edgar Snow, *Red China Today* (New York: Random House, 1970), p. 185.

70. Richard E. Rubenstein, *Alchemists of Revolution: Terrorism in the Modern World* (New York: Basic Books, 1987).

71. Ibid., p. 201.

72. Ivo K. Feierabend, Rosalind L. Feierabend, and Betty A. Nesvold, "Social Change and Political Violence: Cross-National Patterns," in Graham and Gurr, *The History of Violence in America,* pp. 653-68.

73. William A. Gamson, *The Strategy of Social Protest* (Homewood, Ill.: Dorsey Press, 1975).

74. Ibid., p. 82.

75. Gerlach and Hine, *People, Power, Change: Movements of Social Transformation,* pp. 142-54.

76. Charles Tilly, Louise Tilly, and Richard Tilly, *The Rebellious Century, 1830-1930* (Cambridge, Mass.: Harvard University Press, 1975).

77. Ibid., pp. 282-85.

78. James McClenon, "Terrorism As Persuasion: Possibilities and Trends," *Sociological Focus* 21 (1988): 53-66.

79. Walter Laqueur, "Reflections on Terrorism," *Foreign Affairs* 65 (1986): 86-100.

80. Ibid., p. 95.

81. Hofstadter, "Reflections on Violence," p. 38.

82. Joan V. Bondurant, *Conquest of Violence* (Berkeley: University of California Press, 1969), p. 8.

83. Frances Pivan and Richard Cloward, "Disrupting City Services to Change National Priorities," in *Where It's At: Radical Perspectives in Sociology*, ed. Steven E. Deutsch and John Howard (New York: Harper & Row, 1970), pp. 471-80.

84. Barrington Moore, Jr., *Social Origins of Dictatorship and Democracy* (Boston: Beacon Press, 1966), pp. 103-4.

85. Kurt Lang and Gladys Engel Lang, *Collective Dynamics* (New York: Thomas Y. Crowell, 1961), p. 516.

86. Hubert Herring, *A History of Latin America* (New York: Knopf, 1957), pp. 674-75.

87. Martin Luther King, Jr., "Pilgrimage to Nonviolence," in *Instead of Violence*, ed. Arthur and Lila Weinberg (New York: Grossman, 1963), p. 74.

CHAPTER TEN

Structural Sources: Government and Status Anguish

A young woman sat alone in a small room, taking part in an experiment designed to discover the kinds of personal problems faced by college students. She was part of a group, but each member was alone in a small room in order to assure anonymity. They conversed with one another by intercom. One of the students discussed his problem of seizures. When it was his turn to talk again, he suddenly became loud, grew increasingly incoherent, choked, then became silent. Apparently he had had one of his seizures.

What would the young woman do under such circumstances? What do you suppose you would do? The situation just described was actually created by two psychologists in an effort to determine how people react to emergencies. They found that different people responded differently. Some left their cubicles to try to find help for the student who had apparently had the seizure (the seizure was feigned). But others did not. What made the difference? Were some simply more concerned about human beings than others? Were there significant personality differences that explained the different responses? The experimenters found that personality differences did not account for the different responses. Rather, the most significant variable was group size. If the young woman thought that the "group" was composed of only herself and the victim of the seizure, she was far more likely to go for help than if she thought there were six in the group! She was also likely to respond far more quickly alone than if she thought there were six in the group.

To sum up the results of the experiment, 85 percent of subjects in two-person groups, 62 percent in three-person groups, and 31 percent in six-person groups reported the emergency before the victim's voice was cut off. All subjects in the two-person groups eventually reported it, but only 62 percent of those in the six-person groups went for help.[1]

What this experiment stresses is a major point made by sociologists: much of human behavior can be understood in terms of the structure in which it takes place rather than in terms of the personalities of those involved. This same point is made by Jerald Hage and Michael Aiken in their study of program change in welfare agencies. They reported that structural properties such as centralization, formalization, and stratification "were much more highly associated with the rate of program change than attitudes toward change."[2] This implies, they note, that an organization's structure may be far more significant in effecting change than the particular mix of personalities in the organization.

In this and the next chapter, therefore, we shall look at some aspects of the social structure that might account for the direction of change. In every society, there is a government, a group of people who have problems with status (who are, that is, structurally marginal), a group of elites, and youth. These two chapters will show the effect on change of each of these facets of the social structure.

Change from the Center: Government

Government today is pervasive. As Peter Drucker has pointed out, "the most despotic government of 1900 would not have dared probe into the private affairs of its citizens as income-tax collectors now do routinely in the freest society."[3] Drucker also emphasizes the great size of government: 'There is no country in the world today where the entire government establishment of 1910 could not comfortably be housed in the smallest of the new government buildings now going up, with room to spare for a grand-opera house and a skating rink."[4] Every local, state, and federal government agency that existed in the time of Theodore Roosevelt in the United States could easily be put into the regional federal building in Denver.

In other words, both the massiveness and the pervasiveness of government indicate that we ought to examine its effects on change. Books on change generally have little to say about the effect of government, unless the focus is on political change or modernization. Government is indeed an extraordinarily important factor in modernization in the contemporary world; but it is important also in the developed nations—either as a barrier to or as a leader of change. All the levels of government are important, from the local to the national.

• *Government as a Barrier to Change*

In the Marxist view, the state is a reactionary organization that serves the interests of the propertied class and, thereby, impedes necessary change. As Engels put it, the state generally is "the state of the most powerful, economically dominant class, which, through the medium of the state, becomes also the politically dominant class, and thus acquires new means of holding down and exploiting the oppressed class."[5]

This, of course, is completely contrary to the view of government that many American students have acquired in civics courses. Those courses often teach that the government exists to serve us, that it reflects the interests of all of us. It seems historically obvious, however, that the government has hardly served the interests of blacks, or American Indians, or the impoverished. There is a ready explanation for this, of course. For people of higher socioeconomic levels do not support government help for the poor. Despite some popular opinions to the contrary, the evidence shows that one of the most important factors in the voting habits of legislators is their perceptions of the opinions of their constituents. Legislators do not follow public opinion slavishly, of course, but certainly the majority of their votes are consistent with public opinion on the issues involved.[6]

In addition, the composition of the government and the structure of American society should lead us to doubt that the government could effectively serve deprived groups. American politicians have never been representative of a cross section of the American people; rather, they have tended to come more fron the middle and upper classes. Furthermore, the government bureaucracy is composed mainly of middle-class individuals. This is not to say that middle-class individuals are totally insensitive to the needs of the deprived. But in point of fact, while some middle- and upper-class people have always championed the interests of the deprived, historically the poor have not benefited greatly and the middle strata have not been greatly hurt by governmental action. Even programs designed to help the poor generally benefit the nonpoor as much as they do the poor.[7] Medicaid has helped some poor people; it has also made many physicians wealthy. Job-training programs have aided some of the poor; they have also provided high-salaried positions for middle-class administrators.

It is ironic, in view of the evidence, that some Americans describe their government as an example of "creeping socialism." In terms of their share of income, the lower strata of American society were little better off in the 1980s than they were in the early decades of the century.[8] The broad middle strata, on the contrary, have benefited greatly from government action. Perhaps few middle-class Americans have been aware of the extent to which their quality of life has been enhanced by government subsidies for everything from farm products to education to corporations. Such subsidies reflect the intricate relationship between government and business and the extent to which business tends to be unified in support of particular governmental programs and particular politicians.[9]

It is not only in the United States that the government has often been a barrier to enhancing the quality of life for some segments of the population. In Latin America, the combination of the church, the military, the landed elite, and the United States government has frequently proved decisive in maintaining the peasants in a state of oppression.

There are some who would even argue that government programs generally—whatever the intent—are ineffective or even counterproductive in terms of enhancing the economic well-being of people. Looking at economic growth in sixty-five less developed countries between the years 1960 and 1980, an economist found that the greater the governments' expenditures the less their economic growth.[10] In spite of such aggregate findings, however, we shall see below that there are specific instances in which governmental action has greatly facilitated economic growth. The point here is that governmental action can be a barrier to change, and it is particularly likely to be a barrier to those changes that would enhance the well-being of the lower strata of society.

• Government as a Force for Change

In spite of government's role as a barrier to certain kinds of changes, it has directed many other kinds. In the United States, the government has been an important factor in change throughout our history, despite the popular ideology that upholds "free enterprise." Even in the days when the ideology of social Darwinism sat upon the throne of human thought, the government played an important part in the changes that were occurring in the country. The changes were primarily for the benefit of the business elite, and were defined therefore in terms that made the government's role seem negligible. As someone has said, many Americans feel that what the government does for them is progress, while what it does for others is socialism.

Our ignorance of history blinds us to the present as well. Never has government been the disinterested bystander that some ideologies have portrayed it as being. The initial exploration of America resulted from governmental financing, and the first colonists came because of English corporations that were subsidized by the crown. In the days of our early growth, the government seized more and more land from the Indians and employed the military to "protect" the western-bound pioneers; many early farmers were subsidized at the cost of the lives of Indians.

The Homestead Act of 1862 gave farmers great tracts of land. Business was stimulated by the building of canals, subsidies to railroads, and the tolerance of the ruthlessness of the robber barons. Aid to science began at an early date with such things as the Lewis and Clark expedition and the federal grant to Samuel Morse for the building of a telegraph line between Baltimore and Washington, D.C.

The government has been prominent in stimulating education. Before the Constitutional Convention, the government designated large tracts of public land for educational use. The Morrill Act of 1862 gave to each state an amount of public land that was proportionate to its number of Representatives. Money received from the sale of the land could be used for practical education (in fields such as agriculture and engineering).

Thus, the American government has been active in all the major changes that have occurred in our history. The industrialization of the nation, the growth of education and science, the pattern of land usage, and other large new developments have all been given impetus by government action and government aid. In all this, the government has acted on behalf of particular interests; certain groups in the nation have benefited very little from these activities. The point is that the direction of change in America must be understood at least in part in terms of government.

A similar situation occurred in Japan, where the government was, if anything, even more actively involved in the modernization of the nation. The government involved, of course, was a new government created by the Meiji Restoration of 1868. "The new government was in essence an oligarchy in the hands of fewer than one hundred young men."[11] This government embarked on a program to bring Japan swiftly into the modern world. Various tools of modernization were quickly borrowed from the West, including administrative techniques, the Western calendar, religious toleration, a civil service, a national banking system, a modernized currency, a Cabinet, and a Constitution. The Ministry of Education was instituted in 1871, and Japan quickly headed for universal education; it became the first nation in Asia to have a literate population. The government stimulated the industrialization of the nation by creating and controlling such services as railways, the telegraph, and public utilities, and by stimulating enterprise through loans or other methods. The few private capitalists of the early days of development were given government aid and patronage.

In sum, the core of Japanese modernization came through government activity. This may be seen clearly by examining a particular facet of change—the development of science and technology. The Japanese quickly saw science and technology as essential to modernization, and the government took the lead in introducing and developing them. "At huge costs to the national treasury, foreign teachers, specialists, and technology were imported, students sent abroad, foreign books translated."[12] Many of the educational institutions that would further scientific development were established in the Meiji era. Tokyo University was founded in 1877 and was reorganized with the College of Technology in 1886, becoming Tokyo Imperial University.

In 1870 the government set up a Ministry of Engineering which guided the development of railways, telegraphic services, and modern techniques of industrial management. Although foreign advisers were important initially, Japanese scholars and technicians were quickly trained. The aim of the whole process was to create a strong nation, so that military development was also pursued avidly.

The government had a practical end, the building of a great nation, and the swiftness of change toward that end was impressive. Before the end of the Meiji era, the Japanese had developed "an important capacity in heavy industry, with obvious military implications. Facilities for shipbuilding, iron and steel production, coal mining, machine production, and electric power were all given government support for the development of military and industrial power."[13]

More recently, the South Korean government provides an example of how governmental action can facilitate economic growth.[14] The South Korean economic "miracle" began in the early 1960s. For the next decade, the nation had an annual growth rate of 9.5 percent in gross domestic products. Exports increased significantly and domestic savings increased fivefold. The economic expansion continued into the early 1980s.

While many factors were involved in the Korean expansion, certain governmental actions were crucial. The government liberalized the nation's trade policies, largely through a devaluation of currency in 1964. The government also instituted tariff-free imports that would be used in any export production. Goals were established for exports. Firms generally set up their own goals in conjunction with export associations and the government. The goals were comprehensive and specific, including which industries would target which markets with what products. And in the same year that the government devalued currency, it set up the Korean Trade Promotion Corporation to promote exports. It allowed the Korean Traders' Association to collect 1 percent of the value of imports and use the money to promote exports.

The government also involved itself in the regulation of the nation's financial system. It nationalized all commercial banks in 1961. A year later it assumed responsibility for monetary policy (a responsibility previously held by the Bank of Korea).

In order to protect its own industry, the government exercised control over direct foreign investments in Korea. Little competition was allowed with domestic firms. Foreign banks were not permitted to compete with the nation's banks in various ventures. And foreign investors were pressured to consider joint ventures with Koreans rather than pursuing a wholly foreign investment.

The Korean government intervened in the economy in a variety of other ways, including the use of price controls as short-term measures for controlling excess profits. As in the case of Meiji Japan, significant economic growth was integrally tied up with governmental action and policies.

Government, then, is a potent source of change, and much of the direction of change in any society with a strong central government must be understood in terms of the activity of that government. Although, as we have seen, governmental activity tends to benefit the middle and upper classes of any society, the lower strata does benefit occasionally. Action that benefits the lower strata is more likely to result when there is a perception of threat.

An example of change arising out of a perceived threat was the introduction of reforms that occurred in Iran in the early 1960s.[15] In 1963 the Shah launched a "White Revolution" that offered six points of reform. Six additional points were later added to the Revolution. The points included land reform, nationalization of forests and pastures, profit sharing in the industrial sector, inclusion of women in the electoral laws, efforts to improve health and increase literacy, and educational reform.

The threat that impelled this program came not from the peasants but from the new middle class, who rejected the traditional sociopolitical arrangements. The Shah's program, therefore, was aimed at maintaining traditional power patterns by gaining the support of the peasants through the various reform measures. Iranian modernization, like all other modernization in the contemporary world, was centered around the government as the government responded to the threat posed by the new middle class. Ultimately, of course, the Shah's efforts were self-defeating. His promotion of Western-style consumerism, combined with his attacks on Islam (including ridicule of the clergy), came back to haunt him during the Islamic Revolution of 1979. Many of the middle class that had benefited from the reforms of the White Revolution left the country after the Islamic Revolution.

As noted above, it is not only national governments that act as a force for change. Lower level governments may also be quite important in the kinds of changes that occur. An example is provided by Francois Vigier's analysis of Liverpool and Manchester, England, during the period 1750-1850.[16] As a result of the action of the municipal government, Liverpool was transformed from "a slumbering provincial town into one of England's most prosperous cities."[17] Among other actions, the municipal government took the necessary steps to construct port facilities on municipal land and to collect duties on all merchandise passing through the port. As Vigier notes, such a publicly owned enterprise was "a surprisingly modern concept for the time, akin to our own port, bridge, and turnpike authorities."[18] Although the bulk of attention has been paid to the effects of national governments (in part, perhaps, because of the significance of the national government in modernization), the impact of lower level governments should not be ignored.

Of course, the significance of lower level governments will vary from one nation to another and from one time period to another in the same nation. In some Western countries, including the United States, national policies have become increasingly important for the well-being of local areas like cities.[19] Local governments have less autonomy and less discretion in advanced industrial societies. We live in an international economy. And we live in a society that is increasingly service-oriented rather than industrial. The control of economic change in a city, therefore, is no longer as dependent on the local economy or on the state in which the city is located. Both cities and states have become more dependent on the national government, which affects local economies through such things as grants, transfer payments, public employment, federal procurement, and various economic development programs. Local governments still have considerable scope for action, but their ability to control their own economic well-being is far less than it was in the past.

• Type of Government and Change

If we look at the role of government in effecting any particular kind of change at any particular level of social reality, it is immediately evident that the role may vary. For instance, looking at the role of government in economic development at the institutional level, Szymon Chodak points out that we can identify at least three different political ways of shaping that development.[20] First, a government might work to create conditions that facilitate economic development, but not take an active role in that development. This would mean such things as providing a secure social order and supporting various kinds of commercial and industrial developments by private entrepreneurs. Second, the government might attempt to regulate actively the process of development to some extent. For instance, various interest groups might require defense at some point so that they are not overwhelmed by more powerful groups and so that the market can continue to be competitive. Finally, the government might directly engage in the planning and implementation of economic development through such mechanisms as nationalization of some industry, specification of national priorities and goals, and provision of various kinds of resources necessary for development.

Chodak says that the first type described above is characteristic of the early stages of capitalism. The second and third types are characteristic of advanced capitalism and socialism, respectively. In other words, the type of government will make a difference in the course of economic change. By "type" here I refer to governments of differing ideologies (conservative, liberal, radical) and also of differing structures (number of parties, degree of authoritarianism, extent of bureaucratization, and so forth). Types appear to make a difference in the kind of change that occurs, and they make a difference at all levels of government.

For example, in the United States a number of studies have shown the way in which differing kinds of municipal governments bear upon policy. Three results of empirical research have been summarized by Jack Rothman: reformed governments are not as responsive to the goals of minorities and dissidents as are unreformed governments; a city-manager form of government results in a larger proportion of support for education; and a city-manager form of government is more likely to successfully annex suburbs (which can be important to financially pressed and spatially bound urban areas).[21] Similarly, at the national level the type of administration will make a difference in the kinds of programs implemented. When conservative politicians are in power, as during the Reagan administration of the 1980s, the poor are likely to suffer more. Indeed, in the early 1980s millions of Americans were forced into poverty as a result of new federal policies.[22] For example, five million Americans lost some or all of the aid they had been receiving in the form of food stamps; nearly 5 billion dollars were cut from Aid to Families with Dependent Children (AFDC). Medicaid benefits were trimmed; and nearly a million children lost free or reduced-price school breakfasts. At the same time, millions of other Americans profited from changes instituted by the administration. Clearly, it is not true that it makes little difference which party holds power.

• Type of Government and Modernization

It is generally conceded that a strong state is the *sine qua non* of contemporary modernization. To some scholars a "strong" state is equivalent to an authoritarian state, while others argue that a democratic state may achieve the same things and do so more humanely. Some point out that democracy will impede economic growth, because that growth necessarily requires the direction of experts and the willingness of the people to sacrifice current consumption for long-term economic gains. Others argue that authoritarian regimes exact their own cost in both economic and social terms, and that a pluralistic or democratic system provides a creative base for building the economy.

The issue is muddied by the fact that both sides can marshal evidence; both authoritarian and democratic nations have had both low and high rates of growth. One possible way of resolving the question is to say that in the contemporary world there is a need for authoritarianism in the early stages of development and for increasing participation of the citizenry as growth proceeds.

Another possible way of resolving the problem is to distinguish between the form and the activity of the government. We saw with respect to ideology that we could distinguish between function and content; that is, diverse ideologies could create solidarity among people and so facilitate change. We can make the same distinction with government: diverse forms of government can provide the same essential functions that facilitate modernization. Those functions, according to Eugene Staley, fall into three broad categories: "(1) creating the physical and social foundations for development; (2) overall planning and integration of development; (3) bringing about larger and more efficient production and distribution of goods and services."[23]

There seems to be little inherent reason why such functions could not be handled by either a democratic or an authoritarian government. A slightly different approach to the necessary functions of government has been taken by Alexander Eckstein, who specifies five conditions under which the government is likely to play a lesser or greater role in economic growth. Specifically, the role of the government is likely to be greater.

1. The greater the "range of ends" (number and diversity of goals) and the higher the aspirations for attainment.
2. The more rapidly the growth is to be achieved.

3. The "more unfavorable the factor and resource endowments."
4. The stronger the institutional impediments to economic growth.
5. "The more backward the economy in relative terms."[24]

These conditions require governmental intervention if the society is to modernize. Again, there seems to be no inherent reason why different forms of government could not intervene equally well under the above conditions.

In sum, I would not dispute the point that government is essential to modernization among the developing nations today. The government must be a strong one in order to provide the requisite social, political, and economic conditions for modernization to proceed. Whether we opt for an authoritarian or a democratic government must be decided on grounds other than their relative efficiency in economic growth. At least in view of what we now know about modernization, including economic growth, the functions of government appear far more crucial than its form.

Change from the Periphery: Status Anguish

Imagine a psychiatrist, a respected and wealthy man, who is hailed by a policeman one day. The policeman calls the psychiatrist "boy" and treats him with obvious contempt. And this is not an isolated incident, for many people with whom the psychiatrist comes into contact relate to him as though he were their inferior.

The psychiatrist is not really an imaginary character. He is black, and he lives in the United States. The treatment he received from the policeman and from numerous other whites happened in the recent past. How does he respond to this? He has education, a prestigious occupation, and wealth, but his social milieu does not accord him the prestige that is rightfully his. He suffers from what I have called "status anguish," a psychic distress that arises when there is contradiction in the individual's status set.

• Status Anguish and Consistency

It has often been argued that people strive for consistency. Social psychologists have developed a number of theories that explain behavior on the basis of our drive to attain cognitive consistency. Sociologists have pointed to the drive to attain status consistency, which is congruence between various aspects of a status or between differing statuses. As the example of the black psychiatrist illustrates, however, we often face situations and perhaps even an entire existence in which consistency eludes us. We must come to terms then with status anguish. Status anguish includes marginality, status inconsistency, status withdrawal, and relative deprivation. All involve internal contradictions in individuals—perceived contradictions—as they assess their social world and their place in it. We shall now explain these and look at their relation to social change.

Marginality One type of status anguish that has been identified is marginality. The concept was first developed to explain characteristics of second-generation immigrants. An early essay by Everett Hughes linked marginality with social change.[25] Marginality, or the "marginal man," was first defined by Robert Park in 1928. According to Park, a marginal man is one who is "living and sharing intimately in the cultural life and traditions of two distinct peoples; never quite willing to break, even if he were permitted to do so, with his past and his traditions, and not quite accepted, because of racial prejudice, in the new society in which he now sought to find a place."[26] In other words, marginality is existence in two or more social worlds without being fully a part of any of them.

Marginality generates psychic distress, and Hughes noted five different ways in which an individual might strive to reduce his or her marginality. One would be to give up the struggle and return to an earlier status (the black psychiatrist would simply accept his inferior position and identify fully with his own people). A second, requiring societal consent, would be to let one of the statuses disappear as a status (being black would have no relationship per se to status). A third course would be to "resign from the status which interferes with . . . other status aims."[27] If he used this alternative, the black psychiatrist would have to renounce his own people. Fourth, the individual might find one or more of his statuses redefined in such a manner as to resolve the contradiction (psychiatry might degenerate in prestige to the point where the psychiatrist is like a fortune teller in status). Finally, the social system might change or be changed so that the marginal group would become an integral part of the whole (black professionals might be defined differently from other blacks and given a position of prestige within the society). Thus, in Hughes's formulation, some kind of change—at either the individual or the societal level—is required for the reduction of marginality.

Status Inconsistency A second type of status anguish arises from the lack of what has been variously called status crystallization, status congruency, or status consistency. As Gerhard Lenski has argued, this is a "nonvertical dimension" of status.[28] That is, status is not a unidimensional phenemonon but a "series of positions in a series of related hierarchies." An individual may rank consistently or inconsistently in four hierarchies—income, occupation, education, and ethnicity. For instance, in Figure 10-1 we see the relative positions of two individuals, A and B. A is consistent because he ranks high on all four hierarchies. He has a good education, prestigious occupation, high income, and belongs to a high-status ethnic group (let us say he is white and Anglo-Saxon). On the other hand, B has a good education and a fairly prestigious job, but B belongs to a low-status ethnic group (let us say he is black) and suffers discrimination in terms of income. The inconsistency in B's case is along two dimensions—ethnic status and

Figure 10-1 • Status Consistency and Inconsistency (A = consistent individual; B = inconsistent individual)

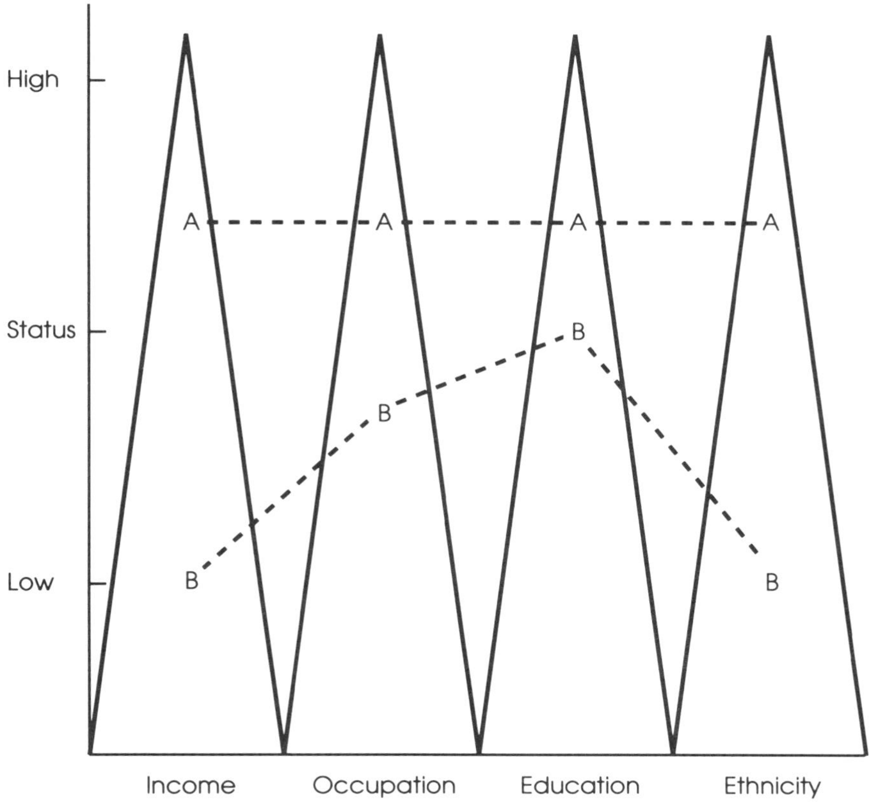

income. An individual may be inconsistent along only one dimension and still feel the effects. Moreover, it is reasonable to assume that if those effects include frustration and psychic stress, the individual will desire to change the social order so that the inconsistency is eliminated. Thus, Lenski asserted that the more people there were who suffered from acute status inconsistency, the more people there would be who would support programs of social change.

Lenski's thesis has been subjected to considerable debate and study. Some researchers report findings that dispute the thesis, while others have reported that individuals suffering status inconsistency may react in a variety of ways, including the development of psychophysiological symptoms.[29] Thus, the actual political consequences, or at least the consequences in terms of political attitudes, of status inconsistency remain ambiguous. Our knowledge in this area is hampered by, among other things, methodological problems in the measurement of status inconsistency.[30]

On the other hand, even if the relationship between status inconsistency and political attitudes is obscure, there is evidence that inconsistency is associated with participation in social movements. Gary Rush found a relationship between status inconsistency (along the dimensions of occupation, income, and education) and right-wing political extremism.[31] James Geschwender found that status inconsistency tends to lead to "symptoms of individual unrest "[32] Other researchers have linked status inconsistency among blacks with participation in the Civil Rights Movement or in civil disturbances. For instance, rioters in Detroit had higher education than nonrioters, but were lower in occupational ranking. This is not to say, of course, that all participants in social movements have inconsistencies in their various statuses, nor that all those with inconsistencies participate in movements. Rather, participation in a social movement is one way in which people can cope with status inconsistency.[33]

Status Withdrawal A third type of status anguish was identified by Hagen in his description of economic development. As we have seen, he placed strong emphasis on the fact that a group in a society may undergo status withdrawal. We need not accept all of the dynamics of Hagen's analysis to see the applicability of his idea in certain historical cases, and we shall examine one of these cases—Japan—in this chapter.

Relative Deprivation The final type of status anguish that we shall examine is relative deprivation, which stresses the importance of the assessment people make of their situation (as opposed to the way it actually is or the way an outsider might assess it). The accent is on the word "relative," for the deprivation is a perceived deprivation in relationship to some standard. For instance, the people who typically participate in a revolutionary movement are not the most deprived—there are few slave revolts in history. Rather, they perceive themselves to be deprived in some way that is intolerable, even though an outsider might point out that they are better off at the time of the movement than they were previously. The concept of relative deprivation, then, demands that we understand the meaning of the situation to the actors involved, for it is how the actors define the situation that is crucial.

Relative deprivation has commonly been used to explain the rise of social movements. Social movements are, by definition collective efforts to implement (or, in some cases, impede) social change.[34] We shall, therefore, explore the meaning of relative deprivation for social change by looking at the former in the context of social movements.

One well-known use of relative deprivation to account for social movements occurs in James Davies's study of revolutions.[35] Davies points out that revolutions do not usually occur in cases of general impoverishment, because the energies of the people are consumed by the basic problem of staying alive. People cannot be concerned about losing their chains, as Marx urged, when they face the choice between losing their chains or their lives. In other words, a revolutionary movement requires at least some people in the society who are above the subsistence level.

Furthermore, the revolutionary impetus arises when there is an expectation of continually increasing opportunities for satisfying individual needs (including those needs that are perceived to be necessary for fullness of life). When a threat arises to this expectation—when it appears that people will be unable to satisfy their needs according to their expectations—a revolutionary situation exists. There is always a gap between expected and actual satisfaction of needs, but when an intolerable gap develops between what people want and what they get, there may be a revolution. Davies illustrates his thesis by applying it to a number of revolutions, in each of which the people were relatively deprived, although they were still better off in absolute terms than they were at an earlier time.

This point was observed by Alexis de Tocqueville with respect to the French Revolution. Tocqueville noted that the French were actually experiencing real gains in economic prosperity prior to the Revolution: "In 1780, there could no longer be any talk of France's being on the downgrade; on the contrary, it seemed that no limit could be set to her advance. . . . Moreover, those parts of France in which the improvement in the standard of living was most pronounced were the centers of the revolutionary movement."[36] Thus, in a situation of relative deprivation there are disparities between legitimate expectations and what is actually obtainable. These disparities may reflect either a worsening of conditions for a group or an exposure to new standards.[37]

An example of revolution in the midst of overall economic growth is Nicaragua.[38] From the 1930s to the 1970s the nation was ruled by the Somoza family, supported by the military and the United States government. The Somozas also retained economic control through their investments in Nicaragua's land, industry, and banking. There was some modernization during their rule, but the modernization benefited only a small minority of the elite. Opposition was generally dealt with by severe repression, including the imposition of martial law. In the 1970s a Marxist guerrilla group, the FSLN (Sandinistas), began armed resistance. The Sandinistas gained increasing support from other nations, and the United States put increasing pressure on Somoza to resign because of his blatant violation of human rights. In 1979, Somoza fled the country and the Sandinistas assumed power.

The Sandinista revolution succeeded because it had mass support in Nicaragua. And it had mass support because of the widespread deprivation that existed in the midst of some economic growth: "A few were benefitting handsomely from the country's modest socioeconomic progress, while the majority were excluded from effective political and economic participation. The Sandinistas succeeded in mobilizing the majority by raising their expectations, their awareness of frustrations, and their level of participation."[39]

There have been some efforts to extend and refine the concept of relative deprivation. Denton Morrison pointed out that much of the evidence for relative deprivation is indirect in the sense that it is evidence that there was no absolute deprivation.[40] Actual data on the perceptions of people involved in a collective effort at change are not often gathered (or available). Morrison used perceptual data he gathered to expand our understanding of relative deprivation.

First, Morrison argued that the discontent implied by the idea of relative deprivation arises from two factors: legitimate expectations and the perception of those expectations as blocked. On the one hand, people feel that they are pursuing legitimate goals. For example, a group such as blacks may feel that they have a right to equal employment opportunities; such a right is a legitimate expectation (as opposed to fantasies such as instant wealth or the seizure of all power). On the other hand, blacks may also perceive their situation as one in which that legitimate expectation is blocked—there is little likelihood of their gaining equal employment opportunities. Both of these elements are necessary for a sense of relative deprivation.

Furthermore, there is a temporal dimension to expectations. People do not expect to reach a certain goal immediately, even if that goal is a legitimate one. Thus, most blacks would probably agree that progress toward equal employment opportunities is their expectation rather than an instant achievement of such opportunities. In order for a sense of relative deprivation to develop, according to Morrison, there must be a sudden increase in the perceived blockage of legitimate goals. Blacks, to return to our example, will not feel a sense of relative deprivation unless they perceive a change in their situation that increases the blockage against equal employment opportunities. The basis for this reasoning is that a long-term blockage is unlikely to lead to legitimate expectations; people only develop the latter when there is a realistic possibility of achieving them. Thus, whereas Davies posited a sudden increase in the gap between what people want and what they get, Morrison said that the crucial factor is a sudden increase between what people believe they have a right to and what they believe they will probably get. In other words, Davies's theory involves an objectively worsening situation (a reversal of the previous trend) combined with a continuing rise in expectations, while Morrison's thesis stresses the perceptions of the people involved (presumably, those perceptions could be incongruous with the actualities of the situation as measured by an outside observer).

Morrison also suggested a number of ways in which people might handle the sudden increase in blockage. An individual might blame himself or herself. A black man who fails to get adequate employment, for example, might decide that he simply does not have the necessary ability to get ahead. An individual might lower his or her aspirations; the black man who suffers job discrimination might lose his ambition for better-paying work. An individual might redefine the blockage as less formidable than it first appeared. Thus, the black man might decide that he must be patient, and that eventually he will reach his goal if only he is persistent.

If, however, the black man becomes involved in the Black Power Movement, he has opted for another alternative identified by Morrison—he has maintained both his legitimate expectation for equal opportunity and his definition of the blockage as intolerable. Such blockage will be defined as a condition of the social structure, and the movement will be defined as the means of effecting structural changes. When will the individual decide to become part of such a movement rather than choose one of the other alternatives? Morrison suggested five structural conditions that facilitate the development of a movement:

1. A substantial number of people must share the experience of deprivation.
2. There must be interaction and communication among those who perceive the deprivation.
3. The deprived must be fairly homogeneous in terms of their roles and statuses. (If the people are very different, it is easier to attribute the problem to individual deficiencies, whereas if many people of the same kind experience the same problem, structural conditions are more likely to be blamed.)
4. The stratification system must have clear boundaries among the strata and observable differences in power.
5. The movement is more likely when there is substantial participation in voluntary associations, for such groups suggest that change can be effected through the collective, voluntary action of people.

The last point mentioned by Morrison may be valid to the extent that nonorganized people recognize the possibility of change through collective action because of voluntary associations in their society. However, there is evidence that those individuals who have successfully participated in existing voluntary associations may not respond to the social movement.[41]

Morrison applied his analysis to power-oriented movements, but expressive movements (such as religious sects) have also been analyzed in terms of relative deprivation. Armand Mauss and Donald Petersen found the concept useful in their study of the "Jesus People."[42] The religious group known as the Jesus People first appeared about 1967, mainly on the West Coast. Mauss and Petersen traced the conversion of many of those in the Jesus People to disillusionment within the hippie community. The hippie notions of love and gentleness were being flagrantly violated by incidents of murder, rape, and drug problems. In order to understand why some of the hippies turned to Christianity and, in particular, to the kind of Christianity represented by the Jesus People, Mauss and Petersen identified the efforts of Pentecostal evangelists (who offered Jesus to the hippies in place of drugs) and the sense of deprivation among the hippies. The evangelists, in essence, arrived on the scene at an appropriate time and capitalized on the experience of deprivation.

The definition of deprivation, as used here, must be enlarged. Too much, argue Mauss and Petersen, has been made of purely economic deprivation. Following Charles Glock, they suggest five different kinds of deprivation that may help to generate new sects and motivate individuals to join a sect. One kind of deprivation is economic. A second is organismic, which refers to bodily deprivation. Many of the recruits to the Jesus People had a variety of physiological and emotional problems that resulted from their previous life-style. Ethical deprivation is a third type, and this was manifested among the recruits in a generalized anti-establishment attitude. A fourth type of deprivation is the psychic, which is similar to anomie, and which appeared among recruits in the form of a searching for identity and purpose. Finally, there is social deprivation, which involves inequalities in the distribution of social rewards such as status, power, and opportunities. The recruits manifested this in their search for belonging and for status.

These various kinds of deprivation were shared by a number of the hippies. Furthermore, there were no channels available to them (or none that they could see) for alleviating the deprivation until the Pentecostal evangelists appeared with a solution. As a result, a number of the hippies became a part of a movement that used argot to express its ideology ("get addicted to God"), stood against the religious establishment as though the latter were virtually the anti-Christ, and generally practiced and expressed a fundamentalistic type of religion. In essence, the aim of the Jesus People was to change the entire world by changing people into their own likeness.

The idea that people who join social movements have experienced some kind of deprivation is both reasonable and congruent with a number of studies. This is particularly true when we expand the notion of deprivation beyond the purely economic. On the other hand, it should be noted that there are a number of problems with the concept of relative deprivation.[43] First, and perhaps foremost, many of the studies have *inferred* the subjective experience of deprivation from evidence about objective circumstances and the ideology of the movement. The fact that a movement's ideology posits a deprivation among its members does not mean that all of those members have actually experienced the deprivation. Furthermore, there are certainly more people who experience the deprivation than join the movement. Why do some of the deprived join a movement while others do not? Undoubtedly, social movements are associated with some kind or kinds of deprivation. We should not conclude that everyone in a particular movement has experienced the same kind of deprivation or is even conscious of any deprivation. Relative deprivation is a useful social psychological tool, but more work needs to be done to determine its overall significance for social movements and social change.

In sum, we have examined briefly four types of status anguish that have been identified as forces of change. The first, marginality, was developed with specific reference to second-generation immigrants. As members of the second generation tried to move from the ethnic community into the mainstream of American life, they commonly found themselves in a marginal position with respect to both. They were involved in two different social worlds but were not fully a part of either, and they endured considerable psychic stress as a result of their marginal status. Hughes argued that such a status was a factor in change as well as a result of rapid change.

The second type, status inconsistency, was formulated by Lenski in an effort to see if political behavior could be illuminated by relating such behavior to inconsistencies in the societal stratification system. Such inconsistency would presumably be applicable to diverse groups and individuals within a society. The inconsistency could be rooted in religious affiliation, ethnic background, a change in occupational prestige without a concomitant change in income, and a number of other factors.

The third type, status withdrawal, involves the loss of status by a particular group that once possessed it. In effect, this group would be downwardly mobile over time. This kind of status anguish differs from the first type, marginality, which implies efforts at upward mobility, and the second type, status inconsistency, which has no *necessary* reference to mobility (though mobility along one dimension could easily create the inconsistency).

Finally, the last type, relative deprivation, has been used frequently to explain social movements. People who feel deprived in comparison to some standard will be potential recruits for movements that attempt to effect change. That change, presumably, will address the deprivation and correct it, thereby reducing the sense of deprivation.

While there are differences, all four types of status anguish indicate problematic status, all four suggest that individuals perceive contradictions in their social world and their places in that world, and all four have been identified with change. I use the term "status anguish" to include the four types of problematic status that may impel a group to strive for change. We shall now examine some additional evidence that supports the notion that status anguish is a driving mechanism of change.

• *Status Anguish and Change*

The thesis that status anguish leads to change is based on the assumption that a moral order prevails with respect to status; that is, people expect consistency between various facets of their status and between various statuses. The business executive does not expect to be, and probably would not be asked to be, an envelope stuffer for a charity drive; rather, the business executive might be the honorary chairperson of the drive. Thus, our experience as well as our intuition tells us that the assumption of a moral order is correct.

When we turn to historical evidence, we find many instances of groups at the cutting edge of change that are characterized by some form of status anguish. The industrialization of England was driven forward by a disproportionate number of religious nonconformists. In Colombia, where three valleys were settled by the Spanish conquerors, only one of the groups of settlers, the Antioquenos, failed to develop landed estates. In modern times, this group became leaders of the economic and political modernization of Colombia; significantly, this group was also viewed with disdain by the other two during the eighteenth and nineteenth centuries. In India, various minority social groups have led the development of business. The examples could be multiplied, but, in general, a traditional society has tended to modernize more quickly "if there was any articulate group of men in it with reason to be unhappy about their position."[44]

This thesis becomes even clearer when we examine in somewhat more detail the leaders of the Meiji Restoration and subsequent modernization of Japan. At this point it is evident that the categories in this chapter overlap; that is, we have already indicated the centrality of the government in Japan's modernization, and now we find it relevant to indicate just who it was that composed that government.

First, it is important to recognize that the moral order has been even stronger in Japan than in the United States, as Ruth Benedict has pointed out. "The Japanese . . . order their world with constant reference to hierarchy. In the family and in personal relations, age, generation, sex, and class dictate proper behavior. In government, religion, the Army, and industry, areas are carefully separated into hierarchies where neither the higher nor the lower may without penalty overstep their prerogatives."[45] Furthermore, the samurai have traditionally occupied a high place in that hierarchy. The sword that symbolized the status of the samurai was not mere decoration; it could be used on the "common" people, the farmers, artisans, and merchants.

The samurai were the warrior class of feudal Japan. Unlike the European knights, the samurai existed on a pension; they were not owners of land or of serfs. The pension was a fixed amount that had been established for the family lines at the beginning of the Tokugawa era.[46] The Tokugawa era (1600-1868) was one of peace, which made a warrior class problematic. Consequently, the samurai "became increasingly the stewards of their overlords' estates and specialists in peaceful arts like the classical drama and the tea ceremony."[47]

In addition to this demilitarization of the functions of the samurai, a number of other important changes occurred during the Tokugawa era. Three of these have been discussed by Thomas Smith: the relationships of the samurai to the land, to political power, and to their feudal lords all changed. Specifically, the first became "purely administrative," the second became bureaucratic, and the third "became distant and impersonal."[48] The samurai possessed certain juridical and social bonds with the land as the lords consolidated their own power. Associated with this was the exercise of a new kind of power by the samurai, whose function became bureaucratic in contrast to the personal and territorial nature of their power in earlier times. Linked with these changes was the third:

> *The relationship between vassal and lord was slowly, silently, and profoundly transformed. It had been an intimate, intensely emotional relationship which existed between men who had fought side by side, grieved together at the loss of comrades, whose safety and families' safety depended on their keeping faith. . . . It became distant and formal . . . the vassal came to look on his lord less as a leader in war (for there was no war) than as an administrative head.*[49]

There was one additional change which was of great significance. The samurai became poorer. In fact, the distribution of wealth in Tokugawa Japan was clearly discordant with the status hierarchy. The merchants, who occupied a low position, became increasingly wealthy even as the samurai—or that group of them known as the "lower samurai"—were becoming increasingly impoverished. That impoverishment resulted from the fact that their pensions were insufficient to support them. It is not surprising, then, that "it was the lower *samurai* more than any other group which was responsible for the Restoration of 1868."[50]

Forces had been impinging upon the Tokugawa regime for some time prior to 1868; the legitimacy of the government was already being challenged when the Western intrusion confronted the nation. The additional challenge of a foreign nation was used to hasten the demise of the Tokugawa government. The powerful Satsuma and Choshu clans called for measures to keep foreigners out of Japan. The shogun, the military ruler of feudal Japan, could neither satisfy the internal opposition nor cope with the external threat. The samurai were able to depose him and establish an imperial government in 1868. This government acted with dispatch to dissolve the feudal system and centralize power. The government also implemented an aggressive, innovative policy of reform that would maintain Japanese independence through economic development, military superiority, and westernization of vital facets of Japanese life.

In concluding our examination of status anguish and change, we ought to reflect on two points. One is that while we have seen that status anguish is a mechanism of change, it is not the only mechanism. Indeed, none of the mechanisms we have studied can account for all change, though sometimes scholars write about a particular one as though it could explain nearly everything. Obviously change can be effected by people who are not subjected to status anguish. People who are free of status anguish engage in strenuous activities designed to facilitate or encourage change.

For example, it would be hard to argue that status anguish was a factor in the motivation of the white, prosperous physician who risked reputation and career in order to participate intensively in the antiwar movement. Nor does status anguish seem to play a role in the life of the white, prosperous lawyer who opts for the radical perspective and who devotes his legal efforts to the defense of radicals. There are innumerable individuals throughout history—some, such as St. Francis of Assisi or Gandhi, are men of note, while others are nameless—who have been motivated by something other than status anguish.

The second point is that, given status anguish, the direction of change is uncertain when change results, and other outcomes are possible besides change. With respect to the first, Andrzej Malewski argued that while status inconsistency did tend to lead people to support change, the change would not necessarily be of the liberal or leftist type envisioned by Lenski. Rightist causes may also offer promise of a change in the problematic status.[51] We noted this previously in Rush's study of the high income–low education type of inconsistency.

The rightist solution is also exemplified in Nazi Germany. A study of the Nazi leadership concludes that "the movement was led and followed by marginal men."[52] For example, a sample of the Nazi propagandists showed 77.4 percent of them to be marginal. Similarly, 82.1 percent of a sample of administrators and 77.1 percent of a sample of police were identified as marginal men.

Finally, with respect to the alternative outcomes of status anguish, we have already noted one study that found an increased incidence of psychophysiological symptoms among people characterized by status inconsistency. In some cases, then, status anguish simply increases psychic disorders rather than leads to change. Further, those who endure status anguish may capitulate to anomie and "become carriers of trends leading towards social disorganization rather than to innovations of a creative type."[53] The consequences of status anguish continue to be a point of debate. While status anguish clearly can result in change, it is not at all clear what circumstances lead to change rather than to psychic disturbance or social disorganization.

Endnotes

1. John M. Darley and Bibb Latané, "Bystander Intervention in Emergencies: Diffusion of Responsibility," in *Confrontation: Psychology and the Problems of Today*, ed. Michael Wertheimer (Glenview, Ill.: Scott, Foresman, 1970), pp. 71-76.
2. Jerald Hage and Michael Aiken, *Social Change in Complex Organizations* (New York: Random House, 1970), p. 122.
3. Peter F. Drucker, *The Age of Discontinuity* (New York: Harper & Row, 1968), p. 212.
4. Ibid., p. 172.
5. From "The Origin of the Family, Private Property and the State," in *Marxist Social Thought*, ed. Robert Freedman (New York: Harcourt, Brace & World, 1968), p. 222.
6. Stuart Oskamp, *Applied Social Psychology* (Englewood Cliffs, N.J.: Prentice-Hall, 1984), pp. 367-69.
7. Robert H. Lauer, *Social Problems and the Quality of Life*, 4th ed. (Dubuque, Iowa: Wm. C. Brown, 1989), pp. 254-55.
8. Ibid., pp. 242-43.
9. Dan Clawson, Alan Neustadtl, and James Bearden, "The Logic of Business Unity: Corporate Contributions to the 1980 Congressional Elections," *American Sociological Review* 51 (1986): 797-811.
10. Daniel Landau, "Government and Economic Growth in the Less Developed Countries: An Empirical Study for 1960-1980," *Economic Development and Cultural Change* 35 (1986): 35-75.
11. Edwin O. Reischauer, *Japan: Past and Present*, 3rd ed. (Tokyo: Charles E. Tuttle, 1964), p. 123. This paragraph follows this work, pp. 123-32.
12. F. Roy Lockheimer, "Prerequisites, Receptivity, and Change: Government and the Development of Science in Japan," in *The Social Reality of Scientific Myth: Science and Social Change*, ed. Kalman H. Silvert (New York: American Universities Field Staff, 1969), p. 163.
13. Ibid., p. 165.
14. M. Shahid Alam, "The South Korean 'Miracle': Examining the Mix of Government and Markets," *The Journal of Developing Areas* 23 (1989): 233-58.
15. James A. Bill, "Modernization and Reform from Above: The Case of Iran," *Journal of Politics* 32 (1970): 19-40.
16. Francois Vigier, *Change and Apathy: Liverpool and Manchester during the Industrial Revolution* (Cambridge, Mass.: MIT Press, 1970).
17. Ibid., p. 37.

18. Ibid., p. 42.

19. Ted Robert Gurr and Desmond S. King, *The State and the City* (Chicago: University of Chicago Press, 1987).

20. Szymon Chodak, *Societal Development* (New York: Oxford University Press, 1973), p. 247.

21. Jack Rothman, *Planning and Organizing for Social Change* (New York: Columbia University Press, 1974), p. 263.

22. Lauer, *Social Problems and the Quality of Life*, p. 255.

23. Eugene Staley, "The Role of the State in Economic Development," in *Modernization: The Dynamics of Growth*, ed. Myron Weiner (New York: Basic Books, 1966), p. 301.

24. Alexander Eckstein, "Individualism and the Role of the State in Economic Growth," *Economic Development and Cultural Change* 6 (1958): 83.

25. Everett C. Hughes, "Social Change and Status Protest: An Essay on the Marginal Man," *Phylon* 10 (1949): 58-65.

26. Ibid., p. 59.

27. Ibid., p. 61.

28. Gerhard E. Lenski, "Status Crystallization: A Non-Vertical Dimension," *American Sociological Review* 19 (1954): 405-13.

29. Examples of research reporting consequences of status inconsistency include Elton Jackson, "Status Consistency and Symptoms of Stress," *American Sociological Review* 27 (1962): 469-80; and Linda Baer et al., "The Consequences of Objective and Subjective Status Inconsistency," *The Sociological Quarterly* 17 (Summer, 1976): 389-400. The latter reported a relationship between both subjective and objective inconsistency and a variety of personality characteristics and political attitudes. The former reported a relationship between inconsistency and stress, a finding supported, with some modification, by Carlton A. Hornung, "Social Status, Status Inconsistency and Psychological Stress," *American Sociological Review* 42 (August, 1977): 623-38. On the other hand, a number of researchers report no relationship between status inconsistency and political attitudes and certain other attitudes and behavior. See, for example, Marvin E. Olsen and Judy Corder Tully, "Socioeconomic-Ethnic Status Inconsistency and Preference for Political Change," *American Sociological Review* 37 (October, 1972): 560-74; and T. Jean Blocker and Paul L. Riedesel, "The Nonconsequences of Objective and Subjective Status Inconsistency: Requiem for a Moribund Concept," *The Sociological Quarterly* 19 (Spring, 1978): 332-39. At some point, it is hoped, someone will sort out the problems involved with the concept and resolve the contradictions.

30. See Keith Hope, "Models of Status Inconsistency and Social Mobility Effects," *American Sociological Review* 40 (1975): 322-43.

31. Gary B. Rush, "Status Inconsistency and Right-Wing Extremism," *American Sociological Review* 32 (1967): 86-92.

32. James A. Geschwender, "Status Inconsistency, Social Isolation, and Individual Unrest," *Social Forces* 46 (1968): 477-84.

33. Status inconsistency can involve overrewarding as well as underrewarding. In their study of antipornography crusades, Zurcher and Kirkpatrick compared members of the antipornography group with those in a counter-

movement (people opposing the efforts of the antipornography crusaders). Out of forty-three underrewarded people, about half were in each movement. But out of the twenty-two overrewarded people in the sample, twenty-one were in the antipornography group and only one was in the opposing group. It appears—as we would expect—that overrewarded people, those who are profiting disproportionately from the existing arrangements, are more likely to be in a change-resisting movement. See Louis A. Zurcher, Jr. and R. George Kirkpatrick, *Citizens for Decency: Antipornography Crusades as Status Defense* (Austin: University of Texas Press, 1976). The work has been criticized by Richard Bland and Roy Wallis, "Comment on Wilson and Zurcher, Jr., and R. George Kirkpatrick, *Citizens for Decency: Antipornography,*" *Sociological Quarterly* 18 (Summer, 1977): 426-29.

34. For a fuller discussion of the relationships between social change and social movements, see Robert H. Lauer, ed., *Social Movements and Social Change* (Carbondale: Southern Illinois University Press, 1976).

35. James C. Davies, "Toward a Theory of Revolution," *American Sociological Review* 27 (1962): 5-19.

36. Alexis de Tocqueville, *The Old Regime and the French Revolution* (New York: Doubleday, 1955), pp. 175-77.

37. David F. Aberle, "A Note on Relative Deprivation Theory as Applied to Millenarian and Other Cult Movements," in *Millennial Dreams in Action*, ed. Sylvia L. Thrupp (New York: Schocken Books, 1970), p. 210.

38. Jacqueline A. Braneboy-Wagner, *Interpreting the Third World* (New York: Praeger, 1986), pp. 204-207.

39. Ibid., p. 207.

40. Denton E. Morrison, "Some Notes Toward Theory on Relative Deprivation, Social Movements, and Social Change," *American Behavioral Scientist* 14 (1971): 675-90.

41. Jack Rothman, *Planning and Organizing for Social Change* (New York: Columbia University Press, 1974), p. 342.

42. Armand L. Mauss and Donald W. Petersen, "The Cross and the Commune: An Interpretation of the Jesus People," in *Social Movements*, ed. Robert R. Evans (Chicago: Rand-McNally, 1973).

43. The critique here follows Roy Wallis, "Relative Deprivation and Social Movements: A Cautionary Note," *British Journal of Sociology* 26 (1975): 360-63.

44. Max F. Millikan and Donald L. M. Blackmer, eds., *The Emerging Nations: Their Growth and United States Policy* (Boston: Little, Brown, 1961), pp. 9-10. The examples in this paragraph are from these pages.

45. Ruth Benedict, *The Chrysanthemum and the Sword* (New York: World Publishing Co., 1946), pp. 95-96.

46. Ibid., p. 63.

47. Ibid., p. 64.

48. Thomas C. Smith, "Japan's Aristocratic Revolution," in *Class, Status, and Power*, 2nd ed., ed. Reinhard Bendix and Seymour Martin Lipset (New York: Free Press, 1966), p. 138.

49. Ibid., p. 137.

50. Robert N. Bellah, *Tokugawa Religion* (New York: Free Press, 1957), p. 45.

51. Andrzej Malewski, "The Degree of Status Incongruence and Its Effects," in Bendix and Lipset, *Class, Status, and Power*, pp. 306-7.

52. Daniel Lerner with Ithiel de Sola Pool and George K. Schueller, "The Nazi Elite," in *World Revolutionary Elites: Studies in Coercive Ideological Movements*, ed. Harold D. Lasswell and Daniel Lerner (Cambridge: MIT Press, 1965), p. 288.

53. Bert F. Hoselitz, "A Sociological Approach to Economic Development," in *Development and Society*, ed. David E. Novack and Robert Lekachman (New York: St. Martin's Press, 1964), pp. 157-58.

CHAPTER ELEVEN

Structural Sources: Elites and Youth

The Western mind seems fond of thinking in dichotomies—something is *either* this or that—but a moment's reflection shows how inadequate this approach may be. Suppose we ask this question: Is our Western level of life due to science or to religion? Although science and religion have often been dichotomous spheres, the question is obviously simplistic. Not only can we point to humane values that derive from religion and technological advances that derive from science, but we can also show how the two spheres overlap. Sometimes they overlap in the same person; the geneticist Mendel, the chemist Boyle, the astronomer Kepler, and the physicist Arthur Holly Compton are but a few of the scientists who have also been devoutly religious. Science and religion are not segregated spheres, but interacting ones.

Likewise, the categories that we are dealing with in this and the previous chapter are not necessarily independent. We have already noted that in Japan the government that implemented modernization was composed of a group that had experienced status anguish. In this chapter we shall examine two other groups in the social structure—elites and youth. Elites and government may overlap. Youth have sometimes been characterized as marginal. Nonpolitical elites and youth may exert pressures that ultimately lead to change through the mediating agency of government, and so forth. Our categories are interacting and overlapping. We focus on each in turn, but we do not mean to suggest thereby that they are separable in reality.

Change from the Top: Elites

Although much elitist thought and writing has focused on political elites, the category is much broader than that. The term elites refers generally to those at the top of the hierarchy of a society, those who hold the high-status positions in various institutions. Most scholars accept the following as elites (not all are present in every society, of course): "full-time professional politicians, senior civil servants, managers and directors of major public and private economic enterprises, top military officials, leading professionals, prominent intellectuals, well-known journalists, religious leaders, and leaders of such mass organizations as labor unions, farm groups, civic associations, and single-issue protest groups."[1] Many thinkers have seen the course of change primarily in terms of the activities of such elites.

• Theories of Elites and Change

We have already examined one theory of change that rested heavily on the activities of elites—that of Toynbee. According to Toynbee, the development of a civilization is crucially linked to the work of creative minorities, who must devise appropriate responses to societal challenges and also lead the society to opt for those responses. When the elites no longer fulfill this function, decline and death result.

To many students of elites, the concept most immediately brings to mind the names of Vilfredo Pareto and Gaetano Mosca. We shall look briefly at Pareto's ideas as representative (and probably more influential).[2] Pareto viewed society as a system of forces in a state of equilibrium. The major categories of any society are two—the elite and the nonelite. Elitist position is maintained by power, so a principal task of the social scientist is to account for the acquisition, exercise, and loss of power.

Pareto explains power by employing psychological variables, the so-called residues and derivations. There is some dispute about the exact meaning of these variables, particularly of the residues. Pareto himself distinguished between them in the context of his effort to analyze ideas that are associated with behavior. Ideas and systems of ideas contain both scientific and nonscientific elements. The latter, in turn, have constant (the residues) and variable (the derivations) facets. Thus, residues are manifestations of sentiments that are associated with stable or recurrent patterns. Derivations are similar to rationalization and are associated with variation.

Throughout history, people have employed innumerable derivations to rationalize their behavior, but certain kinds of residues have remained constant. To be sure, the residues are not distributed in the same proportion among all individuals or among various societies, and this accounts for shifts in the possession of power. Two residues that are of particular importance are the "instinct of combinations" and the "persistence of aggregates." These residues impel people to behave in particular ways.

Thus, depending upon which of the residues is predominant, we have differing types of people who compose the elite (and the nonelite). It is important here to note that Pareto divides the elite itself into two groups—the governing and the nongoverning elite. When the governing elite is composed of people who are predominantly characterized by the "instinct of combinations," change is rapid; when those who rule are predominantly characterized by the "persistence of aggregates," stability tends to prevail.

Pareto applied these ideas to more than the political realm. People who have the persistence of aggregates as a dominant trait are called lions in government, rentiers in the economy, and prophets in the field of ideology. Those who have the instinct of combinations as a dominant trait are called foxes in government, speculators in the economy, and theorists in the field of ideology. In each case, the former act in a stabilizing fashion, while the latter act in a way that impels change.

Pareto felt that an effective elite would require people of both types. As Lewis Coser put it, a "judicious mixture in top elites" of those with the two types of residues "makes for the most stable economic structure, as well as for the most enduring political structure."[3] There is a tendency for elites of the two types to alternate in possessing power. This occurs because there is also a tendency for shifts to occur in the quality of the elite. To some extent, the deficiencies caused in the governing elite by a shift in quality may be remedied by "circulation of the elite," that is, by those who are inferior being replaced by others from the nongoverning elite who are capable of exercising power.

There may also come a time when the judicious balance is no longer maintained. The quality of the governing elite diminishes, and the circulation between the governing and nongoverning elites cannot compensate adequately for it. Then "regimes either degenerate into hidebound and ossified bureaucracies incapable of renewal and adaptation, or into weak regimes of squabbling lawyers and rhetoricians incapable of decisive and forceful action."[4] At that point, the governed will rebel and replace the effete rulers with a more effective group.[5]

More recent theories of elites and change tend to focus on the developing nations. Again, we have already noted two of these in the social-psychological theories of Hagen and McClelland; both emphasized the role of entrepreneurs m the economic development of a society. A more sociological approach is offered by Edward Shils, who identifies the intellectual as the primary initiator of change in Asia and Africa.[6] Intellectuals, according to Shils, have been responsible in large measure for the genesis and development of the new nations in Asia and Africa.

We shall soon examine some evidence relating to elites and change, but we should note one other approach—namely, that of C. Wright Mills. According to Mills, the United States has witnessed a historical development that involves "the rise of an elite of power; that the men of the circles composing this elite, severally and collectively, now make such key decisions as are made; and that, given the enlargement and the centralization of the means of power now available, the decisions that they make and fail to make more consequence for more people than has ever been the case in the world history of mankind."[7]

In other words, Mills saw the American elite as essentially a powerful group maintaining its own power and advantages. This power elite is composed of overlapping cliques of political, economic, and military circles. The elite is a self-serving conglomerate that controls its own destiny and that of the masses. Members of the elite enjoy the full fruits of an affluent society, while those in the masses simply feel "pointless."

Thus, we have the idea that elites direct change and also that they retard change. There is little significant change in Pareto's scheme; the social structure is not transformed but only experiences cycles of change in personnel. In Mills's thought, very little changes unless it is to the advantage of the elite. With Shils and modernization theorists, on the other hand, elites become extraordinarily important in societal development. One might conclude that elites impel change in developing nations and inhibit it in those that are already developed. As we shall see below, the matter is more complex than that.

• *Studies of Elites and Change*

One of the most extensive historical studies of elites and change, which also offers a theory of change, is that of Don Martindale. The theory of change that he sets forth is social-behavioristic, and its basic tenets include the following:

1. All social and cultural change is the work of individuals.
2. The major events in human history consist of the formation and destruction of societies and civilizations.

3. Because of their role in forming and justifying communities and civilizations, the intellectuals represent a strategic reference point for the study of these processes.[8]

Specifically, Martindale examines China, India, Israel, and Greece during the Axial period (900-200 B.C.) and the modern West. In each case, he finds, intellectuals were prime movers of change. The social role of the intellectual has varied widely across these societies. In the Axial period, the primary intellectual roles were the mandarin bureaucrat in China, the Brahman purohita in India, the rabbi in Palestine, and the "moral counselor and jurist" in the Graeco-Roman world. In each case, the intellectuals were highly creative and guided the formation of more complex social orders. In the West, social development has been linked up with the humanists and scientists, who have tended to "establish a sphere of pure expediency"; in particular, the scientific mentality "liquidates every traditional configuration of value with which it comes in contact."[9]

Other historical studies support Martindale's thesis that intellectuals have been crucial sources of change, or at least important sources of pressure toward change (the change agent may be thwarted by opposing forces). In a study of education in nineteenth-century India, China, and Japan, Shanti Tangri concluded that there were a number of differences in the educational systems of the three societies, but that "in all three cases the intellectual was (and is) an activist, deeply committed to the processes of social change, and not an objective bystander."[10]

We pointed out in the last chapter that the Nazi elite included considerable numbers of those suffering from status anguish. Nazi propagandists were identified as marginal men. More specifically, they were identified as alienated intellectuals. Their intellectual identity was established on the basis of their fathers' occupations, the number of their own publications, and the kind of publications they produced. Alienation was measured by unemployment rates. The data lead to the conclusion that Nazi propagandists were typically "a class of intellectuals born and raised with the *elite* of Imperial and Weimar Germany who became *alienated* from the prevailing structure of symbols and sanctions of the elite that nurtured them."[11]

Elites can inhibit as well as facilitate change. In fact, in democratic societies it is the unity or disunity of elites that is crucial for the stability of the regime.[12] Most nation-states have been constructed out of disparate peoples who formerly had at least some autonomy. The result is that most national elites are disunified. That means that the elites have no consensus on appropriate political conduct and tend to remain in disparate groups with minimal interaction. The political consequence is regime instability, with frequent revolutions, uprisings, or coups d'etat that attempt to change the power structure of the society.

In some countries, such as the United States, Britain, and Sweden, there is a consensually unified elite. That means that there is interaction in an integrated structure and that there are shared norms about appropriate political conduct. One of the most important norms is the norm of "restrained partisanship," which includes such things as the recognition of the rights of political opponents and minorities; the willingness to accept disagreement when decisions can't be made; protection of the government as a legitimate authority; and the acceptance of a certain amount of secrecy so that elites can be flexible and bargain and construct innovative solutions to problems.[13]

Countries with disunified elites may experience an "elite transformation" that will lead to political stability. One way that unity can be achieved is by the warring factions to engage in an "elite settlement," in which fundamental differences are resolved and relationships are reorganized. That process occurred in England in the seventeenth century, in Sweden in the nineteenth century, and in Columbia and Venezuela in the late 1950s. Another way in which the transformation can occur is through a two-step process. First, some of the warring factions begin to collaborate in order to gain control of the nation. Second, the remaining factions that are still opposed to those in power 'eventually tire of losing elections and, seeing no other way to gain government power . . . gradually abandon their distinct ideological and policy stances and adopt essentially those of the winning coalition."[14]

A great many studies of elites have focused on their role in the underdeveloped and developing nations of the contemporary world. That role has been a varied one. In some traditional societies, the ruling elite has offered strong resistance to change. In many traditional nations, landowners have linked themselves with political rulers and certain other elites to form a powerful upper stratum.

As nations embark upon the process of modernization we find certain elites actively leading the development, but they are not often the same elites who held sway in the traditional society. In West Africa, for example, the elites in the traditional society included chiefs, priests, and wealthy traders. The nationalist movements were led by Western-educated elites, who "accused their elders of too great an accommodation with European rule, of being 'Uncle Toms.'"[15]

Still other elites may exercise little influence on change; rather, they basically engage in the task of adapting to whatever change occurs. Lawyers in Colombia occupied a position of high status during the traditional days of that nation. Their status became problematic during the process of modernization because they sought to retain traditional values. Those values, however, did not mesh with the modernization process, which offered new opportunities but also demanded such things as a revised curriculum for law students and a changed perspective about being practical with people and things. By 1970, the lawyers found themselves in an ambivalent position with respect to their status; there were too many lawyers for a traditional type of practice and too few lawyers willing to strike out on a new course. Colombian lawyers, therefore, were struggling to adapt to a social order that was changing far more rapidly than they were.[16]

Some sense can be made out of the diverse patterns of behavior of elites by recognizing two important points: (1) there are different kinds of elites, and (2) the consequences of change for the elites are complex and sometimes different from, or even contradictory to, their own aims. As to the first point, we have already noted the two different types of elites involved in African development. A more complex typology has been offered by Lucian Pye, who identified six roles crucial to development: administrators, agitators, amalgamates, transmitters, ideological propagandists, and political brokers.[17] The varied courses of development in different societies, according to Pye, depend upon which combination of the above roles directs the development.

Briefly, the roles may be characterized as follows. The administrators direct the transition from traditional to bureaucratic modes of functioning, often thereby incurring hostility toward themselves. The agitators strive to destroy authoritative systems and increase general participation in political life. The amalgamates function well in both traditional and modern contexts; their ability to make use of traditional sources of power has made them effective in economic development in nations such as Japan and Turkey. The transmitters communicate knowledge and values, facilitating the transition of others from the traditional to the modern context. Ideological propagandists strive to integrate the traditional and modern on some common ideological ground. Political brokers differentiate various special interests and relate them to the system of government.

What the typology points out, among other things, is the heterogeneous nature of elites. A popular notion in the United States equates the intellectual with leftist political views. Intellectuals, however, like all other elites, are varied. In Nazi Germany, for example, some scientists fled, some resisted, and others served Adolph Hitler. A study of political elites from thirty-two countries, covering four centuries of time, looked for differences between loyalist and revolutionary elites.[18] That is, given the fact that elites are heterogeneous, can we identify some reasons why certain elites support the status quo while others revolt against it? Interestingly, the researchers found more similarities than differences between loyalists and revolutionaries. Both tended to come from higher socioeconomic backgrounds (including higher levels of education), urban areas, and mainstream religious and ethnic backgrounds. Both tended to be cosmopolitan and have early socialization into politics. Revolutionaries tended to be more ascetic and puritan, while loyalists tended to be more egotistical. But the primary difference seems to be that the loyalists were more integrated into the existing power structure and had more opportunities for advancement. The revolutionaries were more likely to be blocked in their political aspirations. .Self-interest clearly seems to be an important part of the perspective adopted by elites.

Thus, we may classify elites in various ways, but whatever the scheme of classification, it is important to recognize that elites serve diverse interests (including their own) and function in various ways. In any case, they are important in change and in the particular direction of change in a society. Elitist activity is a part of the change at all levels of social reality. Typologies are important because they direct our attention to the diverse interests and goals and behavior of elites. This, in turn, can help us understand why elites sometimes retard change, sometimes accelerate it, and sometimes simply adapt to it.

These considerations confront us with the second point made above—the complex and sometimes contradictory consequences of change for elites. S. N. Eisenstadt has stressed this in his concept of "split-level" modernization.[19] Split-level modernization is directed by elites—in some cases, foreign elites. The elites are a diverse group and strive for various kinds of modernization. Even the governing elite may have contradictory aims with respect to modernization. For example, it may desire the enhanced power and affluence that come from modernization but may wish to avoid certain social and political consequences such as the erosion of its own power within the nation. Thus, elites sometimes act to counter the effects of their own previous actions, with the result that modernization has often been a spastic process of advance, decline, and turbulence.

Furthermore, elites, like all other people, will experience unanticipated consequences from their actions. Unanticipated consequences (which sometimes may be undesirable as well as unexpected) are common in social life, and a good example of such consequences flowing from the actions of elites is provided by H. Nishio's analysis of early Japanese modernization.[20] Nishio focused on the activities of political elites in Tokugawa Japan (1603-1867) and the economic consequences of those activities. Tokugawa society was highly centralized. Its founder,

Tokugawa Ieyasu, reacted against the weak, decentralized society of his day, and established a political order modeled after the ideal described by the Chinese philosopher Chu Hsi.

In particular, three measures were carried out and institutionalized in order to centralize power. First, there was a policy of isolation, which was implemented by Ieyasu's successors out of their fear of European missionaries and the Japanese Christian community. As a result of the policy, Japan was virtually closed to the outside world far well over two hundred years. The second measure was a system of checks and balances, which was designed to perpetuate the existing power relationships. In order to succeed at this, the central government had to the loyalty of the feudal lords, and Tokugawa achieved this by requiring the lords to live in the Tokugawa castle town every other year. The lords had to leave their wives and children in the castle town when they returned home to administer their own affairs, so that their loyalty was by their captive families. The third measure was a system of class and status, which was intended to implement Chu Hsi's ideal of a hierarchy in which there is loyalty, benevolence, and the awareness of self-limits by all members.

Thus, power was centralized and various mechanisms operated to minimize conflict and power struggles, but what were the consequences of this reorganization by the political elites? 'The policy of isolation cut off foreign trade and tended to create an attitude of economic passivity among merchants. It also may have saved Japanese independence in the face of Western encroachment into the East. Moreover, some scholars have argued that the Japanese were not benefiting from foreign trade in the prior period, so that the policy of isolation may have also saved the Japanese economy. Certainly, the policy of isolation encouraged the conservation of native resources and development of agriculture.

The system of checks and balances also had a number of economic consequences. In order to keep the feudal lords in a weak financial position, the lords were asked on occasion to provide funds and labor for various projects. Some of the projects were religious buildings, but others involved flood prevention measures and the construction of roads. The road system ultimately provided a necessary communication and transportation system for commercial development. The residency requirement also kept the feudal lords weak (both militarily and financially). Because of the travel required of lords every other year, a number of commercial towns grew up on the highways. These towns also became important in commercial development. Moreover, the lords had to use cash for travel expenses, facilitating the transition from a rice to a money economy. In other words, a system that was designed by the elites to stabilize the political order resulted in a growing commercialism that would ultimately weaken the Tokugawa political order.

Finally, the system of class and status had implications for economic developments. Under the Tokugawa system, there was a clear delineation of classes—warriors, farmers, artisans, and merchants. These were also clear occupational roles. The warriors (samurai) were no longer needed on the land, however, so they tended to move into the castle towns of the lords. The number of castle towns grew as the warriors left the land in increasing numbers. This urbanization process required an improved transportation system so that goods could be moved from the rural to the urban areas. With the increased commercial activity, the importance of the merchants increased. The merchants did not attain a higher status, but many of them became affluent.

Thus, the various measures adopted by political elites to create and maintain a stable political order had unanticipated consequences in the form of commercial development. Furthermore, this development would later prove invaluable in the modernization of Japan during the Meiji era. The affluent merchants would provide a source of capital, and the system of roads and money economy would facilitate the rapid industrialization of the nation. The elites had successfully created their centralized, stable political order, but in the process they unwittingly created a dynamic commercialism which facilitated the later economic development of the nation.

• *Elites and Change: Conclusions*

Certain important conclusions can be drawn from existing studies to guide future investigations of the relationship of elites to change. Among them are the following:

1. *The elites of any society are a heterogeneous group.* We may try to understand their behavior with respect to change by analyzing their varied social roles (as exemplified in the work of Pye), by identifying their position on the problem of tradition vs. modernity,[21] by identifying their social origins, and so on. But the important point is that we cannot understand the relationship between elites and change unless we also understand the heterogeneity of the elites of any society.

We must also understand, as noted earlier, that elites may be unified or disunified. *Unified* is a relative term, of course. In any society, including those that are totalitarian, there are at least some of the elite that oppose the status quo. Moreover, various elites may be in or out of depending upon how threatening they are perceived to be by the existing power structure. In Nazi Germany, scientists were viewed with suspicion. In the People's Republic of China, the status of intellectuals has varied considerably.[23] During the Cultural Revolution, the Gang of Four argued that the knowledge of intellectuals was out of touch with the realities of working people and was, therefore, the root of all evil in China. "Thus, from the edifiers of the people, the intellectuals fell to the position of the 'stinking ninth' category in the social strata."[24] Universities were condemned as breeding grounds for harmful ideas and some were closed. But in 1976, the Gang of Four were arrested and the Cultural Revolution came to a close. Intellectuals were restored to positions of honor. They were said to be members of the working class, differing only in the type of work they did.

In the late 1980s, student unrest arose again in China, Supported by the teachings and writings of some intellectuals, students demanded "democracy" and "freedom." We shall take this up later, but here we want to note that one consequence of the 1986 student protests was the expelling of a few intellectuals from the Communist Party. The threat of wider reprisals and a return to some of the horrors of the Cultural Revolution effectively quelled the 1987 protest. In China, the intellectuals maintain a precarious status.

2. *Elites may inhibit as well as impel, and adapt to as well as lead in, change.* An important consideration here is the anticipated consequences of the change for elitist positions. As pointed out earlier, there may also be unanticipated consequences, with the result that the elites may act ambivalently about change. Furthermore, the elites do not exercise absolute control. They themselves may be swept along by currents not of their own making, currents created by technological developments, mass movements, or emergent ideologies, for example. Or the elites may simply be incapable of coping with the demands presented by the social process. One of the reasons Eisenstadt gives for the breakdown of modernization in a number of countries is the inability of political elites to meet effectively the challenges of rapid change.[25] Only where political elites could accomplish their own will in the face of numerous demands from self-seeking, antagonistic interest groups has modernization continued steadily.

3. *Different kinds of leaders may be required for different kinds of change and different types of situations.* For example, many nationalistic movements have been led by charismatic individuals. Whereas charisma may be effective in attaining independence, it is not necessarily effective in building a nation. The people themselves may react against the charismatic leader when they realize that independence has not brought the good -life they anticipated. Indeed, charismatic leadership may contradict the demands of nation building when this

involves the development of citizenship and participation in the political process.

Of course, the viability of charismatic leadership after a revolution depends on the type of society that is being built. In the case of Iran, following the Islamic Revolution of 1979, the charismatic Ayatollah Khomeini not only motivated the people to oust the Shah, but also quickly purged the nation of the bulk of the elite who had helped overthrow the Shah. "Within one year, almost all of the revolutionary leaders who could be considered part of the old elite had been pushed outside the revolution."[26] The old elite consisted of various groups that would not accede to Khomeini's determination to build an Islamic state. Once they had helped to effect the revolution, they were purged from power.

In addition to the differing demands of revolutionary movements and nation-building, various stages of nation-building may also require different kinds of leaders. As economic development proceeds, there is need for the specialist rather than for the "polyvalent" leader.[27] In other words, the social context may demand particular kinds of elites, with the result that there is a circulation of elites with respect to both type and personnel over time. This dependence of elites upon the social context is illustrated by shifts in the elites in Russia following the Revolution. Those with expertise in persuasion were replaced by those with expertise in coercion: "The old Bolshevik intellectuals were executed, assassinated. or "disappeared." . . . In their place came the specialists skilled in violence rather than symbols, the administrators of coercion rather than persuasive ideology. The big change is well characterized by the transition from loquacious Lenin to silent Stalin."[28]

4. *Different kinds of elites may be effective in different cultural and sociohistorical settings.* The third point dealt with elites and change in the same society over time; this one deals with different societies. In other words, the same basic kind of change in differing societies may require different kinds of elites. In the United States. for example, we associate effective change at local levels with democratic procedures. An experiment in land reform in India yielded different results.[29] It was found that the program worked primarily in villages that had a tradition of landlessness. It did not work even in all of those villages; rather, it was effective when the social workers who directed the program were authoritarian rather than democratic!

In other words, however much we may value democracy, where the social order is authoritarian, where the ideology stresses rank positions rather than equality and the stratification system tends to be closed, democratic leaders may totally fail. Thus, in his study of El Pinar, Joseph Aceves points out, "The public concept of the ideal leader can be summarized by noting that the Spaniards here prefer a strong and forceful person who takes charge of an operation and gives the orders in such a way they are carried out quickly and efficiently. The leader who cannot give orders and enforce them is not a leader by village standards."[30]

Similarly, in her study of the Mexican village of Eronganícuaro, Cynthia Nelson identified the traditional superordinate-subordinate pattern of interaction as problematic for effecting change.[31] The United Nations Center for Fundamental Education in Latin America was working in the area of the village and tried to get villagers to assume leadership roles. In this case, the UN people were aware of the traditional modes of interaction, so they tried to get villagers to assume leadership positions in which they would essentially act as patrons over the other villagers. Whereas the traditional relationship with the patrons was one of subservience, the traditional relationships among villagers themselves was basically egalitarian. The villagers had a system of reciprocal obligations and rights among themselves. Thus, even villagers who had leadership qualities (as defined by an outsider) would not accept leadership positions (nor be accepted as leaders by other villagers) because this would disrupt the balanced system of reciprocal rights and obligations and violate the norms regarding roles. In this cultural context, the people could accept an outside authoritarian leader or one within their midst who had a traditional authoritarian role (such as the priest or the mayor), but they could not accept one of their own number being elevated to such a role. The efforts of the UN group to have the people be leaders in planned change were therefore being frustrated by the traditional culture.

In addition to variations in culture, diverse periods of time are also important in terms of the kinds of elites required. There is the argument of some Western economists that economic development—at least of the capitalist variety—hinges upon the activities of entrepreneurs. Elites in the developing nations argue that this is too slow a process for their countries. Furthermore, the world in which a nation must develop today is enormously different from the world in which the West experienced development. If we contrast the Western experience with the problems facing a present-day peasant society, we find the peasant societies in a frustrating situation; they "have no room for major territorial expansion; no technical advantage over competitors; a much higher rate of population growth, and a less differentiated economy, with around 80 percent of population in the agricultural sector."[32] The entrepreneurial elite that effectively led Western development is simply inappropriate for developing nations today.

Change from the Bottom: Youth

"Our civilization is doomed if the unheard-of actions of our younger generations are allowed to continue." These are not the words of a contemporary prophet of doom; they were discovered on an ancient tablet uncovered in Ur. They reflect an opinion of youth that seems rather common in every age—namely, that youth is the' vanguard of change and that change is all for the worse. Youth, on the other hand, has often conceived of itself as the vanguard of change, and has believed that change is all for the better. More than one student has told me that the hope of the world—the *only* hope of the world—lies in the action of youth. How realistic are these contrary views on youth's role in change? As we shall see, the role of youth in change, like that of other groups we have examined is a varied one.

• The Conservatism of Youth

Although the older generation has often looked upon young people as though significant numbers of them were exponents of radical change, there is considerable conservatism among youth. Studies made by H. H. Remmers and D. H. Radler of high-school students during the 1950s found that the students, like adults, tended to be intolerant of divergent viewpoints. They were found to be rather traditional "in the sense that they continue a habit of disrespect for traditional American liberties of conscience, free speech, and the press."[33] All the evidence since then supports the fact that, for the most part, youth maintain the same values and perspectives as their parents. In essence, "for all the hype about generation gaps, on a great many central political issues and concerns, generational differences are modest or nonexistent."[34] Various age groups differ little on such things as priorities of public problems, the proper role of the government in helping the needy, the appropriate amount of military spending, and the use of the death penalty in cases of murder. There has been an increasing liberalization of attitudes as we move from those who matured in the 1950s to those who matured in the 1980s on such matters as race relations and the role of women. But whatever generation we are talking about, the youth cannot on the whole be characterized as radical.

There are some differences depending upon whether we are talking about college or noncollege youth. In general, college youth tend to be more liberal than noncollege youth on many issues. But this is not to say that college youth are radical. Polls of college freshmen taken from 1968 through 1987 show that less than 5 percent ever identified themselves as politically on the "far left."[35] In fact, comparing the earliest with the latest polls, there was a large increase in the proportion who defined themselves as "middle-of-the-road," and a decrease in every other orientation, including far left, liberal, conservative, and far right. In 1987, 83 percent of the freshmen indicated that getting a better job was one of the more important reasons for going to college. Only 16 percent said that influencing the political structure was a very important objective in their lives. Neither radicalism nor support for radicalism has been as widespread in colleges and universities as the public has sometimes tended to believe.

Clearly, differences among young people themselves are as great as those between the young and the old. The student uprisings and campus turmoil of the 1960s seemed to point to a generation of radicals. But the radicals were only a minority of the college students. Moreover, surveys of attitudes of college students suggest that the 1960s group was a "liberal blip": "On issue after issue, that cohort seems particularly liberal relative to other college-educated generations."[36] Finally, even in the 1960s the universities were relatively placid compared with those of the past. In general, then, there is little or no evidence of a generational political revolt, either in the United States or in the developing nations. There is, on the contrary, evidence of a continuing sense of solidarity with the family, a considerable amount of traditionalism among young people, and a degree of continuity between generations that indicates continuing and significant parental influence.

In sum, much of the youth both in the United States and elsewhere is conservative. The majority of students in the United States have always been preparing to fulfill elite positions in society rather than training to transform their society. Nevertheless, college-educated youth are far less conservative than the youth who go directly to work. After studying generational differences in attitudes among both blacks and whites, Ann Brunswick concluded that without question "education is at least as important a divider, or determiner of generations, as age."[37] Education is a liberalizing and, to a small degree, radicalizing force; but conservatism is strong among youth. There is always change between the generations, of course; but the average youth is no flaming radical bent on destroying and recreating the social order at any cost.

• *Radicalism in Youth*

While the majority of youth is either conservative or moderate in outlook, there are probably more extremists among the young than in the adult population. Youth tends to be extreme, but the extremism may be either to the right or to the left. The Weathermen, advocating violent revolution, was a youth organization; but so is the Young Americans for Freedom, which presses for the conservative or reactionary viewpoint.

Our concern in this section, however, is not with extremism but with radicalism, in the sense of commitment to fundamental changes in the social structure. Again, both leftists and rightists may call themselves radicals; an example of the latter are the rational anarchists, who define themselves as radicals because of their commitment to instituting a system of pure laissez-faire capitalism. Our interest here is with the radicalism of the left and the extent of its presence or absence among youth in the United States.

In the decades prior to the 1960s, radicalism tended to be located in a few large, urban universities. It is not a new phenomenon, but one that has existed more or less for the greater part of our history.[38] The Intercollegiate Socialism Society dates back to 1905. By 1921, Calvin Coolidge was deploring radicalism in colleges. Nevertheless, by the 1930s, when the student radical movement reached the peak of intensity—at least until its resurgence in the 1960s—it still included only a relatively small number of adherents. The American Student Union, a leftist-pacifist organization, claimed 20,000 members in 1939, a time when it had reached the pinnacle of its strength. There were other youth organizations, but the total number of students who participated in radical groups was only a small fraction of the total soaring college population, which reached nearly one and one-half million by 1940.

Student radicalism emerged anew in the 1960s. The roots of this radicalism are to be found in a number of movements that began t crystallize in the late 1950s.[39] In England, university intellectuals began to publish two new journals, which merged into the *New Left Review* in 1959. A number of leftist political clubs also arose, composed of both college and working-class youth. In the United States, concern with the racial problem and international peace gained intensity; a number of journals and organizations emerged that reflected leftist concern with these problems.

The mood of student radicals in the 1960s is caught by "An American Student Manifesto," a document compiled from interviews with some five hundred students:

> *We accuse the present society of a perverted frame of mind. A frame of mind that tolerates injustice, insensitivity, lack of candor, and inhumanity. . . . The world's wealthiest nation, America, finds a large part of its population living in poverty. A nation founded on the belief that all men are created equal, it systematically denies civil rights and economic opportunity to its black citizen. . . . The Viet Nam war, since we were the ones who were*

> *called to fight it, led us to make our first moral judgments. We are destroying more than we could possibly reconstruct.*[40]

The resolution. of these problems, of course, depended upon fundamental changes in the social structure, and since the adult generation was seen as the defender of that structure, adults were also seen as enemies of change toward a humane and fully human existence. The casting of adults into the role of the enemy was epitomized in the slogan "don't trust anybody over thirty."

To some observers, the youth of the nation were forging ahead into the new era and there was cause for celebration. The extent of alienation of youth from the existing social order was seen- as so intense that young people could only be understood in terms of a counter culture. Theodore Roszak defined this as a culture that had become "so radically disaffiliated from the mainstream assumptions of our society that it scarcely looks to many as a culture at all, but takes on the alarming appearance of a barbaric intrusion."[41]

A number of events aided the disaffiliation of youth and the growth of radicalism. Jerome Skolnick has suggested that eight events were particularly important.[42] One was the nonviolent southern Civil Rights Movement. Considerable disillusionment followed upon the brutal treatment of civil rights workers and blacks who were only attempting to exercise their rights as citizens. A second event was the war on poverty, which promised much and delivered very little. Third were the events at Berkeley, which cast university administrators in a new light and reshaped the image of the actual functions of the university in the society. The university and its administrators were seen to reflect the same corruption that pervaded the larger society.

Fourth, the escalation of the Vietnam War and the attendant credibility gap regarding governmental policies were blatantly counter to the will of the people which supposedly was sovereign. Fifth, the involvement of the universities with the Vietnam War and with the military establishment in general clearly destroyed the claim of academic neutrality and corroborated the belief in academic corruption.

The draft was the sixth factor. Student deferments were restricted, and many students faced the possibility of being called to participate in a war that they believed was immoral. Moreover, the draft was perceived as violating basic rights of individualism and voluntarism. A seventh factor was the continuing inability of the government to resolve problems of race, poverty, and urban decline. Finally, the eighth factor was confrontation with police on campus. Police violence radicalized a number of students who had been either moderate or uncommitted.

Once radicalized, what were the students like? Todd Gitlin, one of the central participants in Students for a Democratic Society (SDS), recalls the sixties in terms of the ideals and passions of the radical students: "SDS had a passion to make life whole, to bring political commitment into private life, to make private values count in public."[43] Initially, the members of SDS pressed for participatory democracy and the rights of all citizens. They urged change through nonviolent protest against the coalition of government, the military, universities, big business, and the liberal apologists of existing institutions.

But by the mid-1960s, the protest against the war in Vietnam appeared ineffective. Rather than pulling back, President Johnson escalated the war. Young radicals began to consider more extreme methods, and "resistance became the official watchword of the antiwar movement."[44] The youth threatened to burn cities, to overthrow fascist America ("Amerika," as they spelled it), and to bring the system down through various kinds of active and passive resistance.

In 1968, the student movement reached a turning point when rioting broke out in Chicago during the Democratic National Convention. The confrontation between the youth and the authorities was framed in terms of "we" versus "they," of fascism versus revolution, of the necessity of an all-out war against an immoral social order. But the turn toward increasing violence proved to be counterproductive. The movement itself split into various factions, some of whom were willing now to resort to terrorist tactics. Public opinion turned against the radicals. Many states enacted laws to deal with student unrest. Federal and state criminal laws were passed to prosecute those who disrupted public or private facilities. The idealistic, nonviolent youth of the early years of the decade had become the outlawed and outcast rebels of the decade's end.

The next generation of students was far more conservative. The generation of radicals that came of age in the sixties (keep in mind that only a small minority of students even in the sixties identified themselves as radicals) took various turns. Some became a part of the "Establishment" against which they had once fought. Some turned to less violent ways to effect change. Some became part of other movements, including the women's movement and the environmental and antinuclear weapons movements.

In sum, student radicals have been, even in the 1960s, a heterogeneous and relatively small proportion of the total student population. The impact made by the youth of the 1960s has yet to be determined, but at least a few points seem clear. One is that the young have not emerged as the counter-culture ushering in the new age. Only a few years after Roszak celebrated the new generation. newspapers were remarking about the new, quiet atmosphere on the campuses and about the changed mood regarding violence and the possibility of effectively working for change within the system rather than challenging it from without. It seems that those who write about radical youth tend to ignore the existence of large numbers of conservative and moderate youth as well as the historical fluctuations of radicalism.

On the other hand, those who stress the conservatism of the young tend to ignore the radicals and their potential impact. Future historians may identify a number of ways in which the youth of the 1960s and 1970s affected the course of American history, including the influence of the young in the delegitimating of war, in demanding equality of rights for all citizens in fact as well as in ideology, and in reordering national priorities so that human existence becomes a humane existence.

At least one historian has already attempted to assess the leftist movement of the 1960s. Irwin Unger has provided us with the course of the "New Left" from 1959 to 1972 and with an initial assessment of the impact of the New Left.[45] First, he notes that the New Left was composed of large numbers of young people, and his own analysis largely deals with the youth aspect of the movement. The youths who joined the movement were mainly students from middle-class backgrounds who were disillusioned with American society. Various student organizations comprised the movement, perhaps the most well-known of which was the Students for a Democratic Society. The tactics used by the organizations to change American society ranged from educational attempts to violent confrontation with the authorities to, ultimately, guerrilla-type warfare.

Even at the height of the New Left, however, the proportion of young people who belonged to radical organizations, and even the proportion who were sympathetic to radical ideology, was small. The basic conservatism of the college population had not changed much. In some cases, students joined in with radical protesters. but only because they believed the protesters were being unfairly treated by the authorities and not because they accepted radical views. Some youths were radicalized, of course, but there were militant conservatives on the campuses as well as militant radicals during the 1960s. For instance, during the turmoil at Columbia University in New York, when an acting dean was taken hostage by radical students, one of the problems faced by administrators was the possible violent confrontation between leftist and conservative students. The conservatives offered to rescue the acting dean, and later they formed a majority coalition and demanded that the university take action against the radicals who were occupying university buildings.

Eventually, the leftist students and their movement collapsed through internal conflict and fragmentation. Did they achieve anything? Certainly, in some cases they helped strengthen right-wing developments and public acceptance of repressive measures by the authorities. However, Unger argues, and I would agree, that they also forced the United States out of the Vietnam War. Without the antiwar movement, which was fueled to a considerable extent by the students, the war would have been prolonged for perhaps many more years. With respect to the effects on domestic affairs, however, Unger says the question is difficult to answer. There have been changes in life styles and cultural values, but these are hardly the kinds of changes the New Left would have defined as sufficient. Additional research may shed more light on the question. but at this point the effects of the New Left on the United States' domestic life cannot be specified.

• *Youth and Change*

The effects of contemporary American youth on the course of history are not altogether clear, but we may point to a variety of instances in which youth played a decided role in change. In this section, we shall examine the role of the young in a number of nations around the world, paying particular attention to some activities of Chinese youth.

One question we have not yet answered, of course, is what is meant by youth. The answer is not easy to give. To a teenager, the 25-year-old may be an older adult. To the philosopher, one's thoughts as a 40-year-old are part of one's young thoughts. In the political realm, anyone in one's thirties is considered a young politician. As a rule of thumb, therefore, I will be talking about youth in terms of those who are 35 or less.

What impact has this age group made? So far we have been discussing political change and politically directed change, but we must not ignore the contributions to change that the young have made by virtue of their work in science, technology, and ideology. Blaise Pascal was 19 when he invented the adding machine. Einstein was 26 when he started working on his theory of relativity. Whitney invented the cotton gin when he was 28, and Watt had obtained a patent for the first practical steam engine by the time he was 33. The list is long and includes many writers and artists who produced major works in their youth.

Sometimes the young have made significant contributions that differ in some respects from their later ones. the 1960s, great interest developed in the writings of the "young Marx." Before he was 30 years old, Karl Marx had produced a number of writings that were pervaded by a humanitarian social concern. Rediscovery of these early writings provided an ideological basis for a number of purposes, including revisions of the relationship between democracy and socialism and defense of workers' rights against Stalinist bureaucracy.[46]

Youth has been prominent in many social movements and revolutions. The Protestant Reformation in England and revolutions in France, the United States, Cuba, China, and other nations have all been marked by significant participation of youth. Abolitionism in the United States was "a revolt of the young," with the median age of the antislavery leadership of the 1830s being 29.[47] In Meiji Japan, the course of modernization was impelled to a considerable extent by young men. In fact, Japanese youths felt that their elders were little more than an impediment to needed change. As a magazine published by youth in the latter part of the nineteenth century put it, "Today's elders are already useless to society. In a progressive age they are unfortunately a troublesome burden."[48]

Young people were also prominent in Germany prior to World War II, and tended to see themselves as alone being sufficiently pure to create society anew. More recently, studies of youth in a variety of nations show considerable political activity. Numerous governments have been overthrown following major student protests, including those of Venezuela (1958), Japan (1960), South Korea (1960), South Vietnam (1963), Bolivia (1964), the Sudan (1964), and Indonesia (1966). Numerous others successfully withstood student opposition, and those that fell did so because of additional factors. Among the additional factors, intervention of the military ranks high.

Of course, the overthrow of the government *may* be nothing more than a change of the palace guard, while the government *may* remain in power yet initiate important changes in response to youth pressures. That is, the fall or persistence of a particular regime does not in itself indicate a significant change. Rather, we need to examine the course of events in a society after the rebellion of young activists.

Among the many historical examples of significant change effected through the political action of youth is the case of China. In a society that traditionally assigned great respect and deference to the aged, the young have become prominent. A case in point is the Red Guard during the Great Proletarian Cultural Revolution. Here we shall focus on events that preceded the Communist revolution.

China was subservient to and exploited by the West through most of the nineteenth century. It was not until the ideology of nationalism arose—a "prickly, touchy, demanding kind of nationalism" which grew out of China's humiliation by the West—that the Chinese were roused to change their situation.[49] This nationalistic ideology took hold in the student movement in the first years of the twentieth century. The young opposed everything that appeared reactionary, and were determined to liberate themselves and their nation from every form of bondage.

Student activity reached a peak of intensity in the famous May Fourth Movement of 1919, which gave birth to modern China.[50] In order to understand that movement, we must emphasize again the intense interest in national affairs held by Chinese students as the twentieth century dawned. Because of China's repeated humiliation by the West, whom she had previously considered inferior, and because of continuing internal corruption, war, and economic disaster, Chinese students possessed a strong political and social consciousness. In addition, the traditional examination system was abolished in 1905, making professional careers problematic. The road to achievement and power seemed to lie through the organization of mass action rather than through the pursuit of a professional career.

The student leaders were young—in their twenties—and so were their professors. many of whom were in their twenties or thirties. This group confronted the older scholars and warlord leaders with the vision of a new China. The contrast in composition between the two groups was as striking as the contrast in their visions of the nation; in age, education, and ideology, the gap between the new intellectuals and their opposition was unbridgeable.

A number of factors encouraged mass activities. The students lived in very crowded dormitories. Their study and recreation were highly structured by their superiors. They possessed a collective rather than an individualistic perspective. Public opinion indicated an acceptance of the idea of student intervention in political affairs. Finally, the students were already grouped in a number of organizations.

The event that finally triggered mass action was the news from the Paris Conference; this news reached Peking at the end of April, 1919. China had expected that some of the inequities of the past would be rectified at the conference. However, President Wilson's ideas of self-determination and a war without victory were not to apply to the Chinese. Germany's holdings in Shantung, including Tsingtao, were to be given to Japan, who had seized them in 1914.

Students felt that both the West and their own government had sold them out. The student organizations met and declared May 7 a day for mass demonstration. The news from Paris grew worse, and public feelings became increasingly bitter. Efforts of the Peking government to mollify the populace and discourage dissent only intensified the anger. Finally, students in Peking decided that the mass demonstration could not wait until May 7 and moved the time up to May 4.

It was to be a day of orderly protest. Efforts of the Peking government to stop the rally failed. By 1:30 in the afternoon, over 3,000 had gathered. Students distributed a "Manifesto of All the Students of Peking," which called on all of the people to join their protest. The Manifesto left little doubt about the severity of the crisis or depth of commitment of the young. "This is the last chance for China in her life and death struggle. Today we swear two solemn oaths with all our fellow countrymen: (1) China's territory may be conquered, but it cannot be given away; (2) the Chinese people may be massacred, but they will not surrender. Our country is about to be annihilated. Up, brethren!"[51]

The day was significant not only because of the demonstration itself, but because it marked the beginning of organized efforts to gain mass support for radical change. The ideas of the students were disseminated throughout China, and the students themselves made contact with the common people. The incident of May 4 and the subsequent activities of youth were a prophetic microcosm of the new China as well as an important step in attaining the new order.

The continuing influence of youth in development in China is illustrated by the average age of members of the Communist Politburo, which remained at approximately 29 from 1921 through 1931.[52] Moreover, the Chinese leaders have continued to emphasize the role of youth in the ongoing revolution. In 1939, Mao said that the young of China played a vanguard role in the revolution. In a 1973 article, Tan Wen exulted in the commitment of youth to the revolution:

> *Nurtured by Mao Tsetung Thought, the younger generation is the least conservative in its thinking. It is eager for socialist new things and dares to challenge everything decadent. As soon as it grasps the truth, the younger generation will destroy all resistance. . . . In the last few years, millions of educated young people have gone to settle down in the countryside, pounding away at the centuries-old concept of despising manual labour and workers and peasants through their revolutionary actions. All this shows that young people are able to shoulder together with workers and peasants the glorious task of criticizing the bourgeoisie and revisionism. These actions of theirs are good indeed!*[53]

Interestingly enough, as the Chinese leaders have aged they have continued to emphasize and encourage the youth role in China's development. The young created a new China. Now that those young people are old, many of them continue to stress the work of youth in making China a great nation. Ironically, however, the youth frequently challenge rather than support the existing regime. After the death of Mao in 1976, Chinese youth periodically protested events and policies in their nation.[54] In 1976, tens of thousands protested the leadership of the Gang of Four. In 1978 and 1979, protesters put up posters on what became known as the Democracy Wall. In 1986, students throughout China engaged in pro-democracy marches. Their protest led to the downfall of the leader of the Communist Party and, eventually, to a crackdown on the protests. In 1989, more than a hundred thousand students demonstrated in Beijing alone, demanding more freedom and democracy. Again there was a crackdown, with both student protesters and innocent bystanders being killed when the military moved in and opened fire. In China, then, the leaders face the paradox of lauding youth's role in change while at the same time facing periodic efforts by students to change the nation in ways that threaten the existing power structure.

• *Youth and Change: Speculative Conclusions*

How can we account for the role of youth in change? As we have seen, the majority of youth in the United States have been more concerned with securing their own place in the social order than with effecting basic changes in that order. Yet there are many young people who commit themselves to the task of change. What kind of context is likely to generate that commitment? I would offer a number of suggestions.

First, the general status of the young will bear upon their interest in effecting change. It has been argued that youth in America are in a position of "structural marginality," with no socially significant roles available to them. This would mean that the young fall into the category of status anguish discussed in the last chapter, and to the extent that they do, they will be amenable to a commitment to change.

A similar argument has been advanced by F. Musgrove, who says that where the status of adolescents and young adults is high the rate of change will be slow, while a low status will tend to generate a commitment to change.[55] According to Musgrove. high status seems to lead to conservatism even when the young are segregated from the adult world—as they were among the Plains Indians and the Nuer of Africa. When segregation is combined with low status, the young are likely to be leaders in change—as they were among the Tiv of Nigeria and the Manus of New Guinea.

Second, the young are likely to lead in change when there is a clear contradiction between ideology and reality. The events of the 1950s and 1960s which led to the radicalization of many American youth were all clearly contradictory to American ideals. The young radicals did not reject those ideals; they rejected the society that both praised and betrayed the ideals. The young of any society do not generally have economic and psychological commitments to the existing social order; they are. therefore, a potent source of change when ideology and reality conflict.

Third, youth's willingness to engage in change will be a function of certain sociocultural factors. In the United States, "the apex of rebelliousness is reached during the period of youth, before and after which rates of rebelliousness seem considerably lower."[56] At least two factors can help account for this. One is the expectation of rebelliousness during adolescence. Any number of books on parent-child relationships remind us that children advance from the dependence of infancy to the independence of adolescence to the interdependence of adulthood. The adolescent rebels only to establish a more mature relationship; under such conditions, that rebellion is to be expected from any healthy youth. As the anthropologists remind us, however, adolescent rebellion is peculiar to certain cultures. Its frequent occurrence in the United States is due to, among other things, the expectation that it will happen.

A second factor in youthful rebellion in the United States is the influence of the university. The emphasis on universal education means that more and more young people are subjected to more and more education. While that education often serves only to socialize the young into a mindless acceptance of their culture, it sometimes liberalizes and even radicalizes them. The last effect may be an unwitting byproduct of the contradiction between reality and university ideology, but education, nevertheless, is instrumental in transmitting the ideology.

A fourth type of context likely to generate youth commitment to change is a society undergoing rapid change. Historically, revolutionary student movements have arisen in transitional societies.[57] In the contemporary world, student revolt is particularly characteristic of modernizing nations. A number of reasons can account for this, including inevitable and intense conflict between the generations, a high degree of ideological polarization, inadequate employment of educated youth, inferior universities, and the fact that the young may be the only group willing and able to lead in change.[58]

One theme runs throughout the above—generational conflict. We saw this in the cases of Meiji Japan, China, and the United States. It is not clear whether change leads to the conflict, or whether conflict leads to change, or whether (as I think is more likely) this is a chicken-and-egg question, with conflict and change perpetuating each other. Mannheim argued that rapid change is of particular importance in intensifying generational differences.[59] On the other hand, Richard Flacks has asserted that "the emergence of sharp generational conflict and the mass uprising of privileged youth signify that a certain stage of social development is coming to an end and a new one is taking form."[60] Both are correct; change tends to intensify generational conflict and generational conflict leads to change. The young may effect change in collaboration with adults through their contribution to scientific and other kinds of innovation, but they do not seem to effect significant political change without generational conflict. And even then, the conflict tends to occur as a result of a minority of the youth who are vocal, articulate, idealistic, and who are able eventually to gain a broader base of support from the populace.

Endnotes

1. Michael G. Burton, "Elites and Collective Protest," *The Sociological Quarterly* 25 (1984): 51-52.

2. Pareto's thought is elaborated in his massive work *The Mind and Society*. For a concise introduction to Pareto, see Lewis A. Coser, *Masters of Sociological Thought* (New, York: Harcourt Brace Jovanovich, 1971), pp. 387-426.

3. Coser, *Masters of Sociological Thought*, p. 400.

4. Ibid., p. 399.

5. In addition to problems of conceptual definition which we noted. Pareto's thought presents certain difficulties. See T. B. Bottomore, *Elites and Society* (Middlesex: Penguin, 1964), pp. 48-54.

6. Edward A. Shils. "The Intellectuals in the Political Development of the New States," *World Politics* 12 (1960): 329-68.

7. C. Wright Mills, *The Power Elite* (New, York: Oxford University Press. 1986), p. 28.

8. Don Martindale, *Social Life and Cultural Change* (Princeton: Van Nostrand, 1962), p. 60.

9. Ibid., p. 503.

10. Shanti S. Tangri, "Intellectuals and Society in Nineteenth-Century India," *Comparative Studies in Society and History* 3 (1961): 393.

11. Daniel Lerner, with Ithiel de Sola Pool and George K. Schueller, "The Nazi Elite," in *World Revolutionary Elites: Studies in Coercive Ideological Movements*, ed. Harold D. Lasswell and Daniel Lerner (Cambridge, Mass.: MIT Press, 1965) p. 222.

12. See Burton, "Elites and Collective Protest," and John Higley and Michael G. Burton, "The Elite Variable in Democratic Transitions and Breakdowns," *American Sociological Review* 54 (1989): 17-32.

13. Burton, "Elites and Collective Protest," pp. 53-54.

14. Higley and Burton, "The Elite Variable in Democratic Transitions and Breakdowns," p.21.

15. P. C. Lloyd, *Africa in Social Change* (Middlesex: Penguin, 1969), p. 127.

16. Judith Granich Goode, "Responses of a Traditional Elite to Modernization: Lawyers in Colombia," *Human Organization* 29(1970): 70-80.

17. Lucian W. Pye, "Administrators, Agitators, and Brokers," *Public Opin-ion Quarterly* 22 (1958): 342-48.

18. Mostafa Reja and Kay Phillips, *Loyalists and Revolutionaries: Political Leaders Compared* (New York: Praeger, 1988).

19. S. N. Eisenstadt, *Modernization: Protest and Change* (Englewood Cliffs, N.J.: Prentice-Hall, 1966). pp. 67-75.

20. H. Nishio, "Political Centralism and Economic Consequences: An Analysis of Early Japanese Modernization," in *Perspectives on Modernization: Essays in Memory of Ian Weinberg*, ed. Edward B. Harvey (Toronto: University of Toronto Press, 1972), pp. 137-59.

21. Paul E. Sigmund, ed., *The Ideologies of the Developing Nations*, Rev. ed. (New York: Praeger, 1967), pp. 7-8.

22. C. E. Black, *The Dynamics of Modernization* (New York: Harper & Row, 1966), pp. 62-67.

23. Chun-Chan Yeh, "The Role of the Intellectual in China," *Third World Quarterly* 11 (1989): 143-53.

24. Ibid., p. 149.

25. S. N. Eisenstadt, "Breakdowns of Modernization," in *Readings in Social Evolution and Development*, ed. S. N. Eisenstadt (Oxford: Pergamon Press, 1970). pp.421-52.

26. Richard Cottam, "Inside Revolutionary Iran," *Middle East Journal* 43 (1989): 169

27. See the articles on "leadership and economic growth" in the *International Social Science Journal* 16 (1964): 185-274.

28. Daniel Lerner, "The Coercive Ideologists in Perspective," in *World Revolutionary Elites*, ed. Lasswell and Lerner, p. 461.

29. Partha Nath Mukherji, "Study in Induced Social Change: An Indian Experiment." *Human Organization* 29 (1970): 169-77.

30. Joseph Aceves, *Social Change in a Spanish Village* (Cambridge, Mass.: Schenkman, 1971), p. 32.

31. Cynthia Nelson, *The Waiting Village* (Boston: Little, Brown, 1971), pp.100-105.

32. Guy Hunter, *Modernizing Peasant Societies* (New York: Oxford University Press, 1969), pp. 98-99.

33. Reuel Derney, "American Youth Today: A Bigger Cast, a Wider Screen," in *The Challenge of Youth*, ed. Erik H. Erikson (Garden City, N.Y.: Anchor Books, 1965), p. 166.

34. Everett Carll Ladd, "Generation Myths," *Public Opinion*, November/'December, 1986, p. 11.

35. Richard G. Braungart and Margaret M. Braungart, "From Yippies to Yuppies: Twenty Years of Freshman Attitudes," *Public Opinion*, September/October, 1988, p.55.

36. "Gaping at the Generation Gap," *Public Opinion*, February/March, 1980, p. 38. For a theoretical discussion of generational conflict and change, including an examination of student activism in the United States and Canada, see Dan A. Chekki, "Youth and Social Change." *Sociologia Internationalis* 13 (Nos. 1/2, 1975): 89-102. Chekki concludes that the student activism of the 1960s was "a generational revolt which in the long run, most probably, may prove to be transitory."

37. Ann F. Brunswick, "What Generation Gap?" *Social Problems* 17 (1970): 369.

38. Much of the material in this paragraph is drawn from David Matza, "Subterranean Traditions of Youth," *Annals of the American Academy of Political and Social Science* 338 (1961): 109; and Lewis S. Feuer, *The Conflict of Generations* (New York: Basic Books, 1969), p. 318.

39. Paul Jacobs and Saul Landau, *The New Radicals* (New York: Random House, 1966), pp. 11-14.

40. Quoted in Editors of Fortune, *Youth In Turmoil* (New York: Time-Life Books, 1969), pp. 47-55.

41. Theodore Roszak, *The Making of a Counter Culture* (Garden City: Anchor Books, 1969). p. 42.

42. Jerome H. Skolnick, *The Politics of Protest* (New York: Ballantine Books, 1969). pp. 100-105.

43. Todd Gitlin, *The Sixties: Years of Hope, Days of Rage* (New York: Bantam, 1987), p. 365.

44. Ibid., p. 285.

45. Irwin Unger, *The Movement: A History of the American New Left, 1959-1972* (New York: Dodd, Mead, 1974).

46. Loyd D. Easton and Kurt H. Guddat, eds., *Writings of the Young Marx on Philosophy and Society* (Garden City, N.Y.: Anchor Books, 1967), p. 1.

47. David Donald, *Lincoln Reconsidered,* 2nd ed. (New York: Random House, 1961), pp. 26-27.

48. Kenneth B. Pyle, *The New Generation in Meiji Japan* (Stanford: Stanford University Press, 1969), pp. 6-7.

49. Etienne Balazs, *Chinese Civilization and Bureaucracy,* trans. H. M. wright, ed. Arthur F. Wright (New Haven: Yale University Press. 1964), p. 164.

50. Material on the May Fourth Movement is drawn from Chow Tse-tung, *The May Fourth Movement* (Cambridge, Mass.: Harvard University Press, 1960). pp. 92-120.

51. Ibid., p. 108.

52. Robert C. North, "Kuomintang and Chinese Communist Elites," in *World Revolutionary Elites,* ed. Lasswell and Lerner, p. 383.

53. Tan Wen, "Youth Should Stand in the Forefront of the Revolutionary Ranks." *Peking Review,* May 18,1973, p. 8.

54. Nicholas D. Kristof, "China's Leaders Hear the Roar of the Crowd," *New York Times,* April 30, 1989.

55. F.Musgrove, *Youth and the Social Order* (Bloomington: Indiana University Press. 1964), pp. 126-41.

56. Matza, "Subterranean Traditions of Youth," p. 104.

57. Skolnick, *The Politics of Protest,* p. 82.

58. Seymour Martin Lipset, ed., *Student Politics* (New York: Basic Books, 1967), pp. 3-53, 239-45.

59. Karl Mannheim, *Essays on the Sociology of Knowledge,* ed. Paul Kecskemeti (London: Routledge & Kegan Paul, 1952), pp. 309-10.

60. Richard Flacks, *Youth and Social Change* (Chicago: Markham Publishing Company, 1971), p. 14.

PART FOUR

Patterns of Contemporary Change

In Part I we tried to clear away some of the haze surrounding our understanding of change by identifying and rejecting certain false assumptions as well as by defining and illustrating the meaning of change. In Part II we were concerned with various answers to an important question: How can we understand the course of change? Part III dealt with specific factors that seem to impel change. In this part, we shall look at the "how" of change, that is, the form of pattern taken by change in the contemporary world.

Some patterns have already been discussed in earlier parts. In Part I we considered some of the different patterns that can occur and illustrated them by particular examples of change in the United States. In Part II we looked at some cyclical, evolutionary, and dialectical patterns. In this part we will look at industrialization and modernization, the pervasive patterns of change today. As Wilbert Moore has pointed out, "all people everywhere are subject to, and many are actively participating in, a process of social change that is called modernization."[1]

Industrialization and modernization involve extensive changes at all levels in a society. Because the changes are extensive, and because they are pervasive throughout the world today, they have been the subject of a great deal of study. Sociologists and other social scientists have theorized, researched, and debated with one another about the intricate processes of industrialization and modernization. Obviously, it would not be possible within a single chapter to adequately discuss the wealth of books and articles written about these processes. We shall, instead, attempt to cover the fundamental points, including some of the disagreements among social scientists.

Endnote

1. Wilbert E. Moore, *World Modernization: The Limits of Convergence* (New York: Elsevier, 1979), p. 1.

CHAPTER TWELVE

Industrialization and Modernization

"The mass of men lead lives of quiet desperation," wrote Thoreau. There may be many in the contemporary world who are struggling with desperation, but not many appear to be doing so quietly. Rather, the whole world is caught up in that quest that drove Thoreau into the wilderness: "I wanted to live deep and suck out all the marrow of life." Peoples throughout the world are no longer content—if they ever were—to live in quiet desperation; a passion for bread and freedom has swept over the world.[1]

A primary reason for this passion is that the peoples of the world are no longer willing to be paupers, to eke out a wretched existence on crumbs that fall from the well-filled tables of the affluent few. The situation is dramatized by the Indian untouchable who picks undigested pieces of grain out of cow dung in order that he and his family may eat, the thousands of Latin American children dying for lack of water, and the hundreds of millions throughout the world who exist at every moment on the edge of starvation or disease.[2]

In more quantitative terms, we may note the gross inequalities among the world's nations.[3] There are striking differences in goods and services. For instance, in the 1970s the gross national product ranged from about $75 per capita to over $11,000 per capita; in 1974, the developed nations averaged $4,366 per capita, while the developing nations averaged $397 per capita. Similarly, the literacy rate varied from 5 to 99 percent of the adult population of the various nations. The number of people per physician varied from nearly 59,000 in Upper Volta to 361 in the Soviet Union; on a per capita basis, there were seven times as many physicians in the developed nations as there were in the developing nations. The infant mortality rate was over five times higher in the developing than the developed nations. The public expenditure per capita was $4 in the developing nations and $144 in the world's developed nations. In the mid-1980s, the gross national product per capita ranged from an average of $260 among the poorest nations to $1,250 among nations in the middle to $11,430 among the industrialized nations. Ethiopia, the poorest nation, reported $110 per capita, while the United Arab Emirates reported $21,920. The United States had $15,390 per capita. The differences in wealth show up in figures that reflect the quality of life. In the more developed nations of the world, the infant mortality rate in the 1980s was 17 per 1,000 live births, while it was 92 in the less developed nations. Similarly, among the more developed nations, life expectancy was 69.4 years for males and 76.9 years for females, while among the less developed it was 55.5 years for males and 57.7 years for females.

Various other figures underscore the nature and extent of impoverishment in the world:[4]

- One billion people in the Third World, about one out of every five persons on earth, live in poverty.
- At least 100 million people live without any kind of shelter.
- Tens of thousands of infants die unnecessarily each day because of the lack of proper health care.
- At least 700 million people in the world fail to get the proper diet for an active and healthy life.

Because of such disparities, and because of their unwillingness to tolerate them any longer, the peoples of the world are avidly pursuing the pattern of change called modernization. As noted in the first chapter, this does not mean that they are pursuing a course that will lead them to an American type of social order or economic structure. It is a pursuit of bread and freedom rather than of Americanization or Westernization. We have dealt with various facets of this quest at a number of points throughout the book; in this chapter, we shall focus on it as a pattern of change. What is involved in modernization? We must begin by trying to clarify the meaning of the term and of another that is often associated with it—industrialization.

Modernization and Industrialization: Clarifications

Historically, modernization and industrialization have been closely associated, but they are not equivalent terms. *Modernization* is a more inclusive term, for modernization can occur apart from industrialization. As David Apter has noted, in the West modernization proceeded by commercialization and industrialization, while in some non-Western areas modernization has proceeded by commercialization and bureaucracy. Thus, "modernization can . . . be seen as something apart from industrialization—caused by it in the West but causing it in other areas."[5] Obviously, both modernization and industrialization involve the crucial element of economic growth, but that growth can occur apart from industrialization, while it is always integral to modernization.

• Industrialization and Economic Growth

Industrialization, in simple terms, is economic development through a transformation of the sources and quantities of energy employed.[6] In the agrarian society, for the most part, person and animal power were the sources of energy. It has been estimated that in 1850, 65 percent of the energy used in American work was supplied by people and animals. By 1950, 65 percent of the energy was supplied by fossil fuels and hydroelectric power, and energy consumption had soared from 435 horsepower-hours per person in 1850 to 4,470 horsepower-hours per person in 1950.[7]

A number of scholars have wrestled with the problem of defining stages of industrial and economic development. Perhaps one of the best-known efforts is that of Walt Rostow, who has identified five stages of economic growth.[8] These stages include the traditional setting, preconditions for "take-off," the take-off itself, the thrust toward maturity, and the stage of high mass consumption. Since these five stages, at least in their general outline, have been received with some degree of approval by many economists, we shall briefly characterize them.

The traditional setting is characterized by limited potential for productivity; science, technology, and attitudes that prevail in the society all function to put a ceiling on development. Furthermore, agriculture is predominant but not highly productive, little capital is available, few people have any savings, and illiteracy is common.

In the second stage, conditions necessary for industrialization begin to take shape. The people become convinced that economic progress is possible and that it will bring them numerous desirable benefits. Certain changes in the economic structure begin, such as the formation of banks. The content of education shifts so as to prepare people for the coming economic change and to equip them to participate in it. Most important, the polity takes the form of a centralized authority for the nation; it is difficult if not impossible for the next stage to be attained without a strong government.

In the third, or take-off, stage, rapid growth is achieved through the application of modern industrial techniques in a limited number of sectors of the economy. Moreover, this growth becomes self-sustaining. One necessary condition for take-off to occur is the rise of the proportion of net investment to national income to something over 10 percent, "definitely outstripping the likely population pressure . . . and yielding a distinct rise in real output per capita."[9] The noneconomic facets of take-off include the social and political triumph of those committed to modernization over those who tend either to cleave to traditionalism or to pursue other goals.

The fourth stage, the drive to maturity, involves the application of modern technology over the whole range of the economy. In this way, new sectors may supplant older ones as the driving mechanism that sustains growth. In the United States, for example, railways, coal, iron, and heavy engineering dominated the economy and sustained its growth after the middle of the nineteenth century; then steel, ships, chemicals, electricity, and varied manufactured products served the same purpose. During this stage about 10 to 20 percent of national income is invested. As a rule of thumb, maturity is achieved somewhere around sixty years after take-off in the developed nations.

Finally, there is the fifth stage, the age of high mass consumption. Actually, once the state of maturity has been reached and the commitment made to extend technology into all spheres of life, a number of directions are available. A society might focus on welfare for its people, or expand consumption, or strive for enhanced power in the international arena. The United States, according to Rostow, opted for the second of the three in the 1920s. It was then that the movement to suburbia began, the automobile was made available to the masses of people, a proliferation of household gadgets appeared on the market, and a number of other consumption-encouraging trends were started.

As a general outline of economic development that is tied up with industrialization, Rostow's stages apply to a number of nations, though not to all.[10] The important point for our purposes is that industrialization is not simply an economic and technological pattern of change, but a social and cultural one also. We shall examine some of these social and cultural implications after we clarify the meaning of modernization as a process distinct from industrialization.

• *Modernization and Economic Growth*

As pointed out above, modernization also involves economic growth, and that growth may or may not be based upon industrialization. Thus, we shall refer to *industrialization* as economic growth that occurs through the application of technology to industrial development and to *modernization* as a general process involving economic growth along with social and cultural development.

In other words, modernization is a more inclusive term than industrialization and includes the political and social changes that accompany economic growth. There have been differences among scholars as to the meaning of modernization, but there is considerable consensus on the following as characteristics of modernity:

> *(1) a degree of self-sustaining growth in the economy—or at least growth sufficient to increase both production and consumption regularly; (2) a measure of public participation in the polity . . . ; (3) a diffusion of secular-rational norms in the culture . . . ; (4) an increment of mobility in the society . . . ; (5) a corresponding transformation in the modal personality that equips individuals to function effectively in a social order that operates according to the foregoing characteristics.*[11]

Obviously, modernization entails the problem of bread and freedom mentioned earlier. Like industrialization, it involves not only economic growth but a number of social and cultural changes. Again, we must not leap to the erroneous conclusion that there is only one path to modernization or that the process itself leads to a single end. Indeed, since the social context in which modernization occurs has been diverse for various nations, we would expect differences both among nations that have already modernized and among those in the process or yet to begin the process. We shall describe some of these differences in more detail below.

In the following sections I will discuss the problem of the relationship between theories of change and the process of modernization, the international context of modernization, the social and cultural changes that have been associated with modernization, and some of the divergent patterns of modernization. I shall use the term *modernization* rather than *industrialization*, recognizing that most often the latter was a part of the former. The latter term will be used whenever the material applies specifically to that technoeconomic process rather than to the larger process of modernization.

Modernization and Social Change Theory

Since a good part of the world's population is now undergoing the pattern of change that we call modernization, we should raise the question of the adequacy of various theories to account for that pattern. Many of the perspectives we have examined so far have dealt directly with modernization, or with certain aspects of it, including Smelser's structural-functionalist analysis of England's industrialization and the social-psychological approaches of Hagen, McClelland, and the students of individual modernity. There is, however, no generally accepted theory of modernization. In this section we shall see some of the theoretical problems involved in the study of modernization.

The very concept of modernization is relatively new, and modernization theories tend to fall into one of two types, the "critical variable" and the "dichotomous" theories.[12] The first type involves a single kind of change, such as rationalization or industrialization, and the term *modernization* becomes virtually synonymous with the critical variable. The second type is more common and involves the process of transformation of traditional societies into modern ones. The process is defined in terms of an end goal, a goal that is often a nation very like those in the contemporary West. (Recall the myth of unidirectionality and utopia apprehended.)

An example of the critical variable approach is Moore's conclusion that modernization is "the rationalization of the ways social life is organized and social activities performed."[13] Rationalization, in his usage, refers to the use of reason to choose the appropriate means for realizing goals that have been specified. The goals may include anything from a growing economy to better health to a well-functioning government. The goals can never be perfectly realized because there are inherent limits to the human capacity for rational behavior. Nevertheless, Moore argues, the universal pattern of change in the modern world is an increasing rationalization of social life.

The dichotomous approaches are illustrated in the structural-functional and social-psychological theories of change that we discussed earlier. Both approaches have problems. In the critical variable approach, it would seem that little is gained by employing the term *modernization,* for modernization is basically a synonym for the critical variable. The problem with the dichotomous theories is twofold. First, as noted above, they tend to fall into the trap of the myth of utopia apprehended. Second, they tend to ignore factors external to a particular society, viewing modernization as something that involves only elements of that society. That means that every society is perfectly free to modernize or not, depending on what happens within the society.

But nations today are not autonomous entities. We live in a world economy, and a nation that seeks to modernize must do so in a particular kind of world environment. The importance of the world context in a nation's efforts to modernize is incorporated in a theoretical perspective that emerged in the 1960s—world system theory. Where most previous work focused on the characteristics of nations that impeded or facilitated their development, world system theory provided a corrective by stressing the significance of the international context of modernization.

The International Context of Modernization

World system theory, or dependency theory, brings the study of modernization to the highest level of social reality, the international system. As we noted above, a flaw of much of the previous work on modernization is the neglect of the international context. World system theorists argue that so-called underdevelopment is not the result merely of deficiencies or inadequacies in a nation's institutions and values. Rather, location in the international system is the crucial factor bearing upon a nation's development or lack of development. There is some diversity among world system theorists, and their work is scattered throughout the literature of the social sciences. But all agree that modernization must be analyzed at the international level. Let us look more closely at the theory itself. Then we shall examine some empirical evidence that bears upon the theory.

• *World System Theory*

The basic thrust of world system theory may be understood by looking at the work of one of its most important and representative theorists, Immanuel Wallerstein. Wallerstein offers an elaborate, carefully worked out theory by which he proposes to explain the past, present, and future world systems. He takes as his point of departure the assumption that the entire world is the only proper unit of analysis. For the only true social system today is a world system. This follows from the nature of a social system: "We take the defining characteristic of a social system to be the existence within it of a division of labor, such that the various sectors or areas within are dependent upon economic exchange with others for the smooth and continuous provisioning of the needs of the area."[14]

In the past, there were "minisystems," simple agricultural and hunting-and-gathering societies, that had a complete division of labor in the context of a single cultural framework. But minisystems have vanished, so that the only kind of social system today is the world system, which has a single division of labor in the context of numerous and diverse cultural frameworks. There are, in turn, two types of world systems: the world empire, which involves a single political system, and the world economy, which has multiple political systems. It is the world system as a world economy that is the focus of Wallerstein's work.

How did this world economy come into being? In essence, the world economy, or world capitalist system, arose out of dying feudalism in the sixteenth century. There were three essential elements in the emergence of world capitalism (Wallerstein insists that from the first, capitalism was a world phenomenon and not a characteristic of individual nations): "an expansion of the geographical size of the world in question, the development of variegated methods of labor control for different products and different zones of the world-economy, and the creation of relatively strong state machineries in what would become the core-states of this capitalist world-economy."[15] There were other factors that also contributed to the rise of world capitalism. In fact, it appears in retrospect that a remarkable array of events, from various political developments to a shift in the climate of Europe, all contributed to the emergence and triumph of the world capitalist system.

What is the nature of that world system? First, there is a worldwide division of labor. The division is not merely along occupational lines, but is geographical. The varied economic tasks are not distributed equally among the nations of the world. This is largely "a function of the social organization of work, one which magnifies and legitimizes the ability of some groups within the system to exploit the labor of others, that is, to receive a larger share of the surplus."[16] Obviously, Wallerstein uses Marx's analysis of the processes of a capitalist society and applies it to the world as a whole. Thus, the capitalists or exploiters for Marx become the core states for Wallerstein. The core states dominate and exploit the rest of the world, which includes the peripheral and semi-peripheral areas. In the core countries, free labor engages largely in skilled work. In the peripheral areas, labor is coerced and primarily unskilled. The semi-periphery is composed of areas between the core states and the periphery; some of the semi-peripheral areas were core areas in the past, while others moved up from the periphery.

Continuing the analogy with Marx's analysis of capitalist society, Wallerstein says that there is a widening economic and social gap between the various areas of the world system. Technological developments help the world economy to expand and may thereby give the illusion that there is an egalitarian trend in the world system. But it is not theoretically possible for all the nations of the world to develop together: "The so-called 'widening gap' is not an anomaly but a continuing basic mechanism of the operation of the world-economy."[17]

Another characteristic of the world system is a number of cyclical and secular trends. The cyclical economic pattern of a national economy characterizes the world economy as well. Secular trends include the capitalization of world agriculture, technological developments associated with industrialization, and "the strengthening of all organizational structures—the states, the economic corporate structures, and even the cultural institutions—vis-a-vis both individuals and groups."[18] One of the more important of the organizational structures in recent times is the multinational corporation, which is able to function rather independently of national governments. That is, the multinationals have the power to outmaneuver governments when the latter attempt to act in behalf of the interests of their working classes.

A final characteristic of the world system that we should mention is the mechanisms by which the system is maintained. After all, if the gap between the core states and the other areas is widening, if the bulk of the human race is being exploited by a minority, why is the system tolerated? Wallerstein says that there are three basic mechanisms through which the world capitalist system has remained politically stable. First, there is the superior military strength of the core states. Second, the system is stabilized through ideological commitment, through a sense on the part of "the staff or cadres of the system" that their well-being depends upon the system's continuation. Third, and most importantly, the system has survived because of its three layers. The semi-periphery is crucial to political stability. Otherwise, the world would be polarized into two camps (similar to the polarization of capitalist society in Marx's analysis), which would be a revolutionary situation. "The existence of the third category means precisely that the upper stratum is not faced with the *unified* opposition of all the others because the *middle* stratum is both exploited and exploiter."[19] Economically the world system could function well without a semi-periphery, but politically the semi-periphery is essential for system stability.

The stability of the world system cannot be maintained indefinitely, however. Like Marx, Wallerstein sees the future in terms of socialism. There are no socialist systems in existence now, just as there are no longer any feudal systems. There is only the world system, which is capitalist. But socialism lies in the future. It will demand "the creation of a new kind of world-system, neither a redistributive world-empire nor a capitalist world-economy, but a socialist world-government."[20] The new order will not emerge quickly or peacefully. It will be the outcome of a long struggle.

There are a number of other world system theories, each of which is similar to but different to some extent from the above perspective.

Two of the more important points of disagreement are the socialist role in the world system and the question of the number of strata.[21]

With respect to the socialist question, where do the supposedly socialist nations fit into this world capitalist system? We have already noted Wallerstein's argument that there is no socialism today because the system itself is capitalist. The point is that ideology alone does not make a nation socialist. So-called socialist nations function like capitalist nations in the international system regardless of their internal structure. Other theorists take somewhat variant points of view. Daniel Chirot argues that there is no international communist system analogous to the capitalist system, and that communist nations are not necessarily integrated into the capitalist world system. The Soviet Union and China, he contends, "constitute virtually autonomous systems of their own," and the development of communist nations inevitably means an erosion of the power of the core in the world capitalist system.[22] In sum, the theorists all agree that the world system is capitalist, but differ on the extent to which noncapitalist nations are integrated into that system.

The answer to the other question, the number of strata, varies between two and three. Wallerstein insists on three as crucial for the system's survival. Chirot, however, while discussing the three strata, argues that developments during the 1960s and 1970s have made the situation more complicated. The labels of peripheral and semi-peripheral are no longer as applicable as they were.

> *Instead of a world dominated by struggles between core powers, the world has become a battleground between the united capitalist core and its assailants, the two major Communist powers and a growing number of new semi-peripheral societies. In effect, the international relations now consist of a jockeying between the core, the Soviet Union, and China for power and influence in that growing semi-periphery which, however, remains free to play off the major powers against each other.*[23]

While the variations are no doubt of importance to the theorists, they are minor compared with the points of agreement. The world system theorists all offer a conflict model of international stratification. They explain a fact that has both perplexed and distressed a great many observers, the failure of the underdeveloped nations to close the gap between themselves and the developed nations. And they have stimulated a good deal of research to test their theories. Let us look at some of that research.

• World System Research

While not all of the research we shall discuss in this section was stimulated directly by world system theory, all of it bears upon that theory. Basically, the research we shall discuss addresses the question of the consequences for a nation of being economically dependent on other nations. Economic dependence can be related to international trade patterns, to the activities of multinational corporations, to foreign investments, and to foreign aid.

World system theorists see trade patterns as one mechanism by which core or center nations exploit and maintain dominance over the rest of the world. It seems unquestionable that the developed nations benefit far more from trade patterns than do other nations. The disadvantages for the developing nations were noted in an early analysis of trade patterns by Hans Singer.[24] As Singer pointed out, international trade is greatly important to the underdeveloped countries, which have low per capita income and a small margin of income over subsistence (that margin being a source of capital formation). The margin available for capital may depend on a surplus of exports over imports.

Unfortunately, while developing nations require a favorable balance of trade, investments made by the developed nations have made the underdeveloped countries the providers of food and raw materials. That situation is less beneficial than the more rounded industrial development that could have occurred if the underdeveloped nations had not specialized to supply the needs of the developed nations. Moreover, the terms of trade have benefited the developed more than the underdeveloped nations. Technological progress has raised the income of workers in developed nations and kept the prices for raw materials at a low level. The developed nations, therefore, are consumers of primary commodities and producers of manufactured articles, while the underdeveloped nations consume manufactured goods and produce raw materials. Such an arrangement makes progress extremely difficult for the underdeveloped nations. In fact, an analysis of trade patterns concluded that the core nations exploit the semi-periphery which, in turn, exploits the periphery, so that, in accord with world system theory, trade patterns maintain the dominance of some nations over others.[25]

As the pattern suggests, one reason for the disadvantage of the non-core nations is that the exports of the core nations are of much greater value than the imports they receive from the non-core nations.[26] Moreover, the developing nations suffered another blow after the 1973 oil crisis, when the oil-producing nations began to increase the price of crude oil dramatically. The higher oil prices led to a debt crisis for many Third World nations that were trying to develop industry.[27]

They needed the oil, but found themselves in a situation in which imports, increasingly, were of greater value than exports. In Latin America, the loss of domestic savings led to loans from foreign banks. Unfortunately, the money received was not always used wisely. Compounding the problem, some countries have repaid an amount equal to the principal (or several times the principal) but continue to make payments and amass indebtedness. During the latter part of the 1980s, a number of Latin American countries paid out more in principal and interest than they received in new loans, involving them in what economists call a net transfer of resources (and, of course, an ever-growing debt obligation). For example, in 1988, Argentina had a debt that was nearly 80 percent of its gross domestic product and made payments that were nearly $2 billion more than the nation received in new loans.

Thus, the developing nations confront harsh dilemmas as they try to engage in modernization. To the extent that a nation specializes in agricultural exports, it will find its economic development inhibited.[28] But if it seeks to industrialize, it will find its efforts seriously impeded by existing trade patterns and may find itself plunging into the crisis of overwhelming debt.

The second aspect of economic dependence, the multinational corporation, has been a matter of considerable dispute. Indeed, there is even argument about the definition of a multinational. We will accept the United Nations' definition: "all enterprises that control assets—factories, mines, sales offices, and the like—in two or more countries."[29] Such enterprises have existed for a long time, but they have grown dramatically, in number and size, since the end of World War II. Thousands of corporations, headquartered in various nations, maintain an economic interest in companies in two or more countries. Something of the possible economic power available to multinationals may be gathered from the fact that the total dollar sales of General Motors, one of the largest, is greater than the gross national product of the majority of the world's nations.

Some observers have argued that the multinationals are largely beneficial, that they stimulate economic growth in the developing nations. It has been said that they are a source of capital and of advanced technology and of training opportunities and jobs. But a stronger case can be made for the argument that the multinationals, like trade patterns, generally help maintain international inequalities. In the first place, the multinational is likely to provide very little new capital, while it is almost certain to extract considerable profit (which is, after all, the basis for the corporation establishing itself in a host country in the first place). In addition, the host country's economy may be damaged because local investment may be stunted, unemployment may be increased because of capital-intensive methods of production, and the economy may become highly specialized in accord with the needs of the corporation rather than the needs of the nation.

Multinationals have been criticized along other lines as well. We will mention two of them. One is the propensity for the activities of corporations not merely to inhibit economic development but to be economically detrimental to the nation and its people. There is evidence that the greater the penetration of a developing nation's economy by multinationals, the greater the power inequality and the more unequal the income distribution within that nation.[30] Some of the evidence on detrimental effects is logical, though less firm, such as that bearing upon the relationship between elites and masses. That is, the net effect of the multinationals may be to estrange the elites from the masses, weakening the central government and thereby crippling efforts to develop. (Recall in Chapter 10 we noted that there is considerable agreement among theorists that a strong government is essential for economic development today.) This can happen as the elites become more oriented to the corporations than to their own nation. One study of Brazilian businesspeople found that those who worked in firms that were dependent on foreign corporate support believed that their society would function well as long as it had an alliance of upper-class groups, while those in independent firms were far more likely to believe that workers should share in the nation's political power. Thus, multinationals are economic threats to the extent that they lessen political authority in a nation or alienate the masses from their leaders.

The other criticism is that the multinationals not only increase the inequality within nations but also contribute to the amount of political violence in those nations.[31] In fact, it is by intensifying the problem of inequality that the multinationals contribute to the violence. The multinationals pay higher wages than native industries, increasing the income gap between those employed by the multinationals and others, a gap that is not relieved by redistributive governmental policies. Further, the transfer of resources to the home (core) country from the profits of the operation restrict the capital available for investment in the developing country; this intensifies and maintains the problem of inequality. Thus, it is not surprising that the greater the multinational penetration of a developing country, the greater the chance of violence in that country.

Foreign investments and foreign aid are the remaining aspects of economic dependence that we will discuss. As in the case of the multinationals, some observers have argued that they are essential to the well-being of developing nations. But whatever the benefits might be in theory, in practice, foreign investments and foreign aid have not turned out to be the pathway to progress in the Third World. A good portion of foreign investments comes through the multinational corporations, but there is also a substantial amount that arrives through other channels, such as portfolios.

A number of studies have concluded that direct foreign investment and foreign aid increase the economic inequality within countries and decrease the relative rate of economic growth (though they may increase it in the short run).[32] Ironically, the effects seem to be strongest in the developing nations that are better off, suggesting that there may be a limit to how much a developing nation can modernize in the present international context.

It is not only the economy, but the entire way of life that can be affected by the activities surrounding foreign investment. In her study of an Indonesian mining town, Kathryn Robinson showed how a foreign owned nickel mining and processing enterprise changed the lives of the local people.[33] Prior to the enterprise, the people engaged in subsistence agriculture and some regional trade. Each family had access to land and consumed its own products. But the government expropriated the prime irrigated land to make room for the company's site. That forced the people to seek employment in the new enterprise. Many of them became workers in an enterprise run by foreigners, the latter, of course, commanding far higher wages than the former. Going from a traditional agricultural community to an industrial community, in turn, altered such traditions as marriage practices and gender roles.

Whether the Indonesians were better off before or after the change is a matter of debate. In this case, however, the problem was that they did not choose the new way, but had it forced upon them by a governmental decision and the actions of a foreign corporation. People who choose their own path of change are likely to define it as progress, as being better off. Those who are forced upon a path of change, even if it can be shown that they are better off in some sense, are less likely to define the change as a desirable one.

Finally, we should note that not all research supports world system theory, at least as the theory is presently formulated. World system theory indicates that there will be increasing economic convergence within each of the zones—core, semi-periphery, and periphery, and increasing economic divergence between zones. A test of this aspect of the theory, however, showed only partial support.[34] From 1950 to 1980, there was divergence (increasing economic inequality) between zones. However, a good part of the divergence reflected changing population shares and India's slow growth relative to other nations in the semi-periphery. With regard to convergence, on the other hand, only the core nations supported the theory. Within the semi-periphery and periphery zones, the trends indicated divergence or, at best, stability.

Case studies of some nations also show results that differ from what world system theory would predict. A study of Taiwan challenges the notion that foreign investments and aid inevitably retard economic growth and heighten inequality.[35] From the 1950s to the 1980s, Taiwan received enormous amounts of foreign aid and investment and had one of the highest sustained rates of growth in the world. At the same time, income inequality in the nation decreased considerably. There are various reasons for Taiwan's progress: its economic growth was broadly based rather than confined to enclaves, land reform made agricultural income more equal, there were high levels of education and literacy, and its pattern of development was labor-intensive. Without going into detail, the point is that Taiwan demonstrates the fact that foreign aid and investment do not inherently doom a nation to economic problems and subservience.

Similarly, Kenya, one of the peripheral countries, has received a substantial amount of foreign investment and is heavily dependent on the export of raw materials, but has experienced significant economic development.[36] Kenya has been helped by a strong central government, which heavily taxes foreign enterprises and requires them to use local distributors to form joint ventures with domestic capital.

While world system theory does not explain all the results of research, it does underscore the need to put the process of modernization into an international setting. A nation's internal structure and processes are clearly important, but internal factors must be seen in the light of the international environment in which nations necessarily function.

Conditions of Modernization

What is necessary for modernization to occur? Obviously, certain changes must occur within the world system. The theorists differ on how quickly and how peacefully changes in the world system might occur, but there is general agreement on two points: (1) the present system is not immutable but will ultimately give way to a new order, and (2) an altered world system must still be accompanied by changes within nations if those nations are to modernize. With regard to the new international order, the changes that are needed follow directly from the theory and research. The economic dependency of the majority of nations upon the core minority must be broken. Tamas Szentes has suggested that among the necessary principles of a new world system would be the following: (1) research centers must be located within developing nations and must focus on the particular needs and resources of those nations; (2) the "brain drain" must be stopped by preventing educated people from migrating from the developing nations; (3) foreign power over national economies must be regulated; and (4) the activities of multinational corporations must be regulated.[37] Until these and other principles are instituted, there can be no large-scale modernization of the world, at least not in the sense of widespread economic development that leads to diminishing inequality.

Given a world system that is conducive to modernization, non-core nations face a number of dilemmas and issues that must be addressed.[38] The first is whether to even proceed with development. Some Third World thinkers, forced with massive problems and the lack of any immediate benefit, have begun to question the wisdom of development. To return to the question raised above, would the people of the Indonesian town with the nickel mining operation be better off if development had not occurred? Some say yes.

A second problem is the dilemma of self-reliance versus interdependence. Nations like China and India have attempted a high degree of self-reliance in their development efforts. But, as we have seen, no nation can escape the fact that development takes place in an international economy. Interdependence is inevitable. The challenge is to be interdependent without sinking into the patron-client relationship of Third World subservience.

Third is the dilemma of economic growth versus equitable distribution. How can a nation develop without the gross inequalities that characterized the West and that tend to occur in developing nations today? Fourth is the question of whether development can proceed best by centralized planning or by the operation of a free market. Fifth is the dilemma of industrialization versus the environment; can the earth sustain an industrial world?

There are many technical economic questions that must be addressed and, finally, there is the question of the direction of development. How can a nation develop economically and still retain some of its traditions and its uniqueness? Clearly, the issue of development is not a simple one of willingness and perseverance.

The perplexing nature of development today is illustrated by a few comparisons between the contemporary situation and the historical situation in which the first nations began to modernize. The socioeconomic climate of England greatly facilitated that nation's development. English trade was favored by geography and by the lack of destructive wars or political disarray. The size and nature of the market were also "exceptionally favorable. The geographical size of the market available to English manufacturers was wide—transport costs were lower, marketing facilities better, internal tariffs, tolls, etc. . . . were absent" in comparison to the situation in continental countries.[39]

In contrast to England and to other European nations, peasant societies of today face agonizing problems. They do not have the opportunity for significant territorial expansion. They are at a technological disadvantage with respect to competitors. Their economy is less differentiated; about 80 percent of the population is engaged in agriculture. And they have a far greater rate of population growth. The large population increase that typifies the early stages of modernization occurred over the course of a century in Europe, while in many Third World nations it has happened in less than two decades.[40] Thus, "there is no real analogy with the European past; and the labour-saving capital-intensive methods of the European present are even less applicable."[41]

Consequently, it is difficult at best to identify the economic conditions that are necessary for the development of contemporary peasant societies. Clearly the developed nations play a crucial role in contemporary efforts at modernization. The developed nations were literally subsidized in their growth by the territorial and market expansion and the supply of resources afforded by the less developed and underdeveloped nations of today. The fact that some nations have modernized means that the situation in which modernization must occur has completely altered. Recognizing this fact, the Commission on International Development recommended that the industrialized countries each transfer a minimum of 1 percent of their gross national product (with no strings attached) to low-income countries in order to facilitate development.[42] While some of the developed nations have responded to the challenge, the amount given so far has been minimal.

While the economic factors in development are both perplexing and greatly important, the noneconomic factors are equally significant. And there is somewhat more agreement on the noneconomic factors that are necessary. We shall look at some of the important structural and social-psychological factors.

Economic growth is unlikely under certain structural conditions. The system of land tenure can preclude the agricultural development that is crucial to modernization. Popular participation in the affairs of the nation may be minimal and the increase of that participation precluded by a tyrannical government locked in with a rigid system of stratification. Associated with this, there is often little in the way of voluntary associations. The government and its bureaucracy may be unstable, inefficient, ineffective (except in the area of securing benefits for its own members), and corrupt. There may be internal divisions and conflict (such as the long-standing tribal antagonisms in some African nations) that inhibit or preclude significant economic development.

In other words, the structure of some societies may need to be changed before the process of modernization, the economic growth and its attendant social and cultural changes, can occur. This is the point of Marx's work, which emphasizes the continuity as well as the discontinuity between various historical epochs. In the Marxist perspective, modernization requires: "(a) the existence of private property in land and (b) the emerging commercialization of land dependent upon (c) the existence of an individually oriented urban 'burgher' culture."[43] Modernization here means the transition to a capitalist society, however, and we would not posit that as a necessary step for contemporary societies. The point is that the range of alternative directions for change is limited by the existing structural conditions, of both the national and the international varieties. Some kinds of structural conditions are conducive to economic growth, while other kinds inhibit that growth. Some kinds of structural conditions facilitate economic growth but leave the internal distribution of wealth inequitable, while other structural conditions allow economic growth in the context of a more equitable internal distribution of wealth.

When the structure is one that inhibits economic growth, the flaws in the institutional arrangements are likely to be interrelated and, therefore, self-sustaining. Moreover, they are likely to be supported by social-psychological factors. Values and attitudes support the institutions, and vice versa.

Among the social-psychological factors important for modernization, a commitment, or at least a willingness, of the people to modernize is crucial. As noted above, not everyone considers modernization desirable. There are some who press for "de-modernization," or at least a form of development that is different from and independent of the capitalist world economy.[44] Political leaders, therefore, may find that a considerable amount of time and energy is required to gain the commitment or willingness of the populace to modernize. An example of this occurred in Indonesia, where the government allotted "immense resources to creating and maintaining particular attitudes and states of mind" in the post-1958 period.[45] In particular, the government invested heavily in "symbolic activity"—various ceremonial and ritual activities as well as propaganda and indoctrination. The results of this effort were ambiguous. On the one hand, certain economic and administrative problems were resolved; nationalist ideas impelled people to accept undesirable work that needed to be done.

On the other hand, the overall administrative and economic effectiveness of the nation may have suffered. For an atmosphere was created in which "economic tasks are seen as of secondary importance, ideological truth and political enthusiasm being seen as the highest needs of the state."[46] The overall effects of using a nationalist ideology to secure commitment to modernization are problematic in other nations also. Nevertheless, the commitment is an imperative, and securing it may involve a nation in one of those many dilemmas of society in which a course must be pursued that makes the end toward which it seemingly leads more difficult to attain.

One reason why the commitment may be difficult to obtain is that people are called upon to disrupt old ways and, more important, old relationships. People and their families may have to break away from traditional kin relationships and kin responsibilities. (Although, as we shall see below, this is not an inherent demand of the modernization process.) Any change that threatens interpersonal relationships is likely to be resisted. For instance, in the utopian community of Tristan da Cunha, Peter Munch identified a number of values (equality, anarchy, and integrity of the individual) that were tied up with a traditional system of reciprocity in interpersonal relationships.[47] These values and the pattern of reciprocity, in turn, found expression in the traditional subsistence economy. After World War II, some South Africans set up a commercial fishing enterprise on the island. This meant that a cash economy existed along with the traditional subsistence economy, and that the island became more affluent. In order to take advantage of the new economic opportunity, the people had to enter into contract type relationships that contradicted the traditional system. As a result, many of the people rejected the ethos of industrialization, or accepted it only to the extent that traditional values and traditional modes of interaction could be retained.

People everywhere will resist committing themselves to change that disrupts relationships. A second reason why the commitment to modernization may be difficult to secure is that the people are normally called upon to make personal sacrifices in behalf of overall development and economic growth. Their commitment, in other words, is more likely to be in terms of securing for themselves the fruits of modernization rather than in terms of the long-range growth of the economy. In economic terms, the demand for services and consumer goods contradicts the demand for capital accumulation and growth.

A third reason that commitment is difficult to secure is that people may be called upon to work at tasks that for one reason or another involve psychic strain. Industrialization can require individuals to work at jobs that exact heavy psychic costs. Yet commitment to such jobs is important. In fact, labor commitment in general is important for a number of reasons, including the lesser degree of supervision required, the greater predictability of behavior, and the reliability of behavior in crisis situations.

Finally, the commitment may be difficult to secure because the leaders who are calling on their people for sacrifice do not themselves appear to make any sacrifices. When the modernizing elite gains the immediate benefits of economic growth, the rest of the people are less likely to be willing to forgo those benefits until some indeterminate future.

A variety of values and attitudes have been noted as important to attaining modernization, but for the most part they bear upon the problem of commitment. Acceptance of nationalist ideology, willingness to be mobile, approval of secular-rational norms—all ultimately are tied to the commitment to modernization and the kinds of behavior conducive to modernization. Different methods may be employed to secure the commitment, such as ideology, structural change (in addition to other factors, decentralization has been important in China), and symbolic activities. Without the commitment, modernization will probably prove to be abortive.

In addition to the many factors we have already discussed that make modernization problematic—the world capitalist system, internal resources, capital accumulation, commitment, and so on—there are two further issues that must be addressed. First, what is the appropriate model of modernization? I have said that modernization can and must follow diverse paths. But what paths? Social scientists themselves differ on what is necessary for modernization in the contemporary world. Some nations have tried to model their development partly on the West; the results have been counterproductive in many cases. This problem has been well summarized: "The pioneer nations were trebly fortunate. On the whole, their trends of population growth, urbanization, and mechanization helped and reinforced each other. For present day developers the opposite is the case. All the various elements—population, patterns of technology, urban expansion—contradict and impede the others."[48]

A good example of this problem is in education. which many developing nations have associated with the affluence of the West (along with industrialization). A Chinese observer, for instance, pointed out in 1989 that the nation must guarantee primary education to all school-age children in order to deal with its problem of 220 million illiterates: "From a long-term point of view, it is illiteracy and a low education level that will hinder China's modernization drive the most, and eventually exclude it from the world's club of developed countries. . . . Modernization can't be built up in a country where illiterate people make up one fifth of its population."[49] Undoubtedly, a literate population is an integral part of a modern society. But some developing nations have expanded their educational systems too rapidly, with the result that they have a double problem. On the one hand, they are forced to support an expensive system at a time when capital is desperately needed for economic expansion. On the other hand, the populace is achieving an education for which there is little use; the economic opportunities do not match the available educated population. Moreover, all these problems are compounded when the education is geared toward "aristocratic tastes and philosophic concerns," a situation that Irving Horowitz calls "mis-education": "This produces an anti-industrial bias; education too is not geared for industrial concepts of professional training, still harkening back to educating a conversationally stimulating, cultivating leisure class. This deepens the crisis of using 'manpower' with advanced degrees."[50]

The second question that must be addressed is the technical possibility of worldwide modernization. A fair number of observers have warned us that the resources of the earth are insufficient to bring the world's population up to the standard of living enjoyed by much of the West, and, in fact, that even the West's standard will decline in time.[51] At the dawn of the 1990s, the world's population has risen to more than 5 billion.[52] Tropical forests are being cut down at the rate of 26 million acres per year (an area nearly the size of Pennsylvania). Fossil fuels, a major source of environment pollution, are being burned at a 40 percent higher rate than they were in the early 1970s. Natural resources are becoming increasingly scarce, such that no nation, including the United States, has all the natural resources needed to sustain its present level of life.

The outlook is not as gloomy as the above might suggest. A computer simulation suggests that the earth can support about 6 billion people indefinitely at a comfortable European standard of living.[53] But we are rapidly approaching the 6 billion number and a "comfortable European standard" means some decline for a few nations. Furthermore, unanticipated technological developments have nullified dire predictions in the past. Such developments might have particular value for the developing nations. Thus, the poor nations are mainly in the tropics and subtropics, which means that they could benefit greatly from advances in solar energy. This is not to minimize the seriousness of the earth's environmental problems; rather, it is to try to keep a reasonable perspective on both the problems and the possibilities.

In sum, while we can identify some of the conditions that are necessary for modernization, we cannot overstress the enormous problems facing the developing nations. Nor can we overstress the significant role of the developed nations. The future of peace may well hinge upon our understanding of this critical area and upon our willingness to assume our own share of responsibility for the modernization of nations.

The nature of that responsibility is not entirely clear; certainly, it cannot sink into the imperialism of past ages. The future will be perilous and violent if the developed nations have an attitude toward the developing nations that says: "You can modernize if only you want to. If you're willing to work for it, you can get it. After all, we did."

Consequences of Modernization

When we deal with the "consequences" of modernization, we are referring to those changes that have commonly been found to occur along with modernization. By definition, modernization involves change in numerous areas. The changes we shall discuss are typical. This does not mean that they are necessary or determined. Future modernization may well take paths that do not involve the kinds of changes described in the following paragraphs. In fact, those familiar with China will recognize that that nation is pursuing a path of modernization that diverges from some of those discussed below. I shall give later some additional concrete examples of diverse paths.

Keeping in mind, then, that these changes are typical, though not always necessary, we shall outline two broad types of change, structural and social psychological. Structural change involves five areas: demography, the stratification system, the polity, education, and the family. Social-psychological changes include two types: changes in values and attitudes and changes that bear upon the well-being of individuals.

• *Structural Consequences*

Demographic changes that typically have occurred along with modernization include population growth (intensified by a lowered death rate) and a shift from rural to urban areas. In the traditional society, 70 percent or more of the people are involved in agriculture, but a modern society is an urban society. The "mortality revolution" engendered by industrialization has been described by Calvin Goldscheider.[54] Preindustrial mortality rates, he notes, were high, though they fluctuated considerably and varied over space and time. Between the thirteenth and seventeenth centuries, the life expectancy in Europe varied from 20 to 40 years. With the Industrial Revolution, mortality patterns shifted significantly. In developing European countries, life expectancy increased from 45 in 1880 to 51 by 1900 to over 60 by 1930. Not only did the mortality level decline, but the large fluctuations were virtually eliminated because the crises that brought many deaths (crop failures and epidemics) were brought under much greater control. Thus, the typical pattern during modernization has been a growth of population.

Numerous changes occur in the stratification during modernization. Melvin Tumin has described nine general changes in stratification as a society moves toward industrialization:

1. The division of labor becomes more complex, with increasing numbers of specialists.
2. Status tends to be based on achievement instead of ascription (although we should stress the "tends" and keep in mind the points made by Frank in his critique of modernization theories).
3. An adequate means of measuring performance of those engaged in production becomes a central concern.
4. Work shifts from an intrinsically gratifying activity to one that is instrumental, a means to reward rather than the reward itself.
5. The rewards available for distribution increase.
6. Rewards are distributed on a somewhat more equal basis.
7. Some shifts occur in the life chances of those in various social strata.
8. Some shifts occur in the distribution of social prestige, though the advantage of the modern society over the traditional is problematic in this area.
9. Similar shifts and similar problems are to be found in the distribution of power.[55]

As this implies, the middle and upper classes expand during modernization. This expansion is a function of the changing occupational structure, and it means that there is a high rate of mobility. Furthermore, it means that the process tends to become self-sustaining, for the middle class has been typically more oriented to change than the lower class, at least to the type of change involved in modernization. For instance, in the "White Revolution" in Iran, as we noted earlier (Chapter 10), the middle class led the way in pressuring for the changes. The members of the new and growing middle class (professionals and bureaucratic workers) organized and led the two opposition movements—the Communist Tudah party and the National Front—that pressured the government to change the traditional society. The two movements were effectively put down in the mid-1950s. but the work of middle-class opponents continued to press the government.

Similarly, Robert Williamson's studies of Latin Americans affirms the orientation of the middle class toward change.[56] For example, a sample of 229 residents of Bogotá, Colombia, revealed a number of significant differences between middle- and lower-class respondents. When asked about the most important problems to be solved in the nation, a greater proportion of the middle class identified "more and better schools." When asked about the most effective kind of leadership for solving the problems, the middle class was more likely to say a governor, industrialist, or scientist, while the lower class was more likely to choose a religious authority. The middle-class respondents were more certain of their prospects for upward mobility (an important attitude for motivation). Finally, the middle class was more likely to reject traditional ways of life such as orientation toward the family, deference toward authority, an anti-planning attitude, and pessimism about one's chances for mobility.

The growing middle class means not only that the process tends to become self-sustaining, but also that modernization involves a reversal of the usual trend in traditional societies, which is toward increasing inequality. As we go from hunting and gathering to horticultural to agrarian societies, we find ever increasing inequality; the modern society represents the historical reversal of that trend.[57]

Along with these changes in stratification, there is also a tendency for the status of females to rise, for adolescents to gain new positions of status, and for the aged to lose high status. These changes do not always occur in the short run and may even be resisted in the long run by some societies. Consider, for example, the status of women. In some cases, women have not made gains even when they had relatively high status prior to modernization. Thai women traditionally participated actively in family and economic life, but they have not had the same opportunities as men in modern occupations.[58] Those who become civil servants tend to have lower positions and salaries than men. In some areas of India, one of the unexpected consequences of the Green Revolution was a decrease in female labor participation.[59] And women continue to have a subservient role in most Muslim nations: "It appears that neither national prosperity nor independence from foreign political and economic control is sufficient to guarantee female access to emergent opportunities."[60]

The problem of the aged is compounded in the developing nations by the large numbers of elderly people. While some societies, notably China, have tried to retain a reasonably high status for the aged,[61] the sheer numbers will make such efforts extremely difficult. When the West developed, the aged formed a small proportion of the population. Projections are that by 2025 about 11 percent of the population in developing regions will be in the 60-plus age group.[62] That means that by 2025 about 57 percent of all the world's elderly will live in Asia! So many elderly people will be a burden to those trying to forge ahead with economic development.

Modernization brings changes in the polity also. Local interests and loyalties give way to some extent to nationalism. The economy itself demands this shift insofar as it requires an extensive market and modern methods of communication and transportation. Local isolation and purely parochial interests contravene large-scale economic development.

There is also a tendency toward a greater democratization of the political process; political power tends to be more widely distributed (though by no means equalized) among various segments of the modernizing or modern nation. There are, however, variations in the extent to which democratization occurs, and there may also be variations as we move from one level to another in a particular society. This emphasizes a point made in the first chapter—we must be careful to distinguish among the various levels of change and to keep in mind that changes at one level do not necessarily mean changes at other levels.

The state also greatly expands its functions. The enormous increase in size and complexity of government that we have previously noted is associated with proliferation of governmental functions. Some indication of this change may be seen in the data on the number of federal employees. In the United States (similar figures could be shown for other nations), there were nearly 625 times as many federal employees in 1985 as in 1816 (from 4,837 to 3,021,000), while the population was only 27.6 times greater (from 8,659,000 to 239,283,000).[63] In other words, there was one federal employee for every 1,790 Americans in 1816 and one for every 79 Americans in 1985.

Other typical changes in the polity include: urban areas become the focal point of national politics; there is a tendency towards overurbanization, with various problems of alienation and unemployment; and interaction between groups tends to be marked as much by conflict as by consensus. Modernization is a reconstruction of the nation, and people must find new meanings, new symbols, new ways to adapt to the emerging new society.

In other words, just as we must not minimize the extraordinary difficulty of modernizing for contemporary nations, neither must we slight the human agony and social disruption that have been and seemingly will be a part of modernization. Internal political violence (as mentioned in Chapter 9), repressive reactions on the part of governments, and mass movements of various kinds are some of the political problems that have accompanied modernization.[64] Whether developing nations of the present can avoid these remains to be seen.

The fourth area in which significant change occurs in modernization is education. Education changes both quantitatively and qualitatively. Quantitatively, there is often considerable growth of educational organizations and enrollment in schools. One of the initial steps in nations committed to modernization is the establishment of universal primary education. Efforts are made to rapidly expand secondary and university education. Sometimes this expansion is linked with efforts by local areas to enhance their own status by having their own schools.

Qualitatively, education changes because the complex division of labor of the modernizing society requires a means of job preparation that is more efficient and more effective than apprenticeships. Education is geared toward preparing individuals to function in a new type of social structure. Thus, the curriculum is modernized, including a significant number of technical subjects, and the emphasis is on the secular rather than the sacred. Students gain the literacy, learn the skills, and acquire the values needed to function in a modern society.

It appears that the educational system must expand at an appropriate rate; too slow or too rapid an expansion can impede rather than facilitate modernization. According to Alexander Peaslee, economic growth cannot begin until at least 6 percent of the population is enrolled in primary school, and only after about 8 to 10 percent is enrolled in primary school will secondary enrollment correlate with economic growth.[65] On that basis, Peaslee suggests that an ideal model for a developing nation would be Japan, which focused on primary education for about ten years, then spent a number of years expanding secondary enrollment.

The Japanese case is a good example of how education can facilitate economic growth when the former is expanded appropriately. In fact, Ito Ryoji argues that the educational system set up in 1872 has been the primary catalyst in Japanese economic growth.[66] The Japanese had to expand their educational system more rapidly than the European countries because their industrialization was also rapid. The development of heavy industry in Japan was accompanied by an expanding secondary and vocational education system. During the brief time when light industry was established, primary education was the focal point of interest.

Qualitative changes were also made in Japanese education. Initially, the "three R's" were emphasized. Early in the twentieth century, the period of compulsory education was extended to six years and the curriculum was expanded to include history, geography, and science. During the twentieth century, increasing time has been given to science and mathematics in the curriculum. Throughout, the Japanese have spent proportionately more on education than some Western countries, and this has paid off in the higher rate of economic growth experienced by Japan.

Two points are important here. First, in spite of Peaslee's argument, no nation's educational experience is an ideal for all other nations. Japan did not follow the model of the European countries that had industrialized earlier. The point is that the educational system must expand in accord with the needs of the changing economy, which normally means an emphasis on primary education in the early stages of modernization.

Second, the ideal expansion rate is unlikely to occur in any case. According to world system theory, education expands primarily to meet the needs of the elite (to maintain the class system of the nation). Using Thailand as a test case, Anderson and London found that both processes are at work.[67] That is, the distribution of Thai educational resources facilitates modernization to some extent, but also serves the interests of the elite. It is probable that the Thai case is typical.

The family is the fifth area of change. As we noted in Chapter 1, a variety of family forms seems to be compatible with modernization, so that there has not been any universal breakdown of traditional kinship relations. But there are a number of changes occurring in families throughout the world as nations attempt to develop.

Modernization affects family roles, structure, and functions.[68] Emphasis tends to shift toward the nuclear family rather than the extended kin network. Particularly among the poor, however, the extended kin network may continue to be important as individuals pool resources and help each other in their efforts to improve their economic status. Among those who leave the rural areas for opportunities in the cities, maintaining kinship ties also helps to continue various social and cultural traditions.

Within families, there is some tendency for greater equality between men and women though, as noted earlier, this has been minimal in Muslim countries. Family size tends to decline. For example, in East Asia the average number of persons per household dropped from 5.1 in 1965 to 4.3 in 1980, and projections are that the number will be 3.3 in 2000.[69] Smaller family size does not happen immediately or even universally. Traditionally, the rural poor have depended on large families for survival. Furthermore, the health benefits of modernization (improved health care, better nutrition, and reduction of some diseases) may allow some people to have children who were formerly faced with childlessness.[70]

A family change that seems to be universal is a considerable transfer of functions to other social units. In primitive or traditional settings, economic, educational, religious, and emotional needs all tend to be provided in the family. With modernization, much of the responsibility for need fulfillment is transferred to other social units, such as government, schools, and business.

• *Social-Psychological Consequences*

Changes that occur in the area of values, attitudes, and personality are fairly well summed up in the concept of the "modern man." The "modern man," according to Lerner, is one whose personality has been transformed to include "an increment of self-things seeking . . . and 'need-achievement' . . . and an increment of self-others seeking."[71] The latter is what Lerner termed *empathy* in an earlier work. Empathy is "the capacity to see oneself in the other fellow's situation" and is, "an indispensable skill for people moving out of traditional settings."[72] It is the ability to identify with the new and to cope with new demands. Such an ability enables the individual to implement commitment to modernization. This ability to cope with the new is also reflected in Inkeles's portrait of the modern man, which we discussed in Chapter 5.

Obviously, a modern individual is one who is capable of functioning effectively in a nation that is experiencing economic growth, of participating in political development and political decisions, and of ordering behavior and decisions by secular-rational norms. Nevertheless, Inkeles's portrait of the modern individual is general enough that it does not imply uniform human beings. For the most part, the characteristics described by Inkeles would apply to the modern person in China, in Japan, in Nigeria, in Argentina, and elsewhere. Obviously, there are significant differences in both the people and the course of development in these nations. For instance, a most important facet of the personality of the modern person is a commitment to change, to a future that is different from the past and present. The particular future to which one is committed can vary considerably while still requiring the same basic elements of personality.

We pointed out in Chapter 1 that Lerner found that modern individuals were happier. However, we should also take note of a number of studies that identify some deleterious consequences for individual well-being. Various researchers have found that modernization involves higher rates of physical and mental illness, increased anxiety, higher rates of crime and violence, and increased consumption (to excess) of alcohol.

There are both gains and losses in the area of health. As noted above, better health care and a decreased incidence of some kinds of diseases increase the chances for healthy child-bearing. At the same time, a modern civilization is accompanied by its own particular health problems. If modernization brings about the conquest of some infectious diseases, it also leaves people to cope with chronic diseases and with stress-related health problems such as colitis, ulcers, and heart disease. In a modernizing society there may be new social and physical environments created that are conducive to certain kinds of illness. Crowding and lack of proper sanitation facilitated the spread of tuberculosis in the early industrial era. In more recent times, it has been found that there are higher rates of diabetes in the urbanized areas of Africa and Asia, due in part to increased sugar consumption and lower expenditure of energy.[73] Another important change is the breakdown of traditional interpersonal ties and resulting isolation. We have already noted that in some societies there is a tendency for people to maintain their relationships even when they migrate to the cities. Where the individual becomes isolated or marginal, however, his or her health may be jeopardized.[74]

In similar fashion, rates of mental illness may increase in a modernizing society. The higher rates are particularly likely among those who have broken traditional relationships through migration.[75] We should note here that one study found that rates varied among Turkish respondents depending upon the type of illness involved. Children from a traditional group had higher rates of organic disorders and mental retardation, while children from a transitional group had higher rates of psychoses and children from a modern group had higher rates of neuroses.[76] Studies that have not taken into account type of illness may be misleading.

Anxiety has also been associated with modernization and industrialization. Smelser identified anxiety as one of the elements of disturbance in the industrial revolution of England. Various reasons have been given for the anxiety, including marital difficulty from changing roles, conflict between traditional and modern values, the failure to succeed in accord with aspirations, and the perceived threat of the mechanization or automation of work.[77]

A fourth deleterious consequence is an increase in the rates of crime and violence.[78] The level of crime, particularly of violent crime such as homicide, may fall, however, as the modernizing society reaches greater levels of equality among its people.[79] The increased levels of crime and violence that accompany earlier stages of modernization reflect such things as the failure to succeed in accord with aspirations and the disruption of interpersonal relationships.

Finally, excessive alcohol consumption has characterized some people caught up in the process of modernization. In Africa, some migrants to urban areas have not been able to succeed. Alcoholism is one method they may use to attempt to cope with their poverty.[80]

How do the above consequences square with our earlier argument that there is no inherent trauma in change? We have already suggested a part of the answer in reviewing the evidence. It is not modernization per se that leads to the debilitating consequences, but certain other factors that may accompany modernization (but that are not, we must emphasize, intrinsic to modernization). Typically, modernization has occurred by exacting a penalty from the many for the benefit of a few. Certain groups will suffer the deleterious consequences disproportionately. The elites will prosper; the fate of the rest of the populace is more problematic. Those who are deprived are more likely to experience some of the same undesired consequences as the deprived in the developed nations—higher rates of physical and mental illness, anxiety, crime and violence, and alcohol abuse.

On the other hand, those who benefit economically from the modernization and, perhaps as importantly, who are able to make the transition to the new social order without a sense of being wrenched out of their values and traditions are likely to become modern without any of the deleterious health consequences. Thus, in a study comparing 269 urban migrants in Senegal, West Africa, with 300 rural nonmigrants, researchers found no differences in measures of mental health.[81] The two factors that seemed to be important in the health of the migrants were having the skills necessary to succeed in the new environment and maintaining cultural continuity. The migrants maintained a sense of continuity with their values and traditions by banding together in clubs in the city and by maintaining traditions surrounding important events like marriage.

The potential benefits of modernization for individual and societal well-being are great. Some of the more astute leaders in Third World nations are striving to gain those benefits for their people, and to gain them for the bulk of their people rather than allowing the majority to pay the price so that the minority can reap the gains.

The Varied Paths of Modernization

I have argued against the notion of convergence, the idea that all societies that modernize become alike. There are, of course, some similarities. Modernization is not possible without the kinds of structural and social-psychological changes we have noted. For instance, a study of Korean automobile factory workers compared them with automobile workers in four Western-oriented countries.[82] The researchers found that the Korean workers, like those in the other countries, adapted quickly to life as industrial workers, were not hampered in their adaptation by their rural and Confucian background, and developed a working-class mentality in spite of their socialization to support hierarchical relationships. But this does not mean that those in modernizing societies are all becoming alike, only that there are some necessary similarities.

Those who argue for convergence tend to assume a dichotomy of tradition/modernism. In their view, tradition has been obliterated or at least disrupted, and necessarily so, by the process of modernization. But there are a number of flaws in the arguments of those who assert a dichotomy.[83] First, they have attributed a static quality to traditional societies. But, as we have seen, all societies change, all have an inner dynamic. Rates vary, but no society is immutable. Second, they have attributed an unwarranted amount of homogeneity to traditional societies. On the contrary, traditional societies have a range of norms and values. Finally, tradition and modernity are neither "exclusive nor are they inevitably incompatible and perpetually in conflict. They can coexist and mutually adapt to each other."[84] As we shall see in the following examples, the relationships among traditionalism, modernization, and economic development take a variety of forms.

First, traditional ways change apart from modernization. In a study of traditional values in Guatemala, Micklin found that traditionalism was changing faster than modernization was occurring.[85] The changes in the former could not be explained by the latter. In particular, Micklin measured a number of attitudes toward traditional values, and found that his respondents rejected a substantial number of them even though there had not been much change in urbanization, industrialization, or education over a fifty-year period. The values in question related to friendship; importance of instilling respect in, versus a good education for, children; preference for village life; distrust toward people in general; respect for the aged; passivity and acceptance of one's lot in life; and kinship obligations. There was a slight relationship between age and traditionalism, with older people being slightly more traditional. There was a slight inverse relationship between education and traditionalism, and a stronger inverse relationship between first occupation and traditionalism and present occupation and traditionalism. In sum, the younger, better educated respondents with higher-status occupations were less traditional than others. Again, for our purposes, the important point is that these attitudinal changes had occurred independently of any substantial progress in modernization.

On the other hand, if tradition can change without modernization, the latter can occur without substantial change in traditions. Certainly, industrialization can take place without loss of traditional ways, as shown by the experience of Ciudad Industrial, a city built in

Mexico during the 1950s.[86] A study of 97 workers in the factories and 185 farmers from the surrounding rural area showed few differences in attitudes and values (workers who lived in nearby towns and villages were chosen in order to separate out the effects of industrialization from those of urbanization). The farmers were divided into two groups of young (mean age of 35) and old (mean age of over 50) because the workers had a mean age of 32. The three groups differed significantly in educational attainment, with the workers having an average of 3.9 years, the young farmers having 1.8 years, and the old farmers having 0.7 years of schooling on the average. There were also significant differences in income, with the lowest-paid of the workers having an annual income at least double that of the farmers.

What were the differences and similarities between the groups? The workers had greater educational aspirations for their children than did the farmers. Both workers and farmers were basically conservative in their views of sex roles and family life. The workers were somewhat more modern, but not as modern as one would expect if industrialization had modernized them in the sense of altering tradition. For instance, 94 percent of all respondents agreed that a wife should obey her husband in all matters. The respondents evidenced some attitudes that are normally thought of as modern, but both farmers and workers had those attitudes. Farmers and workers both affirmed the importance and power of education and special training. Both groups agreed that it is important to plan for the future. Even the old farmers were basically optimistic and future-oriented.

As John Poggie summarizes these findings:

> *The experience of working in the factories and having more money for purchase of luxury goods has an impact on the people, but it has not led to a striking cleavage between "moderns" and "traditionals." It would seem that the experience of working in the factories does not automatically lead people to become sharply different from the agricultural peasants, if both remain in their traditional villages.*[87]

The people in and around Ciudad Industrial seemed to be changing together. They retained some traditional ways (or, more accurately, some traditional ways were changing more rapidly than others), but industrial work experience did not make a difference in this process.

It is also possible for pockets of traditionalism to be maintained in the face of change in the larger society. Neyl, a peasant village near Cologne, Germany, remained traditional for seventy years while the larger society moved from the preindustrial into an industrial age.[88]

There has been a close relationship between the village and the city from at least the thirteenth century, for the villagers traditionally sold their produce and fish in the city market.

Cologne was transformed by industrialization. How did this affect the village? The village was helped economically, because the expanding city provided an ever growing market. Furthermore, the peasants accepted technical innovations that made agricultural production more efficient and profitable. Nevertheless, they did not find the urban way of life appealing and therefore refused to be assimilated by the city. Neyl was affected by Cologne's industrialization and growth, however. The village was annexed by the city and linked to it by a trolley line. The population of the village increased over fourfold from 1871 to 1925. Some farmland was turned over to other uses, such as a sewage plant, a race track, and a military training field. Those who were displaced by the reduced amount of farmland available were forced to take jobs in factories. This enabled the villagers to maintain their peasant ways! The wages earned in the city factories were sufficient so that they could continue their peasant way of life, including clothes, homes, food habits, and relationships. The traditional attachment to the land was maintained by vegetable gardens, which also enabled them to continue the traditional preference for home-produced food. Education was not particularly valued. Traditional practices of religion and medicine (much to the chagrin of the local doctor) were followed. Traditional forms of recreation, mainly drinking, cards, and dancing in village taverns, were pursued. Far from being disrupted by the industrial civilization, the people of Neyl used it as an economic base to maintain their peasant traditions.

A similar case of modernization actually facilitating the maintenance of traditional patterns is provided by C. S. Whitaker in his study of Northern Nigeria.[89] We will look at one of his many examples. In examining the social composition of the parliament from 1956 to 1961, he learned the social background of those elected from the areas of traditional, autocratic rulers. He found that 75 percent of the members belonged to the traditional ruling class (in terms of the status of their fathers). In the subsequent period of 1961-1966, all members were elected by direct procedures and on the basis of adult male suffrage (only a minority had been elected on these bases in the previous period). Nevertheless, a spot check of about half of the new members from emirate constituencies indicated that the proportion of those from the traditional ruling class may have increased.

In other words, the hereditary ruling class maintained its elite position into the 1960s. In part, this reflected the fact that ascriptive positions were sustained by achievement, as Whitaker put it. For members of the traditional ruling class were also elites in terms of education. Although less than 2 percent of the population was literate in the 1956-1961 period, the parliamentarians had an average of 7.5 years of formal, Western-type education. Thus, the modern educational system reinforced the power of the traditional ruling class.

Thus, change in tradition and the process of modernization can occur independently, and the latter may even strengthen or help to sustain aspects of the former. This is not to deny the typical kinds of changes that have been involved in modernization; rather, it is to stress the divergent paths that modernization may take. Among the important reasons for the divergent paths are the differing traditional systems in which the process begins, the diverse bases upon which modernization proceeds, and the varying ideologies that guide the process.

In sum, the consequences of modernization are diverse. Although modernization took a particular form in the West, it does not follow that other societies will take that course. Nor does modernization obliterate the traditional. Elements of tradition and pockets of traditional culture may be maintained within the modernizing society. In some cases, traditional elements may provide a firm base upon which to modernize.

Many of the preceding points about the relationships between tradition and modernization may be illustrated by a more detailed consideration of a single society—India. More particularly, we will look at one city in that society. Milton Singer has provided us with a comprehensive portrait of the consequences of modernization in the city of Madras.[90] In essence, Singer argues that there is an ongoing process of reciprocal adaptation between traditional and modernizing tendencies. There is no dichotomy between the two, for tradition affects the modern as well as vice versa. Moreover, the modern is not to be equated with that which comes to India from the outside, for there have been important innovations that have arisen within the traditional culture (in accord with the argument that change is normal).

Singer points out that the problems associated with the question of whether traditional religion in India hinders or facilitates social change are rooted in a common approach to the study of India. Namely, many of the scholars, who have argued that Indian religion has impeded change base their analyses on their interpretation of Hindu scriptures. Westerners may fail to grasp the significance of the meaning of those scriptures and of the way in which they affect the thinking and behavior of Indians. Furthermore, Western scholars have often failed to recognize the individualism of Indian religion.

Two aspects of traditional Hindu religion that have been said (by Max Weber, among others) particularly to hinder social change are caste ritualism and the beliefs in fate, rebirth, duty, and salvation through escape from the present world. Weber claimed that within such a system a rational economy is impossible. Singer says that when he related Weber's theory to orthodox Hindus, they replied that if Weber were correct, "'how could we have lived and done so many things—built temples, ships, and empires, fought wars and organized agriculture, crafts, and trade?' There must be some misunderstanding, they feel, of the relations of religious belief and ritual to daily life."[91]

If, then, traditional beliefs are not incongruous with modernization, what happens when the processes of modernization intersect with the Hindu tradition? We may get some ideas from the experiences of industrial leaders in Madras. One issue that interested Singer was the fate of the joint family. He found that the joint family did not break down and become a pattern of nuclear families. Rather, the urban, industrial members of a family continued their ties and obligations to those of the family who remained in the village or who moved elsewhere. Within the urban area, a modification of the joint-family type was emerging. Singer concludes that the joint family is not incompatible with urban, industrial life. In fact, he argues, there are some advantages to the joint family, for it can provide capital for the education of its members and for entrepreneurial activities.

An interesting fact about the industrial leaders is that nearly half of them were Brahmans (a reading of the orthodox literature would lead one to believe that the daily ritual requirements for Brahmans would preclude an industrial career). This again emphasizes the lack of inherent incompatibility between the Hindu tradition and a modern industrial career. Not only did the industrial leaders not experience "soul-shattering conflicts" between their religious beliefs and the demands of their careers, but they adapted the two spheres to each other in a fashion similar to that used by the Puritan capitalists described by Weber. Basically, the leaders have learned to compartmentalize the industrial and the domestic spheres. The former is considered the leader's modern culture, although it contains some traditional elements; and the latter is considered the traditional culture, although it contains modern elements.

This makes for some interesting patterns, though they are not as unusual as they might at first appear. For example, at work a leader might participate in intercaste teams, eat in an intercaste setting, and use common washing and medical facilities. The traditional prohibitions against intercaste contact, with the consequent ritual pollution for those who break the prohibitions, are not operative in the work situation. The same person who interacts with other castes at work, however, will not do so at home. The interaction patterns of the workplace are shed, along with the Western clothing, when the individual arrives home. This is not as unusual as some might think—compare the white American worker who works with blacks, eats with them and uses the same rest rooms, but who staunchly resists the movement of blacks into the same neighborhood and social life generally. To some extent, compartmentalization is a familiar mechanism to all people.

For the orthodox Hindu, compartmentalization means that the work sphere is "ritually neutralized." The laws of intercaste contact and pollution simply do not apply there. In addition, some of the leaders maintain their religious commitment through "vicarious ritualization." We pointed out above that the traditional time demands for the Brahmans would seem to preclude an industrial career. "Vicarious ritualization" means that a shorter rite or ceremony is substituted for the longer, traditional form, or even that a proxy takes the place of the industrialist and performs the ritual. For example, in place of four to six hours a day for rituals, the Hindus take from one-quarter to one-half of an hour. Some rise early to perform the rituals; others pray while they shave and wash; and still others say they will perform their ritual obligations when they are older.

Thus, various adaptations are made by the industrial leaders so that they can fulfill the requirements of industry and still continue to be good Hindus. Singer summarizes the adaptations to industry and urban life in seven points:

1. The leaders are modernizing by accepting and developing the innovations of urban, industrial life.
2. The leaders are also adapting and restructuring traditional ways in order to maintain and strengthen what they regard as the core of their traditions.
3. Ritual observances have been altered the most and joint-family organization the least.
4. The restructuring has occurred the most in the industrial sphere; in the domestic sphere, traditional ways are maintained to a great extent.
5. The adaptations do *not* mean that Madras is becoming like a Western city.
6. The general trend is one of "experimentation with and a gradual incorporation of innovative changes . . . into an indigenous culture that is already both 'traditional' and 'modern.'"
7. The indigenous culture is restructured as innovations are accepted. For example, ritual becomes more vicarious and symbolic, and traditional ritual is replaced to some extent by devotional and cultural performances.[92]

To sum up his study, Singer argues that the traditions of India are actually a system of built-in mechanisms for accepting and adapting to change. Through the traditional beliefs and practices, new ways are assimilated, given meaning, and made legitimate. Tradition helps to shape the innovations and, in turn, is influenced by those innovations. Modern urban and industrial life does not obliterate tradition. On the contrary, the traditional and the modern continue to flourish and to exert reciprocal influences on each other.

Modernization and Urbanization

We are living in an increasingly urban world. From 1750 to 1960 the population of the world increased by about 300 percent, from 728 million to almost 3 billion. The number of people living in towns of 5,000 or more increased about 1,400 percent, from 22 million to over 900 million. In 1800, one city had a population of 1 million or more—London. More than a hundred cities now have that many residents, and the growth of the largest cities has been faster than the overall rate of urbanization. Between 1950 and 1980, Mexico City's population went from 3 to 15 million. By the mid-1980s, about 42 percent of the world's population lived in urban areas. The proportion of people living in urban areas ranged from 72 percent in developed countries to 26 percent in Asia.[93]

Urbanization does not necessarily mean modernization, but the latter has been marked by urbanization wherever it has occurred. There are, of course, instances of economic development in local communities; factories have been located in essentially rural areas. In general, though, all modern societies are highly urbanized and modernizing societies are generally characterized by a process of urbanization.

Why does urbanization occur with modernization? And why has urbanization been so rapid in Third World countries in recent decades? There is considerable controversy over answers to these questions.[94] Modernization theorists have argued that urban expansion is an inherent part of the transition from a traditional, agrarian society to a modern, industrial society. Rural people are attracted to the cities by the economic opportunities. Furthermore, urban life helps develop the modern ideas and the skills necessary for an industrial society. As a result, there will be a positive relationship between urbanization and economic growth.

Urban bias theorists, on the other hand, assert that government policies favor urban areas. Various groups located in urban areas have political power, and they influence government to pass legislation concerning such things as investments, taxes, and pricing that will favor the urban dwellers. The resultant higher standard of living in the cities thereby attracts the poorer rural dwellers to the urban areas. But such a reason for migration to the urban areas may inhibit rather than enhance economic efficiency. The cities become glutted with people for whom there is no work. People migrate faster than the economy can absorb them, and they become economic liabilities rather than assets. Furthermore, governmental bias for urban areas may mean that aid to agriculture is neglected; there may be a tendency towards an unbalanced kind of growth. Thus, over-urbanization is a sign of economic ill health in a nation.

Finally, world system theorists argue along a number of lines. They have noted such things as foreign investment reducing the amount of land available to farmers and expanding the service sector too early in the process of development. According to Rodriguez and Feagin, many major cities have grown because they perform a specialized function in the world system as, for example, producers or financial markets.[95] In other words, Third World urbanization occurs because in some way it serves the interests of the core nations. At the same time, the periphery and semi-periphery maintain their subservient positions.

Examining data from sixty-one underdeveloped countries between 1960 and 1980, Bradshaw concluded that there is some validity to all three theories.[96] Urbanization did occur. Basically, the nations seemed to be in a process of transition from agrarian to service economies (a transition that inhibits rather than facilitates economic development); urban migrants were finding more jobs in low-paying service and informational areas than in industry. Government policy making did favor urban areas somewhat. All three theories are correct, at least in part:

> *In support of modernization theory, the level of relative urbanization in 1960 has a positive impact on rate of economic growth. In support of urban bias and dependency/world system arguments, change in relative urbanization has a deleterious impact on the rate of economic expansion. The urban population of Third World nations is expanding too quickly, given their level of economic development.*[97]

Thus, there is an optimum rate of urbanization for economic development. In China, which may be the only nation that has ever actively promoted a shift of urban dwellers out into the countryside, over-urbanization has occurred despite efforts to impede it. As an editor put it, with nearly a fourth of the one billion population living in urban areas, the problems are serious: "The over-concentration of population in the big cities puts a strain on transportation, housing, energy supplies, services, and commodities, and can cause problems in employment, education, and other areas as well. The 26 big cities in northern China are all having difficulties finding enough water for their factories and their residents."[98] The editor suggested that people will inevitably move into cities as modernization proceeds, but that they must begin to move mainly into smaller cities and townships.

In sum, urbanization seems invariably to accompany modernization in a nation. Urbanization can facilitate modernization through such things as centralized political control, the stimulation of literacy and education, the enhanced ease of coordination, and the breaking down of localism. But over-urbanization impedes economic growth. Any nation committed to modernization, therefore, must deal with the serious problems presented by—and take advantage of the opportunities offered by—the process of urbanization.

Modernization and Secularization

According to Max Weber, we live in an age that is "characterized by rationalization and intellectualization and, above all, by the 'disenchantment of the world.'"[99] The world is no longer a sacred phenomenon. Life is no longer an unfathomable mystery. The fate of humanity is no longer in the hands of some ethereal, superhuman being. Indeed, the religion that may at one time have abetted human development is no longer needed. Protestantism facilitated the rise of capitalism, but capitalism is now triumphant, resting upon "mechanical foundations," and no longer needs the support of religion.[100]

Many writers would agree with Weber that modernization is a process that slowly but surely pushes religion to the periphery of human existence. Like Dmitri in Dostoyevsky's *The Brothers Karamazov,* they see the acceptance of science as the loss of God. While modernization does involve secularization, it does not necessarily involve the decline of religion. The polarity between modernization and religion, like that between modernization and tradition, is a distortion of reality.

First, what do we mean by secularization? In essence, secularization involves two related trends: "the diminishing role of traditional religious agencies in daily routine and in the exercise of public authority," and "the diminishing significance of supernatural ('super-empirical') concerns as a basis for moral order and the corresponding intensification of a rational and empirical moral orientation."[101] In other words, secularization is a process in which people increasingly think and act in rational ways, so that laws and norms constructed by reason and governments rather than by religious authorities become the governing standards of life.

Was Weber correct in arguing that such secularization is not only an inevitable part of the modern world but a process that necessarily displaces religion? On both theoretical and empirical grounds, we find that religion can flourish even while a people are becoming increasingly modern (including increasingly rational in such areas of life as the economy). Theoretically, we could argue that religion will always be a part of people's lives because humans search for meaning, and religion gives a transcendent meaning to human existence. Religion can also specify and justify moral codes and provide people with support during various social and personal crises.

Empirically, religion has not disappeared nor even diminished as a result of modernization. In the United States, for example, religion is strong, and has been for many decades. Consider the following facts:[102]

- More than 90 percent of Americans say that they believe in God.
- Church membership changed little between the mid-1930s and mid-1980s, ranging from 67 to 76 percent in various years.
- Church attendance remained fairly stable at around 40 percent for most of the years between the mid-1930s and mid-1980s.
- In 1985, 87 percent of Americans said that they prayed, and the proportion who said they read the Bible daily increased by 50 percent over the number in 1942.
- Charitable contributions are higher in the United States than in any other country, and 45 to 50 percent of the contributions go to religious organizations.

Even some of the presumed evidence for religious decline may be seen as transformation rather than decline. That is, religion is taking some new forms in the modern world, including the "sacred ideology" of governments who lead people in ritual commitment to such things as democracy, equality, and justice.[103] Finally, throughout the world, there is evidence of renewed vitality in many traditional religions. Liberation theology among Roman Catholics in Latin America, Islamic fundamentalism, militant Judaism in Israel, and the Christian Right in the United States all exemplify the continuing influence of religion.

How, then, do religion and modernization affect each other? Modernization does not eliminate religion, but it may lead to some changes in religious practices and/or beliefs. We have already noted the extent to which the industrial leaders of Madras maintained their traditional religious faith while engaging in modern careers. Singer argued that the religious culture was democratized rather than secularized, for while there was a decline in ritual observance, there was a concomitant increase in devotional religion.[104]

Religion, on the other hand, even the same religion in different contexts, may have contrary effects on modernization. Some religious systems inhibit economic development. But others, as we saw in our discussion of ideology and change, facilitate that development. Religion is not inherently opposed to the rationality demanded by modernization. Terrance Carroll, a political scientist, has looked at the role of various religions in a modern state. [105] First, he notes that the minimum requirements for a modern state are "well-developed capabilities" in terms of communication, coercion, legitimation, planning, and policy implementation. The state must be able to communicate regularly with most of the citizenry and, at the same time, receive feedback from that citizenry. Coercive and legitimate power is necessary in order to ensure compliance with policies. Planning includes the ability to identify problems and to formulate policies to deal with those problems. And, finally, the modern state must be able to implement the policies it has formulated so that it is at least partly successful in achieving the goals it has set.

How does religion affect such capabilities in a modern state? For the most part, the effects are either positive or neutral. Catholicism has a very positive effect, being negative only in the area of coercion. (The Church will oppose what it regards as brutal measures by the state.) Buddhism and Islam also have a positive effect. Islam's effect is likely to be negative in the planning area, since there is still some resistance in Islamic countries to scientific education. Buddhism has a positive effect in its impact on legitimation of the state and has a neutral effect in the other areas. Finally, Hinduism's effect is neutral overall. It tends to have a positive impact on legitimation and a negative impact on implementation (the caste system can inhibit equal treatment of people in business and government), but it is neutral with regard to the other areas.

In sum, modernization and religion are not incompatible. There is likely to be secularization with modernization, but at most that means some changes in religion rather than the demise of religion. The modern person uses reason as a primary tool for comprehending and controlling his or her experience. This, rather than an assault on religion, is the core meaning of secularization.

Modernization and Bureaucratization

For many Americans who put a premium on getting things done, bureaucracy is virtually a four-letter word. It is thought to be the pinnacle of irrationality and inefficiency. It is conceived of as a barrier and a harassment to the "go-getter." These popular connotations reflect the extent to which a bureaucratic organization can diverge from what it is in theory—the most rational and efficient form of large-scale administration. It is rational and efficient because, in its ideal form, it involves carefully trained people who are expert in what they do and who function within a context of written rules and regulations that allow all clients to be treated fairly and equally.

Whether the popular or the theoretical image is more correct in actuality is important because the modern world is increasingly bureaucratic as well as urban and secular. Some observers have talked about the "end of bureaucracy" in the modern world, arguing that continued social development necessitates that bureaucratic organization be replaced by a different type. But evidence from sixty-two nations, including both the developing and the developed nations, shows that bureaucratic activity is still increasing throughout the world.[106]

Weber noted a number of reasons for the bureaucratization of the modern world.[107] One was the development of a money economy. Weber argued that if officials were paid in produce or commodities rather than money, the bureaucratic structure would gradually change. A second reason was the quantitative and qualitative increase of administrative tasks in the modern state. The technical requirements of administering a large, complex state, with all the social, political, and economic demands made upon it, are such as to demand a bureaucratic type of administration. Finally, bureaucratization has occurred because it is technically superior to any other form of administration (in terms of efficiency).

As far as the developing nations of the world are concerned, we can add a couple of reasons to this list. First, these nations are seeking to carve out a place for themselves in a world dominated by legal-rational societies; their only hope is to develop quickly a legal-rational form of state for themselves. Second, there are pressures arising from the populace in terms of demand for services and, equally important, demands for jobs on the part of the educated. In some cases, this has led to inefficiency as more civil servant jobs than are necessary have been created. It is a political dilemma, of course, since resistance to the pressures for employment and services would place the government in a precarious position.

Thus, in both modern and modernizing nations there has been a process of bureaucratization. The force with which modernization seems to demand bureaucratization is reflected in the bureaucratic nature of communist states where, theoretically, the state is withering away. When the Bolsheviks came to power in the Soviet Union, they promised a purge of the bureaucracy. Lenin even declared that "the whole inherited administrative apparatus would have to be destroyed and replaced by 'a new one, consisting of the armed workers.'" [108] As early as April, 1918, he recognized that the management of industry demanded a revision of his ideas. Socialism could not be achieved without administrative skills and the guidance of specialists in various fields.

Gradually, the Bolshevik leaders became an industrializing elite. Lenin led the way. In 1918, he said: "The possibility of building Socialism will be determined precisely by our success in combining the Soviet government and the Soviet organization of administration with the modern achievements of capitalism."[109]

The problems of industrialization generated considerable controversy among Russian leaders. As bureaucratization proceeded along with industrialization, theoreticians tried to account for that unanticipated outcome. Trotsky argued, for example, that the oppressive bureaucracy was due to the lack of worldwide proletarian revolution rather than to the immaturity of socialism in Russia. Socialism cannot be achieved in one country while capitalism flourishes in the other. Under such conditions, the bureaucracy will grow stronger. Nevertheless, Trotsky, like Lenin, was optimistic about the future—ultimately, he believed, the bureaucracy would vanish as socialism triumphed.

Since bureaucracy is an integral part of the modern world, we must ask about its effects. On the one hand, it is apparent that the popular image of bureaucracy as an impediment to change holds true in some cases. In both the developed and developing nations, and in both communist and capitalist countries, bureaucracies can thwart the intent of politicians and exploit and abuse the people that are supposedly served by the bureaucracies.[110] In the developing nations, the bureaucracy may impede effective political development by expanding too rapidly, thereby becoming too strong while other aspects of the polity are still weak. Finally, in some cases where there have been pressures to change the situation, the bureaucracy has responded by adding additional units that will supposedly bring about the change. In other words, efforts to change the public bureaucracy resulted in a larger bureaucratic structure and increased administrative costs rather than the changes that were sought.[111]

In spite of its potential for stifling change, however, bureaucracy has been important in modernization; in fact, at this point it would appear that bureaucratization is an indispensable element in modernization. The recognition of this paradoxical nature of bureaucracy led Mao to be somewhat ambivalent about the bureaucratization of China.[112] Mao grew up in the midst of the disintegration of the traditional bureaucracy, and he saw the corruption that pervaded the bureaucratic organization of the Kuomintang. Moreover, his own ideological commitment was antibureaucratic. Nevertheless, bureaucratization proceeded along with modernization following the 1949 establishment of the People's Republic; the Cultural Revolution of the late 1960s, however, seemed to represent an effort to stop and even reverse the tendency toward increasing bureaucratization. Perhaps Mao thought that through the Cultural Revolution he might be able to fulfill an old hope of tossing the "great evil" of bureaucracy into the cesspool. This is not to say that all organization must be cast off, of course. Economic development cannot proceed without organizations. Mao tried to offer an alternative to the Weberian bureaucracy. In simple terms, as Martin Whyte has put it, while the basic concern in the Weberian bureaucracy is for "internal efficiency through the maximum use of technical knowledge," the basic concern of the Maoist model is "to maximize the involvement and commitment of organizational participants, particularly the 'masses' at the bottom of organizations."[113] As Whyte has shown, this divergence in basic concern means that there are a number of differences (and some similarities) in the Western and Maoist conceptions. Mao stressed the priority of politics over technical competence, the participation of the masses rather than a hierarchy of authority, the equalization of rewards, comradeship rather than impersonality, and flexibility and change rather than the establishment of rules and procedures. In spite of this, one could argue from observing the organization of the Chinese economy and Chinese society in general that it is as bureaucratized as any nation in the world. We shall not enter into that argument, however. We will only note that Mao vigorously attempted to debureaucratize Chinese society while implementing economic development.

In other modernizing nations, bureaucratization has been accepted as a necessary part of development, and the problem is seen in terms of making the bureaucracy work as it ought rather than in terms of minimizing or halting its growth. The fact that bureaucracy can be an effective tool for modernizing is illustrated by Japan, whose development can be explained in terms of an exceptionally bureaucratic state.[114] Japan's dramatic economic growth was directed by the bureaucracy. Of course, the mere presence of a bureaucracy does not guarantee such growth. In some developing nations today, the bureaucracy is a political and patronage system. The kinship and friendship ties that presumably are discounted in bureaucratic operations play a dominant role, thereby impeding rather than aiding development.

In sum, bureaucracy seems to be an integral part of modernization. It can provide the legal context and social order necessary for modernization. It can implement various political decisions and government policies that aid economic growth. But it can only do these things to the extent that it approaches the ideal-typical form outlined by Weber. In no society, of course, does the bureaucracy function in the completely impersonal, rational, and efficient way set forth by Weber. The point is, however, that the more it approximates that ideal, the more it can facilitate the nation's modernization. Despite the limitations and problems of actual bureaucracies, no other form of large-scale organization appears to work any better.

Endnotes

1. For a brief description of the meaning of the hunger for bread and freedom, as well as the dilemmas involved in trying to secure both of them simultaneously, see William McCord, *The Springtime of Freedom* (New York: Oxford University Press, 1965), pp. 3-18.

2. Ibid., pp. 11, 20.

3. *Global Development Report*, Fall, 1987, pp. 62-63. Other figures in this paragraph are taken from the same report.

4. Ruth Leger Sivard, *World Military and Social Expenditures: 1986* (Washington, D.C.: World Priorities, 1986), pp. 19-23.

5. David E. Apter, *The Politics of Modernization* (Chicago: University of Chicago Press, 1965), pp. 43-44.

6. Gerhard E. Lenski, *Power and Privilege* (New York: McGraw-Hill, 1966), pp. 298-99.

7. Ibid.

8. Walt W. Rostow, *The Stages of Economic Growth* (New York: Cambridge University Press, 1960).

9. Ibid., p. 37.

10. See, for example, John K. Fairbank, Alexander Eckstein, and L. S. Yang, "Economic Change in Early Modern China: An Analytic Framework," *Economic Development and Cultural Change* 9 (1960): 1-26. The authors suggest five phases of industrialization that are similar to some extent to the scheme of Rostow: traditional equilibrium, the appearance of disequilibrating forces, gestation, breakthrough (take-off), and self-sustaining growth. This fits China, India, and most other Far Eastern economies with the exception of Japan. Modifications are necessary for England and other West European countries and for Japan. In England, for example, the framework for gestation

was provided by the traditional setting itself without the necessity of the "prolonged pre-industrial period of tension and gestation as in the Far Eastern case" (p. 2).

11. Daniel Lerner, "Modernization, Social Aspects," in *International Encyclopedia of the Social Sciences,* vol. 10 (New York: Free Press, 1968), p. 387.

12. Dean C. Tipps, "Modernization Theory and the Comparative Study of Societies: A Critical Perspective," *Comparative Studies in Society and History* 15 (1973): 199-226.

13. Wilbert E. Moore, *World Modernization: The Limits of Convergence* (New York: Elsevier, 1979), p. 1.

14. Immanuel Wallerstein, *The Capitalist World-Economy* (New York: Cambridge University Press, 1979), p. 5.

15. Immanuel Wallerstein, *The Modern World-System* (New York: Academic Press, 1974), p. 38.

16. Ibid., p. 349.

17. Wallerstein, *The Capitalist World-Economy,* p. 73. There is some mobility of nations, as indicated by the nature of the semi-periphery. However, particular countries can only develop at the expense of others that decline. There is no expansion of core states. An interesting aspect of mobility is the argument that individual modernity inhibits rather than facilitates a nation's development, for, among other things, the modern individual may emigrate to greener pastures. See Alejandro Portes, "Modernity and Development: A Critique," *Studies in Comparative International Development* 8 (Fall, 1973): 247-79; and Jacques Delacroix and Charles Ragin, "Modernizing Institutions, Mobilizations, and Third World Development: A Cross-National Study," *American Journal of Sociology* 84 (July, 1978): 123-50.

18. Wallerstein, *The Capitalist World-Economy,* p. 63.

19. Ibid., p. 23.

20. Ibid., p. 35.

21. Steven R. Steiber, "The World System and World Trade: An Empirical Exploration of Conceptual Conflicts," *The Sociological Quarterly* 20 (Winter, 1979): 25-26.

22. Daniel Chirot, *Social Change in the Twentieth Century* (New York: Harcourt Brace Jovanovich, 1977), pp. 232-33.

23. Ibid., p. 181.

24. Hans Singer, "The Distribution of Gains Between Borrowing and Investing Counties," in *Economic Development and Social Change: The Modernization of Village Communities,* ed. George Dalton (Garden City, N.Y.: Natural History Press, 1971), pp. 336-50.

25. Steiber, 'The World System and World Trade," pp. 34-35. See also Elisabeth L. Gidengil, "Centres and Peripheries: An Empirical Test of Galtung's Theory of Imperialism," *Journal of Peace Research* 15 (No. 1, 1978): 51-66.

26. Roger J. Nemeth and David A. Smith, "International Trade and World-System Structure: A Multiple Network Analysis," *Review* 8 (1985): 538.

27. See, e.g., Sarah Bartlett, "A Vicious Circle Keeps Latin America in Debt," *The New York Times,* January 15, 1989. Figures in this paragraph come from this article.

28. Harvey Marshall, Michael Schwartz, and James Ziliak, "Agricultural Specialization and Economic Growth," *Sociological Focus* 21 (1988).

29. United Nations Department of Economic and Social Affairs, *Multinational Corporations in World Development* (New York: Praeger, 1974), p. 3.

30. Volker Bornschier and Thanh-Huyen Ballmer-Cao, "Income Inequality: A Cross-National Study of the Relationships Between MNC-Penetration, Dimensions of the Power Structure and Income Distribution," *American Sociological Review* 44 (June, 1979): 487-506.

31. Bruce London and Thomas D. Robinson, "The Effect of International Dependence on Income Inequality and Political Violence," *American Sociological Review* 54 (1989): 305-308.

32. Volker Bornschier, Christopher Chase-Dunn, and Richard Rubinson, "Cross-National Evidence of the Effects of Foreign Investment and Aid on Economic Growth and Inequality: A Survey of Findings and a Reanalysis," *American Journal of Sociology* 84 (1978): 677; and Steve Chan, "Income Inequality Among LDCs: A Comparative Analysis of Alternative Perspectives," *International Studies Quarterly* 33 (1989): 45-65.

33. Kathryn May Robinson, *Stepchildren of Progress: The Politics of Development in an Indonesian Mining Town* (Albany, N.Y.: SUNY Press, 1986).

34. Walter Gillis Peacock, Greg A. Hoover, and Charles D. Killian, "Divergence and Convergence in International Development: A Decomposition Analysis of Inequality in the World System," *American Sociological Review* 53 (1988): 838-52.

35. Richard E. Barrett and Martin King Whyte, "Dependency Theory and Taiwan: Analysis of a Deviant Case," *American Journal of Sociology* 87 (1982): 1064-89.

36. York W. Bradshaw, "Reassessing Economic Dependency and Uneven Development: The Kenyan Experience," *American Sociological Review* 53 (1988): 693-708.

37. Tamas Szentes, "International Trade and the Developing Countries: Will the New International Economic Order Be Really New?" *Labour and Society* 1 (July-Oct., 1976): 39-51.

38. S. C. Dube, *Modernization and Development: The Search for Alternative Paradigms* (Tokyo: The United Nations University, 1988), pp. 6-10.

39. H. J. Habakkuk, "The Historical Experience on the Basic Conditions of Economic Progress," in *Comparative Perspectives on Social Change,* ed. S. N. Eisenstadt (Boston: Little, Brown, 1968), p. 33.

40. Phillips Cutright and William R. Kelly, "Modernization and Other Determinants of National Birth, Death, and Growth Rates: 1958-1972," *Comparative Studies in Sociology* 1 (1978): 17-46.

41. Guy Hunter, *Modernizing Peasant Societies* (New York: Oxford University Press, 1969), pp. 98-99.

42. See Lester B. Pearson et al., *Partners in Development: Report of the Commission on International Development* (New York: Frederick A. Praeger, 1969).

43. Shlomo Avineri, "Marx and Modernization," *Review of Politics* 31 (1969): 188.

44. Mats Friberg and Bjorn Hettne, "Local Mobilization and World System Politics," *International Social Science Journal* 40 (1988): 341-60.

45. Herbert Feith, "Indonesia's Political Symbols and Their Wielders," in *Political Development and Social Change,* eds. Jason L. Finkle and Richard W. Gable (New York: Wiley,1966), pp. 365-78.

46. Ibid., p. 370.

47. Peter A. Munch, "Economic Development and Conflicting Values: A Social Experiment in Tristan Da Cunha," *American Anthropologist* 72 (1970): 1300-18.

48. Barbara Ward, Lenore D'Anjou, and J. D. Runnalls, eds., *The Widening Gap: Development in the 1970's* (New York: Columbia University Press, 1971), p. 3.

49. Li Haibo, "Illiteracy Threatens Modernization," *Beijing Review,* January 16-22, 1989, pp. 7-8.

50. Irving Louis Horowitz, Three Worlds of Development, 2nd ed. (New York: Oxford University Press, 1972), p. 470.

51. Donella Meadows, Dennis L. Meadows, Jorgen Randers, and William W. Behrens III, *The Limits to Growth* (New York: Universe Books, 1972).

52. Data in this paragraph are from Donella H. Meadows, "Futures Terrible and Terrific," *Los Angeles Times,* January 29, 1989.

53. Ibid.

54. . Calvin Goldscheider, *Population, Modernization, and Social Structure* (Boston: Little, Brown, 1971), pp. 104-14.

55. Melvin M. Tumin, "Competing Status Systems," in *Labor Commitment and Social Change,* ed. Wilbert E. Moore and Arnold S. Feldman (New York: Social Science Research Council, 1960), pp. 280-82.

56. Robert C. Williamson, "Social Class and Orientation to Change: Some Relevant Variables in a Bogota Sample," *Social Forces* 46 (1968): 317-28.

57. Lenski, *Power and Privilege,* p. 308.

58. J. Fred Springer and Richard W. Gable, "Modernization and Sex Roles: The Status of Women in the Thai Bureaucracy," *Sex Roles* 7 (1981): 723-37.

59. Milica Zarkovic, "The Effects of Economic Growth and Technological Innovation on the Agricultural Labor Force in India," *Studies in Comparative International Development* 22 (1987): 103-20.

60. Susan E. Marshall, "Politics and Female Status in North Africa: A Reconsideration of Development Theory," *Economic Development and Cultural Change* 32 (1984): 517.

61. Philip Olson, "Modernization in the People's Republic of China: The Politicization of the Elderly," *The Sociological Quarterly* 29 (1988) 241-62.

62. "Aging: An Update On the Elderly Worldwide," *UN Chronicle* 22 (1985): xxi.

63. The figures are from *Historical Statistics of the United States* and U.S. Bureau of the Census, *Statistical Abstract of the United States, 1987* (Washington, D.C.: U.S. Government Printing Office, 1987), pp. 8, 280.

64. Political turmoil and mass movements occurred in England, the first nation to modernize. See Neil J. Smelser, *Social Change in the Industrial Revolution* (Chicago: University of Chicago Press, 1959), p. 245. There is some dispute about whether violence always accompanies modernization, and, if so, whether it occurs at the beginning or at some intermediate level of development. See Ivo K. Feierabend, Rosalind L. Feierabend, and Betty A. Nesvold, "Social Change and Political Violence: Cross-National Patterns," *The History of Violence in America*, ed. H. D. Graham and T. R. Gurr (New York: Bantam, 1969), pp. 632-87; Mark N. Cooper, "A Reinterpretation of the Causes of Turmoil: The Effects of Culture and Modernity," *Comparative Political Studies* 7 (October, 1974): 267-91; and Charles Tilly, Louise Tilly, and Richard Tilly, *The Rebellious Century: 1830-1930* (Cambridge, Mass.: Harvard University Press, 1975), pp. 83, 236.

65. Alexander L. Peaslee, "Elementary Education as a Prerequisite for Economic Growth," *International Development Review* 7 (1965): 19-21; and "Education's Role in Development," *Economic Development and Cultural Change* 17 (1969): 293-318.

66. Ito Ryoji, "Education as a Basic Factor in Japan's Economic Growth," *Developing Economies* 1 (1963): 37-54.

67. Kristine L. Anderson and Bruce London, "Modernization, Elites, and the Distribution of Educational Resources in Thailand," *Social Forces* 63 (1985): 775-94.

68. "Development and the Family," *UN Chronicle* 22 (#5, 1985): xix-xx.

69. Ibid., p. xx.

70. Dudley L. Poston, Jr., Elizabeth Briody, Katherine Trent, and Harley L. Browning, "Modernization and Childlessness in the States of Mexico," *Economic Development and Cultural Change* 33 (1985): 503-19.

71. Lerner, "Modernization, Social Aspects," *International Encyclopedia of the Social Sciences*, p. 387.

72. Daniel Lerner, *The Passing of Traditional Society* (Glencoe, Ill.: Free Press, 1958), p. 50.

73. Cynthia Eaton, "Diabetes, Culture Change, and Acculturation: A Biocultural Analysis," *Medical Anthropology* 1 (Spring, 1977): 41-63.

74. See, for example, M. Assael and G. A. German, "Changing Society and Mental Health in Eastern Africa," *The Israel Annals of Psychiatry and Related Disciplines* 8 (April, 1970): 52-74; J. H. Abramson, "Observations on the Health of Adolescent Girls in Relation to Culture Change," *Psychosomatic Medicine* 23 (1961): 156-65; and John G. Bruhn, Billy U. Philips, and Stewart Wolf, "Social Readjustment and Illness Patterns: Comparison Between First, Second and Third Generation Italian-Americans Living in the Same Community," *Journal of Psychosomatic Research* 16 (October, 1972): 387-94.

75. Assael and German, "Changing Society and Mental Health in Eastern Africa;" and M. F. M. El Sendiony, M. G. M. Abou-El-Azaem, and F. Luza, "Culture Change and Mental Illness," *International Journal of Social Psychiatry* 23 (Spring, 1977): 20-25.

76. R. Cebiroglu et al., "A Survey on the Distribution of Psychiatric Syndromes Seen in Children in Three Major Groups of Changing Turkish Culture, *Acta Paedopsychiatrica* 39 (No. 6, 1973): 155-61.

77. I. B. Amara, "Detribalization and Neuroses Among the Africans," *Bulletin of the Mennenger Clinic* 35 (No. 5, 1968): 298; Beatrice B. Whiting, "Rapid Social Change: Threat or Promise?" *Ekistics* 43 (February, 1977): 66; Engin Inel Holmstrom, "Changing Sex Roles in a Developing Country," *Journal of Marriage and the Family* 35 (August, 1973): 550; and M. H. Beaubrun, "Discussion: Socioeconomic Change, Population Explosion and the Changing Phases of Mental Health Programs in Developing Countries," *American Journal of Orthopsychiatry* 36 (January, 1966): 87.

78. Lamin Sesay, "Crime and Development in Africa," *The Annals of the American Academy of Political and Social Science* 432 (July, 1977): 42-51.

79. Steven F. Messner, "Societal Development, Social Equality, and Homicide: A Cross-National Test of a Durkheimian Model," *Social Forces* 61 (1982): 225-40.

80. Amara, "Detribalization and Neuroses Among the Africans," p. 299; and Assael and German, "Changing Society and Mental Health in Eastern Africa," p. 73.

81. Morton Beiser and Henri Collomb, "Mastering Change: Epidemiological and Case Studies in Senegal, West Africa," *American Journal of Psychiatry* 138 (1981): 455-59.

82. William Form and Kyu-Han Bae, "Convergence Theory and the Korean Connection," *Social Forces* 66 (1988): 618-44.

83. S. C. Dube, "Cultural Dimensions of Development," *International Social Science Journal* 118 (1988): 505-11.

84. Ibid., p. 507.

85. Michael Micklin, "Urbanization, Technology, and Traditional Values in Guatemala: Some Consequences of a Changing Social Structure," *Social Forces* 47 (1969): 438-46.

86. John J. Poggie, Jr., "Ciudad Industrial: A New City in Rural Mexico," in *Technology and Social Change*, ed. H. Russell Bernard and Pertti Pelto (New York: Macmillan, 1972), pp. 10-38.

87. Ibid., p. 32.

88. Emilio Willems, "Peasantry and City: Cultural Persistence and Change in Historical Perspective, a European Case," *American Anthropologist* 72 (1970): 528-44.

89. C. S. Whitaker, Jr., "A Dysrhythmic Process of Political Change," *World Politics* 29 (1967): 190-217.

90. Milton Singer, *When a Great Tradition Modernizes* (New York: Praeger, 1972).

91. Ibid., p. 275.

92. Ibid., p. 359.

93. Data in this paragraph were taken from *Habitat* 12 (1969): 4-5, and *UN Chronicle* 22 (#5, 1985), p. xvi.

94. This discussion follows York W. Bradshaw, "Urbanization and Underdevelopment: A Global Study of Modernization, Urban Bias, and Economic Dependency," *American Sociological Review* 52 (1987) 224-39.

95. Nestor P. Rodriguez and Joe R. Feagin, "Urban Specialization in the World-System: An Investigation of Historical Cases," *Urban Affairs Quarterly* 22 (1986): 187-220.

96. Bradshaw, "Urbanization and Underdevelopment."

97. Ibid., p. 236

98. An Zhiguo, "Controlled Urbanization Vital," *Beijing Review*, May 6, 1985, p. 4.

99. H. H. Gerth and C. Wright Mills, *From Max Weber: Essays in Sociology* (New York: Oxford University Press, 1946), p. 155.

100. Max Weber, *The Protestant Ethic and the Spirit of Capitalism*, trans. Talcott Parsons (New York: Scribner's, 1958), pp. 181-82.

101. Timothy Crippen, "Old and New Gods in the Modern World: Toward a Theory of Religious Transformation," *Social Forces* 67 (1988): 316-36.

102. From Jeffrey K. Hadden, "Toward Desacralizing Secularization Theory," *Social Forces* 65 (1987): 587-611.

103. Crippen, "Old and New Gods in the Modern World," p. 332.

104. Singer, *When a Great Tradition Modernizes*, pp. 149-96.

105. Terrance G. Carroll, "Secularization and States of Modernity," *World Politics* 36 (1984): 362-82.

106. Clifford J. Clarke, "The End of Bureaucratization? Recent Trends in Cross-National Evidence," *Social Science Quarterly* 64 (1983): 127-35.

107. Gerth and Mills, *From Max Weber*, pp. 204-16.

108. Merle Fainsod, "Bureaucracy and Modernization: The Russian and Soviet Case," in *Bureaucracy and Political Development*, ed. Joseph LaPalombara (Princeton: Princeton University Press, 1963), p. 249.

109. Ibid., p. 252.

110. See Ronald M. Glassman, William H. Swatos, Jr., and Paul L. Rosen, eds., *Bureaucracy Against Democracy and Socialism* (Westport, Conn.: Greenwood Press, 1987), for case studies of bureaucracies that impeded progress.

111. William B. Stevenson, "Change In the Structure of Bureaucracy," *Sociological Perspectives* 29 (1986): 307-36.

112. Richard M. Pfeffer, "Mao Tse-tung and the Cultural Revolution," in *National Liberation*, ed. Norman Miller and Roderick Aya (New York: Free Press, 1971), pp. 264-68.

113. Martin King Whyte, "Bureaucracy and Modernization in China: The Maoist Critique," *American Sociological Review* 38 (1973): 156.

114. James Fulcher, "The Bureaucratization of the State and the Rise of Japan," *British Journal of Sociology* 39 (1988): 228-54.

PART FIVE

Applied Sociology: How to Bring about Change

All history, according to Oswald Spengler, is not the same kind of history. For example: "What the conspicuously historical West calls 'Indian history' achieved itself without the smallest consciousness of what it was doing. . . . Western history was willed and Indian history happened."[1] In other words, there always will be a history of a people, but the people may have consciously shaped that history or merely unthinkingly adapted to it.

Spengler's estimation of the extent to which people controlled the course of change in the West is disputed by others. Michael Harrington argues that the twentieth-century crisis of the West is the result of our "accidental revolution." We are a living paradox, for "these most conscious and man-made of times have lurched into the unprecedented transformation of human life without thinking about it. And in a sense, this century, this scientific, technological, and utterly competent century, has happened accidentally."[2] The transformation must continue, Harrington believes, but it must stop being an accident, and rather must result from human intervention in and control of the social process.

While their assessments differ somewhat, both Spengler and Harrington stress the fact that people can control change as well as respond to it. In fact, unless we strive to control the course of development, we will become slaves to our own history. "If men do not make history," as C. Wright Mills put it, "they tend increasingly to become the utensils of history-makers as well as the mere objects of history."[3]

Suppose, then, that you wish to make history and not simply understand it. Suppose you want to effect change rather than simply gain insight into it. Suppose you have the desire to change an individual (including yourself), a group, an organization, or some facet of social existence. How do you proceed? Much of the material in the preceding chapters either implicitly or explicitly bears upon this question. In our final chapters, however, we will show the applications of sociology in the area of change. We will discuss specifically the ways in which people can take control of the process of change at the various levels of social life.

Endnotes

1. Oswald Spengler, *The Decline of the West,* vol. 1, trans. Charles Francis Atkinson (New York: Knopf, 1926), p. 133.

2. Michael Harrington, *The Accidental Century* (New York: Macmillan, 1965), p. 41.

3. C. Wright Mills, *Power, Politics & People,* ed. Irving Louis Horowitz (New York: Oxford University Press, 1963), p. 25.

CHAPTER THIRTEEN

General Considerations for Practitioners

Applied sociology is not a "quick fix," a simple formula for easily bringing about change. Anyone who strives to control change, to direct the process in a particular way, needs to be ready to face resistance and frustration with the effort. There are likely to be many forces acting on people in addition to the efforts of the practitioner. It is necessary, therefore, to be both knowledgeable and patient, both understanding and persistent. Successful practitioners of the craft of change are able to weather some failures in order to finally achieve the desired result.

Consider, for example, Stephen Richer's study of the attempt to change traditional conceptions of gender in a Canadian elementary school.[1] It would appear that changing gender stereotypes could be achieved with relative ease at the elementary school level. In addition, all the force of the educational system was behind the change. The Ontario Ministry of Education had issued a guide to help teachers create a learning environment free of sex-role stereotyping. A consultant visited each school and helped teachers understand how biased materials and unconscious attitudes could perpetuate stereotypes. Sexist materials were removed from the classrooms.

To measure the amount of sexual stereotyping, the researcher asked the children in grades one through six to draw themselves engaged in their favorite sport, game, or other activity. Two groups of children drew the pictures. One group was tested before the change effort began. The second group was tested some six years after the program had been initiated. Surprisingly, the researcher found that the group that participated in the change effort had more gender-stereotyped ideas than the early group. The disparity between the proportion of boys and girls who drew themselves in competitive activities had increased. After six years of a deliberate, well-planned effort at change, boys were still far more likely than girls to picture themselves in a competitive activity, to draw themselves as the prominent figure in the sketch, and to put themselves in an outdoor rather than an indoor activity.

The researcher concluded that the experiment shows "the futility of attempting change (a) through discourse alone and (b) by using the school as the central change agent."[2] Even at the elementary school level, it is not a simple matter to bring about change in people. Let us, then, look at some of the considerations involved if a change effort is to be successful. We will begin with one of the more vexing questions—why do people seem to resist change?

Why People Resist Change

In Chapter 1, we dismissed the idea that humans inherently resist change. Still, it is undeniable that there is an enormous amount of resistance. It is important to understand two factors about that resistance. First, there are times when people *should* resist change. Sometimes practitioners talk as though resistance is an impediment to progress that must be broken down, or even an unhealthy reaction that must be overcome for the sake of the people.

While it is true that people sometimes resist change that will enhance their well-being (for reasons we shall discuss below), it is also true that they appropriately resist change that will be detrimental to their well-being. For example, one of the more traumatic experiences of human life is the sudden, unexplained death of an infant. For a long time, physicians believed that an enlarged thymus gland pressed against the windpipe, resulting in coughing, choking, and, in extreme cases, even death. In the early part of the twentieth century, American physicians used the relatively new technology of X rays to reduce the thymus in thousands of infants.[3] Not all physicians accepted the innovation, and not all parents allowed the procedure to be done on their children. Eventually, physicians agreed that the thymus could not be responsible for sudden infant deaths, and the practice eventually stopped. Unfortunately, by the 1950s researchers reported significant numbers of thyroid cancers among those who had been x-rayed for a supposedly enlarged thymus.

There are times when change should be resisted for the sake of people's well-being, whether it's the case of adopting a medical innovation, using a new drug like crack, or the rise of a dictator like Hitler. In discussing resistance, therefore, I am not assuming that resistance is always something negative that must be overcome.

The second factor about resistance is that it normally has rational bases. Some practitioners believe that people react emotionally, unthinkingly to change efforts. While it may be true that resistance sometimes occurs without much thought, a close examination will show that there are usually reasonable bases for that resistance. That is, the resistance is reasonable if you look at it from the point of view of those resisting. Their point of view may be rooted in misunderstanding or inadequate information, but that does not make it irrational.

In sum, it is best to approach the problem of resistance by addressing two factors. Is the resistance appropriate in terms of the potential impact of the change on the people? What are the reasonable bases on which the resistance stands? If the answer to the first question is no, the practitioner needs to inquire into the reasonable bases and deal with them as a part of the change effort. Let us examine those bases.

• *Resistance to Threats*

We all will resist those changes that are defined as a threat in some sense. The anthropologist, Spicer, pointed out that people are always changing their ways, but they will resist any change that is defined as a threat to basic securities.[4] Actually, people resist change that threatens them in other ways as well.

For instance, the change may threaten our values. In his study of a Spanish village, Joseph Aceves points out that a number of planned changes were accepted "willingly and often eagerly," including new varieties of seed, new kinds of crops, and modern methods of farming."[5] Other proposed changes, however, were resisted vigorously. Aceves notes that the Spanish villagers hold a primary loyalty to the family rather than the village; in fact, a basic mistrust pervades village life, and peace and security are believed to lie in maintaining the advantage of one's own family. Consequently, villagers accepted those changes that were beneficial to them and their families but resisted or rejected changes that compelled them to engage in "long-term contractual relationships . . . long-term being anything over ten days or two weeks according to local reckoning."[6] The people were not opposed to change, and they did value an enhanced economic status. Their value on primary loyalty to the family and their mistrust of fellow villagers led them, however, to resist change that would force them into more extended relationships and obligations, even when they were told that the latter would lead to economic improvement.

The unknown is also threatening to some extent, and change may involve a transition from the familiar to the unknown. We can never, after all, be certain that the change effort will produce the results that were planned. As noted earlier, there are always unanticipated consequences to change. Why take a chance on changing that which is familiar and, therefore, comfortable? Most of us are hesitant to leave the familiar behind, particularly when we are reasonably satisfied with the situation.[7] Given a choice between remaining in an acceptable situation or moving to one that has the promise of being better but also the potential for undesirable outcomes, many if not most people will prefer the former. Therefore, the more that the practitioner can minimize the perception that unknown and unanticipated consequences will occur, the lower the resistance is likely to be.

In many cases, however, it is not the unknown that poses the threat but the potential loss of tangible possessions. Addressing the question of why employees in organizations resist change, Donald Kirkpatrick notes that one reason is the threat of personal loss.[8] Among other things, they may define the change as a threat to their job security, income, work satisfaction, interpersonal relationships on the job, and status.

Such perceptions of threat are not without a basis in reality. People have lost jobs through automation or other changes in the workplace. Changing jobs or changing positions in an organization can result in loss of pay (or greater expenses, which amounts to a loss of spendable income), lower status, altered relationships, and diminished satisfaction.

In some cases, the threat may be even more severe. It may literally be a threat to people's lives. For example, it is one thing to convince an American farmer to try a new hybrid grain, and quite another to convince a Third World peasant. The American farmer may risk a year's crop and deeper debt, perhaps even the loss of the farm. The peasant, however, who is living at the margin of life already, may be risking the survival of himself and his family.

Similarly, it may appear to an outsider to be helpful to urge peasants to opt for cash crops rather than for subsistence farming. As long as the peasants simply grow food for their own consumption, they obviously will remain at the subsistence level. But it may be more important to the peasants to ensure subsistence than to risk their minimal security on the altar of a capricious market. Again, the threat to the peasants is not merely a loss of income but a potential loss of life.

• *Resistance Based on a Cost/Benefit Analysis*

In the example just given, the peasants were not only reacting to a threat, but, in essence, making a cost/benefit analysis of the situation. A cost/benefit analysis is simply a weighing of the potential gains with the potential losses, and deciding whether it is worthwhile to risk the change. It is important to keep two things in mind here. First, a cost/benefit analysis does not necessarily provide clear directives. Rather, the analysis may simply indicate the degree of risk involved. Individuals must still decide whether the potential gains are worth the risks involved. Second, individuals do not necessarily make correct analyses. They may not have sufficient information to know the potential for either loss or gain. Practitioners, then, can help by providing an accurate cost/benefit analysis.

In some cases, the cost/benefit analysis may indicate to people that the proposed change will do more harm than good, that the change will cause more problems than it is worth. This is a common outcome when "people at the 'bottom' of an organization feel that top management makes changes without knowing what's going on 'down on the line.'"[9] In other cases, people may simply feel that the benefits are not worth the cost of bringing about the change. Many changes, for example, demand a certain amount of psychophysiological restructuring on the part of people. Paul Alcorn illustrates the problem with regard to learning how to write computer programs:

> *A young child can learn BASIC in a very short period of time. . . . Adults can and many do learn to use a computer as well, but the task is far harder. . . . They have strongly reinforced patterns of neuronic interaction in their brain that determine the predominance of their mode of thinking. In many cases this is not a mode of thinking that easily lends itself to learning computer programming. It is hard work for the adult, not play. It requires effort, time, and concentration in the adult just to load and execute a canned program, constantly adjusting the adult's thinking to what the computer is doing. For the child, it is, what else, "child's play."*[10]

For an adult to accept the "work" of the change, whether that be the Westerner learning a computer language or a peasant learning to use a new method of irrigation, there must be a sense that the benefits to be derived outweigh the cost. Again, it is the change agent, the practitioner, who can help people make an accurate cost/benefit analysis.

There is one other aspect to the cost/benefit analysis that is important to keep in mind. People generally make such an analysis from their personal point of view, not from the point of view of an organization or a society. An analysis from the group's point of view may indicate that a particular change is desirable, while the same analysis from the individual's (or the individual and his or her family) point of view may indicate that the change is undesirable.

As an example of the conflict between individual and group analyses, consider efforts in the People's Republic of China to limit population growth.[11] In 1979, Chinese leaders began an intensive campaign to promote a one-child policy. They touted the slogan, "one is best, at most two, never a third." Prior to 1979, the emphasis had been on a maximum of two children per family, but the leaders came to believe that even two children per family would be detrimental to the nation's economic well-being. If China were to develop rapidly and minimize the strain on its natural resources, it would be important to closely control population growth. Because of the large numbers of young people coming into the child-bearing years, the one-child-per-family policy seemed the only way to reach national economic goals.

Thus, from the national point of view, a cost/benefit analysis indicated the need for severe restrictions on family size. The government attempted to make the changed policy acceptable to the people by providing incentives to those who agreed to limit their families to one child. In urban areas, couples received monthly cash payments for fourteen years and got preferred treatment in housing and jobs. Only children would also get special privileges, such as priority medical care and preferred schooling and jobs after graduation. Rural couples, on the other hand, were promised extra shares of their commune's income for fourteen years, more private land, and larger grain rations.

By the mid-1980s, the government estimated that 78 percent of urban but only 31 percent of rural couples had signed an agreement to limit their families to one child. The greater resistance to the change in the rural areas was rooted in part in a cost/benefit analysis based on the family's place in the rural context. In rural China, the family's success still depends on the number of children available to help tend the fields. Moreover, most rural Chinese are not covered by the state-funded pension system. Rural townships must guarantee food, shelter, clothing, medical care, and burial to elderly couples without a son, but the provisions are minimal. The only way a rural couple can ensure a comfortable old age is to have sons, for the sons have been, and still are, responsible for caring for their aged parents.

Thus, a cost/benefit analysis makes the one-child policy desirable from the nation's point of view, and even from urban dwellers' point of view. Of course, other factors, such as the traditional importance to the Chinese of having at least one son, also enter the calculations for many people. But in the rural areas, it is not only family honor and family continuity that are a part of the analysis but also the need for farm labor and well-being in old age. Whatever the group benefits may be, people tend to resist that change for which their personal or family costs appear to be higher than the benefits.

• Resistance Based on Reactance

We have noted that change that is imposed is likely to be resisted even when it seems to be in people's best interests. Such resistance reflects psychological *reactance*. As framed by Jack Brehm, reactance theory states that people resist any perceived infringement on their freedom.[12] If any individual believes that one of his or her free behaviors has been eliminated, or is threatened with elimination, that individual will be motivated to act in order to restore his or her freedom. Reactance theory helps explain such things as the effectiveness of ads that proclaim a "limited number available" or "for a limited time only." People may respond because they do not want to lose the freedom of purchasing the item after the limited number or limited time has been exhausted.

In terms of resisting change, reactance theory sheds light on such things as China's attempt to control inflation in the 1980s. Responding to inflationary pressures in 1988, the government took two steps that turned out to be counterproductive.[13] First, the government increased prices on a number of foods, and, at the same time, raised wages to compensate people for the higher prices. Second, the leaders announced a policy of immediate and major price reforms, though the nature of the reforms was unclear. Public statements by leaders attempted to prepare the people for the reforms by assuring them that their incomes would increase sufficiently to offset the additional costs.

To the people, it appeared that the government's actions confirmed the fact of inflation. And they believed that inflation would reduce their buying options. In order to avoid the loss of that freedom, they took their money out of their savings and rushed to purchase various consumer goods. The resulting panic buying, of course, only intensified inflation, frustrating the government's attempts at control.

In sum, people invariably resist those changes that threaten their freedoms. The peasants who perceive that an agricultural innovation will reduce their freedom to sow as much seed as they want, the workers who perceive that an organizational change will reduce their freedom to chat with co-workers, and the urbanites who define new legislation as restricting their right to sell their homes to whomever they please, will resist changes in these directions. To gain acceptance, change agents must show that the perceptions are wrong, or that whatever loss of freedom is involved is compensated for by new benefits.

Choosing the Appropriate Target

In addition to being sensitive to the reasons that people resist change, the practitioner must make important decisions about a number of matters. In the remainder of this chapter, we will look at two of those decisions—what is the target of change and who will be the agent of the change?

As far as the target is concerned, we may aim at individuals, at groups, or at the social structure. Ultimately, of course, we are interested in changing the behavior of individuals. The behavior to be changed may be any one of an endless number of problems and situations, such as the dictator who exploits people, the peasant who uses outmoded and inefficient farming methods, the businessperson who treats minorities unfairly, or the worker who is unproductive. But in changing human behavior, there is still the question of the proximate target of the change efforts. Will the behavior be changed best by focusing on individuals themselves, some aspect of a group to which people belong, or the social structure in which the people function? In the long run, all may change. In fact, the long-run target may be a holistic one of changing individuals, their groups, and the social structure; the short-run decision, however, involves identifying which part of the whole to attack.

In selecting the target, a number of questions must be addressed. What is the problem? What are the sources of the problem? What needs to be changed in order to resolve the problem? From a sociological perspective, the problem is frequently rooted in group or social-structural factors, even when the problem is defined as individual behavior of some kind. For example, suppose that a plant manager discovers that the first-line supervisors are not spending enough time responding to the needs of their workers. How can the manager bring about change in the supervisors' behavior? What are the sources of the problem? Are the supervisors insensitive? Are they ignorant of the situation? Do their attitudes or values need to be changed? In a study of 160 first-line supervisors in a pharmaceutical plant, two researchers found that the allocation of time to various tasks was a function of technology, labor union strength, and pressures from upper management.[14] It was not the supervisors' attitudes or values but various aspects of the organization that determined their behavior. Clearly, in such a situation, it would be pointless to try to change behavior by improving attitudes or altering the supervisors' values.

Once, then, the above questions are clearly addressed, the change agent can better decide on the appropriate target. If, for example, the problem is low farm productivity, and the sources are antiquated methods and peasant attitudes that resist innovation, the question becomes one of which target will best effect change in the peasants' attitudes. Is it possible that the social structure supports their attitudes by failing to provide support if an innovation means crop failure rather than success? Might local groups to which the peasants belong perpetuate their attitudes by accepting and diffusing erroneous information? Or can the attitudes be changed by working directly with the peasants in some way?

As the above example indicates, the selection of the target is not an easy task. It should be made only after considerable analysis of a particular situation. Recall the earlier discussion about birth control efforts in China. How effective could the government's efforts be to convince people when the social structure in which the rural Chinese functioned made the one-child policy appear hazardous to their well-being?

On the other hand, there are cases where it is not the social structure or the group but the individual that is the appropriate target. An organization may be functioning with an unacceptable amount of inefficiency because of the lack of productivity on the part of a number of workers scattered throughout the organization. An analysis may show that the problem with some workers is that they are having marital and family problems, while others are unmotivated because they do not feel that their jobs make full use of their abilities. In such cases, the change agent may decide to make those individuals the target of change. But in all cases, it is imperative to identify all possible factors at all levels—the individual, group, and social structural—that may account for the situation that is to be changed. Only then can a rational decision be made about the appropriate target.

• *The Individual as Target*

If the individual is the appropriate proximate target of change, it is necessary that the number of people to be changed is relatively small and/or the resources are sufficient to give the required attention to each individual. The change effort may be aimed directly at certain patterns of behavior or at attitudes or values that have behavioral consequences. The ultimate goal is changed behavior, but that goal may best be reached in some cases by attacking the behavior directly and in others by first addressing people's attitudes and/or values.

For example, if the goal is to eliminate discrimination in an organization in which a few people have failed to treat others equitably regardless of sex or race, efforts to first erase the prejudice may be exceedingly slow and even fruitless. Establishing a rule that imposes severe penalties for discriminatory acts goes to the heart of the matter—behavior. Once the behavior changes, as we shall discuss in the next chapter, the attitudes and values are more likely to change as well. In other cases, it may be necessary to bring about attitudinal change first. Efforts to get peasants to adopt an agricultural innovation may first require the change agent to convince an opinion leader in the community. Once the opinion leader's attitudes have changed, so that the leader adopts the innovation, the desired diffusion may occur rapidly.

As we shall see in the next chapter, there are a number of differing strategies that can be employed to change individuals, ranging from individual therapy to small-group processes. While all of the various individual approaches have demonstrated some degree of success, choosing the individual as a target can be a painstakingly slow method of seeking change, even if it succeeds. For example, a therapist may help an individual cope with a stressful existence, but that individual may be incapable of doing anything other than coping. Not only may he or she be unable to effect any changes beyond himself or herself, but the therapist will be faced with a continuing stream of others who must exist in the same debilitating social structure. The therapist has succeeded in helping the individual, but has not thereby effected any larger changes. This is not to demean the work of therapists; multitudes could be psychologically shredded to pieces while we wait for the creation of a new social structure. While humans suffer, all strategies are important. By the same token, no one strategy is sufficient by itself, and some are limited in their consequences.

• *The Group as Target*

When the group or the social structure is selected as a target, it generally is assumed that a changed context will effect changes in individuals as well. Individual values, attitudes, and behavior will be modified by changing the group or the social structure in which individuals think and act. Again, both individuals and the social entities are to be changed in the long run; but the group and social-structural approaches choose the supraindividual entity as the proximate target of change on the premise that changes in individuals will follow.

Selecting the group as a target is appropriate when there are larger numbers of people to be changed and/or when it is the composition or structure and processes of the group that primarily cause the behavior that is to be changed. Usually, the "group" is an organization of some kind. But the group could also be a subunit of an organization, a family, a network of friends, or a neighborhood.

There are cases, however, where even the group as a target is inadequate. Just as it may be necessary to change the group in which an individual functions in order to change the individual, it may be necessary to change the social structure in which the group is embedded in order to change the group. For example, the students at a particular university may be generally convinced that the grading system impedes learning. It would not be feasible for that university to abolish grades while it continues to function in a competitive social milieu where grades are used for securing employment, gaining admission to graduate school, and maintaining enrollment at a manageable level. For some kinds of change, then, only the social structure itself is an appropriate target.

• *The Social Structure as Target*

When the social structure is the target, change will be more extensive, diffusing throughout a larger part of the society than a group or a few groups, or an organization or a few organizations. Furthermore, we are talking about changes that affect more than a single mode of interaction; that is, these changes would affect people in more than a single setting such as a particular group or organization. Examples of this kind of change include such things as alterations in the power structure of a society, cultural change, and changes in one or more social institutions.

Let us look at an example of social structural change: the transition from an agrarian to an industrial society as illustrated by Mexico following the 1910 revolution.[15] The changes experienced in Mexico are typical of other nations making the transition. At the preindustrial level, there is a long-term trend toward increasing inequality. With rare exceptions, agricultural societies exhibit sharp inequalities. In Mexico, a very small upper class existed prior to 1910. Power derived from ownership of the land, and about 1 percent of the population owned 97 percent of the land. About 80 percent of Mexicans were rural people, living at a subsistence level; most existed as semi-serfs on large haciendas.

During Mexico's transition to an industrial society following the 1910 revolution, certain trends were established that are typical of societies making the transition. First, individuals began to be evaluated on the basis of achievement. Education, occupation, and income began to displace ascribed memberships as criteria of evaluation. Second, the occupational structure changed. There was an upgrading, with a demand for increasing numbers of people with some skill. The proportion of the Mexican population engaged in nonagricultural activities changed from about 25 percent in 1910 to almost 50 percent in 1960 to 63 percent in 1980.

Third, individual mobility increased. The urban population in Mexico rose from 29 percent in 1910 to 51 percent in 1960 to 66 percent by 1980. Associated with mobility has been a rising income for a greater proportion of the people. In the early 1960s, 0.5 percent of rural families and 6.3 percent of urban families were at the highest of five income levels, while 39.9 percent of rural families and only 6.6 percent of urban families were at the lowest level. Unfortunately, however, the reduction in inequality has not been as dramatic as many Mexicans would have liked. In the late 1970s, those in the highest of the five income levels got 57.7 percent of the total income, while those at the lowest level got only 2.9 percent.

Education, an essential tool for mobility, has grown more widespread over the years. By 1965, 4 percent of the school-age population was enrolled in higher education; by 1983, 15 percent were in higher education. While still relatively small compared with some other nations, Mexico's middle class has grown and is more than double what it was at the turn of the century.

In sum, while there continues to be considerable inequality in Mexico, the nation's people have made considerable progress during this century. The important point here is that the Mexican peasants could not have changed their situation through an individual or group approach. It is of little use to tell an individual to work hard and be diligent if the structure of society ensures continued deprivation.

• *Secondary Targets: The Wisdom of Aiming Low*

Someone has called compromise one of the greatest human inventions. The so-called true believer might disdain compromise and insist upon rigid adherence to the strategy demanded by an ideology, but the true believer might also founder upon the rocks of unrealistic aspirations. History-makers need to consider carefully the wisdom of aiming low while not losing sight of higher aims; that is, they need to consider compromising their loftier aims in order to achieve short-run and more realistic goals. They need to consider the wisdom of backing away from the primary target and aiming at a secondary and more accessible target. They can do this in at least two different ways. First, they can treat symptoms rather than the disease. Second, they can shift from attempts to change the whole to efforts to change a part of the whole.

The first way has been suggested by Etzioni.[16] Because of the medical analogy, we may have an aversion to the notion of treating symptoms, but Etzioni has persuasively argued that the choice may be one of treating symptoms or doing nothing rather than one of treating symptoms or the disease. Some radicals, for example, may oppose, or at least be disappointed by, worker-benefits legislation on the grounds that such legislation will inhibit the development of a revolutionary consciousness among workers. The whole structure of the society, they will say, must be altered before workers (and other oppressed people) will truly benefit. In the United States, the choice may not be between legislation and revolution, but between legislation and continued deprivation.

Etzioni has argued that many social problems can be attacked by "shortcuts," by treating the symptoms even though that treatment will not get at the deeper causes of the problems. These shortcuts at least have the value of reducing the cost of the problem to the society. For example, the introduction of tranquilizers reduced the number of patients in state mental hospitals after 1955. Tranquilizers do not get at the root of the problem of emotional distress, but they have reduced the cost of that distress (including the cost to the disturbed individual, who may remain at home rather than being confined in a hospital).

It is no doubt true that increased street lighting only gets at the symptoms and not the root causes of crime, that affirmative action programs do not eliminate racism, and that methadone clinics will not strike at the heart of the drug problem. It is equally true that such measures are probably preferred by most people to doing nothing at all about the problems. The true believers may insist on waiting for the needed revolution, but the victims will welcome the treatment of symptoms.

Furthermore, the treatment of symptoms can be a cumulative process that ultimately results in the achievement of the higher aims. This seems to be occurring in the case of nonwhites in the United States. Many of the laws designed to attack discrimination aimed at specific areas—voting, education, and job opportunities. In most cases, a series of laws has been required, since various ways were found to subvert the law. One could argue that any particular law, such as an open housing ordinance, does not get at the heart of the racial problem. Nevertheless, a whole series of laws, dealing with housing and other matters, has changed the structural position of nonwhites. Nonwhites could have made greater and quicker gains by a violent overthrow of the government and the seizure of political power, but that would be an unrealistic goal in the United States. Moreover, the continual attack on secondary targets has brought nonwhites a good deal closer to the primary target of universal equity in American society.

The second way of aiming low that we mentioned above involved the shift from efforts to change the whole to efforts to change some part of the whole. This seems to be the course taken by a number of radical leaders of the 1960s. During their work with the New Left, they confronted the larger society and attempted to change it by remaining "outside of the system." In the 1970s, however, some of the leaders decided to work within the system by running for political office or becoming involved in the support of political candidates. They shifted from efforts to change the whole of American society in one fell swoop to efforts to change the polity. The latter change would ultimately, of course, result in broader changes. In the meantime, considerable effort and time would be spent on the secondary target of the polity.

Harry Edwards has called this approach "revolutionary conformity": "Its main feature is that rather than dropping out or engaging in the most ludicrous kinds of confrontation since the lions ate lunch at the Colosseum, you get involved in the system, you use established channels."[17] Edwards argues that such an approach actually demands more effort than conformity itself and equal energy to that consumed by radicalism. The cost is less while the rewards are greater. In other words, the switch from unrealistic efforts to change the whole to the more realistic attempt to change a part of the whole is both more realistic and more likely to bring desired results.

The practicality of aiming at a part rather than at the whole has been demonstrated by William Gamson, who calls it the "strategy of thinking small."[18] In analyzing various kinds of protest groups and their effectiveness in the United States, Gamson identified the consequences of three choices: the pursuit of a single issue versus multiple demands, the advocacy of radical demands versus those that accept the legitimacy of the social order, and the effort to influence elites versus attempts to replace elites. He found that the groups that tried to displace elites (through elections or more militant means) had little success in terms of gaining new advantages for group members. Groups that pursued multiple demands had no success in gaining new advantages (compared with a 59 percent success rate of single-issue groups). Finally, he found that having radical or nonradical goals was not a factor in success as long as the radical goals did not include the goal of replacing or destroying an antagonist.[19] Gamson concludes that there is a "modest advantage" to thinking small. Groups with more limited goals, pursuing a single issue, and not aiming at the displacement of their antagonists were more likely to succeed.

Selecting an Appropriate Agent

A second crucial question must also be faced by practitioners. Who makes the change? Does the change come about by one group imposing it on others, or by the participation of all those involved? The question is a pertinent one whatever the target happens to be.

At the individual level, therapists have employed both authoritarian and participative techniques. At group and structural levels, both elitist and democratic strategies have been advocated and employed. The elites may be experts of some kind: entrepreneurs, intellectuals, or political revolutionaries, for example. In any case, the task of the elites is to effect the change with or without the willingness of others involved in the change. In democratic strategies, there may still be experts, but they work with the people, so that all those affected by the change have the opportunity to participate in the decisions.

Many social scientists and consultants have argued that change must be democratic to some extent in order to be effective. As an executive put it, one of the fundamental principles of management is that "employees at all levels should be involved in decisions that affect their work, and management should work at developing a consensus on key change issues."[20] Participation, then, doesn't mean total control or that managers turn over crucial decisions to workers. It does require at a minimum the opportunity to have input into the decision-making process. Reactance is likely wherever there is the failure to observe such minimal participation.

Participation, in other words, gives organizational members some control over their lives. The sense of control, in turn, is important to their well-being and to their functioning in the organization. Those who participate in the decision-making process report a higher quality of communication with their superiors than those who lack such participation.[21] They also report higher levels of satisfaction.[22] Finally, productivity is likely to be higher where there is participatory management.[23]

The above suggests that change efforts will be more effective where people are able to participate in the decision-making process. Research supports such a conclusion. Let us look at two examples of participation in organizational change. In a study of workers in various industries, Nurick found that those who had participated in changes in their organizations (by being members of a Quality of Work Committee or task force) benefited in a number of ways.[24] Compared with other workers, they perceived themselves to have more influence and had more positive attitudes toward their jobs and their organizations. In another study, researchers looked at the effects of trying to implement a 3-day/38-hour work schedule among eighty-four employees working with information systems.[25] The changed schedule was important to the organization, because it was expected to (and did) reduce sick time, overtime, and personal leave time, making the organization more efficient. Eighteen months after the new schedule had been implemented, those most likely to favor it were the workers who had participated in the decision to implement it.

The insistence that democratic processes are more successful has not been limited to the organizational context, however. A similar argument has been advanced with respect to entire societies. Whatever the size of the group, according to the advocates of democratic change, and whatever the context, some members must be included in the planning of any change.

Just how much participation constitutes democratic procedures is problematic. At the very least, people must feel that the change is being effected on their behalf. Mao correctly noted that the Chinese revolution depended on the support of the peasants. Long before the revolution succeeded, he wrote: "Without the poor peasants there would be no revolution. To deny their role is to deny the revolution."[26] That role was a supportive one, facilitating the survival and ultimate triumph of the Red Army.

At the most, democratic procedure will involve active participation of all those involved in the change. When the size of the group concerned becomes large, this obviously is impossible. If diverse groups are involved, all or the majority of the people must sense that their interests are adequately represented and/or that some of them have been consulted. Failure in this, again, may lead to reactance even when the proposed change is in the best interests of the people. Consider, for instance, an effort in Zimbabwe to implement a program for raising crop yields among the peasant farmers.[27] An agrochemical company in Zimbabwe developed the program, which was supported by the government's extension service. The company planned to give the peasants enough herbicides, pesticides, and fertilizers for a half-acre crop. The company also provided training in preparing the land and the use of sprayers. Finally, the peasants would be given financial aid and help in marketing the crops. "It was a tidy, perfectly planned package except for one thing. Nobody asked the *masvikiro* for advice or support."[28]

The *masvikiro* are the men, including spirit mediums, medicine makers, and village leaders, who led the peasants in their struggle for independence from Britain. Many are now opinion leaders in their communities. Angry because no one consulted them about something as fundamental to their way of life as farming, they decided to defend the existing ways of farming. They told the people that artificial fertilizers would ruin the land and reminded them that their forefathers had gotten all the food they needed without the help of artificial fertilizers.

The company eventually cancelled the program. Moreover, *masvikiro* opposition frustrated subsequent government efforts at such things as crop rotation and conservation. Eventually, Zimbabwe's extension officers realized that they could not simply dictate new methods to the people. They began a program of working with, and trying to enlist the cooperation of, the *masvikiro*. Eventually, they hope that participation will bring about what efforts to dictate or impose could not—modernization of farming.

In spite of the high value we place on democratic change, however, there are a number of problems involved in choosing between it and elitist-led change. One problem has to do with the relative effectiveness of the two approaches. The above statements notwithstanding, the democratic approach is not the only and not always the most rapid way to effect change. In a previous chapter, we noted that changes in a number of cultural contexts required an elitist approach, including those changes in Indian villages that were wrought by authoritarian leaders who succeeded where democratic leaders had failed. A number of studies have indicated that authoritarian regimes are particularly effective in the early stages of modernization. Others have shown that in a context where peasants expect authoritarian procedures from the government, they may ignore or resist more democratic efforts at change.

For example, in contrast to the Zimbabwe situation noted above, research on Nigerian workers questioned the utility of participatory management.[29] The research raised the question of whether employees' self-esteem and morale, both important in how workers function on the job, improved as the workers became more involved in decision-making processes. In a survey of 1,865 workers from five occupations, only front-line managers indicated that participative management was important to them. In a study of eighty-four bricklayers, morale and production were highest among those who did not participate but who got cash bonuses for high production. And a study of six college principals with differing leadership styles showed that teachers were absent less under authoritarian than under democratic principals.

In other words, however much we may value the democratic approach, it is not necessarily the most effective in all cultures or in all situations. A second problem is the meaning of the democratic approach. In a word, has democratic change taken place or has a potential critic been co-opted? People may be brought into the decision-making process only in the sense of confirming, and thereby legitimating, decisions that have already been made. People may be given a voice in relatively trivial matters in order to allow an authority to maintain control over more significant decisions.

All participation, then, is not participatory democracy. As a minimum, democratic approaches to change should include the following:

1. An actual, not apparent, sharing in decisions relevant to the existence of those involved;
2. Full political rights and representation for all segments of the relevant population in order to achieve the above;
3. Action based on consensus rather than coercion; and
4. Planning that is, in Mannheim's words, "planning for freedom."

A third problem is choosing a democratic strategy is posed by certain dilemmas. For one thing, "it is always easier to organize in an elitist fashion and then simply dictate to the rest."[30] Those who are impatient to get something done may find themselves strongly tempted to take an elitist approach even when they prefer the democratic.

Another dilemma is the extent to which organizations and movements tend to reflect the larger society. The same inequalities that characterize the society generally will tend to appear in any group that organizes for change. High status in the larger society, for example, will tend to command a certain amount of deference within the group seeking change in spite of a commitment to democratic structure.

One other dilemma involves the need for expertise. A particular change may demand certain expert knowledge and that expert knowledge may demand the kind of change that would not be chosen in a democratic setting. In the context of a business firm, the dilemma takes the form of a question: "To what extent should managers rely on technical expertise to guide their decisions, in which event they limit their own influence over the outcome, and to what degree should they insist on being involved, in which case there will be a less informed decision based more on political compromise?"[31] In the context of industrialization, the dilemma means that considerable technical skills are required to initiate enterprises; only later can workers take over or participate in the management.

Because of these dilemmas, it should not surprise us that some efforts at democratic change fail.[32] Other efforts indicate very positive results.[33] Perhaps the basic problem is the first dilemma mentioned above—the elitist approach is easier. Even assuming that most changes may be effected democratically, there may be an unwillingness to expend the time and energy necessary for democratic procedures. From the point of view of human well-being, the democratic approach is superior. From the point of view of efficiency or profit, the elitist approach is superior. As a business executive once told me: "If we tried to be democratic in our corporation, we would be broke in two weeks."

Endnotes

1. Stephen Richer, "Schooling and the Gendered Subject: An Exercise in Planned Social Change," *Canadian Review of Sociology and Anthropology* 25 (1988): 98-108.

2. Ibid., p. 104.

3. Allan Mazur, *The Dynamics of Technical Controversy* (Washington, D.C.: Communications Press, Inc., 1981), pp. 2-5.

4. Edward H. Spicer, ed., *Human Problems in Technological Change* (New York: Russell Sage Foundation, 1952), p. 18.

5. Joseph Aceves, *Social Change in a Spanish Village* (Cambridge, Mass.: Schenkman, 1971), p. 126.

6. Ibid.

7. Abraham Sagie, Dov Elizur, and Charles W. Greenbaum, "Job Experience, Persuasion Strategy and Resistance to Change," *Journal of Occupational Behavior* 6 (1985): 157-62.

8. Donald L. Kirkpatrick, *How to Manage Change Effectively* (San Francisco: Jossey-Bass Publishers, 1985), pp. 85-86.

9. Ibid., p. 86.

10. Paul A. Alcorn, *Social Issues in Technology: A Format for Investigation* (Englewood Cliffs, N.J.: Prentice-Hall, 1986), p. 27.

11. The following materials are taken from Jodi L. Jacobson, "Baby Budget," *World-Watch*, September/October, 1989, pp. 21-31.

12. Jack W. Brehm, *A Theory of Psychological Reactance* (New York: Academic Press, 1966).

13. Barry Naughton, "Inflation and Economic Reform in China," *Current History* 88 (September, 1989): 269-72, 289-91.

14. Tove H. Hammer and Jay M. Turk, "Organizational Determinants of Leader Behavior and Authority," *Journal of Applied Psychology* 72 (1987): 674-82.

15. Data about Mexico are taken from Joseph A. Kahl, ed., *Comparative Perspectives on Stratification: Mexico, Great Britain, Japan* (Boston: Little, Brown, 1968), pp. ix-82, and *Current History* 86 (March, 1987): 126.

16. Amitai Etzioni, "'Shortcuts' to Social Change?" *The Public Interest* 12 (1968): 40-51.

17. Harry Edwards, "To Drop Out, or Not To," *Intellectual Digest* 3 (1972): 20-21.

18. William A. Gamson, *The Strategy of Social Protest* (Homewood, Ill.: Dorsey Press, 1975), pp. 38-54.

19. Because of the difficulty of defining the meaning of radical or nonradical goals, Gamson divided the groups into those with "limited" and those with "more-than-limited" goals. A group was categorized as more-than-limited if it was concerned with one or more of four aims: changing the scope of authority of antagonists, changing procedures of antagonists, changing personnel of antagonists, and destroying or replacing antagonists. If the group had none of these aims, it was classified as one with limited goals.

20. Charles W. Joiner, Jr., *Leadership For Change* (Cambridge, Mass.: Ballinger Publishing Company, 1987), p. 7.

21. Teresa M. Harrison, "Communication and Participative Decision Making: An Exploratory Study," *Personnel Psychology* 38 (1985): 93-116.

22. Katherine I. Miller and Peter R. Monge, "Participation, Satisfaction, and Productivity: A Meta-Analytic Review," *Academy of Management Journal* 29 (1986): 727-43.

23. Ibid.

24. Aaron J. Nurick, "Participation in Organizational Change: A Longitudinal Field Study," *Human Relations* 35 (1982): 413-30.

25. Janina C. Latack and Lawrence W. Foster, "Implementation of Compressed Work Schedule: Participation and Job Redesign as Critical Factors for Employee Acceptance," *Personnel Psychology* 38 (1985): 75-92.

26. Mao Tse-tung, *Selected Works of Mao Tse-tung*, vol. 1 (Peking: Foreign Languages Press, 1967), p. 33.

27. Charles Creekmore, "Misunderstanding Africa," *Psychology Today*, December, 1986, pp. 39-42.

28. Ibid., p. 39.

29. Aloy M. Ejiogu, "Participative Management in a Developing Economy: Poison or Placebo?" *Journal of Applied Behavioral Science* 19 (1983): 239-47.

30. C. George Benello, "Participatory Democracy and the Dilemma of Change," in *The New Left*, ed. Priscilla Long (Boston: Porter Sargent, 1969), p. 410.

31. Neil W. Chamberlain, *Enterprise and Environment: The Firm in Time and Place* (New York: McGraw-Hill, 1968), p. 155.

32. Walter Gove and Herbert Costner, "Organizing the Poor: An Evaluation of a Strategy," in *Planned Social Intervention*, ed. Louis A. Zurcher, Jr., and Charles M. Bonjean (Scranton, Pa.: Chandler Publishing Co., 1970), pp. 275-88.

33. See Zurcher and Bonjean, eds., *Planned Social Intervention*, pp. 289-338.

CHAPTER FOURTEEN

Stategies of Change

"The progress of the world is like that of a fleet horse, galloping and galloping onward. Whatever cannot skillfully change itself and progress along with the world will find itself eliminated by natural selection."[1] This 1915 plea of Ch'en Tu-hsiu to Chinese youth is thoroughly applicable to practitioners today. We live in a world of ongoing change. We will either help guide change, adapt to changes that occur, or find ourselves outmoded and passed by. At the level of the business organization, Sayles has argued, "introducing change and management effectiveness are almost synonymous."[2] I agree, but would extend the idea to all levels of social reality. That is, the proper management of change is the essence of effective life at the individual, group, and societal levels of human existence.

But the task of change is complex and demanding. We have seen the reasons why people resist change. We have noted the importance of choosing an appropriate target and selecting an appropriate agent. In this chapter, we will discuss some strategic considerations that must be faced, and then look at ways that people can bring about change at various levels of human life.

We have already encountered ideas about strategies for changing. Various theorists assert or imply that change will be effected by revolution, by nonintervention, by elites, by the solidarity of the group making the change, by marginal groups or individuals, and so on. We have seen that technology, ideas, conflict, and social-structural factors may all influence the direction of change.

Obviously, there are incompatible and contradictory elements in these ideas. That is why the task of the practitioner is difficult—there is no one strategy of change that is universally applicable. Each situation must be carefully assessed before a strategy is selected. For many, if not most, situations, a variety of strategies may be called for.

As a first step, we should distinguish between strategy and tactics. Strategy refers to the general design or plan of action, while tactics refer to the concrete and specific actions that flow from the strategy. For instance, the strategy might be educational—teaching people something that will change them and/or lead them to change their social environment. An educational strategy can be pursued by a variety of tactics, including propaganda, classes, paid advertisements, and speeches.

The activities of the John Birch Society illustrate the various tactics that may be pursued within an educational strategy. Robert Welch, the founder of the Society, set forth a ten-point program of action, which basically falls within the realm of an educational strategy.[3] First, he advocated the establishment of reading rooms throughout the country. These rooms would provide anti-Communist literature for the public. Second, the reading rooms would be used to extend the circulation of various right-wing periodicals. The periodicals would also be placed in doctors' offices, barbershops, and anywhere else literature is normally available to people who are waiting. Third, right-wing radio programs would be supported and increased. Fourth, a letter-writing campaign would be established that would continually reach people in positions of influence with impressive amounts of mail supporting anti-Communist positions. Fifth, various front organizations would be set up which would pursue such specific purposes as keeping Communist China out of the United Nations.

Sixth, various "shock" techniques would be used in the Society's journal, *American Opinion*, to force the public to recognize the insidious nature of communism. For instance, a public official might be asked a question in the journal, a question suggesting the official's connections with communism. Seventh, public speakers who are part of the communist conspiracy would be challenged by members of the Society. Eight, dedicated anti-communist speakers would be made available for local organizations such as churches, PTAs, and business groups. The speakers would not necessarily give explicitly anti-communist talks, but would always deal with subjects that the Society considered anti-communist in nature. Ninth, various activities would be encouraged to promote anti-communism on an international scale. For instance, anti-communist governments-in-exile could be set up, using refugees from communist nations. Finally, the Birchers would infiltrate the political process by getting involved at the precinct level, ultimately striving to influence national politics.

Thus, there are numerous tactics that may be employed to pursue a particular strategy. The practitioner must not only decide on which strategy to employ but also on which of varied tactics might be most effective in a particular situation. First, then, what are the different types of strategies that can be employed and what are some of the factors that need to be considered in selecting a strategy?

Strategic Considerations

There are assumptions made in any choice of strategy. For example, Robert Chin and Kenneth Benne identify three types of strategies, which they call the rational-empirical, the normative-re-educative, and the power-coercive.[4] The first assumes that people are rational and that they will follow their self-interest when it is shown to them. The second also assumes that people are rational but recognizes that they act on the basis of social norms as well as from knowledge and self-interest. Consequently, this approach endeavors to change values and attitudes as well as to give knowledge. The third strategy assumes that people act on the basis of power relationships—legitimate or coercive.

A simpler classification has been proposed by Richard Walton, who suggests that all strategies may be categorized as power or attitude types.[5] This is a useful distinction, although some methods may combine power and attitude tactics. The basic assumptions relate to the desired outcome of the change effort; with power tactics substantive concessions are sought, while with attitude tactics improved relationships are sought. Obviously, both outcomes may be desired, and, as we shall see below, that poses some dilemmas.

We shall discuss methods of change by using the distinction between power and attitude approaches as well as one other distinction—that between violent and nonviolent approaches. Violence is a power strategy, but advocates of violence often anticipate new and improved relationships arising out of the new social order. In the Marxist view, for example, the violence of revolution is a necessary prelude to the building of a humane society. Nonviolence may also be a power strategy, but it tends to emphasize the creation of new relationships. In other words, violence versus nonviolence cuts across the power versus attitude distinction.

• *Power versus Attitude Strategies*

To many students of social life, power is the name of the game. A society is a network of groups and individuals bound together in superior-subordinate relationships. Any effort to direct change, therefore, requires the mobilization and manipulation of power over others. Power strategies are simply plans for directing change that recognize this fundamental fact of social life.

The need for power strategies attests to the resistance of those who benefit from the status quo to changes that could alter their power or their benefits. There seems to be a universal law in human society that the "haves" tend to keep what they have and even gain more. The elites of any society are not easily moved from their positions. Thus, in her study of a Nepalese village, A. Caplan found that economic changes that in principle could have benefited the lower castes had somewhat different outcomes.[6] A land-reform act of the government changed credit procedures and could have reduced the indebtedness of many untouchables, but the wealthy Brahmins found ways to circumvent the law. A cobbler, for example, reported that his grandfather had mortgaged his land to a wealthy Brahmin who refused to allow the cobbler to pay off the loan and receive the land back. Unfortunately, the cobbler had no copy of the original agreement.

Similarly, in 1951 the government ordered untouchables to be admitted to all government-sponsored and government-aided schools. Eighteen years later, at the time of Caplan's study, few untouchables were actually in the schools. Basically, the schools had helped the high-caste members of the area to become literate and thereby to take advantage of employment opportunities. The untouchables had to be content with unskilled jobs. The net result was an increasing amount of inequality in the village and surrounding area—those who had were keeping and increasing, while those who lacked were becoming worse off relative to the "haves."

The tendency for the powerful to retain and even increase their power, and to resist any efforts to alter the power distribution, is a characteristic of all societies. Those who seek to change the social order, therefore, must use a power strategy. Gamson found that "unruly" protest groups, those that resorted to such tactics as violence, boycotts, and strikes, have had more success in the United States than other groups:

> *Of the 21 groups that use some form of constraint, fully two-thirds win new advantages and 71 percent win acceptance. Among the ten groups that use no constraints but receive either violence or arrests, none are successful on either criterion. The 22 groups that neither experience nor use constraints fall in the middle, 54 percent (12) win new advantages and half win acceptance.*[7]

Similarly, a study of protest activities on college campuses in 1969 pointed out that the more sustained the protest activities were, the more likely the success. The evidence, said the study, suggests that "institutions are unyielding unless threats of disruption are levied."[8]

The evidence also indicates, however, that protest can be carried too far and become counterproductive. In a study of a large number of cases in which militant tactics were used in urban protest, Schumaker raised the question of the extent to which such tactics resulted in positive policy responses from politicians.[9] That is, were those groups that used more militant (including violent) actions more successful in getting government action that was consistent with their demands? The answer is somewhat complicated. In general, contrary to the findings of Gamson and the Tillys, Schumaker found that the more militant tactics seemed to reduce rather than facilitate government responsiveness. But he also noted a number of qualifications to that finding.

First, some of the tactics are more effective than others. Boycotting public services and local businesses can be effective. But such things as demonstrating and obstructing (e.g., blocking entrance to a building by a sit-in) are unlikely to get the kind of response desired by the protesters. Second, militant tactics may be effective under certain specific conditions, such as their use by groups that have no other resources and no support from other sectors of the community. It may be that the perception by officials that a group has resorted to militancy because it has no other way to air its grievances is sufficient to elicit a sympathetic response.

Third, the effectiveness of militancy may vary over time. This could account for the apparent contradiction with the findings of Gamson and the Tillys. "It may well be that unconventional strategies go through cycles of relative effectiveness followed by relative ineffectiveness. When unconventional strategies are novel experiences for targets, their coercive aspects may be effective. But as these experiences become commonplace and targets learn to exert counter-control, the effectiveness of unconventional strategies may wane."[10] We could add that the cycle of effectiveness may also be related to the degree of conservatism among politicians and in the society.

Finally, the effectiveness of militancy is related to the type of society in which it occurs. Interestingly, protest militancy seems to be more effective in societies that are less pluralistic and less open. In open societies such as the United States, Canada, and others with democratic forms of government, the state has such legitimacy that militant protesters have difficulty getting a wider base of support. By contrast, in more closed societies, such as the Soviet Union has been, militant protest may be more effective.

Kowalewski showed the efficacy of militancy in a relatively closed society in his study of 382 protest demonstrations in the Soviet Union between 1965 and 1978.[11] The protests were conducted by twenty-four different groups, including nationals (Jews, Crimean Tatars, Ukranians, and others), religious groups, industrial workers, peasants, artists, intellectuals, and students. Kowalewski measured protest efficacy in terms of whether the target of the protest granted any concessions to the demonstrators' explicit demands. He found that all twenty-four groups were able to get at least some concessions. "Regardless of the particular condition of geography, group, or target, militance always works better than nonmilitance."[12] There were some differences, however, in the amount of concessions gained. Protests outside the large cities were more effective than those within the capitals and centers of government control. And older and larger groups of dissidents were more effective than younger, smaller groups.

In sum, militancy seems to work better in some societies than others. Within a particular society, the effectiveness of militancy varies over time, and some tactics are more effective than others. Those who opt for militant protest must face the possibility that their efforts may be counterproductive if the circumstances are not right.

Not everyone would agree that change involves a power struggle, of course. Some students, notably those who lean in a social-psychological or human relations direction, see society in terms of a plexus of groups and individuals bound together by certain attitudes and values. Change efforts require a restructuring of relationships based on attitudes and values, which generally means a changing of the attitudes and values themselves.

Thus, the power strategy assumes a different view of the nature of society than that implied by the attitude strategy. Moreover, the two strategies assume different outcomes—concessions or surrender in the case of the power strategy, and qualitatively heightened relationships in the case of the attitude strategy. Obviously, there are times when both outcomes are desired. Martin Luther King, Jr., as a leader of a movement, wished to gain both substantial concessions and improved relationships from white society. Workers striving for economic gains also may want to improve, or at least not worsen, relationships with supervisors and management. Students may desire to gain some voice in university affairs and at the same time to relate more meaningfully to faculty and administration.

Can both outcomes be achieved? They can, but, as Walton points out, the two strategies "place contradictory tactical demands on a leader."[13] For example, the power strategy would lead one to overstate one's aim, stressing differences between the two groups involved, while the attitude strategy would lead one to minimize differences (e.g., "you're taking more than your share of the pie" versus "after all, we're all Americans who want the best for our country and deserve the best it has to offer"). The power strategy would emphasize the ability to coerce, while the attitude strategy would stress trust. The power strategy would involve the control of information and creation of ambiguity for the other group, while the attitude strategy would declare for openness and honest communication.

Walton suggests three ways of coping with these and other dilemmas posed by the two strategies. First, there is the "freeze-thaw" approach, in which power and attitude tactics are alternated. Thus, in East-West relationships, both sides have tended to employ power to gain concessions and to follow that with overtures of peace and friendship. Second, different persons or subgroups can use different strategies. There is little doubt, for example, that blacks who appear to be committed to an attitude approach have used the threat of more militant groups to gain concessions and also to maintain or improve relationships.

Finally, the dilemmas may be dealt with by recognizing them and carefully choosing actions that minimize them. One might pursue a power strategy in different ways, some of which are counterproductive. A group that engages in what appears to the public to be irrational violence may quickly lose its mass support and, therefore, its cause. Lewis Feuer has criticized student movements on this basis, pointing out that they have often chosen strategies that have virtually guaranteed the failure of their objectives.[14]

• *Violent versus Nonviolent Strategies*

In order to "resolve old contradictions and produce new things" in a class society, Mao told us, "revolutions and revolutionary wars are inevitable."[15] For class societies contain "antagonistic" contradictions that must be resolved in the violence of revolution. Under socialism, there will still be contradictions, but they will be "non-antagonistic"; thus, further bloodshed will not be required.

In Mao's view, then, some kinds of change demand violence while others clearly must be effected in nonviolent ways. In handling controversial issues among the people, "we can only use democratic methods, methods of discussion, of criticism, of persuasion, and education, not coercive, high-handed methods."[16] In fact, even certain antagonistic contradictions, such as that between the national bourgeoisie and the working class in China, "can be transformed into a non-antagonistic one and resolved in a peaceful way" if properly handled.[17]

Thus, even those with great expertise in the use of violence to effect change do not see violence as a universal prod to social evolution. In our earlier discussion of violence, we noted that under certain conditions it was effective and in at least a few contexts it has seemed to be necessary. For the most part, violence is an alternative method rather than the necessary one for effecting a particular change. Some violence—such as indiscriminate killings by terrorists or abuse of people trying to protest peacefully—can be counterproductive.

What, then, is the nonviolent alternative? Can change come about through nonviolent methods? The examples of Gandhi, Martin Luther King, Jr., and Cesar Chavez, among others, show the usefulness of the nonviolent alternative. This alternative tends to incorporate both power and attitude tactics. For example, *satyagraha*, the method of Gandhi, means "the Force which is born of Truth and Love or non-violence."[18] Nonviolence here means force or power, for a fundamental rule of the method is the refusal to compromise "basic principles or essential portions of valid objectives."[19]

At the same time, the attitude strategy is employed. For another fundamental rule of *satyagraha* is the "persistent search for avenues of cooperation with the adversary on honorable terms," including making every effort "to win over the opponent by helping him . . . thereby demonstrating sincerity to achieve an agreement with, rather than a triumph over, the adversary."[20]

The same mixture of elements of power and attitude strategies was evident in Martin Luther King, Jr. The enemy who had to be overcome was clearly identified: "The policy-makers of the white society have caused the darkness: they created discrimination; they created slums; they perpetuate unemployment, ignorance, and poverty."[21] At the same time, King deplored certain kinds of behavior on the part of blacks and noted that "white man" was only a general description of the enemy. For there are "millions who have morally risen above prevailing prejudices" and who "are willing to share power and to accept structural alterations of society."[22] This kind of distinction between a group and its leaders is a common way of following both the power and the attitude strategies.

Thus, nonviolence does not imply a less forceful course of action than violence. Joan Bondurant outlined nine steps in a *satyagraha* campaign:

1. Try to resolve the conflict or grievance by negotiation and arbitration (without compromising fundamentals).

2. Prepare the group for direct action (including preparation to suffer the consequences of the action).
3. Engage in propaganda and demonstrations.
4. Try once again to persuade the opponent to accede to the demands, explaining further action to be taken if he refuses.
5. Begin economic boycotts and various kinds of strikes.
6. Initiate a program of noncooperation with established authorities and institutions.
7. Engage in civil disobedience to selected laws.
8. Take over some of the functions of government.
9. Establish a parallel government to handle those functions.[23]

The above is a progressive type of strategy; it could stop at any point at which the opponent acceded to the demands. Obviously, many of the steps were used by Martin Luther King, Jr., who acknowledged his own indebtedness to Gandhi. In India, *satyagraha* has been used by various groups, including Muslims who had traditionally resorted to violence to achieve their ends.

Nonviolent methods have been successfully used to effect change in other situations also. The effort of Cesar Chavez to organize field laborers in California during the late 1960s and early 1970s was a nonviolent crusade. The effort began as a strike of the grape pickers—mainly Mexican-American farm workers. In spite of harassment by the police, strikebreaking efforts by the growers, hostile and contemptuous statements by the governor, and increased purchase of grapes by the Defense Department when other Americans were pressing for a nationwide boycott, the growers eventually agreed to negotiate and sign a union contract.

Other alternatives were open to Chavez, of course. He could have tried violent tactics against growers, strikebreaking workers, or the crops. Whether this would have enabled him to gain more or to gain it more quickly is an open question; we can only speculate on the basis of other historical change efforts. The point here is that the nonviolent method did work. The course of history may be shaped by methods other than the heavy hand of violence.

In sum, the practitioner must analyze each situation on its own merits in order to make appropriate strategic decisions. Once the target is identified, the agent is selected, and a decision made about attitude versus power and violent versus nonviolent strategies, the practitioner has a wide range of methods to use. Let us examine some of the methods that have been effective in changing individuals, organizations, and the larger society.

Changing Individuals

There are a variety of methods by which individuals can be changed. One is psychotherapy. It is not possible to discuss therapy in detail here. However, we should note two things about it. First, there are different kinds of therapy, ranging from long-term psychoanalysis to short-term behavior modification techniques. Second, no particular kind of therapy works better than others, though some problems are better treated through some kinds of therapy than others. For example, behavior modification techniques, which employ rewards and, in some cases, punishments, can help people stop smoking or change annoying habits or get rid of some irrational fears. But behavior modification would be inappropriate for someone who is questioning the meaning of life or who has deep-seated anxieties rooted in childhood experiences.

Therapy is appropriate when the behavior to be changed is rooted in some kind of emotional disturbance or disorder. But the behavior to be changed may be based on habit, values, or attitudes, and as such can be attacked by various other methods. Let us look at three strategies that have proven effective.

• Education

Generally, when education is selected as the basis for change, there is an assumption that humans are rational creatures who will act logically or at least in their own interests on the basis of knowledge they receive. Education can occur through formal schooling, through training classes in organizations or the community, and through other mechanisms such as home-study courses and the mass media.

The effectiveness of education can be illustrated by the socialization of factory workers in England in the early days of the Industrial Revolution.[24] Agrarian people typically work in patterns that are independent of clock time, while industrial society requires considerable conformity to clock time. During the industrialization of England, there was an intense struggle between the owners and the workers as the former sought to impose the new pattern of clock time on the latter. The workers resisted in various ways, some resorting to religion and some to gin in an effort to alleviate the stress of factory work. Many of the English peasants even preferred poverty to the relatively well-paying factory during the eighteenth and nineteenth centuries.

The owners tried various methods to instill clock-regulated habits of work, including time sheets, timekeepers, informers, and fines. Ultimately, it was education that seemed most effective in changing the peasants into methodical factory workers. Both religion and the schools cooperated in the educational effort. In churches, Sunday Schools, religious writings, and charity schools, the value of time was stressed. Wasting time became an affront at best, a sin at worst. For example, a children's hymn underscored the value of diligence:

> How doth the busy little bee
> Improve each shining hour
> And gather honey all the day
> From every opening flower.
>
> In works of labour or of skill,
> I would be busy too;
> For Satan finds some mischief still
> for idle hands to do.

Thus, people were systematically educated to willingly work hard for long hours. A new breed of worker emerged in England. By the 1830s, the English worker was noted for "his regularity, his methodical paying-out of energy," and for his suppression "of the capacity to relax in the old, uninhibited ways."[25]

Educating the English peasants to become industrial workers took a considerable amount of time. And, of course, the effort proceeded as much for the benefit of the owners as the workers. Education is most effective and most efficient when it appeals to the self-interest of the students. Thus, efforts to educate people to stop smoking, to take precautions against sexually transmitted diseases, and to adopt more healthy diets have all appealed to self-interest and have all been successful to some extent. Similarly, training in an organization will be more successful to the extent that the trainees see their self-interests furthered by the process. Employees can be trained to be more productive, more loyal, and more creative, but only if the training intersects with their own interests and not simply with the good of the organization as a whole.

• *Self-Management*

Self-management is essentially applying behavior modification techniques to yourself in order to change yourself in some way. An educational strategy assumes that people need to be convinced to change. Self-management begins at the point of the individual's desire to change in a specific way. The two may be combined when education makes an individual want to change and self-management gives that individual the tools necessary for him or her to change.

One important type of self-management is "management by consequences."[26] In essence, the individual uses some kind of reward or punishment to change behavior. The reward should be extrinsic (buying something or going somewhere or doing something that is enjoyable) rather than intrinsic (feeling good about the change), and it should follow closely after the individual changes the behavior. If punishment is used, it can be anything from snapping the wrist with a rubber band to giving money to a cause with which the individual disagrees. Consider, for instance, those who have problems daydreaming at work. They want to be more productive but have difficulty concentrating. These individuals could set the goal of increasing their productivity (decreasing daydreaming) by a specified amount each day, then reward themselves each day they achieve the goal (or punish themselves each time they exceed their daydreaming allotment).

Management by consequence can be used to control the individual's thoughts as well as behavior. People, for example, who find themselves obsessed by worries or who are concerned about negative thoughts about someone with whom they frequently interact can change their thinking patterns by using a punishment such as the rubberband on the wrist each time the unwanted thought comes to mind or by using some kind of reward for each period of time that is free of the unwanted thought.

Self-instructions are one other example of self-management: "The things we say to ourselves before and after a behavior, a feeling, or a thought are cognitions. Although we don't always listen to this 'self-talk,' it seems to control both our actions and our reactions to what is happening to us. . . . Often the difference between successful and unsuccessful self-management seems to be the things one says to oneself."[27] For example, an individual who fears speaking before a group is engaging in self-sabotage by thinking such things as: "They're not going to like what I say; I can't be convincing; they'll think I'm stupid." Rather, the individual should use a different set of self-instructions, such as: "This is my job, and I'm going to do it. My only responsibility is to communicate my ideas to them, not to make them like me or my ideas."

Self-management includes various other techniques that any individual can learn and use. Thinking, feelings, and behavior can all be changed by self-management techniques. The techniques are not a cure-all, of course, but they are very useful for achieving a considerable number of goals.

• *Change through Small Groups*

While the individual may be the target of change, the medium through which the change is effected is often a group—whether the group is the family, the classroom, or some other group created for the purpose of change. In particular, the small group has been employed to make specific changes in individuals. This technique has worked successfully in "thought reform" in China,[28] in the conversion of individuals to the Pentecostal movement,[29] and in the T-group and Lewinian-type discussion groups.[30] This lasts method falls into the general category of "group dynamics."

The group dynamics approach to change stems from the notion that the norms governing behavior are fashioned in group interaction; the logical place to change norms, therefore, is in a group. Thus, Kurt Lewin and his colleagues used the small group to persuade housewives to purchase and use foods such as beef hearts, sweetbreads, and kidneys during World War II. Since the housewife is the "gatekeeper" who channels the food into the family, groups of housewives were brought together. It was found that group discussion and group decision were far more effective in changing norms than a lecture; a follow-up study found that 32 percent of women in the group decision context as opposed to only 3 percent in the lecture situation served one of the meats never used before.[31]

A variety of other kinds of behavior have been attacked through this method. Studies have reported change in alcoholics, in industrial productivity, in skill levels, in various attitudes, and in personality. The groups can be structured in various ways, and there are now some "classic" types of small-group processes for bringing about change.[32] The format used by Alcoholics Anonymous has been taken up by a variety of other groups that help individuals change anything from eating habits to ways of relating to others.

The small group can be extremely effective, though some groups fail in their objectives. In good part, the group's effectiveness depends on the skills of the leader. The leader should be a well-trained person, one who has participated extensively in groups and who has "the ability to diagnose and design" as well as "technical and methodological knowledge about groups."[33]

Change in an Organization

A good deal of the literature on how to bring about change focuses on organizational change. People today, after all, spend a good part of their lives in the context of various organizations. Thus, there may be a need to bring about change in a political organization, such as a city government; an educational organization, such as a high school; a religious organization, such as a denominational center or a local church; or a business organization, such as an insurance company or a chemical plant.[34]

Whatever the type of organization, however, there are certain principles of change that apply.

• General Principles of Organizational Change

In the last chapter, we underscored the importance of *participation* in change efforts. While not universally valid, it is most often true that participation is an essential element of effective organizational change. As Lewin's studies showed, people who participate are far more likely to support the change than those who do not. (Recall that we all tend to resist those changes that are imposed on us, even if the changes are conducive to our well-being.)

When people do not participate, then, they are likely to either subvert the change effort or minimize its effectiveness. For example, when managers tried to implement a change in work procedures in a clothing factory, they used two different methods.[35] They told one group of workers why and how the procedures would be changed. They worked with another group to discuss how the procedures could be changed, and jointly developed new procedures. Among the first group, output dropped dramatically after the new procedures were implemented, and it never reached previous levels. Among the second group, output dropped slightly at first then increased beyond previous levels.

Numerous studies have shown that participatory change in business organizations brings about such things as increased productivity, decreased costs, and lower turnover and absenteeism.[36] In other organizations, it also tends to ensure goal attainment. Whether the aim is greater efficiency, more effective achievement of organizational goals, or a new direction for the organization, participation can make the difference between a blunted effort and a successful one.

Second, the practitioner must be *sensitive to human needs*. It is all too easy to become so engrossed in the effects on the organization that the people who comprise the organization are forgotten. In many organizations and in many decisions that are made, it isn't possible for everyone who will be affected to participate. How, then, will the people be affected? Attempting to answer that question can help the practitioner anticipate some possible resistance to the change. It can also help the practitioner formulate the change in a way that will meet the needs of those affected.

For example, one need that all of us have is for meaningful relationships with others. For many people, one of the more gratifying aspects of work is the interaction with co-workers. Ignoring the importance of existing patterns of relationships caused problems when management decided to introduce new technology into the British mining industry.[37] At the time of the change, the industry was hampered by low productivity and high costs. The mechanized "long-wall" organization of work teams was introduced in the hope that productivity could be increased and the costs of operations reduced. The long-wall technology used groups of forty to fifty workers, who were spread out over a distance of some 200 yards. The prior short-wall work teams had been composed of two to eight self-selected individuals who frequently interacted with one another on the job. The new method, therefore, increased the distance and reduced the interaction between workers, greatly increased the size of the groups, and made them more specialized. In the past, the workers could see how their own contribution led to the output of their team and, consequently, to their income (pay was based on team output). With the new method, there were too many individuals in the team for any single worker to see how his efforts affected the total output. Moreover, management became much more involved in the work. Formerly, the teams had been virtually autonomous work units that required little supervision; under the new system, management was needed to coordinate the teams.

Contrary to the hopes of the sponsors of the new technology, productivity did not increase and, worse, the workers became dissatisfied, voiced numerous grievances, and developed high absentee rates. Finally, management was forced to deal with the situation. The new technology was retained, but the groups were broken down into small units again. The former solidarity, based on interaction among a few workers, returned. Productivity increased and the absentee rate declined.

A third principle involves the *expectations* of those seeking to bring about the change. Long ago, W. I. Thomas formulated the dictum "If men define situations as real, they are real in their consequences." Robert Merton used Thomas's statement as the foundation for his discussion of the self-fulfilling prophecy.[38] In essence, the self-fulfilling prophecy begins with "a *false* definition of the situation," which then evokes "a new behavior which makes the originally false conception come *true*."[39] The basic idea of the self-fulfilling prophecy has been incorporated into so-called "interpersonal expectancy effects," the idea that our expectations for other people's behavior tend to affect that behavior in accord with the expectations.[40]

Basically, through various verbal and nonverbal cues we convey our expectations to others, and they tend to respond accordingly. Thus, if a manager expects workers to be lazy and, therefore, to require close supervision, they may act in a way that confirms the expectations. Actually, they may only be reacting to the manager's negative view of them, but the manager will define it as confirmation of his or her viewpoint.

For the practitioner, this means that any change effort needs to be approached with positive expectations. If the practitioner enters an organization expecting people to resist all change efforts, the expectations will probably be confirmed in some way. If the practitioner begins with the expectation that people are likely to be interested in useful change and to cooperate with it, those expectations are also likely to be confirmed.

Finally, the practitioner must be *knowledgeable about the structure of the organization*. An organization is a social system. When change occurs in a part of that system, it is likely to affect the total system. Contrariwise, when you attempt to change a part of a system, you must be aware of how other parts of the system will affect the change effort. A.T.& T. once attempted to initiate a marketing philosophy into its traditionally service-oriented business.[41] The corporation set up a school to teach managers how to create products for specific customer needs. But the managers who completed the course discovered that they functioned in a system that didn't support their efforts. Mass sales of standardized products continued to be most important, and the reward system in the corporation discouraged managers from spending time and effort on customized products and individual needs. Eventually, A.T.& T. disbanded the school, and most of the managers who had graduated from it left the corporation. Those responsible for trying to make the change had ignored the organizational structure that eventually doomed the effort.

An important part of the organizational structure is the power structure. An effective practitioner discovers both the the formal and informal power structures and acts accordingly:

> *If an organization is a political system composed of different groups each competing for power, then the most obvious action step is* assuring or developing the support of key power groups. *For a change to occur successfully, a critical mass of power groups needs to be assembled and mobilized in support of the change. Those groups that may oppose the change have to in some way be compensated for or have their effects neutralized.*[42]

In other words, just as a change agent in a peasant society does well to identify and use opinion leaders, the practitioner in an organization does well to know and make use of those groups that have power, whether the power is formal (organizational position) or informal (organizational influence).

• Methods of Organizational Change

There are a great many ways of bringing about change in an organization, including a number of commonly used techniques. Any of the techniques can be successful when based on the above principles. We should note, however, that people may or may not employ the principles in using the techniques. The techniques themselves do not necessarily require all of the principles. But those who ignore the principles do so at the peril of a failed effort.

There are, then, six techniques most commonly employed in organizational change: (1) organizational behavior modification, (2) management by objectives, (3) managerial development, (4) organizational development, (5) management auditing, and (6) the control cycle of planning, implementing, and evaluating operations.[43] In *organizational behavior modification* there are five steps:

1. Identifying behavior(s) to be changed;
2. Measuring the behavior(s) in some way to see if frequency is high enough to demand change;
3. Analyzing the behavior to determine what antecedents or consequences might change it;
4. Intervening with appropriate positive responses (rewards of some kind); and
5. Evaluating the results.

For instance, the behavior to be changed might be the unscheduled break in work and socializing that occurs with the entry of a mail clerk in an office. The intervention could be the supervisor entering at the same time and complimenting those employees who do not interrupt their work. An evaluation would take place at some point to determine if this intervention addressed the problem.

Management by objectives strives for change through planning discussions between superiors and subordinates regarding the latter's work. The discussions are used to generate objectives, plans, and programs that bring about change of some kind. This technique is particularly useful with those engaged in nonroutine work, such as professional and technical personnel. Clearly, it is a technique that maximizes participation.

Managerial development involves the training of managers to enhance their skills and thereby alter their behavior. Managerial development may be appropriate where a performance appraisal has shown some deficiency or where larger organizational change (introduction of new technology or policies) suggests the need for new managerial behavior.

Organizational development is an effort to change the collective behavior of all or a subset of the members of the organization. In organizational development, a typical program involves improving interpersonal skills, resolving common problems, and team building (enhancing group solidarity). Normally an outside expert (which may be an individual or a group) comes in and conducts the development. The expert collects data in order to diagnose the situation. Once the data are collected, there is feedback to members of the organization. The expert uses the reaction of the members, along with the original data and analysis, to formulate a program of intervention. A variety of interventions can be employed, including structural changes, team building, conflict resolution, training, role playing, and so on. Following the intervention, there is an evaluation of the effects on the organization.

Management auditing is an evaluation of managers designed to anticipate, identify, and solve organizational problems. The auditors usually have a checklist of factors that need to be reviewed and evaluated. The checklist is based on the auditors' knowledge of good management practice. The outcome of the audit is a set of recommended changes for improving the organization.

Finally, the *control cycle* "provides for the planning, implementation, and evaluation of changes in operations and organizational arrangements to bring about or maintain an appropriate fit between the organization and its environment."[44] In the control cycle, there is ongoing monitoring, evaluation, planning, and changing in order to maintain a healthy organization in a changing environment. In other words, the control cycle is a technique that stresses looking at the organization in its social context and not just at the organization's internal processes.

Surveying seventy-one Fortune 500 companies, Michael found that all of them used the control cycle.[45] About three-fourths used management by objectives and managerial development. Approximately half used organizational development and management auditing, and 11 percent used organizational behavior modification. Other kinds of organizations also use these techniques, and there are additional techniques that could be used. The above, however, have been tried and found to be effective.

Change at the Institutional/Societal Level

For those people who are living in a state of oppression or deprivation, and for those who are morally outraged by some aspect of society, neither individual nor organizational change is sufficiently wide-ranging.

It is necessary to bring about change at a larger level, in the power structure of the society or its laws or culture or institutions. Such changes can be brought about through a commitment on the part of the polity, as happened in Meiji Japan; or through a mass movement culminating in revolution, as happened in China; or through organizations or social movements that exert sufficient pressure on those in power to effect change, as the Civil Rights and Women's movements have done in the United States to some extent.

One important way to bring about more wide-ranging change is through the law. Particularly in democratic societies, some social change may be effected by altering the legal basis of the society. In the United States, for example, Congress passed a number of equal employment opportunity laws in the 1960s and 1970s. Enforcement of those laws led to some gains in employment and income by black Americans.[46] Bringing about social change through legal change, however, is not always effective even in democratic societies. Laws can be changed in order to reverse the direction of change. And laws can be ignored or subverted as well as enforced.

The difficulty of bringing about change at the institutional or societal level is illustrated by the history of black people's efforts to gain equality. Black protest movements in the United States have gone through four phases: the transition from accommodation to protest, legal protest, nonviolent direct action, and black power strategy. Associated with each of these, and with the continuing work of certain organizations, is a considerable amount of legislative action. Protest first emerged out of the context of severe oppression and deprivation, which was given at least temporary legitimacy by Booker T. Washington. A number of blacks, including W. E. B. DuBois, took strong issue with Washington. Segregation in public accommodations and the successful disenfranchisement of large numbers of blacks around the turn of the century were among the conditions that outraged the militants.

The protest quickly took the form of legal efforts and was greatly aided by the formation of the N.A.A.C.P. in 1909. In the early part of the century this organization won a number of cases, including the noted 1954 Supreme Court decision on school segregation. The failure of local, state, and federal governments to implement effectively the legal victories led to other forms of protest, including the nonviolent direct action of Martin Luther King, Jr., and the more militant action of certain black power advocates.

A series of civil rights acts and the Voting Rights Act of 1965 were among the legislative consequences of the protest movements. It would be foolish to think that such legislation has solved the problem. The laws have been circumvented and even ignored. Continuing legal changes have been necessitated by continuing circumvention. Nevertheless, it would be equally foolish to think that the overall structure is unchanged, that the situation of the black is no better than it was in the nineteenth century.

By 1970, black people in America were in the process of being fully enfranchised (though not without resistance), were gaining some measure of political power, and were showing economic achievements. However, with respect to the latter, progress has been slow and marked by periods of reversals. The income gap between white and nonwhite workers, aged 14 and over, for example, has fluctuated since the end of World War II, but by 1985 it had dropped down to just below the level it was in 1948![47] In 1948, blacks earned about 60 percent as much as whites, while in 1985 black income was about 59.5 percent that of whites. It had risen to a high of 67 percent in 1969, but conservative government policies and a fluctuating economy led to reversals in the late 1970s and 1980s. Of course, blacks are better off than they were just prior to the World War II; in 1939, black income was 41 percent that of whites.

Nevertheless, what the figures underscore is the fact that gains made as a result of a social movement and legal change can be erased by subsequent events. Then the people must, in effect, begin anew in their effort to gain equality.

One thing is clear. Any effort to bring about change in the larger society by the citizenry requires an organized effort. Americans have been told frequently to redress their grievances at the ballot box. But voting only works if a sufficiently large number of politicians who support the change are running for office. In general, bringing about institutional/societal change requires an organized effort of some kind.

Grass-roots organizations, then, are the appropriate method. The organizations may opt for either an attitude or power strategy, or both. Foes of abortion have attempted to oppose the practice by such attitude strategies as educating the public and such power strategies as pressure on politicians and sit-ins at abortion clinics. Pro-choice advocates, similarly, have also engaged in educational efforts and have had their counter-demonstrations and confrontations with the right-to-life groups.

One of the primary advocates of the power strategy was Saul Alinsky, who devoted years to mobilizing people to effectively use power. He defined a radical as one who uses power to effect needed change. "Liberals dream dreams; radicals build the world of men's dreams."[48] Alinsky conceived of power in terms of organizing and engaging in conflict:

> *A People's Organization is not a philanthropic plaything nor a social service's ameliorative gesture. . . . It thinks and acts in terms of social surgery and not cosmetic cover-ups. . . . A People's Organization is dedicated to an eternal war. It is a war against poverty, misery, delinquency, disease, injustice, hopelessness, and unhappiness. . . . A war is not an intellectual debate, and in the war against social evils there are no rules of fair play.*[49]

A pure power strategy could hardly be more clearly expressed than that. And Alinsky's tactics illustrate the extent to which he disdains the attitude strategy; he did everything from organizing boycotts to dumping garbage on an alderman's driveway. As a national magazine put it, Alinsky "has possibly antagonized more people . . . than any other living American."[50] It is evident that Alinsky had contempt—in both his words and his actions—for the attitude strategy. Changes are effected by power, not by trust and persuasion.

Alinsky's influence has continued among grass-roots community organizers.[51] His followers have organized efforts in cities across the nation to achieve change of all kinds through grass-roots action. One organization, the Midwest Academy, was set up to train organizers. The organizers generally create the community organizations out of preexisting cohesive neighborhood groups (such as members of a church). They develop a number of issues that reflect the concerns of the people and that demand action, and then confront the authorities with demands for change.

Interestingly, people throughout the world who are pressing for change have discovered the value of grass-roots organizations. In India, for example, the self-help movement sprang out of Gandhi's village development work, dating from the 1920s.[52] Gandhi tried to construct a new and more humane social order by helping villagers become self-reliant. After India gained its independence in 1948, one of Gandhi's followers, Vinoba Bhave, led the Village Awakening movement. That was followed in the 1960s by "a new wave of community organizing," so that "tens if not hundreds of thousands of local groups in India now wage the day-by-day struggle for development."[53]

Grassroots self-help organizations thrive all over the world. They are engaged in all kinds of change: political, social welfare, economic, environmental, and social norms and values. Most commonly, they are attempting to bring about change that they perceive to be conducive to the well-being of the larger society as well as some segment of that society.

As organizations, it is important that these groups incorporate the principles identified earlier. We can illustrate this by what happened with the movement Bhoomi Sena (Land Army) in India.[54] Bhoomi Sena was a reaction against the illegal usurpation of peasant land by money-lending *sawkars*. The first effort to deal with the expropriation of the land occurred in 1970, when left-wing parties led some peasants in the Thane district of India in a "land-grab" movement. The movement ended with many of the participants being jailed and without a resolution of the land question. After their release from jail, some of the leaders formed Bhoomi Sena and took a few thousand acres of land back by force. The leaders had no clear plans for extending their work, so they deferred to outside social workers who brought in new technology and large bank loans to help the people. But the outsiders ran their program in a paternalistic way, without any participation on the part of the people. Mismanagement caused the effort to end in financial disaster.

In 1975, a new phase of Bhoomi Sena began. This time the peasants were committed to full participation in the planning and execution of the change effort. A few of the outsiders from the earlier failure had remained because they saw the need for a participatory movement. The peasants met in small groups to discuss their problems and to find ways to attack those problems. The movement's leadership encouraged people to take action in their own villages and in accord with their own collective decisions. As a result of these developments, the movement gained power. And power is precisely what is needed in the effort to change a situation of inequity.

In sum, people are not pawns in the hands of vast, impersonal forces of history. People can change themselves, their organizations, and aspects of the larger society in which they live. There are many proven methods to bring about change. But the person who would implement change must analyze each situation on its own merits in order to determine such things as the appropriate target of change, who will be involved in the effort, and what method will most likely lead to the desired outcome.

We now live in the history of the future. The way that history will be written depends upon the extent to which, and the manner in which, we strive to shape ourselves, our organizations, and our society, and thus the future. Pascal said that man is both "the pride and refuse of the universe."[55] A moral commitment demands that we select those methods that will lead future historians to write about humanity in terms of the former rather than the latter.

Endnotes

1. Ch'en Tu-hsiu, "Call to Youth," in *China's Response to the West,* ed. Ssu-yu Teng and John K. Fairbank (New York: Atheneum, 1967), p. 242.

2. Leonard R. Sayles, *Leadership: What Effective Managers Really Do . . . And How They Do It* (New York: McGraw-Hill, 1979), p. 151.

3. Robert Welch, *The Blue Book* (Belmont, Mass.: Robert Welch, 1961).

4. Robert Chin and Kenneth D. Benne, "General Strategies for Effecting Changes in Human Systems," in *The Planning of Change,* ed. Warren G. Bennis, Kenneth D. Benne, and Robert Chin, 2nd ed. (New York: Holt, Rinehart & Winston, 1969), pp. 32-59.

5. Richard E. Walton, "Two Strategies of Social Change and Their Dilemmas," *The Journal of Applied Behavioral Science* 1(1965): 167-79.

6. A. Patricia Caplan, *Priests and Cobblers* (San Francisco: Chandler, 1972).

7. William A. Gamson, *The Strategy of Social Protest* (Homewood, Ill.: Dorsey Press, 1975), p. 87.

8. Quoted in Gil Green, *The New Radicalism: Anarchist or Marxist?* (New York: International Publishers, 1971), p. 96.

9. Paul D. Schumaker, "The Effectiveness of Militant Tactics in Contemporary Urban Protest," *Journal of Voluntary Action Research* 9 (1980): 131-48.

10. Ibid., p. 144.

11. David Kowalewski, "Protest Militancy in the USSR: When Does It Work?" *The Social Science Journal* 24 (1987): 169-79.

12. Ibid., p. 176.

13. Walton, "Two Strategies of Social Change," *The Journal of Applied Behavioral Science,* p. 171.

14. Lewis S. Feuer, *The Conflict of Generations* (New York: Basic Books, 1969), pp. 529-31.

15. Mao Tse-tung, *Selected Works of Mao Tse-tung,* vol. 1 (Peking: Foreign Languages Press, 1967), pp. 343-44.

16. From the essay, "On the Correct Handling of Contradictions among the People," in *Mao Tse-tung: An Anthology of His Writings,* ed. Anne Fremantle (New York: Mentor Books, 1962), p. 269.

17. Ibid., p. 266.

18. Joan V. Bondurant, *Conquest of Violence* (Berkeley: University of California Press, 1969), p. 8.

19. Ibid., p. 39.

20. Ibid.

21. Martin Luther King, Jr., *The Trumpet of Conscience* (New York: Harper & Row, 1967), p. 8.

22. Ibid.

23. Bondurant, *Conquest of Violence,* pp. 40-41.

24. These materials follow Robert H. Lauer, *Temporal Man: The Meaning and Uses of Social Time* (New York: Praeger, 1981), pp. 61-62.

25. E. P. Thompson, "Time, Work-Discipline, and Industrial Capitalism," *Past and Present* 38 (1967): 92.

26. Brian T. Yates, *Self-Management: The Science and Art of Helping Yourself* (Belmont, Calif.: Wadsworth, 1985), pp. 27-58.

27. Ibid., pp. 63-64.

28. Robert J. Lifton, "Brainwashing in Perspective," *New Republic*, May 13, 1957, pp. 21-25.

29. Luther P. Gerlach and Virginia H. Hine, *People, Power, Change: Movements of Social Transformation* (Indianapolis: Bobbs-Merrill, 1970).

30. Examples of T-group studies may be found in Hornstein et al., *Social Intervention*, pp. 31-90. Examples of the discussion groups may be found in Kurt Lewin, *Field Theory in Social Science*, ed. Dorwin Cartwright (New York: Harper & Bros., 1951).

31. Kurt Lewin, "Group Decision and Social Change," in *Readings in Social Psychology*, ed. Eleanor E. Maccoby, Theodore M. Newcomb, and Eugene L. Hartley, 3rd ed. (New York: Holt, Rinehart & Winston, 1958), p. 202.

32. See Rodney W. Napier and Matti K Gershenfeld, *Making Groups Work: A Guide for Group Leaders* (Boston: Houghton Mifflin, 1983).

33. Ibid., p. 44.

34. For examples of studies of change in various kinds of organizations, see: William B. Stevenson, "Change in the Structure of Bureaucracy: A Longitudinal Analysis," *Sociological Perspectives* 29 (1986): 307-36; John R. Earle, Dean D. Knudsen, and Donald W. Shriver, Jr., *Spindles & Spires: A Re-Study of Religion and Social Change in Gastonia* (Atlanta: John Knox Press, 1976); Bill R. Hampton and Robert H. Lauer, *Solving Problems in Secondary School Administration: A Human Organization Approach* (Boston: Allyn and Bacon, 1981); and Donald L. Kirkpatrick, *How to Manage Change Effectively* (San Francisco: Jossey-Bass Publishers, 1985).

35. Reported in Neil R. Sweeney, *For Those Who Would Be President: 16 Management Skills for the Top Job* (Glenview, Ill.: Scott, Foresman, 1986), pp. 79-80.

36. See, e.g., Kirkpatrick, *How to Manage Change Effectively*, pp. 133-34.

37. See William Foote Whyte, *Organizational Behavior: Theory and Application* (Homewood, Ill.: Dorsey Press, 1969), pp. 561-62.

38. Robert K. Merton, *Social Theory and Social Structure* (Glencoe, Ill.: Free Press, 1957), pp. 421-36.

39. Ibid., p. 423.

40. For a review of the research and some of the important results regarding how expectations affect the behavior of others, see Monica J. Harris and Robert Rosenthal, "Mediation of Interpersonal Expectancy Effects: 31 Meta-Analyses," *Psychological Bulletin* 97 (1985): 363-86.

41. Reported in Paul F. Buller, Borje O. Saxberg, and Howard L. Smith, "Institutionalization of Planned Organizational Change: A Model and Review of the Literature," in *Developing Human Resources*, ed. Leonard D. Goodstein and J. William Pfeiffer (San Diego: University Associates, 1985), p. 193.

42. David A. Nadler, "Managing Organizational Change: An Integrative Perspective," *The Journal of Applied Behavioral Science* 17 (1981): 204.

43. Stephen R. Michael, "Organizational Change Techniques: Their Present, Their Future," *Organizational Dynamics* 11 (1982): 67-80.

44. Ibid., p. 75.

45. Ibid., p. 77.

46. Paul Burnstein, "Equal Employment Opportunity Legislation and the Income of Women and Nonwhites," *American Sociological Review* 44 (1979): 367-91.

47. Data on black-white income disparity may be found in Robert H. Lauer, *Social Problems and the Quality of Life,* 4th ed. (Dubuque, Iowa: Wm. C. Brown, 1989), pp. 351-52, and in recent editions of the *Statistical Abstract of the United States.*

48. Saul D. Alinsky, *Reveille for Radicals* (Chicago: University of Chicago Press, 1946), p. 30.

49. Ibid., p. 154.

50. *Time,* March 2, 1970, p. 56.

51. See Donald C. Reitzes and Dietrich C. Reitzes, *The Alinsky Legacy: Alive and Kicking* (Greenwich, Conn.: JAI Press, 1987).

52. Alan B. Durning, "Mobilizing at the Grassroots," in Lester R. Brown et al., eds., *State of the World: 1989* (New York: Norton, 1989), p. 156.

53. Ibid.

54. Muhammad Anisur Rahman, "The Theory and Practice of Participatory Action Research," in Orlando Fals Borda, ed., *The Challenge of Social Change* (Beverly Hills, Calif.: Sage, 1985), pp. 108-10.

55. Blaise Pascal, *Pensees,* trans. W. F. Trotter (New York: Modern Library, 1941), p. 143.

Name Index

Subject Index